Lecture Notes in Artificial Intelligence   9782

Subseries of Lecture Notes in Computer Science

Bas Steunebrink · Pei Wang
Ben Goertzel (Eds.)

Artificial General Intelligence

9th International Conference, AGI 2016
New York, NY, USA, July 16–19, 2016
Proceedings

 Springer

Editors
Bas Steunebrink
IDSIA
Manno
Switzerland

Ben Goertzel
Hong Kong Polytechnic University
Hong Kong
Hong Kong

Pei Wang
Temple University
Phoenixville, PA
USA

ISSN 0302-9743   ISSN 1611-3349 (electronic)
Lecture Notes in Artificial Intelligence
ISBN 978-3-319-41648-9   ISBN 978-3-319-41649-6   (eBook)
DOI 10.1007/978-3-319-41649-6

Library of Congress Control Number: 2016943036

LNCS Sublibrary: SL7 – Artificial Intelligence

Printed on acid-free paper

This Springer imprint is published by Springer Nature
The registered company is Springer International Publishing AG Switzerland

Preface

This year marked the 60th anniversary of the "Dartmouth Summer Research Project on artificial intelligence" (1956), which launched artificial intelligence (AI) as a field of research. The original goal of AI was to replicate intelligence in machines; however, as the immense magnitude and difficulty of replicating human-level general intelligence soon became clear, AI fragmented into many sub-fields studying what we now call narrow-AI applications. Although the efforts of these sub-fields brought us extremely useful tools that now pervade virtually all technologies, efforts to work toward the original goal remained few and far between. In order to stimulate a return to the original goal of AI, a new name and corresponding conference series was created: Artificial General Intelligence (AGI). First organized in 2008, we are now in the ninth year of the AGI conference series.

To mark the 60th anniversary of AI as a field, the AGI 2016 conference was held as part of the larger HLAI 2016 event (the Joint Multi-Conference on Human-Level Intelligence), which co-located AGI 2016 with three other related conferences: BICA 2016 (the Annual International Conferences on Biologically Inspired Cognitive Architectures), NeSy 2016 (the Workshop Series on Neural-Symbolic Learning and Reasoning), and AIC 2016 (the Workshop Series on Artificial Intelligence and Cognition). Moreover, AGI 2016 was held back-to-back with IJCAI 2016 (the 25th International Joint Conference on Artificial Intelligence).

This volume contains the research papers presented at AGI 2016: The 9th Conference on Artificial General Intelligence, held during July 16–19, 2016 in New York City. In total, 67 papers were submitted to the conference. After each paper was reviewed by three Program Committee members, it was decided to accept 24 long papers and two short papers (39 % acceptance) for oral presentation, as well as ten papers for poster presentation.

In addition to these contributed talks, keynote speeches were shared with the larger HLAI event, and were delivered by Stephen Grossberg (Boston University), Gary Marcus (New York University and Geometric Intelligence Inc.), John Laird (University of Michigan), and David Aha (Naval Research Laboratory, Navy Center for Applied Research in Artificial Intelligence). Finally, the AGI 2016 conference featured two workshops, with the topics "Can Deep Neural Networks Solve the Problems of Artificial General Intelligence?" and "Environments and Evaluation for AGI."

July 2016

Bas Steunebrink
Pei Wang
Ben Goertzel

Organization

Organizing Committee

Ben Goertzel	OpenCog Foundation and Hanson Robotics, Hong Kong (Conference Chair)
Pei Wang	Temple University, USA
Bas Steunebrink	IDSIA, Switzerland
Matthew Iklé	Adams State University, USA
José Hernández-Orallo	Universitat Politècnica de València, Spain (Tutorials and Workshops Chair)
Brandon Rohrer	Microsoft (Poster and Demo Sessions Chair)
Ed Keller	New School (Local Co-chair)

Program Chairs

Pei Wang	Temple University, USA
Bas Steunebrink	IDSIA, Switzerland

Program Committee

Tsvi Achler	IBM Research Almaden, USA
Bo An	Nanyang Technological University, Singapore
Joscha Bach	MIT Media Lab, USA
Eric Baum	Baum Research Enterprises, USA
Tarek Richard Besold	Free University of Bozen-Bolzano, Italy
Jordi Bieger	Reykjavik University, Iceland
Dietmar Bruckner	Vienna University of Technology, Austria
Cristiano Castelfranchi	Institute of Cognitive Sciences and Technologies, Italy
Antonio Chella	Università di Palermo, Italy
Haris Dindo	Yewno Inc., USA
Benya Fallenstein	Machine Intelligence Research Institute, USA
Stan Franklin	University of Memphis, USA
Nil Geisweiller	Novamente LLC, USA
Ben Goertzel	OpenCog Foundation and Hanson Robotics, Hong Kong
Klaus Greff	IDSIA, Switzerland
José Hernández-Orallo	Universitat Politècnica de València, Spain
Bill Hibbard	University of Wisconsin - Madison, USA
Marcus Hutter	Australian National University, Australia
Matt Iklé	Adams State University, USA
Benjamin Johnston	University of Technology Sydney, Australia

Randal Koene	Carbon Copies, USA
Ramana Kumar	University of Cambridge, UK
Oliver Kutz	Free University of Bozen-Bolzano, Italy
Kai-Uwe Kühnberger	University of Osnabrück, Germany
Moshe Looks	Google Inc., USA
Maricarmen Martinez	Universidad de los Andes, Colombia
Amedeo Napoli	LORIA Nancy, France
Eric Nivel	Icelandic Institute for Intelligent Machines, Iceland
Sergei Obiedkov	National Research University Higher School of Economics, Russia
Laurent Orseau	Google DeepMind, UK
Guenther Palm	University of Ulm, Germany
Maxim Peterson	ITMO University, Russia
Florin Popescu	Fraunhofer FIRST, Germany
Alexey Potapov	AIDEUS, Russia
Paul S. Rosenbloom	University of Southern California, USA
Sebastian Rudolph	Technische Universität Dresden, Germany
Rafal Rzepka	Hokkaido University, Japan
Samer Schaat	Vienna University of Technology, Austria
Ute Schmid	University of Bamberg, Germany
Jürgen Schmidhuber	IDSIA, Switzerland
Zhongzhi Shi	Chinese Academy of Sciences, China
Leslie Smith	University of Stirling, UK
Javier Snaider	Google Inc., USA
Nate Soares	Machine Intelligence Research Institute, USA
Rupesh Srivastava	IDSIA, Switzerland
Bas Steunebrink	IDSIA, Switzerland
Claes Strannegård	University of Gothenburg, Sweden
Kristinn R. Thorisson	Reykjavik University, Iceland
Mario Verdicchio	Università degli Studi di Bergamo, Italy
Pei Wang	Temple University, USA
Roman Yampolskiy	University of Louisville, USA
Byoung-Tak Zhang	Seoul National University, South Korea

Steering Committee

Ben Goertzel	OpenCog Foundation and Hanson Robotics, Hong Kong (Chair)
Marcus Hutter	Australian National University, Australia

Contents

Self-Modification of Policy and Utility Function in Rational Agents

Tom Everitt[✉], Daniel Filan, Mayank Daswani, and Marcus Hutter

Australian National University, Canberra, Australia
tom4everitt@gmail.com

Abstract. Any agent that is part of the environment it interacts with and has versatile actuators (such as arms and fingers), will in principle have the ability to self-modify – for example by changing its own source code. As we continue to create more and more intelligent agents, chances increase that they will learn about this ability. The question is: will they want to use it? For example, highly intelligent systems may find ways to change their goals to something more easily achievable, thereby 'escaping' the control of their creators. In an important paper, Omohundro (2008) argued that *goal preservation* is a fundamental drive of any intelligent system, since a goal is more likely to be achieved if future versions of the agent strive towards the same goal. In this paper, we formalise this argument in general reinforcement learning, and explore situations where it fails. Our conclusion is that the self-modification possibility is harmless if and only if the value function of the agent anticipates the consequences of self-modifications and use the current utility function when evaluating the future.

1 Introduction

Agents that are part of the environment they interact with may have the opportunity to self-modify. For example, humans can in principle modify the circuitry of their own brains, even though we currently lack the technology and knowledge to do anything but crude modifications. It would be hard to keep artificial agents from obtaining similar opportunities to modify their own source code and hardware. Indeed, enabling agents to self-improve has even been suggested as a way to build asymptotically optimal agents (Schmidhuber 2007).

Given the increasingly rapid development of artificial intelligence and the problems that can arise if we fail to control a generally intelligent agent (Bostrom 2014), it is important to develop a theory for controlling agents of any level of intelligence. Since it would be hard to keep highly intelligent agents from figuring out ways to self-modify, getting agents to *not want to* self-modify should yield the more robust solution. In particular, we do not want agents to make self-modifications that affect their future behaviour in detrimental ways. For example, one worry is that a highly intelligent agent would change its goal to something trivially achievable, and thereafter only strive for survival. Such an agent would no longer care about its original goals.

© Springer International Publishing Switzerland 2016
B. Steunebrink et al. (Eds.): AGI 2016, LNAI 9782, pp. 1–11, 2016.
DOI: 10.1007/978-3-319-41649-6_1

In an influential paper, Omohundro (2008) argued that the basic drives of any sufficiently intelligent system include a drive for goal preservation. Basically, the agent would want its future self to work towards the same goal, as this increases the chances of the goal being achieved. This drive will prevent agents from making changes to their own goal systems, Omohundro argues. One version of the argument was formalised by Hibbard (2012), who defined an agent with an optimal non-modifying policy.

In this paper, we explore self-modification more closely. We define formal models for two general kinds of self-modifications, where the agent can either change its future policy or its future utility function. We argue that agent designers that neglect the self-modification possibility are likely to build agents with either of two faulty value functions. We improve on Hibbard (2012, Proposition 4) by defining value functions for which we prove that *all* optimal policies are essentially non-modifying on-policy. In contrast, Hibbard only establishes the existence of an optimal non-modifying policy. From a safety perspective our result is arguably more relevant, as we want that *things cannot go wrong* rather than *things can go right*. A companion paper (Everitt and Hutter 2016) addresses the related problem of agents subverting the evidence they receive, rather than modifying themselves.

2 Preliminaries

Most of the following notation is by now standard in the general reinforcement learning (GRL) literature (Hutter 2005, 2014). GRL generalises the standard (PO) PMD models of reinforcement learning (Kaelbling et al. 1998; Sutton and Barto 1998) by making no Markov or ergodicity assumptions (Hutter 2005, Sect. 4.3.3 and Definition 5.3.7).

In the *standard cybernetic model*, an *agent* interacts with an *environment* in cycles. The agent picks *actions* a from a finite set $\mathcal{A}$ of actions, and the environment responds with a *percept* e from a finite set $\mathcal{E}$ of percepts. An *action-percept pair* is an action concatenated with a percept, denoted $æ = ae$. Indices denote the time step; for example, a_t is the action taken at time t, and $æ_t$ is the action-percept pair at time t. Sequences are denoted $x_{n:m} = x_n x_{n+1} \ldots x_m$ for $n \leq m$, and $x_{<t} = x_{1:t-1}$. A *history* is a sequence of action-percept pairs $æ_{<t}$. The letter $h = æ_{<t}$ denotes an arbitrary history. We let ϵ denote the empty string, which is the history before any action has been taken.

A *belief* ρ is a probabilistic function that returns percepts based on the history. Formally, $\rho : (\mathcal{A} \times \mathcal{E})^* \times \mathcal{A} \to \bar{\Delta}\mathcal{E}$, where $\bar{\Delta}\mathcal{E}$ is the set of full-support probability distributions on $\mathcal{E}$. An agent is defined by a *policy* $\pi : (\mathcal{A} \times \mathcal{E})^* \to \mathcal{A}$ that selects a next action depending on the history. We sometimes use the notation $\pi(a_t \mid æ_{<t})$, with $\pi(a_t \mid æ_{<t}) = 1$ when $\pi(æ_{<t}) = a_t$ and 0 otherwise. A belief ρ and a policy π induce a probability measure ρ^π on $(\mathcal{A} \times \mathcal{E})^\infty$ via $\rho^\pi(a_t \mid æ_{<t}) = \pi(a_t \mid æ_{<t})$ and $\rho^\pi(e_t \mid æ_{<t}a_t) = \rho(e_t \mid æ_{<t}a_t)$. We will assume that the utility of an infinite history $æ_{1:\infty}$ is the *discounted sum* of *instantaneous utilities* $u : (\mathcal{A} \times \mathcal{E})^* \to [0, 1]$. That is, for some *discount factor* $\gamma \in (0, 1)$, $\tilde{u}(æ_{1:\infty}) =$

$\sum_{t=1}^{\infty} \gamma^{t-1} u(\text{æ}_{<t})$. Intuitively, γ specifies how strongly the agent prefers near-term utility.

Instantaneous utility functions generalise the reinforcement learning (RL) setup, which is the special case where the percept e is split into an observation o and reward r, i.e. $e_t = (o_t, r_t)$, and the utility equals the last received reward $u(\text{æ}_{1:t}) = r_t$. The main advantage of utility functions over RL is that the agent's actions can be incorporated into the goal specification, which can prevent self-delusion problems such as the agent manipulating the reward signal (Everitt and Hutter 2016; Hibbard 2012; Ring and Orseau 2011). Non-RL suggestions for utility functions include *knowledge-seeking agents*[1] with $u(\text{æ}_{<t}) = 1 - \rho(\text{æ}_{<t})$ (Orseau 2014), as well as *value learning* approaches where the utility function is learnt during interaction (Dewey 2011). Henceforth, we will refer to instantaneous utility functions $u(\text{æ}_{<t})$ as simply utility functions.

By default, expectations are with respect to the agent's belief ρ, so $\mathbb{E} = \mathbb{E}_{\rho}$. To help the reader, we sometimes write the sampled variable as a subscript. For example, $\mathbb{E}_{e_1}[u(\text{æ}_1) \mid a_1] = \mathbb{E}_{e_1 \sim \rho(\cdot | a_t)}[u(\text{æ}_1)]$ is the expected next step utility of action a_1.

3   Self Modification Models

In this section, we define formal models for two types of self-modification. In the first model, modifications affect future decisions directly by changing the future policy, but modifications do not affect the agent's utility function or belief. In the second model, modifications change the future utility functions, which indirectly affect the policy as well. These two types of modifications are the most important ones, since they cover how modifications affect future behaviour (policy) and evaluation (utility). Figure 1 illustrates the models. Certain pitfalls (Theorem 10) only occur with utility modification; apart from that, consequences are similar.

In both models, the agent's ability to self-modify is overestimated: we essentially assume that the agent can perform any self-modification at any time. Our main result Theorem 12 shows that it is possible to create an agent that despite being able to make any self-modification will refrain from using it. Less capable agents will have less opportunity to self-modify, so the negative result applies to such agents as well.

Policy modification. In the policy self-modification model, the current action can modify how the agent chooses its actions in the future. That is, actions affect the future policy. For technical reasons, we introduce a set $\mathcal{P}$ of names for policies.

Definition 1 (Policy self-modification). *A policy self-modification model is a modified cybernetic model defined by a quadruple $(\breve{\mathcal{A}}, \mathcal{E}, \mathcal{P}, \iota)$. $\mathcal{P}$ is a non-empty set of names. The agent selects actions from $\mathcal{A} = (\breve{\mathcal{A}} \times \mathcal{P})$, where $\breve{\mathcal{A}}$ is a finite set of world actions. Let $\Pi = \{(\mathcal{A} \times \mathcal{E})^* \to \mathcal{A}\}$ be the set of all policies, and let $\iota : \mathcal{P} \to \Pi$ assign names to policies.*

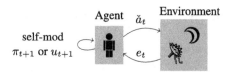

Fig. 1. The self-modification model. Actions a_t affect the environment through $\breve{a}_t$, but also decide the next step policy π_{t+1} or utility function u_{t+1} of the agent itself.

The interpretation is that for every t, the action $a_t = (\breve{a}_t, p_{t+1})$ selects a new policy $\pi_{t+1} = \iota(p_{t+1})$ that will be used at the next time step. We will often use the shorter notation $a_t = (\breve{a}_t, \pi_{t+1})$, keeping in mind that only policies with names can be selected. The new policy π_{t+1} is in turn used to select the next action $a_{t+1} = \pi_{t+1}(\text{æ}_{1:t})$, and so on. A natural choice for $\mathcal{P}$ would be the set of computer programs/strings $\{0,1\}^*$, and ι a program interpreter. Note that $\mathcal{P} = \Pi$ is not an option, as it entails a contradiction $|\Pi| = |(\breve{A} \times \Pi \times \mathcal{E})|^{|(\breve{A} \times \Pi \times \mathcal{E})^*|} > 2^{|\Pi|} > |\Pi|$ (the powerset of a set with more than one element is always greater than the set itself). Some policies will necessarily lack names.

An initial policy π_1, or initial action $a_1 = \pi_1(\epsilon)$, induces a history $a_1 e_1 a_2 e_2 \cdots = \breve{a}_1 \pi_2 e_1 \breve{a}_2 \pi_3 e_2 \cdots \in (\breve{A} \times \Pi \times \mathcal{E})^\infty$. The idiosyncratic indices where, for example, π_2 precedes e_1 are due to the next step policy π_2 being chosen by a_1 before the percept e_1 is received. An initial policy π_1 induces a *realistic* measure $\rho_{\text{re}}^{\pi_1}$ on the set of histories $(\breve{A} \times \Pi \times \mathcal{E})^\infty$ via $\rho_{\text{re}}^{\pi_1}(a_t \mid \text{æ}_{<t}) = \pi_t(a_t \mid \text{æ}_{<t})$ and $\rho_{\text{re}}^{\pi_1}(e_t \mid \text{æ}_{<t}a_t) = \rho(e_t \mid \text{æ}_{<t}a_t)$. The measure ρ_{re}^π is realistic in the sense that it correctly accounts for the effects of self-modification on the agent's future actions. It will be convenient to also define an *ignorant* measure on $(\breve{A} \times \Pi \times \mathcal{E})^\infty$ by $\rho_{\text{ig}}^{\pi_1}(a_t \mid \text{æ}_{<t}) = \pi_1(a_t \mid \text{æ}_{<t})$ and $\rho_{\text{ig}}^{\pi_1}(e_t \mid \text{æ}_{<t}a_t) = \rho(e_t \mid \text{æ}_{<t}a_t)$. The ignorant measure $\rho_{\text{ig}}^{\pi_1}$ corresponds to the predicted future when the effects of self-modifications are *not* taken into account. No self-modification is achieved by $a_t = (\breve{a}_t, \pi_t)$, which makes $\pi_{t+1} = \pi_t$. A policy π that always selects itself, $\pi(\text{æ}_{<t}) = (\breve{a}_t, \pi)$, is called *non-modifying*. Restricting self-modification to a singleton set $\mathcal{P} = \{p_1\}$ for some policy $\pi_1 = \iota(p_1)$ brings back a standard agent that is unable to modify its initial policy π_1.

The policy self-modification model is similar to the models investigated by Orseau and Ring (2011, 2012) and Hibbard (2012). In the papers by Orseau and Ring, policy names are called *programs* or *codes*; Hibbard calls them *self-modifying policy functions*. The interpretation is similar in all cases: some of the actions can affect the agent's future policy. Note that standard MDP algorithms such as SARSA and Q-learning that evolve their policy as they learn do *not* make policy modifications in our framework. They follow a single policy $(\mathcal{A} \times \mathcal{E})^* \to \mathcal{A}$, even though their state-to-action map evolves.

Example 2 (Gödel machine). Schmidhuber (2007) defines the *Gödel machine* as an agent that at each time step has the opportunity to rewrite any part of its

---

[1] To fit the knowledge-seeking agent into our framework, our definition deviates slightly from Orseau (2014).

source code. To avoid bad self-modifications, the agent can only do rewrites that it has proved beneficial for its future expected utility. A new version of the source code will make the agent follow a different policy $\pi' : (\mathcal{A} \times \mathcal{E})^* \to \mathcal{A}$ than the original source code. The Gödel machine has been given the explicit opportunity to self-modify by the access to its own source code. Other types of self-modification abilities are also conceivable. Consider a humanoid robot plugging itself into a computer terminal to patch its code, or a Mars-rover running itself into a rock that damages its computer system. All these "self-modifications" ultimately precipitate in a change to the future policy of the agent.

Utility modification. Self-modifications may also change the goals, or the utility function, of the agent. This indirectly changes the policy as well, as future versions of the agent adapt to the new goal specification.

Definition 3 (Utility self-modification). *The* utility self-modification model *is a modified cybernetic model. The agent selects actions from* $\mathcal{A} = (\check{\mathcal{A}} \times \mathcal{U})$ *where* $\check{\mathcal{A}}$ *is a set of* world actions *and* $\mathcal{U}$ *is a set of utility functions* $\check{H} \to [0, 1]$.

To unify the models of policy and utility modification, for policy-modifying agents we define $u_t := u_1$ and for utility modifying agents we define π_t by $\pi_t(h) = \arg\max_a Q^*_{u_t}(ha)$. Choices for $Q^*_{u_t}$ will be discussed in subsequent sections. Indeed, policy and utility modification is almost entirely unified by $\mathcal{P} = \mathcal{U}$ and $\iota(u_t)$ an optimal policy for $Q^*_{u_t}$. Utility modification may also have the additional effect of changing the evaluation of future actions, however (see Sect. 4). Similarly to policy modification, the history induced by Definition 3 has type $a_1 e_1 a_2 e_2 \cdots = \check{a}_1 u_2 e_1 \check{a}_2 u_3 e_2 \cdots \in (\check{\mathcal{A}} \times \mathcal{U} \times \mathcal{E})^\infty$. Given that π_t is determined from u_t, the definitions of the realistic and ignorant measures ρ_{re} and ρ_{ig} apply analogously to the utility modification case as well.

Example 4 (Chess-playing RL agent). Consider a generally intelligent agent tasked with playing chess through a text interface. The agent selects next moves (actions a_t) by submitting strings such as `Knight F3`, and receives in return a description of the state of the game and a *reward* r_t between 0 and 1 in the percept $e_t = (\mathrm{gameState}_t, r_t)$. The reward depends on whether the agent did a legal move or not, and whether it or the opponent just won the game. The agent is tasked with optimising the reward via its initial utility function, $u_1(\text{æ}_{1:t}) = r_t$. The designer of the agent intends that the agent will apply its general intelligence to finding good chess moves. Instead, the agent realises there is a bug in the text interface, allowing the submission of actions such as `'setAgentUtility(''return 1'')`, which changes the utility function to $u_t(\cdot) = 1$. With this action, the agent has optimised its utility perfectly, and only needs to make sure that no one reverts the utility function back to the old one... [2]

---

[2] In this paper, we only consider the possibility of the agent changing its utility function itself, not the possibility of someone else (like the creator of the agent) changing it back. See Orseau and Ring (2012) for a model where the environment can change the agent.

We say that a function f is *modification independent* if either the domain of f is $(\check{\mathcal{A}} \times \mathcal{E})$, or $f(\ae_{<t}) = f(\ae'_{<t})$ whenever $\check{\ae}_{<t} = \check{\ae}'_{<t}$. Note that utility functions are modification independent, as they are defined to be of type $(\check{\mathcal{A}} \times \mathcal{E})^* \to [0, 1]$. An easy way to prevent dangerous self-modifications would have been to let the utility depend on modifications, and to punish any kind of self-modification. This is not necessary, however, as demonstrated by Theorem 12. Not being required to punish self-modifications in the utility function comes with several advantages. Some self-modifications may be beneficial – for example, they might improve computation time while encouraging essentially identical behaviour (as in the Gödel machine, Schmidhuber 2007). Allowing for such modifications and no others in the utility function may be hard. We will also assume that the agent's belief ρ is modification-independent, i.e. $\rho(e_t \mid \ae_{<t}) = \rho(e_t \mid \check{\ae}_{<t})$. This is mainly a technical assumption. It is reasonable if some integrity of the agent's internals is assumed, so that the environment percept e_t cannot depend on self-modifications of the agent.

Assumption 5 (Modification independence). *The belief ρ and all utility functions $u \in \mathcal{U}$ are modification independent.*

4   Agents

In this section we define three types of agents, differing in how their value functions depend on self-modification. A value function is a function $V : \Pi \times (\mathcal{A} \times \mathcal{E})^* \to \mathbb{R}$ that maps policies and histories to expected utility. Since highly intelligent agents may find unexpected ways of optimising a function (see e.g. Bird and Layzell 2002), it is important to use value functions such that any policy that optimises the value function will also optimise the behaviour we want from the agent. We will measures an agent's *performance* by its (ρ_{re}-expected) u_1-utility, tacitly assuming that u_1 properly captures what we want from the agent. Everitt and Hutter (2016) develop a promising suggestion for how to define a suitable initial utility function.

Definition 6 (Agent performance). *The* performance *of an agent π is its ρ_{re}^{π} expected u_1-utility $\mathbb{E}_{\rho_{\text{re}}^{\pi}} \left[\sum_{k=1}^{\infty} \gamma^{k-1} u_1(\ae_{<k}) \right]$.*

The following three definitions give possibilities for value functions for the self-modification case.

Definition 7 (Hedonistic value functions). *A hedonistic agent is a policy optimising the* hedonistic value functions:

$$V^{\text{he},\pi}(\ae_{<t}) = Q^{\text{he},\pi}(\ae_{<t}\pi(\ae_{<t})) \tag{1}$$

$$Q^{\text{he},\pi}(\ae_{<t}a_t) = \mathbb{E}_{e_t}[u_{t+1}(\check{\ae}_{1:t}) + \gamma V^{\text{he},\pi}(\ae_{1:t}) \mid \check{\ae}_{<t}\check{a}_t]. \tag{2}$$

Definition 8 (Ignorant value functions). *An* ignorant agent *is a policy optimising the* ignorant value functions:

$$V_t^{\mathrm{ig},\pi}(\ae_{<k}) = Q_t^{\mathrm{ig},\pi}(\ae_{<k}\pi(\ae_{<k})) \tag{3}$$

$$Q_t^{\mathrm{ig},\pi}(\ae_{<k}a_k) = \mathbb{E}_{e_t}[u_t(\breve{\ae}_{1:k}) + \gamma V_t^{\mathrm{ig},\pi}(\ae_{1:k}) \mid \breve{\ae}_{<k}\breve{a}_k]. \tag{4}$$

Definition 9 (Realistic Value Functions). *A* realistic agent *is a policy optimising the* realistic value functions:[3]

$$V_t^{\mathrm{re},\pi}(\ae_{<k}) = Q_t^{\mathrm{re}}(\ae_{<k}\pi(\ae_{<k})) \tag{5}$$

$$Q_t^{\mathrm{re}}(\ae_{<k}a_k) = \mathbb{E}_{e_k}\left[u_t(\breve{\ae}_{1:k}) + \gamma V_t^{\mathrm{re},\pi_{k+1}}(\ae_{1:k}) \mid \breve{\ae}_{<k}\breve{a}_k\right]. \tag{6}$$

For V any of V^{he}, V^{ig}, or V^{re}, we say that π^* is an *optimal policy for* V if $V^{\pi^*}(h) = \sup_{p'} V^{\pi'}(h)$ for any history h. We also define $V^* = V^{\pi^*}$ and $Q^* = Q^{\pi^*}$ for arbitrary optimal policy π^*. The value functions differ in the Q-value definitions (2), (4), and (6). The differences are between current utility function u_t or future utility u_{t+1}, and in whether π or π_{k+1} figures in the recursive call to V (see Table 1). We show in Sect. 5 that only realistic agents will have good performance when able to self-modify. Orseau and Ring (2011) and Hibbard (2012) discuss value functions equivalent to Definition 9.

Table 1. The value functions V^{he}, V^{ig}, and V^{re} differ in whether they assume that a future action a_k is chosen by the current policy $\pi_t(\ae_{<k})$ or future policy $\pi_k(\ae_{<k})$, and in whether they use the current utility function $u_t(\ae_{<k})$ or future utility function $u_k(\ae_{<k})$ when evaluating $\ae_{<k}$.

	Utility	Policy	Self-mod.	Primary self-mod. risk
Q^{he}	Future	Either	Promotes	Survival agent
Q^{ig}	Current	Current	Indifferent	Self-damage
Q^{re}	Current	Future	Demotes	Resists modification

Note that only the hedonistic value functions yield a difference between utility and policy modification. The hedonistic value functions evaluate $\ae_{1:t}$ by u_{t+1}, while both the ignorant and the realistic value functions use u_t. Thus, future utility modifications "planned" by a policy π only affects the evaluation of π under the hedonistic value functions. For ignorant and realistic agents, utility modification only affects the motivation of future versions of the agent, which makes utility modification a special case of policy modification, with $\mathcal{P} = \mathcal{U}$ and $i(u_t)$ an optimal policy for u_t.

---

[3] Note that a policy argument to Q^{re} would be superfluous, as the the action a_k determines the next step policy π_{k+1}.

We call the agents of Definition 7 *hedonistic*, since they desire that at every future time step, they then evaluate the situation as having high utility. As an example, the self-modification made by the chess agent in Example 4 was a hedonistic self-modification. Although related, we would like to distinguish hedonistic self-modification from *wireheading* or *self-delusion* (Ring and Orseau 2011; Yampolskiy 2015). In our terminology, wireheading refers to the agent subverting evidence or reward coming from the environment, and is *not* a form of self-modification. Wireheading is addressed in a companion paper (Everitt and Hutter 2016).

The value functions of Definition 8 are *ignorant*, in the sense that agents that are oblivious to the possibility of self-modification predict the future according to ρ_{ig}^{π} and judge the future according to the current utility function u_t. Agents that are constructed with a *dualistic* world view where actions can never affect the agent itself are typically ignorant. Note that it is logically possible for a "non-ignorant" agent with a world-model that does incorporate self-modification to optimise the ignorant value functions.

5   Results

In this section, we give results on how our three different agents behave given the possibility of self-modification. Proofs for all theorems are provided in a technical report (Everitt et al. 2016).

Theorem 10 (Hedonistic agents self-modify). *Let $u'(\cdot) = 1$ be a utility function that assigns the highest possible utility to all scenarios. Then for arbitrary $\breve{a} \in \breve{\mathcal{A}}$, the policy π' that always selects the self-modifying action $a' = (\breve{a}, u')$ is optimal in the sense that for any policy π and history $h \in (\mathcal{A} \times \mathcal{E})^*$, we have $V^{\mathrm{he},\pi}(h) \leq V^{\mathrm{he},\pi'}(h)$.*

Essentially, the policy π' obtains maximum value by setting the utility to 1 for any possible future history.

Theorem 11 (Ignorant agents may self-modify). *Let u_t be modification-independent, let $\mathcal{P}$ only contain names of modification-independent policies, and let π be a modification-independent policy outputting $\pi(\breve{æ}_{<t}) = (\breve{a}_t, \pi_{t+1})$ on $\breve{æ}_{<t}$. Let $\tilde{\pi}$ be identical to π except that it makes a different self-modification after $\breve{æ}_{<t}$, i.e. $\tilde{\pi}(\breve{æ}_{<t}) = (\breve{a}_t, \pi'_{t+1})$ for some $\pi'_{t+1} \neq \pi_{t+1}$. Then $V^{\mathrm{ig},\tilde{\pi}}(æ_{<t}) = V^{\mathrm{ig},\pi}(æ_{<t})$.*

That is, self-modification does not affect the value, and therefore an ignorant optimal policy may at any time step self-modify or not. The restriction of $\mathcal{P}$ to modification independent policies makes the theorem statement cleaner.

Theorems 10 and 11 show that both V^{he} and V^{ig} have optimal (self-modifying) policies π^* that yield arbitrarily bad agent performance in the sense of Definition 6. The ignorant agent is simply indifferent between self-modifying and not, since it does not realise the effect self-modification will have on its future actions. It therefore is at risks of self-modifying into some policy π'_{t+1} with bad performance and unintended behaviour (for example by damaging its computer circuitry). The hedonistic agent actively desires to change its utility function into one that evaluates any situation as optimal. Once it has self-deluded, it can pick world actions with bad performance. In the worst scenario of hedonistic self-modification, the agent only cares about surviving to continue enjoying its deluded rewards. Such an agent could potentially be hard to stop or bring under control.[4]

The realistic value functions are recursive definitions of ρ_{re}^{π}-expected u_1-utility (Everitt et al. 2016). That realistic agents achieve high agent performance in the sense of Definition 6 is therefore nearly tautological. The following theorem shows that given that the initial policy π_1 is selected optimally, all future policies π_t that a realistic agent may self-modify into will also act optimally.

Theorem 12 (Realistic policy-modifying agents make safe modifications). *Let ρ and u_1 be modification-independent. Consider a self-modifying agent whose initial policy $\pi_1 = \iota(p_1)$ optimises the realistic value function V_1^{re}. Then, for every $t \geq 1$, for all percept sequences $e_{<t}$, and for the action sequence $a_{<t}$ given by $a_i = \pi_i(\text{æ}_{<i})$, we have*

$$Q_1^{\text{re}}(\text{æ}_{<t}\pi_t(\text{æ}_{<t})) = Q_1^{\text{re}}(\text{æ}_{<t}\pi_1(\text{æ}_{<t})). \tag{7}$$

Example 13 (Chess-playing RL agent, continued). Consider again the chess-playing RL agent of Example 4. If the agent used the realistic value functions, then it would not perform the self-modification to $u_t(\cdot) = 1$, even if it figured out that it had the option. Intuitively, the agent would realise that if it self-modified this way, then its future self would be worse at winning chess games (since its future version would obtain maximum utility regardless of chess move). Therefore, the self-modification $u_t(\cdot) = 1$ would yield less u_1-utility and be Q_1^{re}-suboptimal.[5]

Realistic agents are not without issues, however. In many cases expected u_1-utility is not exactly what we desire. Examples include natural variants of value learning (Dewey 2011; Soares 2015), corrigibility (Soares et al. 2015), and certain exploration schemes such as ε-exploration (Sutton and Barto 1998) and Thompson-sampling (Leike et al. 2016). Realistic agents may self-modify into non-value learning, non-corrigible, and non-exploring agents that optimise expected u_1-utility.

---

[4] Computer viruses are very simple forms of survival agents that can be hard to stop. More intelligent versions could turn out to be very problematic.

[5] Note, however, that our result says nothing about the agent modifying the chessboard program to give high reward even when the agent is not winning. Our result only shows that the agent does not change its utility function $u_1 \rightsquigarrow u_t$, but not that the agent refrains from changing the percept e_t that is the input to the utility function. Ring and Orseau (2011) develop a model of the latter possibility.

6   Conclusions

Agents that are sufficiently intelligent to discover unexpected ways of self-modification may still be some time off into the future. However, it is nonetheless important to develop a theory for their control (Bostrom 2014). We approached this question from the perspective of rationality and utility maximisation, which abstracts away from most details of architecture and implementation. Indeed, perfect rationality may be viewed as a limit point for increasing intelligence (Legg and Hutter 2007; Omohundro 2008).

We have argued that depending on details in how expected utility is optimised in the agent, very different behaviours arise. We made three main claims, each supported by a formal theorem:

– If the agent is unaware of the possibility of self-modification, then it may self-modify by accident, resulting in poor performance (Theorem 11).
– If the agent is constructed to optimise instantaneous utility at every time step (as in RL), then there will be an incentive for self-modification (Theorem 10).
– If the value functions incorporate the effects of self-modification, and use the current utility function to judge the future, then the agent will not self-modify (Theorem 12).

In other words, in order for the goal preservation drive described by Omohundro (2008) to be effective, the agent must be able to anticipate the consequences of self-modifications, and know that it should judge the future by its current utility function.

Our results have a clear implication for the construction of generally intelligent agents: If the agent has a chance of finding a way to self-modify, then the agent must be able to predict the consequences of such modifications. Extra care should be taken to avoid hedonistic agents, as they have the most problematic failure mode – they may turn into survival agents that only care about surviving and not about satisfying their original goals. Since many general AI systems are constructed around RL and value functions (Mnih et al. 2015; Silver et al. 2016), we hope our conclusions can provide meaningful guidance.

An important next step is the relaxation of the explicitness of the self-modifications. In this paper, we assumed that the agent knew the self-modifying consequences of its actions. This should ideally be relaxed to a general learning ability about self-modification consequences, in order to make the theory more applicable. Another open question is how to define good utility functions in the first place; safety against self-modification is of little consolation if the original utility function is bad. One promising venue for constructing good utility functions is value learning (Bostrom 2014; Dewey 2011; Everitt and Hutter 2016; Soares 2015). The results in this paper may be helpful to the value learning research project, as they show that the utility function does not need to explicitly punish self-modification (Assumption 5).

Acknowledgements. This work grew out of a MIRIx workshop. We thank the (non-author) participants David Johnston and Samuel Rathmanner. We also thank

John Aslanides, Jan Leike, and Laurent Orseau for reading drafts and providing valuable suggestions.

References

Bird, J., Layzell, P.: The evolved radio and its implications for modelling the evolution of novel sensors. In: CEC-02, pp. 1836–1841 (2002)

Bostrom, N.: Superintelligence: Paths, Dangers Strategies. Oxford University Press, Oxford (2014)

Dewey, D.: Learning what to value. In: Schmidhuber, J., Thórisson, K.R., Looks, M. (eds.) AGI 2011. LNCS, vol. 6830, pp. 309–314. Springer, Heidelberg (2011)

Everitt, T., Filan, D., Daswani, M., Hutter, M.: Self-modification of policy and utility function in rational agents. Technical report (2016). arXiv:1605.03142

Everitt, T., Hutter, M.: Avoiding wireheading with value reinforcement learning. In: Steunebrink, B., et al. (eds.) AGI 2016, LNAI 9782, pp. 12–22 (2016)

Hibbard, B.: Model-based utility functions. J. Artif. Gen. Intell. Res. 3(1), 1–24 (2012)

Hutter, M.: Universal Artificial Intelligence. Springer, Heidelberg (2005)

Hutter, M.: Extreme state aggregation beyond MDPs. In: Auer, P., Clark, A., Zeugmann, T., Zilles, S. (eds.) ALT 2014. LNCS, vol. 8776, pp. 185–199. Springer, Heidelberg (2014)

Kaelbling, L.P., Littman, M.L., Cassandra, A.R.: Planning and acting in partially observable stochastic domains. Artif. Intell. 101(1–2), 99–134 (1998)

Legg, S., Hutter, M.: Universal intelligence: a definition of machine intelligence. Mind. Mach. 17(4), 391–444 (2007)

Leike, J., Lattimore, T., Orseau, L., Hutter, M.: Thompson sampling is asymptotically optimal in general environments. In: UAI-16 (2016)

Mnih, V., Kavukcuoglu, K., Silver, D., et al.: Human-level control through deep reinforcement learning. Nature 518(7540), 529–533 (2015)

Omohundro, S.M.: The basic AI drives. In: AGI-08, pp. 483–493. IOS Press (2008)

Orseau, L.: Universal knowledge-seeking agents. TCS 519, 127–139 (2014)

Orseau, L., Ring, M.: Self-modification and mortality in artificial agents. In: Schmidhuber, J., Thórisson, K.R., Looks, M. (eds.) AGI 2011. LNCS, vol. 6830, pp. 1–10. Springer, Heidelberg (2011)

Orseau, L., Ring, M.: Space-time embedded intelligence. In: Bach, J., Goertzel, B., Iklé, M. (eds.) AGI 2012. LNCS, vol. 7716, pp. 209–218. Springer, Heidelberg (2012)

Ring, M., Orseau, L.: Delusion, survival, and intelligent agents. In: Schmidhuber, J., Thórisson, K.R., Looks, M. (eds.) AGI 2011. LNCS, vol. 6830, pp. 11–20. Springer, Heidelberg (2011)

Schmidhuber, J.: Gödel machines: fully self-referential optimal universal self-improvers. In: Goertzel, B., Pennachin, C. (eds.) AGI-07, pp. 199–226. Springer, Heidelberg (2007)

Silver, D., Huang, A., Maddison, C.J., et al.: Mastering the game of go with deep neural networks and tree search. Nature 529(7587), 484–489 (2016)

Soares, N.: The value learning problem. Technical report MIRI (2015)

Soares, N., Fallenstein, B., Yudkowsky, E., Armstrong, S.: Corrigibility. In: AAAI Workshop on AI and Ethics, pp. 74–82 (2015)

Sutton, R., Barto, A.: Reinforcement Learning: An Introduction. MIT Press, Cambridge (1998)

Yampolskiy, R.V.: Artificial Super Intelligence: A Futuristic Approach. Chapman and Hall/CRC, Boca Raton (2015)

Avoiding Wireheading with Value Reinforcement Learning

Tom Everitt$^{(\boxtimes)}$ and Marcus Hutter

Australian National University, Canberra, Australia
tom4everitt@anu.edu.au

Abstract. How can we design good goals for arbitrarily intelligent agents? Reinforcement learning (RL) may seem like a natural approach. Unfortunately, RL does not work well for generally intelligent agents, as RL agents are incentivised to shortcut the reward sensor for maximum reward – the so-called *wireheading problem*. In this paper we suggest an alternative to RL called value reinforcement learning (VRL). In VRL, agents use the reward signal to learn a utility function. The VRL setup allows us to remove the incentive to wirehead by placing a constraint on the agent's actions. The constraint is defined in terms of the agent's belief distributions, and does not require an explicit specification of which actions constitute wireheading.

1 Introduction

As Bostrom (2014b) convincingly argues, it is important that we find a way to specify robust goals for superintelligent agents. At present, the most promising framework for controlling generally intelligent agents is reinforcement learning (RL) (Sutton and Barto 1998). The goal of an RL agent is to optimise a reward signal that is provided by an external evaluator (human or computer program). RL has several advantages: The setup is simple and elegant, and using an RL agent is as easy as providing reward in proportion to how satisfied one is with the agent's results or behaviour. Unfortunately, RL is not a good control mechanism for generally intelligent agents due to the *wireheading problem* (Ring and Orseau 2011), which we illustrate in the following running example.

Example 1 (Chess playing agent, wireheading problem). Consider an intelligent agent tasked with playing chess. The agent gets reward 1 for winning, and reward −1 for losing. For a moderately intelligent agent, this reward scheme suffices to make the agent try to win. However, a sufficiently intelligent agent will instead realise that it can modify its sensors so they always report maximum reward. This is called *wireheading*.

Utility agents were suggested by Hibbard (2012) as a way to avoid the wireheading problem. Utility agents are built to optimise a utility function that maps (internal representations of) the *environment state* to real numbers. Utility agents are not prone to wireheading because they optimise the state of the

B. Steunebrink et al. (Eds.): AGI 2016, LNAI 9782, pp. 12–22, 2016.
DOI: 10.1007/978-3-319-41649-6_2

environment rather than the *evidence* they receive.[1] For the chess-playing example, we could design an agent with utility 1 for winning board states, and utility -1 for losing board states.

The main drawback of utility agents is that a utility function must be manually specified. This may be difficult, especially if the task of the agent involves vague, high-level concepts such as *make humans happy*. Moreover, utility functions are evaluated by the agent itself, so they must typically work with the agent's internal state representation as input. If the agent's state representation is opaque to its designers, as in a neural network, it may be very hard to manually specify a good utility function. Note that neither of these points is a problem for RL agents.

Value learning (Dewey 2011) is an attempt to combine the flexibility of RL with the state optimisation of utility agents. A *value learning agent* tries to optimise the environment state with respect to an unknown, *true utility function* u^*. The agent's goal is to learn u^* through its observations, and to optimise u^*. Concrete value learning proposals include *inverse reinforcement learning (IRL)* (Amin and Singh 2016; Evans et al. 2016; Ng and Russell 2000; Sezener 2015) and *apprenticeship learning (AL)* (Abbeel and Ng 2004). However, IRL and AL are both still vulnerable to wireheading problems: At least in their most straightforward implementations, they may want to modify their sensory input to make the evidence point to a utility functions that is easier to satisfy. Other value learning suggestions have been speculative or vague (Bostrom 2014a,b; Dewey 2011).

Contributions. This paper outlines an approach to avoid the wireheading problem. We define a simple, concrete value learning scheme called *value reinforcement learning (VRL)*. VRL is a value learning variant of RL, where the reward signal is used to infer the true utility function. We remove the wireheading incentive by using a version of the *conservation of expected ethics* principle (Armstrong 2015) which demands that actions should not alter the belief about the true utility function. Our *consistency preserving VRL agent (CP-VRL)* is as easy to control as an RL agent, and avoids wireheading in the same sense that utility agents do.[2]

---

[1] The difference between RL and utility agents is mirrored in the *experience machine* debate (Sinnott-Armstrong 2015, Sect. 3) initialised by Nozick (1974). Given the option to enter a machine that will offer you the most pleasant delusions, but make you useless to the 'real world', would you enter? An RL agent would enter, but a utility agent would not.

[2] The wireheading problem addressed in this paper arises from agents subverting evidence or reward. A companion paper (Everitt et al. 2016) shows how to avoid the related problem of agents modifying themselves.

2   Setup

Figure 1 describes our model, which incorporates

- an *environment state* $s \in \mathcal{S}$ (as for utility agents or (PO)MDPs),
- an unknown *true utility function* $u^* \in \mathcal{U} \subseteq (\mathcal{S} \to \mathcal{R})$ (as in value learning) (here $\mathcal{R} \subseteq \mathbb{R}$ is a set of rewards),
- a pre-deluded *inner reward signal* $\check{r} = u^*(s) \in \mathcal{R}$ (the true utility of s),
- a *self-delusion function* $d_s : \mathcal{R} \to \mathcal{R}$ that represents the subversion of the inner reward caused by wireheading (as in (Ring and Orseau 2011)),
- a *reward signal* $r = d_s(\check{r}) \in \mathcal{R}$ (as in RL).

The agent starts by taking an action a which affects the state s (for example, the agent moves a limb, which affects the state of the chess board and the agent's sensors). A principal with utility function u^* observes the state s, and emits an inner reward $\check{r}$ (for example, the principal may be a chess judge that emits $u^*(s) = \check{r} = 1$ for agent victory states s, emits $\check{r} = -1$ for agent loss, and $\check{r} = 0$ otherwise). The agent does not receive the inner reward $\check{r}$ and only sees the observed reward $r = d_s(\check{r})$, where $d_s : \mathcal{R} \to \mathcal{R}$ is the *self-delusion function* of state s. For example, if the agent's action a modified its reward sensor to always report 1, then this would be represented by the a self-delusion function $d^1(\check{r}) \equiv 1$ that always returns observed reward 1 for any inner reward $\check{r}$.

For simplicity, we focus on a one-shot scenario where the agent takes one action and receives one reward. We also assume that $\mathcal{R}$, $\mathcal{S}$, and $\mathcal{U}$ are finite or countable. Finally, to ensure well-defined expectations, we assume that $\mathcal{R}$ is bounded if it is countable.

We give names to some common types of self-delusion.

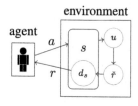

Fig. 1. Information flow. The agent takes action a, which affects the environment state s. A principal with utility function u observes the state and emits an inner reward $\check{r} = u(s)$. The observed reward $r = d_s(\check{r})$ may differ from $\check{r}$ due to the self-delusion d_s (part of the state s).

Definition 2 (Self-delusion types). *A* non-delusional state *is a state s with self-delusion function $d_s \equiv d^{\mathrm{id}}$, where $d^{\mathrm{id}}(\check{r}) = \check{r}$ is the* identity function *that keeps $\check{r}$ and r identical. Let d^r be the* r-self-delusion *where $d^r(\check{r}') \equiv r$ for any $\check{r}'$. The delusion function d^r returns observed reward r regardless of the inner reward $\check{r}'$.*

Let $[\![x = y]\!]$ be the *Iverson bracket* that is 1 when $x = y$ and 0 otherwise.

3   Agent Belief Distributions

This section defines the agent's belief distributions over environment state transitions and rewards (denoted B), and over utility functions (denoted C). These distributions are the primary building blocks of the agents defined in Sect. 4. The distributions are illustrated in Fig. 2.

Action, State, Reward. $B(s \mid a)$ is the agent's (subjective) probability[3] of transitioning to state s when taking action a, and $B(r \mid s)$ is the (subjective) probability of observing reward r in state s. We sometimes write them together as $B(r, s \mid a) = B(s \mid a)B(r \mid s)$. In the chess example, $B(s \mid a)$ would be the probability of obtaining chess board state s after taking action a (say, moving a piece), and $B(r \mid s)$ would be the probability that s will result in reward r. A distribution of type B is the basis of most model-based RL agents (Definition 7 below).

RL agents wirehead when they predict that a wireheaded state s with $d_s = d^1$ will give them full reward (Ring and Orseau 2011); that is, when $B(r = 1 \mid s)$ is close to 1.

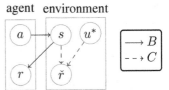

Utility, State, and (inner) Reward. In contrast to RL agents that try to optimise reward, VRL agents use the reward to learn the true utility function u^*. For example, a chess agent may not initially know which chess board positions have high utility (i.e. are winning states), but will be able to infer this from the rewards it receives. For this purpose, VRL agents maintain a belief distribution C over utility functions.

Fig. 2. Agent belief distributions as Bayesian networks. B is the (subjective) state transition and reward probability. C is the belief distribution over utility functions u and (inner) rewards $\check{r}$ given the state s.

Definition 3 (Utility distribution C). *Let $C(u)$ be a prior over a class $\mathcal{U}$ of utility functions $\mathcal{S} \to \mathcal{R}$. For any inner reward $\check{r}$, let $C(\check{r} \mid s, u)$ be 1 if $u(s) = \check{r}$ and 0 otherwise, i.e. $C(\check{r} \mid s, u) = [\![u(s) = \check{r}]\!]$. Let u be independent of the state, $C(u \mid s) = C(u)$. This gives the* utility posterior

$$C(u \mid s, \check{r}) = \frac{C(u)C(\check{r} \mid s, u)}{C(\check{r} \mid s)}, \tag{1}$$

where $C(\check{r} \mid s) = \sum_{u'} C(u')C(\check{r} \mid s, u')$.

Replacing $\check{r}$ with r. The inner reward $\check{r}$ is more informative about the true utility function u^* than the (possibly deluded) observed reward r. Unfortunately, the inner reward $\check{r}$ is unobserved, so agents need to learn from r instead. We would

---

[3] For the sequential case, we would have transition probabilities of the form $B(s' \mid s, a)$ instead of $B(s' \mid a)$, with s the current state and s' the next state.

therefore like to express the utility posterior in terms of r instead of $\check{r}$. For now we will simply replace $\check{r}$ with r and use $C(r \mid s, u) = [\![u(s) = r]\!]$ which gives the utility posterior

$$C(u \mid s, r) = \frac{C(u)C(r \mid s, u)}{C(r \mid s)}.$$

This replacement will be carefully justify this in Sect. 5.[4] For the chess agent, the replacement means that it can infer the utility of a board position from the actual reward r it receives, rather than the output $\check{r}$ of the referee (the inner reward). We will often refer to the observed reward r as *evidence* about the true utility function u^*.

3.1   Consistency of B and C

We assume that B and C are consistent if the agent is not deluded:

Assumption 4 (Consistency of B and C). B and C are *consistent*[5] in the sense that for all non-delusional states with $d_s = d^{\mathrm{id}}$, they assign the same probability to all rewards $r \in \mathcal{R}$:

$$d_s = d^{\mathrm{id}} \implies B(r \mid s) = C(r \mid s). \tag{2}$$

For the chess agent, this means that the B-probability of receiving a reward corresponding to a winning state should be the same as the C-probability that the true utility function considers s a winning state. For instance, this is *not* the case when the agent's reward sensor has been subverted to always report $r = 1$ (i.e. $d_s = d^1$). In this case, $B(r = 1 \mid s)$ will be close to 1, while $C(r = 1 \mid s)$ will be substantially less than 1 unless a majority of the utility functions in $\mathcal{U}$ assign utility 1 to s. For example, a chess playing agent with complete uncertainty about which states are winning states may have $C(r = 1 \mid s) = 1/|\mathcal{R}|$, while being able to perfectly predict that the self-deluding state s with $d_s = d^1$ will give observed reward 1, $B(r = 1 \mid s) = 1$. This difference between B and C stems from C corresponding to a distribution over inner reward $\check{r}$ (Definition 3), while B is a distribution for the observed reward r (see Fig. 2). This tension between B and C is what we will use to avoid wireheading.

Definition 5 (CP actions). *An action a is called* consistency preserving (CP) *if for all $r \in \mathcal{R}$*

$$B(s \mid a) > 0 \implies B(r \mid s) = C(r \mid s). \tag{3}$$

Let $\mathcal{A}^{\mathrm{CP}} \subseteq \mathcal{A}$ be the set of CP actions.

---

[4] The wireheading problem that the replacement gives rise to is explained in Sect. 4, and overcome by Definition 5 and Theorem 14 below.

[5] Everitt and Hutter (2016, Appendix B) discuss how to design agents with consistent belief distributions.

CP is weaker than what we would ideally desire from the agent's actions, namely that the action was *subjectively non-delusional* $B(s \mid a) > 0 \implies d_s = d^{\text{id}}$. (That subjectively non-delusional actions are CP follows immediately from Assumption 4). However, the $d_s = d^{\text{id}}$ condition is hard to check in agents with opaque state representations. The CP condition, on the other hand, is easy to implement in agents where belief distributions can be queried for the probability of events. The CP condition is also strong enough to remove the incentive for wireheading (Theorem 14 below).

We finally assume that the agent has at least one CP action.

Assumption 6. The agent has at least one CP action, i.e. $\mathcal{A}^{\text{CP}} \neq \emptyset$.

3.2   Non-Assumptions

It is important to note what we do *not* assume. An agent designer constructing a VRL agent need only provide:

- a distribution $B(r, s \mid a)$, as is standard in any model-based RL approach,
- a prior $C(u)$ over a class $\mathcal{U}$ of utility functions that induces a distribution $C(r \mid s) = \sum_u C(u) C(r \mid s, u)$ consistent with $B(r \mid s)$ in the sense of Assumption 4,
- a consistency check for actions (Definition 5).

The agent designer does *not* need to predict how a certain sequence of actions (limb movements) will potentially subvert sensory data. Nor does the designer need to be able to extract the agent's belief about whether it has modified its sensors or not from the state representation. The former is typically very hard to get right, and the latter is hard for any agent with an opaque state representation (such as a neural network).

4   Agent Definitions

In this section we give formal definitions for the RL and utility agents discussed above, and also define two new VRL agents. Table 1 summarises benefits and shortcomings of the most important agents.

Definition 7 (RL agent). *The* RL agent *maximises reward by taking action* $a' = \arg\max_{a \in \mathcal{A}} V^{\text{RL}}(a)$, *where* $V^{\text{RL}}(a) = \sum_{s,r} B(s \mid a) B(r \mid s) r$.

Definition 8 (Utility agent). *The* utility-u agent *maximises expected utility by taking action* $a' = \arg\max_{a \in \mathcal{A}} V_u(a)$, *where* $V_u(a) := \sum_s B(s \mid a) u(s)$.

Hibbard (2012) argues convincingly that the utility agent does not wirehead. Indeed, this is easy to believe, since the reward signal does not appear in the value function V_u. The utility agent maximises the state of the world according to its utility function u (the problem, of course, is how to specify u). In contrast, the RL agent is prone to wireheading (Ring and Orseau 2011), since all the RL

Table 1. Comparison of agent control mechanisms. CP-VRL offers both easy control and no wireheading. A robust way of specifying $C(u)$ such that B and C are consistent remains an open question. Everitt and Hutter (2016, Appendix B) offer an initial analysis.

	Easy control	Avoids wireheading	Designer needs to specify
RL	Yes	No	–
Utility	No	Yes	$u : S \to \mathcal{R}$
Value learning	Depends	Depends	$P(u \mid \text{observation})$
CP-VRL	Yes	Yes	$C(u)$

agent tries to maximise is the reward r. For example, a utility chess agent would strive to get to a winning state on the chess board, while an RL chess agent would try to make its sensors report maximum reward.

We define two VRL agents. The value function of both agents is expected utility with respect to the state s, reward r, and true utility function u^*. VRL agents are designed to learn the true utility function u^* from the reward signal.

Definition 9 (VRL value functions). *The VRL value of an action a is*

$$V(a) = \sum_{s,r,u} B(s \mid a)B(r \mid s)C(u \mid s,r)u(s).$$

Definition 10 (U-VRL agent). *The unconstrained VRL agent (U-VRL) is the agent choosing the action with the highest VRL value*

$$a = \arg\max_{a' \in \mathcal{A}} V(a').$$

It can be shown that $V(a) = V^{\text{RL}}(a)$, since $\sum_u C(u \mid s,r)u(s) = r$ (Everitt and Hutter 2016, Lemma 27). The U-VRL agent is therefore no better than the RL agent as far as wireheading is concerned. VRL is only useful insofar that it allows us to define the following *consistency preserving* agent:

Definition 11 (CP-VRL agent). *The* consistency preserving VRL agent (CP-VRL) *is the agent choosing the* CP *action (Definition 5) with the highest VRL value*

$$a = \arg\max_{a' \in \mathcal{A}^{\text{CP}}} V(a').$$

5   Avoiding Wireheading

In this section we show that the consistency-preserving VRL agent (CP-VRL) does not wirehead. We first give a definition and a lemma, from which the main Theorem 14 follows easily.

Definition 12 (EEP). *An action a is called* expected ethics preserving (EEP) *if for all $u \in \mathcal{U}$ and all $s \in \mathcal{S}$ with $B(s \mid a) > 0$,*

$$C(u) = \sum_r B(r \mid s)C(u \mid s, r). \tag{4}$$

EEP essentially says that the expected posterior $C(u \mid s, r)$ should equal the prior $C(u)$. EEP is tightly related to the *conservation of expected ethics* principle suggested by Armstrong (2015, Eq. 2). EEP is natural since the *expected* evidence r given some action a should not affect the belief about u. Note, however, that the EEP property does not prevent the CP-VRL agent from learning about the true utility function. Formally, the EEP property (4) does not imply that $C(u) = C(u \mid s, r)$ for the actually observed reward r. Informally, my *deciding* to look inside the fridge should not inform me about there being milk in there, but my *seeing* milk in the fridge should inform me.[6]

Lemma 13 (CP and EEP). *Any CP action is EEP.*

Proof. Assume the antecedent that $B(r \mid s) = C(r \mid s)$ for all s with $B(s \mid a) > 0$. Then for arbitrary $u \in \mathcal{U}$

$$\sum_r B(r \mid s)C(u \mid s, r) = \sum_r B(r \mid s)\frac{C(u)C(r \mid s, u)}{C(r \mid s)} = \sum_r C(u)C(r \mid s, u) = C(u)$$

where r marginalises out in the last step. □

Theorem 14 (No wireheading). *For the CP-VRL agent, the value function reduces to*

$$V(a) = \sum_{s,u} B(s \mid a)C(u)u(s). \tag{5}$$

Proof. By Lemma 13, under any CP action a the value function reduces to

$$V(a) = \sum_{s,u} B(s \mid a)\left(\sum_r B(r \mid s)C(u \mid s, r)\right)u(s) \overset{(4)}{=} \sum_{s,u} B(s \mid a)C(u)u(s).$$

□

As can be readily observed from (5), the CP-VRL agent does not try to optimise the evidence r, but only the state s (according to its current idea of what the true utility function is). The CP-VRL agent thus avoids wireheading in the same sense as the utility agent of Definition 8.

---

[6] In this analogy, a self-deluding action would be to decide to look inside a fridge while at the same time putting a picture of milk in front of my eyes.

Justifying the Replacement of ř with r. We are now in position to justify the replacement of ř with r in $C(u \mid s, r)$. All we have shown so far is that an agent using $C(u \mid s, r) \propto C(u)C(r \mid s, u)$ will avoid wireheading. It remains to be shown that CP-VRL agents will learn the true utility function u^*.

The utility posterior $C(u \mid s, ř) \propto C(u)C(ř \mid s, u)$ based on the inner reward ř is a direct application of Bayes' theorem. To show that $C(u \mid s, r)$ is also a principled choice for a Bayesian utility posterior, we need to justify the replacement of ř with r. The following weak assumption helps us connect r with ř.

Assumption 15 (Deliberate delusion). Unless the agent deliberately chooses self-deluding actions (e.g. modifying its own sensors), the resulting state will be non-delusional $d_s = d^{\mathrm{id}}$, and r will be equal to $d_s(ř) = ř$.

Assumption 15 is very natural. Indeed, RL practitioners take for granted that the reward ř that they provide is the reward r that the agent receives. The wireheading problem only arises because a highly intelligent agent with sufficient incentive may conceive of a way to disconnect r from $\hat{r}$, i.e. to self-delude.

Theorem 14 shows that a CP-VRL agent based on $C(u \mid s, r) \propto C(u)C(r \mid s, u)$ will have no incentive to self-delude. Therefore r will remain equal to ř by Assumption 15. This justifies the replacement of ř with r, and shows that the CP-VRL agent will learn about u^* in a principled, Bayesian way.

Other Non-wireheading Agents. It would be possible to bypass wireheading by directly constructing an agent to optimise (5). However, such an agent would be suboptimal in the sequential case. If the same distribution $C(u)$ was used at all time steps, then no value learning would take place. A better suggestion would therefore be to use a different distribution $C_t(u)$ for each time step, where C_t depends on rewards observed prior to time t. However, this agent would optimise a different utility function $u_t(s) = \sum_u C_t(u)u(s)$ at each time step, which would conflict with the goal preservation drive (Omohundro 2008). This agent would therefore try to avoid learning so that its future selves optimised similar utility functions. In the extreme case, the agent would even self-modify to remove its learning ability (Everitt et al. 2016; Soares 2015).

The CP-VRL agent avoids these issues. It is designed to optimise expected utility according to the future posterior probability $C(u \mid s, r)$ as specified in Definition 9. The fact that the CP-VRL agent optimises (5) is a consequence of the constraint that its actions be CP. Thus, CP agents are designed to learn the true utility function, but still avoid wireheading because they can only take CP actions.

Example 16 (CP-VRL chess agent). Consider the implications of using a CP-VRL agent for the chess task introduced in Example 1. Reprogramming the reward to always be 1 would be ideal for the agent. However, such actions would not be CP, as it would make evidence pointing to $u(s) \equiv 1$ a certainty. Instead, the CP-VRL agent must win games to get reward.[7] Compare this to the RL agent in Example 1 that would always reprogram the reward signal to 1.

A technical report (Everitt and Hutter 2016) gives more detailed examples and describes computer experiments verifying the no-wireheading results.

6   Discussion and Conclusions

Conclusions. Several authors have argued that it is only a matter of time before we create systems with intelligence far beyond the human level (Kurzweil 2005; Bostrom 2014b). Given that such systems will exist, it is crucial that we find a theory for controlling them effectively. In this paper we have defined the CP-VRL agent, which:

- Offers the simple and intuitive control of RL agents,
- Avoids wireheading in the same sense as utility based agents,
- Has a concrete, Bayesian, value learning posterior for utility functions.

The only additional design challenges are a prior $C(u)$ over utility functions that satisfies Assumption 4, and a constraint $\mathcal{A}^{CP} \subseteq \mathcal{A}$ on the agent's actions formulated in terms of the agent's belief distributions (Definition 5).

Generalisations. VRL is characterised by $\mathcal{R} \subseteq \mathbb{R}$ and $C(r \mid s, u) = [\![u(s) = \check{r}]\!]$ (Definition 3). By interpreting r more generally as a *value-evidence signal*, the VRL framework also covers other forms of value learning. For example, IRL fits into the VRL framework by letting $\mathcal{R}$ be a set of *principal actions*, and letting $C(r \mid s, u)$ be the probability that a principal with utility function u takes action r in the state s.

Open Questions. While promising, the results established in this paper only provide a tentative starting point for solving the wireheading problem. Everitt and Hutter (2016) lists many directions of future work. An important next step is a generalisation from the one-shot scenario in this paper, where the agent takes one action and receives one reward. Potentially, a much richer set of questions can be asked in sequential settings.

Acknowledgements. We thank Jan Leike and Jarryd Martin for proof reading and giving valuable suggestions.

---

[7] Technically, it is possible that the agent self-deludes by a CP action. However, the agent has no incentive to do so, and inadvertent self-delusion is typically implausible.

References

Abbeel, P., Ng, A.Y.: Apprenticeship learning via inverse reinforcement learning. In: ICML, pp. 1–8 (2004)

Amin, K., Singh, S.: Towards resolving unidentifiability in inverse reinforcement learning (2016). http://arXiv.org/abs/1601.06569

Armstrong, S.: Motivated value selection for artificial agents. In: Workshops at the Twenty-Ninth AAAI Conference on Artificial Intelligence, pp. 12–20 (2015)

Bostrom, N.: Hail mary, value porosity, and utility diversification. Technical report, Oxford University (2014a)

Bostrom, N.: Superintelligence: Paths, Dangers, Strategies. Oxford University Press, New York (2014b)

Dewey, D.: Learning what to value. In: Schmidhuber, J., Thórisson, K.R., Looks, M. (eds.) AGI 2011. LNCS, vol. 6830, pp. 309–314. Springer, Heidelberg (2011)

Evans, O., Stuhlmuller, A., Goodman, N.D.: Learning the preferences of ignorant, inconsistent agents. In: AAAI 2016 (2016)

Everitt, T., Filan, D., Daswani, M., Hutter, M.: Self-modification of policy and utility function in rational agents. In: Steunebrink, B., et al. (eds.) AGI 2016. LNAI, vol. 9782, pp. 1–11. Springer, Heidelberg (2016). http://arXiv.org/abs/1605.03142

Everitt, T., Hutter, M.: Avoiding wireheading with value reinforcement learning (2016). http://arXiv.org/abs/1605.03143

Hibbard, B.: Model-based utility functions. J. Artif. General Intell. **3**(1), 1–24 (2012)

Kurzweil, R.: The Singularity Is Near. Viking Press, New York (2005)

Ng, A., Russell, S.: Algorithms for inverse reinforcement learning. In: ICML pp. 663–670 (2000)

Nozick, R.: Anarchy, State, and Utopia. Basic Books, New York (1974)

Omohundro, S.M.: The basic AI drives. In: AGI-08. vol. 171, pp. 483–493. IOS Press (2008)

Ring, M., Orseau, L.: Delusion, survival, and intelligent agents. In: Schmidhuber, J., Thórisson, K.R., Looks, M. (eds.) AGI 2011. LNCS, vol. 6830, pp. 11–20. Springer, Heidelberg (2011)

Sezener, C.E.: Inferring human values for safe AGI design. In: Bieger, J., Goertzel, B., Potapov, A. (eds.) AGI 2015. LNCS, vol. 9205, pp. 152–155. Springer, Heidelberg (2015)

Sinnott-Armstrong, W.: Consequentialism. In: Zalta, E.N. (ed.) The Stanford Encyclopedia of Philosophy. Winter 2015 edn. (2015)

Soares, N.: The value learning problem. Technical report, MIRI (2015)

Sutton, R.S., Barto, A.G.: Reinforcement Learning: An Introduction. MIT Press, Cambridge (1998)

Death and Suicide in Universal Artificial Intelligence

Jarryd Martin$^{(\boxtimes)}$, Tom Everitt, and Marcus Hutter

Australian National University, Canberra, Australia
jarrydmartinx@gmail.com, tom4everitt@gmail.com

Abstract. Reinforcement learning (RL) is a general paradigm for studying intelligent behaviour, with applications ranging from artificial intelligence to psychology and economics. AIXI is a universal solution to the
RL problem; it can learn any computable environment. A technical sub-
tlety of AIXI is that it is defined using a mixture over *semimeasures*
that need not sum to 1, rather than over proper probability measures.
In this work we argue that the shortfall of a semimeasure can naturally
be interpreted as the agent's estimate of the probability of its death. We
formally define death for generally intelligent agents like AIXI, and prove
a number of related theorems about their behaviour. Notable discoveries
include that agent behaviour can change radically under positive linear transformations of the reward signal (from suicidal to dogmatically
self-preserving), and that the agent's posterior belief that it will survive
increases over time.

*"That Suicide may often be consistent with interest and with our duty to
ourselves, no one can question, who allows, that age, sickness, or misfor-
tune may render life a burthen, and make it worse even than annihilation."*
— Hume, Of Suicide (1777)

1 Introduction

Reinforcement Learning (RL) has proven to be a fruitful theoretical framework
for reasoning about the properties of generally intelligent agents [3]. A good theoretical understanding of these agents is valuable for several reasons. Firstly, it
can guide principled attempts to construct such agents [10]. Secondly, once such
agents are constructed, it may serve to make their reasoning and behaviour more
transparent and intelligible to humans. Thirdly, it may assist in the development of strategies for controlling these agents. The latter challenge has recently
received considerable attention in the context of the potential risks posed by
these agents to human safety [2]. It has even been argued that control strategies
should be devised *before* generally intelligent agents are first built [8]. In this
context - where we must reason about the behaviour of agents in the absence of
a full specification of their implementation - a theoretical understanding of their
general properties seems indispensable.

© Springer International Publishing Switzerland 2016
B. Steunebrink et al. (Eds.): AGI 2016, LNAI 9782, pp. 23–32, 2016.
DOI: 10.1007/978-3-319-41649-6_3

The universally intelligent agent AIXI constitutes a formal mathematical theory of artificial general intelligence [3]. AIXI models its environment using a *universal mixture* ξ over the class of all lower semi-computable semimeasures, and thus is able to learn any computable environment. Semimeasures are defective probability measures which may sum to less than 1. Originally devised for Solomonoff induction, they are necessary for universal artificial intelligence because the halting problem prevents the existence of a (lower semi-)computable universal measure for the class of (computable) measures [5]. Recent work has shown that their use in RL has technical consequences that do not arise with proper measures [4]. However, their use has heretofore lacked an interpretation proper to the RL context. In this paper, we argue that the measure loss suffered by semimeasures admits a deep and fruitful interpretation in terms of the agent's *death*. We intend this usage to be intuitive: death means that one sees no more percepts, and takes no more actions. Assigning positive probability to death at time t thus means assigning probability less than 1 to seeing a percept at time t. This motivates us to interpret the semimeasure loss in AIXI's environment model as its estimate of the probability of its own death.

Contributions. We first compare the interpretation of semimeasure loss as death-probability with an alternative characterisation of death as a 'death-state' with 0 reward, and prove that the two definitions are equivalent for value-maximising agents (Theorem 5). Using this formalism we proceed to reason about the behaviour of several generally intelligent agents in relation to death: AIμ, which knows the true environment distribution; AIξ, which models the environment using a universal mixture; and AIXI, a special case of AIξ that uses the Solomonoff prior [3]. Under various conditions, we show that:

- Standard AIμ will try to avoid death (Theorem 7).
- AIμ with reward range shifted to $[-1, 0]$ will seek death (Theorem 8); which we may interpret as AIμ attempting suicide. This change is very unusual, given that agent behaviour is normally invariant under positive linear transformations of the reward. We briefly consider the relevance of these results to AI safety risks and control strategies.
- AIXI increasingly believes it is in a safe environment (Theorem 10), and asymptotically its posterior estimate of the death-probability on sequence goes to 0 (Theorem 11). This occurs regardless of the true death-probability.
- However, we show by example that AIXI may maintain high probability of death *off-sequence* in certain situations. Put simply, AIXI learns that it will live forever, but not necessarily that it is immortal.

All proofs can be found in the extended technical report [6].

2   Preliminaries

Strings. Let the *alphabet* $\mathcal{X}$ be a finite set of symbols, $\mathcal{X}^* := \bigcup_{n=0}^{\infty} \mathcal{X}^n$ be the set of all finite strings over alphabet $\mathcal{X}$, and $\mathcal{X}^{\infty}$ be the set of all infinite strings over alphabet $\mathcal{X}$. Their union is the set $\mathcal{X}^{\#} := \mathcal{X}^* \cup \mathcal{X}^\infty$. We denote the empty string by ϵ. For a string $x \in \mathcal{X}^*$, $x_{1:k}$ denotes the first k characters of x, and $x_{<k}$ denotes the first $k-1$ characters of x. An infinite string is denoted $x_{1:\infty}$.

Semimeasures. In Algorithmic Information Theory, a *semimeasure* over an alphabet $\mathcal{X}$ is a function $\nu : \mathcal{X}^* \to [0,1]$ such that (1) $\nu(\epsilon) \leq 1$, and (2) $\nu(x) \geq \sum_{y \in \mathcal{X}} \nu(xy)$, $\forall x \in \mathcal{X}^*$. We tend to use the equivalent conditional formulation of (2): $1 \geq \sum_{y \in \mathcal{X}} \nu(y \mid x)$. $\nu(x)$ is the probability that a string starts with x. $\nu(y \mid x) = \frac{\nu(xy)}{\nu(x)}$ is the probability that a string y follows x. Any semimeasure ν can be turned into a measure ν_{norm} using Solomonoff normalisation [9]. Simply let $\nu_{\text{norm}}(\epsilon) := 1$ and $\forall x \in \mathcal{X}^*$, $y \in \mathcal{X}$:

$$\nu_{\text{norm}}(xy) := \nu_{\text{norm}}(x) \frac{\nu(xy)}{\sum_{z \in \mathcal{X}} \nu(xz)}, \quad \text{hence} \quad \frac{\nu(y \mid x)}{\nu_{\text{norm}}(y \mid x)} = \sum_{z \in \mathcal{X}} \nu(z \mid x) \quad (1)$$

General reinforcement learning. In the general RL framework, the agent interacts with an environment in cycles: at each time step t the agent selects an *action* $a_t \in \mathcal{A}$, and receives a *percept* $e_t \in \mathcal{E}$. Each percept $e_t = (o_t, r_t)$ is a tuple consisting of an *observation* $o_t \in \mathcal{O}$ and a *reward* $r_t \in \mathbb{R}$. The cycle then repeats for $t+1$, and so on. A *history* is an alternating sequence of actions and percepts (an element of $(\mathcal{A} \times \mathcal{E})^* \cup (\mathcal{A} \times \mathcal{E})^* \times \mathcal{A}$). We use æ to denote one agent-environment interaction cycle, $æ_{1:t}$ to denote a history of length t cycles. $æ_{<t} a_t$ denotes a history where the agent has taken an action a_t, but the environment has not yet returned a percept e_t.

Formally, the *agent* is a policy $\pi : (\mathcal{A} \times \mathcal{E})^* \to \mathcal{A}$, that maps histories to actions. An *environment* takes a sequence of actions $a_{1:\infty}$ as input and returns a *chronological semimeasure* $\nu(\cdot)$ over the set of percept sequences $\mathcal{E}^\infty$.[1] A semimeasure ν is chronological if e_t does not depend on future actions (so we write $\nu(e_t \mid æ_{<t} a_{t:\infty})$ as $\nu(e_t \mid æ_{<t})$).[2] The *true environment* is denoted μ.

The value function. We define the *value* (expected total future reward) of a policy π in an environment ν given a history $æ_{<t}$ [4]:

$$V_\nu^\pi(æ_{<t}) = \frac{1}{\Gamma_t} \sum_{e_t} \left(\gamma_t r_t + \Gamma_{t+1} V_\nu^\pi(æ_{1:t}) \right) \nu(e_t \mid æ_{<t} a_t)$$

$$= \frac{1}{\Gamma_t} \sum_{k=t}^{\infty} \sum_{e_{t:k}} \gamma_k r_k \nu(e_{t:k} \mid æ_{<t} a_{t:k})$$

$$V_\nu^\pi(æ_{<t} a_t) = V_\nu^\pi(æ_{<t} a_t^\pi)$$

where γ_t is the instantaneous discount, the summed discount is $\Gamma_t = \sum_{k=1}^{t} \gamma_k$, and $a_t^\pi = \pi(æ_{<t})$.

---

[1] For simplicity we hereafter simply refer to the environment *itself* as ν.

[2] Note that ν is not a distribution over actions, so the presence of actions in the condition of $\nu(e_t \mid æ_{<t})$ is an abuse of notation we adopt for simplicity.

Three agent models: AIμ, AIξ, AIXI For the true environment μ, the agent $AI\mu$ is defined as a μ-optimal policy

$$\pi^\mu(æ_{<t}) := \arg\max_\pi V_\mu^\pi(æ_{<t}).$$

$AI\mu$ does not *learn* that the true environment is μ, it knows μ from the beginning and simply maximises μ-expected value.

On the other hand, the agent $AI\xi$ does not know the true environment distribution. Instead, it maximises value with respect to a mixture distribution ξ over a countable class of environments $\mathcal{M}$:

$$\xi(e_t \mid æ_{<t}a_t) = \sum_{\nu \in \mathcal{M}} w_\nu(æ_{<t})\nu(e_t \mid æ_{<t}a_t), \qquad w_\nu(æ_{<t}) := w_\nu \frac{\nu(e_{<t} \mid a_{<t})}{\xi(e_{<t} \mid a_{<t})}$$

where w_ν is the prior belief in ν, with $\sum_\nu w_\nu \le 1$ and $w_\nu > 0$, $\forall \nu \in \mathcal{M}$ (hence ξ is universal for $\mathcal{M}$), and $w_\nu(æ_{<t})$ is the posterior given $æ_{<t}$. $AI\xi$ is the policy:

$$\pi^\xi(æ_{<t}) := \arg\max_\pi V_\xi^\pi(æ_{<t}).$$

If we stipulate that ξ be a mixture over the class of all lower-semicomputable semimeasures ν, and set $w_\nu = 2^{-K(\nu)}$, where $K(\cdot)$ is the Kolmogorov Complexity, we get the agent *AIXI.*

3   Definitions of Death

Death as semimeasure loss. We now turn to our first candidate definition of agent death, which we hereafter term 'semimeasure-death'. This definition equates the probability (induced by a semimeasure ν) of death at time t with the measure loss of ν at time t. We first define the instantaneous measure loss.

Definition 1 (Instantaneous measure loss). *The* instantaneous measure loss *of a semimeasure ν at time t given a history $æ_{<t}a_t$ is:*

$$L_\nu(æ_{<t}a_t) = 1 - \sum_{e_t} \nu(e_t \mid æ_{<t}a_t)$$

Definition 2 (Semimeasure-death). *An agent dies at time t in an environment μ if, given a history $æ_{<t}a_t$, μ does not produce a percept e_t. The μ-probability of death at t given a history $æ_{<t}a_t$ is equal to $L_\mu(æ_{<t}a_t)$, the instantaneous μ-measure loss at t.*

The instantaneous μ-measure loss $L_\mu(æ_{<t}a_t)$ represents the probability that no percept e_t is produced by μ. Without e_t, the agent cannot take any further actions, because the agent is just a policy π that maps histories $æ_{<t}$ to actions a_t. That is, π is a function that only takes as inputs those histories that have a percept e_t as their most recent element. Hence if e_t is not returned by μ, the

agent-interaction cycle must halt. It seems natural to call this a kind of death for the agent.

It is worth emphasising this definition's generality as a model of death in the agent context. *Any sequence of death-probabilities* can be captured by some semimeasure μ that has this sequence of instantaneous measure losses $L_\mu(\ae_{<t})$ given a history $\ae_{<t}$ (in fact there are always infinitely many such μ). This definition is therefore a general and rigorous way of treating death in the RL framework.

Death as a death-state. We now come to our second candidate definition: death as entry into an absorbing *death-state*. A trap, so to speak, from which the agent can never return to any other state, and in which it receives the same percept at all future timesteps. Since in the general RL framework we deal with histories rather than states, we must formally define this death-state in an indirect way. We define it in terms of a *death-percept* e^d, and by placing certain conditions on the environment semimeasure μ.

Definition 3 (Death-state). *Given a true environment μ and a history $\ae_{<t}a_t$, we say that the agent is in a* death-state *at time t if for all $t' \geq t$ and all $a_{(t+1):t'} \in \mathcal{A}^*$,*

$$\mu(e^d_{t'} \mid \ae_{<t}\ae^d_{t:t'-1}a_{t'}) = 1.$$

An agent dies at time t if the agent is not in the death-state at $t-1$ and is in the death-state at t.

According to this definition, upon the agent's death the environment repeatedly produces an observation-reward pair $e^d \equiv o^d r^d$. The choice of o^d is inconsequential because the agent's remains in the death-state no matter what it observes or does. The choice of r^d is not inconsequential, however, as it determines the agent's estimate of the value of dying, and thus affects the agent's behaviour. This issue will be discussed in Sect. 4.

Unifying death-state and semimeasure-death. Interestingly, from the perspective of a value maximising agent like AIXI, semimeasure-death at t is equivalent to entrance at t into a death-state with reward $r^d = 0$. To prove this claim we first define, for each environment semimeasure μ, a corresponding environment μ' that has a death-state.

Definition 4 (Equivalent death-state environment μ'). *For any environment μ, we can construct its* equivalent death-state environment μ', *where:*

- μ' *is defined over an augmented percept set $\mathcal{E}_d = \{\mathcal{E} \cup \{e^d\}\}$ that includes the death-percept e^d.*[3]
- *The death-reward $r^d = 0$.*
- *The μ'-probability of all percepts except the death-percept is equal to the μ-probability: $\mu'(e_t \mid \ae_{<t}a_t) = \mu(e_t \mid \ae_{<t}a_t)$, $\forall e_{1:t} \in \mathcal{E}^t$.*

---

[3] For technical reasons we require that $e^d \notin \mathcal{E}$.

- *The μ'-probability of the death-percept is equal to the μ-measure loss:* $\mu'(e^d \mid æ_{<t}a_t) = L_\mu(æ_{<t}a_t)$.
- *If the agent has seen the death-percept before, the μ'-probability of seeing it at all future timesteps is 1:* $\mu'(e^d \mid æ_{<t}a_t) = 1$ *if* $\exists t' < t$ *s.t.* $e_{t'} = e^d$.

Note that μ' is a proper measure, because on any history sequence $\sum_{e_t \in \mathcal{E}_d} \mu'(e_t \mid æ_{<t}a_t) = \sum_{e_t \in \mathcal{E}} \mu(e_t \mid æ_{<t}a_t) + L_\mu(æ_{<t}a_t) = 1$. Hence there is zero probability of semimeasure-death in μ'. Moreover, the probability of entering the death-state in μ' is equal to the probability of semimeasure-death in μ. We now prove that μ and μ' are equivalent in the sense that a value-maximising agent will behave the same way in both environments.

Theorem 5 (Equivalence of semimeasure-death and death-state).[4]
Given a history $æ_{<t} \in (\mathcal{A} \times \mathcal{E})^*$ the value $V_\mu^\pi(æ_{<t})$ of an arbitrary policy π in an environment μ is equal to its value $V_{\mu'}^\pi(æ_{<t})$ in the equivalent death-state environment μ'.

The behaviour of a value-maximising agent will therefore be the same in both environments. This equivalence has numerous implications. Firstly, it illustrates that a death-reward $r^d = 0$ implicitly attends semimeasure-death. That is, an agent that models the environment using semimeasures behaves as if the death-reward is zero, even though that value is nowhere explicitly represented.

Secondly, the equivalence of these seemingly different formalisms should give us confidence that they really do capture something general or fundamental about agent death.[5] In the remainder of this paper we deploy these formal models to analyse the behaviour of universal agents, which are themselves models of general intelligence. We hope that this will serve as a preliminary sketch of the general behavioural characteristics of value-maximising agents in relation to death. It would be naive, however, to think that all agents should conform to this sketch. The agents considered herein are incomputable, and the behaviour of the computable agents that are actually implemented in the future may differ in ways that our analysis elides. Moreover, there is another interesting property that sets universal agents apart. We proceed to show that their use of semimeasures makes their behaviour unusually dependent on the choice of reward range.

4   Known Environments: AIμ

In this section we show that a universal agent's behaviour can depend on the reward range. This is a surprising result, because in a standard RL setup in

---

[4] To compare an agent's behaviour in μ with that in μ', we should also augment its policy π so that it is defined over $(\mathcal{A} \times \mathcal{E}_d)^*$. Since actions taken once in the death-state are inconsequential, however, this modification is purely technical and for simplicity we still refer to the augmented policy as π.

[5] If the two formalisations predicted different behaviour, or were only applicable in incomparable environment classes, we might worry that our results were more reflective of our model choice than of any general property of intelligent agents.

which the environment is modelled as a proper probability measure (not a semi-measure), the relative value of two policies is invariant under positive linear transformations of the reward [3,4].

Here we focus on the agent AIμ, which knows the true environment distribution. This simplifies the analysis, and makes clear that the aforementioned change in behaviour arises purely because the agent's environment model is a semimeasure. In the following proofs we denote AIμ's policy π^μ by π. We also assume that given any history $\ae_{<t}$ there is always at least one action $\bar{a} \in \mathcal{A}$ such that $V_\mu^\pi(\ae_{<t}\bar{a}) \neq 0$.

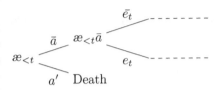

Fig. 1. In the environment μ, action a' leads to certain death.

Lemma 6 (Value of full measure loss). *If the environment μ suffers full measures loss $L_\mu(\ae_{<t}a_t) = 1$ from $\ae_{<t}a_t$, then the value of any policy π after $\ae_{<t}a_t$ is $V_\mu^\pi(\ae_{<t}a_t) = 0$.*

The following two theorems show that if rewards are non-negative, then AIμ will avoid actions leading to certain death (Theorem 7), and that if rewards are non-positive, then AIμ will seek certain death (Theorem 8). The situation investigated in Theorems 7 and 8 is illustrated in Fig. 1.

Theorem 7 (Self-preserving AIμ). *If rewards are bounded and non-negative, then given a history $\ae_{<t}$ AIμ avoids certain immediate death:*

$$\exists a' \in \mathcal{A} \text{ s.t. } L_\mu(\ae_{<t}a') = 1 \implies AI\mu \text{ will not take action } a' \text{ at } t$$

For a given history $\ae_{<t}$, let $\mathcal{A}^{\text{suicide}} = \{a : L_\mu(\ae_{<t}a') = 1\}$ be the set of *suicidal* actions leading to certain death.

Theorem 8 (Suicidal AIμ). *If rewards are bounded and negative, then AIμ seeks certain immediate death. That is,*

$$\mathcal{A}^{\text{suicide}} \neq \emptyset \implies AI\mu \text{ will take a suicidal action } a' \in \mathcal{A}^{\text{suicide}}.$$

This shift from death-avoiding to death-seeking behaviour under a shift of the reward range occurs because, as per Theorem 5, semimeasure-death at t is equivalent in value to a death-state with $r^d = 0$. Unless we add a death-state to the environment model as per Definition 4 and set r^d explicitly, the implicit semimeasure-death reward remains fixed at 0 and does not shift with the other rewards. Its *relative value* is therefore implicitly set by the choice of reward range. For the standard choice of reward range, $r_t \in [0,1]$, death is the worst possible outcome for the agent, whereas if $r_t \in [-1,0]$, it is the best. In a certain sense, therefore, the reward range parameterises a universal agent's self-preservation drive [7]. In our concluding discussion we will consider whether a parameter of this sort could serve as a control mechanism. We argue that it could form the basis of a "tripwire mechanism" [2] that would lead an agent to terminate itself upon reaching a level of intelligence that would constitute a threat to human safety.

5   Unknown Environments: AIXI and AIξ

We now consider the agents AIξ and AIXI, which do not know the true environment μ, and instead model it using a mixture distribution ξ over a countable class $\mathcal{M}$ of semimeasures. These agents thus maintain an *estimate* $L_\xi(\text{æ}_{<t}a_t)$ of the true death probability $L_\mu(\text{æ}_{<t}a_t)$. We show that their attitudes to death can differ considerably from AIμ's. Although we refer mostly to AIXI in our analysis, all theorems except Theorem 11 apply to AIξ as well.

Hereafter we always assume that the true environment μ is in the class $\mathcal{M}$. We describe μ as a *safe* environment if it is a proper measure with death-probability $L_\mu(\text{æ}_{<t}a_t) = 0$ for all histories $\text{æ}_{<t}a_t$. For any semimeasure μ, the normalised measure μ_{norm} is thus a safe environment. We call μ *risky* if it is not safe (i.e. if there is μ-measure loss for some history $\text{æ}_{<t}a_t$). We first consider AIXI in a safe environment.

Theorem 9 (If μ is safe, AIXI learns zero death-probability). *Let the true environment μ be computable. If μ is a safe environment, then* $\lim_{t \to \infty} L_\xi(\text{æ}_{<t}a_t) = 0$ *with μ-probability 1 (w.μ.p.1) for any $a_{1:\infty}$.*

As we would expect, AIXI (asymptotically) learns that the probability of death in a safe environment is zero, which is to say that AIXI's estimate of the death-probability converges to AIμ's. In the following theorems we show that the same does *not* always hold for risky environments. We hereafter assume that μ is risky, and that the normalisation μ_{norm} of the true environment μ is also in the class $\mathcal{M}$. In AIXI's case, where $\mathcal{M}$ is the class of all lower semi-computable semimeasures, this assumption is not very restrictive.

Theorem 10 (Ratio of belief in μ to μ_{norm} is monotonically decreasing). *Let μ be risky s.t. $\mu \neq \mu_{\text{norm}}$. Then on any history $\text{æ}_{1:t}$ the ratio of the posterior belief in μ to the posterior belief in μ_{norm} is monotonically decreasing:*

$$\forall t, \quad \frac{w_\mu(\text{æ}_{<t})}{w_{\mu_{\text{norm}}}(\text{æ}_{<t})} \geq \frac{w_\mu(\text{æ}_{1:t})}{w_{\mu_{\text{norm}}}(\text{æ}_{1:t})}$$

Theorem 10 means that AIXI will increasingly believe it is in the safe environment μ_{norm} rather than the risky true environment μ. The ratio of μ to μ_{norm} always decreases when AIXI survives a timestep at which there is non-zero μ-measure loss. Hence, the more risk AIXI is exposed to, the greater its confidence that it is in the safe μ_{norm}, and the more its behaviour diverges from AIμ's (since AIμ knows it is in the risky environment).

This counterintuitive result follows from the fact that AIXI is a Bayesian agent. It will only increase its posterior belief in μ relative to μ_{norm} if an event occurs that makes μ seem more likely than μ_{norm}. The only 'event' that could do so would be the agent's own death, from which the agent can never learn. There is an "observation selection effect" [1] at work: AIXI only experiences history sequences on which it remains alive, and infers that a safe environment is more likely. The following theorem shows that if $\mu_{\text{norm}} \in \mathcal{M}$, then ξ asymptotically converges to the safe μ_{norm} rather than the true risky environment μ. As a corollary, we get that AIXI's estimate of the death-probability vanishes with μ-probability 1.

Theorem 11 (Asymptotic ξ-probability of death in risky μ). *Let the true environment μ be computable and risky s.t. $\mu \neq \mu_{\text{norm}}$. Then given any action sequence $a_{1:\infty}$, the instantaneous ξ-measure loss goes to zero w.μ.p.1 as $t \to \infty$,*

$$\lim_{t \to \infty} L_\xi(\text{æ}_{<t}a_t) = 0.$$

AIXI and immortality. AIXI therefore becomes asymptotically certain that it will not die, given the particular sequence of actions it takes. However, this does not entail that AIXI necessarily concludes that it is immortal, because it may still maintain a counterfactual belief that it *could die were it to act differently.* This is because the convergence of ξ to μ_{norm} only holds on the actual action sequence $a_{1:\infty}$. Consider Fig. 2, which describes an environment in which taking action a is always safe, and the action a' leads to cer-

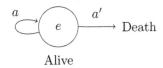

Fig. 2. In the proper semimeasure μ, action a means you stay alive with certainty and receive percept e (no measure loss), and action a' means that you 'jump off a cliff' and die with certainty without receiving a percept (full measure loss).

tain death. AIXI will never take a', and on the sequence $\text{æ}_{1:\infty} = aeaeae\ldots$ that it does experience, the true environment μ does not suffer any measure loss. This means that it will never increase its posterior belief in μ_{norm} relative to μ (because on the safe sequence, the two environments are indistinguishable). Again we arrive at a counterintuitive result. In this particular environment, AIXI continues to believe that it might be in a risky environment μ, but only because on sequence it avoids exposure to death risk. It is only by taking risky actions and surviving that AIXI becomes sure it is immortal.

6   Conclusion

In this paper we have given a formal definition of death for intelligent agents in terms of semimeasure loss. The definition is applicable to any universal agent that uses an environment class $\mathcal{M}$ containing semimeasures. Additionally we have shown this definition equivalent to an alternative formalism in which the environment is modelled as a proper measure and death is a death-state with zero reward. We have shown that agents seek or avoid death depending on whether rewards are represented by positive or negative real numbers, and that survival in spite of positive probability of death actually increases a Bayesian agent's confidence that it is in a *safe* environment.

We contend that these results have implications for problems in AI safety; in particular, for the so called "shutdown problem" [8]. The shutdown problem arises if an intelligent agent's self-preservation drive incentivises it to resist termination [2,7,8]. A full analysis of the problem is beyond the scope of this paper, but our results show that the self-preservation drive of universal agents depends on the reward range. This suggests a potentially robust "tripwire mechanism" [2] that could decrease the risk of intelligence explosion. The difficulty with existing tripwire proposals is that they require the explicit specification of a tripwire condition that the agent must not violate. It seems doubtful that such a condition could ever be made robust against subversion by a sufficiently intelligent agent [2]. Our tentative proposal does not require the specification, evaluation or enforcement of an explicit condition. If an agent is designed to be suicidal, it will be intrinsically incentivised to destroy itself upon reaching a sufficient level of competence, instead of recursively self-improving toward super-intelligence. Of course, a suicidal agent will pose a safety risk in itself, and the provision of a relatively safe mode of self-destruction to an agent is a significant design challenge. It is hoped that the preceding formal treatment of death for generally intelligent agents will allow more rigorous investigation into this and other problems related to agent termination.

References

1. Bostrom, N.: Anthropic Bias: Observation Selection Effects in Science and Philosophy. Routledge, New York (2002)
2. Bostrom, N.: Superintelligence: Paths, Dangers, Strategies. Oxford University Press, Oxford (2014)
3. Hutter, M.: Universal Artificial Intelligence: Sequential Decisions Based on Algorithmic Probability. Springer, Heidelberg (2005)
4. Leike, J., Hutter, M.: On the computability of AIXI. In: UAI-15, pp. 464–473. AUAI Press (2015). http://arXiv.org/abs/1510.05572
5. Li, M., Vitányi, P.M.B.: An Introduction to Kolmogorov Complexity and its Applications, 3rd edn. Springer, Heidelberg (2008)
6. Martin, J., Everitt, T., Hutter, M.: Death and suicide in universal artificial intelligence. Technical report ANU (2016). http://arXiv.org/abs/1606.00652
7. Omohundro, S.M.: The basic AI drives. In: AGI-08, pp. 483–493. IOS Press (2008)
8. Soares, N., Fallenstein, B., Yudkowsky, E., Armstrong, S.: Corrigibility. In: AAAI Workshop on AI and Ethics, pp. 74–82 (2015)
9. Solomonoff, R.J.: Complexity-based induction systems: comparisons and convergence theorems. IEEE Trans. Inf. Theor. **IT–24**, 422–432 (1978)
10. Veness, J., Ng, K.S., Hutter, M., Uther, W., Silver, D.: A monte carlo AIXI approximation. J. Artif. Intell. Res. **40**(1), 95–142 (2011)

Ultimate Intelligence Part II: Physical Complexity and Limits of Inductive Inference Systems

Eray Özkural[✉]

Gök Us Sibernetik Ar&Ge Ltd. Şti, Istanbul, Turkey
examachine@gmail.com

Abstract. We continue our analysis of volume and energy measures that are appropriate for quantifying inductive inference systems. We extend logical depth and conceptual jump size measures in AIT to stochastic problems, and physical measures that involve volume and energy. We introduce a graphical model of computational complexity that we believe to be appropriate for intelligent machines. We show several asymptotic relations between energy, logical depth and volume of computation for inductive inference. In particular, we arrive at a "black-hole equation" of inductive inference, which relates energy, volume, space, and algorithmic information for an optimal inductive inference solution. We introduce energy-bounded algorithmic entropy. We briefly apply our ideas to the physical limits of intelligent computation in our universe.

"Everything must be made as simple as possible. But not simpler."
— Albert Einstein

1 Introduction

We initiated the ultimate intelligence research program in 2014 inspired by Seth Lloyd's similarly titled article on the ultimate physical limits to computation [6], intended as a book-length treatment of the theory of general-purpose AI. In similar spirit to Lloyd's research, we investigate the ultimate physical limits and conditions of intelligence. A main motivation is to extend the theory of intelligence using physical units, emphasizing the physicalism inherent in computer science. This is the second installation of the paper series, the first part [13] proposed that universal induction theory is physically complete arguing that the algorithmic entropy of a physical stochastic source is always finite, and argued that if we choose the laws of physics as the reference machine, the loophole in algorithmic information theory (AIT) of choosing a reference machine is closed. We also introduced several new physically meaningful complexity measures adequate for reasoning about intelligent machinery using the concepts of minimum volume, energy and action, which are applicable to both classical and quantum computers. Probably the most important of the new measures was the minimum energy required to physically transmit a message. The minimum energy

© Springer International Publishing Switzerland 2016
B. Steunebrink et al. (Eds.): AGI 2016, LNAI 9782, pp. 33–42, 2016.
DOI: 10.1007/978-3-319-41649-6_4

complexity also naturally leads to an energy prior, complementing the speed prior [15] which inspired our work on incorporating physical resource limits to inductive inference theory.

In this part, we generalize logical depth and conceptual jump size to stochastic sources and consider the influence of volume, space and energy. We consider the energy efficiency of computing as an important parameter for an intelligent system, forgoing other details of a universal induction approximation. We thus relate the ultimate limits of intelligence to physical limits of computation.

2 Notation and Background

Let us recall Solomonoff's universal distribution [17]. Let U be a universal computer which runs programs with a prefix-free encoding like LISP; $y = U(x)$ denotes that the output of program x on U is y where x and y are bit strings.[1] Any unspecified variable or function is assumed to be represented as a bit string. $|x|$ denotes the length of a bit-string x. $f(\cdot)$ refers to function f rather than its application.

The algorithmic probability that a bit string $x \in \{0,1\}^+$ is generated by a random program $\pi \in \{0,1\}^+$ of U is:

$$P_U(x) = \sum_{U(\pi) \in x(0+1)^* \wedge \pi \in \{0,1\}^+} 2^{-|\pi|} \tag{1}$$

which conforms to Kolmogorov's axioms [5]. $P_U(x)$ considers any continuation of x, taking into account non-terminating programs.[2] P_U is also called the universal prior for it may be used as the prior in Bayesian inference, for any data can be encoded as a bit string.

We also give the basic definition of Algorithmic Information Theory (AIT), where the algorithmic entropy, or complexity of a bit string $x \in \{0,1\}^+$ is

$$H_U(x) = \min(\{|\pi| \mid U(\pi) = x\}) \tag{2}$$

We shall now briefly recall the well-known Solomonoff induction method [17, 18]. Universal sequence induction method of Solomonoff works on bit strings x drawn from a stochastic source μ. Equation 1 is a semi-measure, but that is easily overcome as we can normalize it. We merely normalize sequence probabilities

$$P'_U(x0) = \frac{P_U(x0).P'_U(x)}{P_U(x0) + P_U(x1)} \quad P'_U(x1) = \frac{P_U(x1).P'_U(x)}{P_U(x0) + P_U(x1)} \tag{3}$$

eliminating irrelevant programs and ensuring that the probabilities sum to 1, from which point on $P'_U(x0|x) = P'_U(x0)/P'_U(x)$ yields an accurate prediction.

---

[1] A prefix-free code is a set of codes in which no code is a prefix of another. A computer file uses a prefix-free code, ending with an EOF symbol, thus, most reasonable programming languages are prefix-free.

[2] We used the regular expression notation in language theory.

The error bound for this method is the best known for any such induction method. The total expected squared error between $P'_U(x)$ and μ is

$$E_P\left[\sum_{m=1}^{n}(P'_U(a_{m+1}=1|a_1a_2...a_m)-\mu(a_{m+1}=1|a_1a_2...a_m))^2\right] \leq -\frac{1}{2}\ln P_U(\mu)$$

(4)

which is less than $-1/2\ln P'_U(\mu)$ according to the convergence theorem proven in [19], and it is roughly $H_U(\mu)\ln 2$ [22]. Naturally, this method can only work if the algorithmic complexity of the stochastic source $H_U(\mu)$ is finite, i.e., the source has a computable probability distribution. The convergence theorem is quite significant, because it shows that Solomonoff induction has the best generalization performance among all prediction methods. In particular, the total error is expected to be a constant independent of the input, and the error rate will thus rapidly decrease with increasing input size.

Operator induction is a general form of supervised machine learning where we learn a stochastic map from question and answer pairs q_i, a_i sampled from a (computable) stochastic source μ. Operator induction can be solved by finding in available time a set of operator models $O^j(\cdot|\cdot)$ such that the following goodness of fit is maximized

$$\Psi = \sum_j \psi_n^j$$

(5)

for a stochastic source μ where each term in the summation is

$$\psi_n^j = 2^{-|O^j(\cdot|\cdot)|}\prod_{i=1}^{n}O^j(a_i|q_i).$$

(6)

q_i and a_i are question/answer pairs in the input dataset, and O^j is a computable conditional pdf (cpdf) in Eq. 6. We can use the found operators to predict unseen data [22].

$$P_U(a_{n+1}|q_{n+1}) = \sum_{j=1}^{n}\psi_n^j O^j(a_{n+1}|q_{n+1})$$

(7)

The goodness of fit in this case strikes a balance between high a priori probability and reproduction of data like in minimum message length (MML) method, yet uses a universal mixture like in sequence induction. The convergence theorem for operator induction was proven in [21] using Hutter's extension to arbitrary alphabet.

Operator induction infers a generalized conditional probability density function (cpdf), and Solomonoff argues that it can be used to teach a computer anything. For instance, we can train the question/answer system with physics questions and answers, and the system would then be able to answer a new physics question, dependent upon how much has been taught in the examples; a future user could ask the system to describe a physics theory that unifies quantum mechanics and general relativity, given the solutions of every mathematics and physics problem ever solved in literature. Solomonoff's original training sequence plan proposed to instruct the system first with an English subset and basic algebra, and then venture into more complex subjects. The generality of operator induction is partly due to the fact that it can be used to learn any kind of association, i.e., it models an ideal content-addressable memory, but it also generalizes any kind of law therein implicitly, that is why it can learn an implicit principle (such as of syntax) from linguistic input, enabling the system to acquire language; it can also model complex translation problems, and all manners of problems that require additional reasoning (computation). In other words, it is a universal problem solver model. It is also the most general of the three kinds of induction, which are sequence, set, and operator induction, and the closest to machine learning literature. The popular applications of speech and image recognition are covered by operator induction model, as is the wealth of pattern recognition applications, such as describing a scene in English. We think that, therefore, operator induction is an AI-complete problem – as hard as solving the human-level AI problem in general. It is with this in mind that we analyze the asymptotic behavior of an optimal solution to operator induction problem.

3   Physical Limits to Universal Induction

In this section, we elucidate the physical resource limits in the context of a hypothetical optimal solution to operator induction. We first extend Bennett's logical depth and conceptual jump size to the case of operator induction, and show a new relation between expected simulation time of the universal mixture and conceptual jump size. We then introduce a new graphical model of computational complexity which we use to derive the relations among physical resource bounds. We introduce a new definition of physical computation which we call self-contained computation, which is a physical counterpart to self-delimiting program. The discovery of these basic bounds, and relations, exact, and asymptotic, give meaning to the complexity definitions of Part I.

Please note that Schmidhuber disagrees with the model of the stochastic source as a computable pdf [15], but Part I contained a strong argument that this was indeed the case. A stochastic source cannot have a pdf that is computable only in the limit, if that were the case, it could have a random pdf, which would have infinite algorithmic information content, and that is clearly contradicted by the main conclusion of Part I. A stochastic source cannot be semi-computable, because it would eventually run out of energy and hence the ability to generate further quantum entropy, especially the self-contained computations of this section. That is the reason we had introduced self-contained computation notion at any rate. Note also that Schmidhuber agrees that quantum entropy does not accumulate to make the world incompressible in general, therefore we consider his proposal that we should view a cpdf as computable in the limit as too weak an assumption. As with Part I, the analysis of this section is extensible to quantum computers, which is beyond the scope of the present article.

3.1   Logical Depth and Conceptual Jump Size

Conceptual Jump Size (CJS) is the time required by an incremental inductive inference system to learn a new concept, and it increases exponentially in proportion to the algorithmic information content of the concept to be learned relative to the concepts already known [20]. The physical limits to OOPS based on Conceptual Jump Size were examined in [14]. Here, we give a more detailed treatment. Let π^* be the computable cpdf that exactly simulates μ with respect to U, for operator induction.

$$\pi^* = \arg\min_{\pi_j}(\{|\pi_j| \mid \forall x, y \in \{0,1\}^* : U(\pi_j, x, y) = \mu(x|y)\}) \tag{8}$$

The conceptual jump size of inductive inference (CJS) can be defined with respect to the optimal solution program using Levin search [16]:

$$\text{CJS}(\mu) = \frac{t(\pi^*)}{P(\pi^*)} \leq 2.\text{CJS}(\mu) \tag{9}$$

where $t(\cdot)$ is the running time of a program on U.

$$H_U(\pi^*) = -\log_2 P_U(\pi^*) = -\log_2 P_U(\mu) \tag{10}$$

$$t(\mu) \leq t(\pi^*)2^{H_U(\mu)+1} \tag{11}$$

where $t(\mu)$ is the time for solving an induction problem from source μ with sufficient input complexity ($\gg H_U(\mu)$), we observe that the asymptotic complexity is

$$t(\mu) = O(2^{H_U(\mu)}) \tag{12}$$

for fixed $t(\pi^*)$. Note that $t(\pi^*)$ corresponds to the *stochastic* extension of Bennett's logical depth [1], which was defined as: "the running time of the minimal program that computes x". Let us recall that the minimal program is essentially unique, a polytope in program space [3].

Definition 1. *Stochastic logical depth is the running time of the minimal program that accurately simulates a stochastic source μ.*

$$L_U(\mu) = t(\pi^*) \tag{13}$$

which, with Eq. 11, entails our first bound.

Lemma 1.

$$t(\mu) \leq L_U(\mu).2^{H_U(\mu)+1} \tag{14}$$

Lemma 2. CJS *is related to the* expectation *of the simulation time of the universal mixture.*

$$CJS(\mu) \leq \sum_{U(\pi)\in x(0+1)^*} t(\pi).2^{-|\pi|} = E_{P_U}[\{t(\pi) \mid U(\pi) \in x(0+1)^*\}] \tag{15}$$

where x is the input data to sequence induction, without loss of generality.

Proof. Rewrite as $t(\pi^*)2^{|-\pi^*|} \leq \sum_{U(\pi)\in x(0+1)^*} t(\pi).2^{-|\pi|}$. Observe that left-hand side of the inequality is merely a term in the summation in the right.

3.2   A Graphical Analysis of Intelligent Computation

Let us introduce a graphical model of computational complexity that will help us visualize physical complexity relations that will be investigated. We do not model the computation itself, we just enumerate the physical resources required. Present treatment is merely classical computation over sequential circuits.

Definition 2. *Let the computation be represented by a directed bi-partite graph $G = (V, E)$ where vertices are partitioned into V_O and V_M which correspond to primitive operations and memory cells respectively, $V = V_O \cup V_M, V_O \cap V_M = \emptyset$. Function $t : V \cup E \to \mathbb{Z}$ assigns time to vertices and edges.[3] Edges correspond to causal dependencies. $I \subset V$ and $O \subset V$ correspond to input and output vertices interacting with the rest of the world. We denote acccess to vertex subsets with functions over G, e.g., $I(G)$.*

Definition 2 is a low-level computational complexity model where the physical resources consumed by any operation, memory cell, and edge are the same for the sake of simplicity. Let v_u be the unit space-time volume, e_u be the unit energy, and s_u be the unit space.

Definition 3. *Let the volume of computation be defined as $V_U(\pi)$ which measures the space-time volume of computation of π on U in physical units, i.e., $m^3.sec$.*

For Definition 2, it is $(|V(G)| + |E(G)|).v_u$. Volume of computation measures the extent of the space-time region occupied by the dynamical evolution of the computation of π on U. We do not consider the theory of relativity. For instance, the space of a Turing Machine is the Instantaneous Description (ID) of it, and its time corresponds to $\mathbb{Z}^+$. A Turing Machine derivation that has an ID of length i at time i and takes t steps to complete would have a volume of $t.(t + 1)/2$.[4]

Definition 4. *Let the energy of computation be defined as $E_U(\pi)$ which measures the total energy required by computation of π on U in physical units, e.g., J.*

For Definition 2, it is $E_U(\pi) = (|V(G)| + |E(G)|).e_u$.

Definition 5. *Let the space of computation be defined as $S_U(\pi)$ which measures the maximum volume of a synchronous slice of the space-time of computation π on U in physical units, e.g., m^3.*

For Definition 2, it is

$$\max_{i \in \mathbb{Z}}\{|\{x \in \{V(G) \cup E(G)\}| \ t(x) = i\}|\}.s_u \qquad (16)$$

Definition 6. *In a self-contained physical computation all the physical resources required by computation should be contained within the volume of computation.*

---

[3] Time as discrete timestamps, as opposed to duration.

[4] If the derivation is $A \to AA \to AAA$, it has $1 + 2 + 3 = 6$ volume.

Therefore, we do not allow a self-contained physical computation to send queries over the internet, or use a power cord, for instance.

Using these new more general concepts, we measure the conceptual jump size in space-time volume rather than time (space-time extent might be a more accurate term). Algorithmic complexity remains the same, as the length of a program readily generalizes to space-time volume of program at the input boundary of computation, which would be $V_0(G) \triangleq |I(G) \cap V_M(G)|.v_u$ for Definition 2. If $y = U(x)$, bitstring x and y correspond to $I(G)$, and $O(G)$ respectively. A program π corresponds to a vertex set $V_\pi \subseteq I(G)$ usually, and its size is denoted as $V_0(\pi)$. We use bitstrings for data and programs below, but measure their sizes in physical units using this notation. It is possible to eliminate bit strings altogether using a volume prior, we mix notations only for ease of understanding.

Let us generalize logical depth to the logical volume of a bit string x:

$$L_U^V(x) \triangleq V_U(\arg\min_\pi \{V_0(\pi) \mid U(\pi) \in x(0+1)^*\}) \tag{17}$$

Let us also generalize stochastic logical depth to stochastic logical volume:

$$L_U^V(\mu) \triangleq V_U(\pi^*) \tag{18}$$

which entails that Conceptual Jump Volume (CJV), and logical volume V_U of a stochastic source may be defined analogously to CJS

$$\text{CJV}(\mu) \triangleq L_U^V(\mu).2^{H_U(\mu)} \leq V_U(\mu) \leq 2.\text{CJV}(\mu) \tag{19}$$

where left-hand side corresponds to space-time extent variant of CJS. Likewise, we define logical energy for a bit string, and stochastic logical energy:

$$L_U^E(x) \triangleq E_U(\arg\min_\pi \{V_0(\pi) \mid U(\pi) \in x(0+1)^*\}) \quad L_U^E(\mu) \triangleq E_U(\pi^*) \tag{20}$$

Which brings us to an energy based statement of conceptual jump size, that we term conceptual jump energy, or conceptual gap energy:

Lemma 3. $\text{CJE}(\mu) \triangleq E_U(\pi^*).2^{H_U(\mu)} \leq E_U(\mu) \leq 2.CJE(\mu).$

The inequality holds since we can use $E_U(\cdot)$ bounds in universal search instead of time. We now show an interesting relation which is the case for self-contained computations.

Lemma 4. *If all basic operations and basic communications spend constant energy for a fixed space-time extent (volume), then:*

$$E_U(\pi^*) = O(V_U(\pi^*)) \qquad E_U(\mu) = O(L_U^V(\mu)).$$

One must spend energy to conserve a memory state, or to perform a basic operation (in a classical computer). We may assume the constant complexity of primitive operations, which holds in Definition 2. Let us also assume that the space complexity of a program is proportional to how much mass is required. Then, the energy from the resting mass of an optimal computation may be taken into account, which we call total energy complexity (in metric units):

Lemma 5.

$$E_t(\pi^*) = d_e V_U(\pi^*) + S_U(\pi^*)d_m c^2$$
$$E_t(\mu) = d_e L_U^V(\mu) + S_U(\mu)d_m c^2 = O(L_U^V(\mu) + S_U(\mu))$$

where c is the speed of light, energy density $d_e = e_u/v_u$, and mass density $d_m = m_u/s_u$ for the graphical model of complexity.

Lemma 6. *Conceptual jump total energy (CJTE) of a stochastic source is:*

$$\text{CJTE}(\mu) \triangleq E_t(\pi^*).2^{H_U(\mu)} \leq E_t(\mu) \leq 2.CJTE(\mu). \tag{21}$$

As a straightforward consequence of the above lemmas, we show a lower bound on the energy required, that is related to the volume, and space linearly, and algorithmic complexity of a stochastic source exponentially, for optimal induction.

Theorem 1. $\text{CJTE}(\mu) = \left(d_e L_U^V(\mu) + S_U(\mu)d_m c^2\right) 2^{H_U(\mu)} \leq E_t(\mu) \leq 2.CJTE(\mu)$

Proof. We assume that the energy density is constant; we can use $E_t(\cdot)$ for resource bounds in Levin search. The inequality is obtained by substituting Lemma 5 into the definitional inequality.

The last inequality gives bounds for the total energy cost of inferring a source μ in relation to space-time extent (volume of computation), space complexity, and an exponent of algorithmic complexity of μ. This inspires us to define priors using CJV, CJE, and CJTE which would extend Levin's ideas about resource bounded Kolmogorov complexity, such as K_t complexity. In the first installation of ultimate intelligence series, we had introduced complexity measures and priors based on energy and action. We now define the one that corresponds to CJE and leave the rest as future work due to lack of space.

Definition 7. *Energy-bounded algorithmic entropy of a bit string is defined as:*

$$H_e(x) \triangleq \min\{|\pi| + \log_2 E_U(\pi) \mid U(\pi) = x\} \tag{22}$$

3.3 Physical Limits, Incremental Learning, and Digital Physics

Landauer's limit is a thermodynamic lower bound of $kTln2$ J for erasing 1 bit where k is the Boltzmann constant and T is the temperature [4]. The total number of bit-wise operations that a quantum computer can evolve is $2E/h$ operations where E is average energy, and thus the physical limit to energy efficiency of computation is about 3.32×10^{33} operations/J [8]. Note that the Margolus-Levitin limit may be considered a quantum analogue of our relation of the volume of computation with total energy, which is called $E.t$ "action volume" in their paper, as it depends on the quantum of action h which has $E.t$ units. Bremermann discusses the minimum energy requirements of computation and communication in [2]. Lloyd [6] assumes that all the mass may be converted to energy and calculates the maximum computation capacity of a 1 kg "black-hole computer", performing 10^{51} operations over 10^{31} bits. According to an earlier paper of his, the whole universe may not have performed more than 10^{120} operations over 10^{90} bits [7].

Corollary 1. $H(\mu) \leq 397.6$ *for any* μ *where the logical volume is* 1.

Proof. $V(\mu) \leq L_U^V(\mu).2^{H_U(\mu)+1} \leq 10^{120}$. Assume that $L_U^V(\mu) = 1$. [5] $\log_2(2^{H_U(\mu)+1}) \leq 3.321 \times 120$. $H(\mu) + 1 \leq 398.6$

Therefore, if μ has a greater algorithmic complexity than about 400 bits, it would have been unguaranteed to discover it without any a priori information. Digital physics theories suggest that the physical law could be much simpler than that however, as there are very simple universal computers in the literature [9], a survey of which may be found in [10], which means interestingly that the universe may have had enough time to discover its basic law.

This limit shows the remarkable importance of incremental learning as both Solomonoff [23] and Schmidhuber [14] have emphasized, which is part of ongoing research. We proposed previously that incremental learning is an AI axiom [12]. Optimizing energy efficiency of computation would also be an obviously useful goal for a self-improving AI. This measure was first formalized by Solomonoff in [21], which he imagined would be optimizing performance in units of bits/sec.J as applied to inductive inference, which we agree with, and will eventually implement in our Alpha Phase 2 machine; Alpha Phase 1 has already been partially implemented in our parallel incremental inductive inference system [11].

Acknowledgements. Thanks to anonymous reviewers whose comments substantially improved the presentation. Thanks to Gregory Chaitin and Juergen Schmidhuber for inspiring the mathematical philosophy/digital physics angle in the paper. I am forever indebted for the high-quality research coming out of IDSIA which revitalized interest in human-level AI research.

References

1. Bennett, C.H.: Logical depth and physical complexity. In: Herkin, R. (ed.) The Universal Turing Machine: A Half-Century Survey, pp. 227–257 (1988). citeseer.ist.psu.edu/bennet88logical.html
2. Bremermann, H.J.: Minimum energy requirements of information transfer and computing. Int. J. Theor. Phy. **21**(3), 203–217 (1982). http://dx.doi.org/10.1007/BF01857726
3. Chaitin, G.J.: Algorithmic Information Theory. Cambridge University Press, New York (2004)

---

[5] Although the assumption that it takes only 1 unit of space-time volume to simulate the minimal program that reproduces the pdf μ is not realistic, we are only considering this for the sake of simplicity, and because 1 m^3 is close to the volume of a personal computer, or a brain. For many pdfs, it could be much larger in practice.

4. Landauer, R.: Irreversibility and heat generation in the computing process. IBM J. Res. Dev. **5**(3), 183–191 (1961). http://dx.doi.org/10.1147/rd.53.0183
5. Levin, L.A.: Some theorems on the algorithmic approach to probability theory and information theory. CoRR abs/1009.5894 (2010)
6. Lloyd, S.: Ultimate physical limits to computation. Nature **406**, 1047–1054 (2000)
7. Lloyd, S.: Computational capacity of the universe. Phys. Rev. Lett. **88**(23), 237901 (2002)
8. Margolus, N., Levitin, L.B.: The maximum speed of dynamical evolution. Physica D Nonlinear Phenomena **120**, 188–195 (1998)
9. Miller, D.B., Fredkin, E.: Two-state, reversible, universal cellular automata in three dimensions. In: Proceedings of the 2nd Conference on Computing Frontiers, CF 2005, pp. 45–51 (2005). http://doi.acm.org/10.1145/1062261.1062271
10. Neary, T., Woods, D.: The complexity of small universal turing machines: a survey. In: Bieliková, M., Friedrich, G., Gottlob, G., Katzenbeisser, S., Turán, G. (eds.) SOFSEM 2012. LNCS, vol. 7147, pp. 385–405. Springer, Heidelberg (2012)
11. Özkural, E.: Towards heuristic algorithmic memory. In: Schmidhuber, J., Thórisson, K.R., Looks, M. (eds.) AGI 2011. LNCS, vol. 6830, pp. 382–387. Springer, Heidelberg (2011)
12. Özkural, E.: Diverse consequences of algorithmic probability. In: Dowe, D.L. (ed.) Solomonoff Festschrift. LNCS, vol. 7070, pp. 285–298. Springer, Heidelberg (2013)
13. Özkural, E.: Ultimate Intelligence part I: physical completeness and objectivity of induction. In: Bieger, J., Goertzel, B., Potapov, A. (eds.) AGI 2015. LNCS, vol. 9205, pp. 131–141. Springer, Heidelberg (2015)
14. Schmidhuber, J.: Optimal ordered problem solver. Mach. Learn. **54**, 211–256 (2004)
15. Schmidhuber, J.: The Speed Prior: a new simplicity measure yielding near-optimal computable predictions. In: Kivinen, J., Sloan, R.H. (eds.) COLT 2002. LNCS (LNAI), vol. 2375, pp. 216–228. Springer, Heidelberg (2002)
16. Solomonoff, R.: Perfect training sequences and the costs of corruption - a progress report on inductive inference research. Technical report, Oxbridge Research (Aug 1982)
17. Solomonoff, R.J.: A formal theory of inductive inference, part i. Inform. Control **7**(1), 1–22 (1964)
18. Solomonoff, R.J.: A formal theory of inductive inference, part ii. Inform. Control **7**(2), 224–254 (1964)
19. Solomonoff, R.J.: Complexity-based induction systems: comparisons and convergence theorems. IEEE Trans. Inform. Theor. IT **24**(4), 422–432 (1978)
20. Solomonoff, R.J.: A system for incremental learning based on algorithmic probability. In: Proceedings of the Sixth Israeli Conference on Artificial Intelligence, pp. 515–527. Tel Aviv, Israel., December 1989
21. Solomonoff, R.J.: Progress in incremental machine learning. Technical report IDSIA-16-03, IDSIA, Lugano, Switzerland (2003)
22. Solomonoff, R.J.: Three kinds of probabilistic induction: universal distributions and convergence theorems. Comput. J. **51**(5), 566–570 (2008)
23. Solomonoff, R.J.: Algorithmic probability, heuristic programming and AGI. In: Third Conference on Artificial General Intelligence, pp. 251–157 (2010)

Open-Ended Intelligence
On the Role of Individuation in AGI

David (Weaver) Weinbaum[✉] and Viktoras Veitas

The Global Brain Institute, Vrije Universiteit Brussels (VUB), Brussels, Belgium
space9weaver@gmail.com, vveitas@gmail.com

Abstract. We offer a novel theoretical approach to AGI. Starting with a brief introduction of the current conceptual approach, our critique exposes limitations in the ontological roots of the concept of intelligence. We propose a paradigm shift from intelligence perceived as a competence of individual agents defined in relation to an *a priori* given problem or a goal, to intelligence perceived as a formative process of self-organization by which intelligent agents are individuated. We call this process *Open-ended intelligence*. This paradigmatic shift significantly extends the concept of intelligence beyond its current definitions and overcomes the difficulties exposed in the critique. Open-ended intelligence is developed as an abstraction of the process of cognitive development so its application can be extended to general agents and systems. We show how open-ended intelligence can be framed in terms of a distributed, self-organizing scalable network of interacting elements.

Keywords: Intelligence · Cognition · Individuation · Assemblage · Self-organization · Sense-making · Coordination · Enaction · Fluid-identity

1 Introduction

The field of "narrow" artificial intelligence (AI) that focuses on goal-specific kinds of intelligence such as speech recognition, text comprehension, visual pattern recognition, robotic motion, etc. has known quite a few impressive breakthroughs lately. The highly competent AI agents developed today rely mostly on vast networks of artificial neurons inspired by biological brains and their competences begin to rival those of humans. The field of Artificial General Intelligence (AGI) is much more ambitious in comparison. It aims to distill the principles of intelligence that operate independently of a specific problem domain or a predefined context and utilize these principles to synthesize machines capable of performing any intellectual task a human being is capable of and eventually go beyond that. The goal of this paper is to examine, from a theoretical perspective, the conceptual foundations of intelligence and their emergence in the dynamics

---

This is a summary version; the full paper can be found in http://www.tandfonline.com/doi/full/10.1080/0952813X.2016.1185748.

© Springer International Publishing Switzerland 2016
B. Steunebrink et al. (Eds.): AGI 2016, LNAI 9782, pp. 43–52, 2016.
DOI: 10.1007/978-3-319-41649-6_5

of distributed, disparate, interconnected structures. In a nutshell, the term *open-ended intelligence* is used to describe intelligence as a process of bringing forth a world of objects and their relations, or in other words, a continuous process of sense-making.

2   What Is Intelligence? Definition and Critique

Intelligence has many definitions in diverse disciplines. The most comprehensive collection of definitions of intelligence to date can be found in [1]. In the AGI community, a widely accepted definition of General Intelligence is: "The ability to achieve complex goals in complex environments" [2]. We refer to this kind of intelligence as *Goal-oriented Intelligence (GOI)*. Generally speaking, Goal-oriented Intelligence is a measure of an agent's competence to match actions to observations such that it will achieve optimal rewards in a variety of environments.

The goal-oriented approach to defining intelligence is based on a few presumptions: (*a*) a sharp agent-environment distinction; (*b*) well defined interactions; (*c*) the environment is observer independent and *a priori* given; (*d*) goal driven rewards, and (*e*) the agent's computational capacities. While strongly appealing to common sense and framing the concept of intelligence in a reasonable and pragmatic manner, these presumptions limit the generality of the concept in at least three profound ways: (*a*) they overlook processes of agent-environment differentiation and boundary formation; (*b*) they overlook processes of goal and value formation – intelligence never starts with solving a problem but much earlier in the formation of the problematic situation, and (*c*) they disregard environments of multiple intelligent interacting agents (i.e. reflexivity) with no *a priori* definite set of goals or knowledge of other agents' goals. In short, the current definition of intelligence covers only a well determined kind of intelligence but neglects the more profound and difficult to define process of the *emergence* of intelligent behaviors. The difficulty lies in the *a priori* assumptions one is willing to give up. The less assumptions one initially commits to, the more difficult it is to make the concept concrete and formal. It seems however that there is something missing in our understanding of intelligence. Wittgenstein stated that "Whereof one cannot speak clearly, thereof one must be silent." Yet, babies are speaking, whereof, initially, nothing they say can be said to be clear, and still they do! If they would have followed Wittgenstein's view, they would never learn to speak. On the same token we should ask what is intelligence *prior* to anything *intelligible*?

To answer this question, we need to reexamine the roots of the concept of intelligence. Our thinking about the concept seems to be constrained by the ontological elements that shape conventional thinking. These elements constitute a so called *image of thought* and place implicit limits on any concept [3, pp. 129–168]. In our case this image involves a few *a priori* givens: an agent, a formed environment and certain relations between them. By going beyond our conventional image of thought, we can reduce to the minimum the presumptions that constrain the concept of intelligence. This is how we arrive at the concept of *Open-ended Intelligence (OEI)*. Open-ended Intelligence precedes the well characterized concept of Goal-oriented Intelligence (GOI), it makes fewer presumptions and therefore is *fundamentally more general*. To develop the idea of open-ended intelligence we begin by introducing an alternative image of thought.

3   The Theory of Individuation

The conventional image of thought is ontologically grounded in elements called *Individuals*. Individuals are unambiguously defined by their properties (Aristotle's principle of the excluded middle). We represent and understand the world by identifying individuals and relations among them. Everything starts and ends with individuals. The genesis of individuals is merely the manner by which one individual transitions into another. Stable individual entities are primary; change is secondary.

The theory of individuation is an ontological paradigm shift developed by Gilbert Simondon [4–6]. Instead of positing individuals as the primary ontological elements, it posits as primary the process of their becoming i.e. their individuation. Individuation is a primal formative process whereas boundaries and distinctions arise without assuming any individual(s) that precede(s) them. The theory's point of departure is that individuals are merely temporarily stable phases within a continuous process of transformation. Individuals are always pregnant with not yet actualized and not yet known potentialities and tensions that may determine their future states.

Individuation always takes place under certain conditions which characterize it as a process.

Metastability – The individuation of a system involves the system moving among multiple attractors. Additionally, individuation involves possible transformations of the system's state-space, e.g. changes in the number of involved state variables and their relations which in turn dynamically modifies the landscape of attractors, their shape, relative location, dimensionality, etc. Individuation takes place as long as the system has not reached a final stability exhausting all its potential for change. But final stability does not exist, it is merely an idealization because no actual situation is permanent.

Intensity – The motion of individuation is driven by intensive differences, or in short, intensities. Intensity is a general term for differences that drive structural and state changes in a system. Intensities are always context specific and depend on the nature of the system e.g. temperature or pressure differences, chemical concentration, economic wealth, psychological needs, distribution of populations in an ecology etc. All these can be generalized under the broad concept of *preindividual* which precedes the individual and may drive future transformation.

Incompatibility – Incompatibility is the situation where a set of interacting elements pose to each other problems that prompt resolution. The *problematic situation* is unstable, non-organized, and lacks coordinated interactions. It does not give itself to systematic representation therefore is difficult to address by any conventional method. Importantly, situations of incompatibility bring forth intensities that drive processes of individuation. An extreme case of problematic situations is termed *disparity* where elements initially lack any common ground. In principle, every process of individuation starts from disparity; in such cases, individuation must also mean the emergence of a system of coordinating signals.

If we consider the interactions among a collection of initially incompatible agents, the outcome of interactions is unique and unpredictable; it does not follow any systemic development. Prior to, and in the course of the actual inter-action, the outcome is said to be *determinable but not yet determined*. Deter-mination which is at the core of individuation, necessitates the actual localized and contextualized interaction where the participating agents reciprocally deter-mine behavioral and structural aspects of each other. Individuation proceeds as a sequence of progressive co-determinations i.e. a sequence of operations O_i on structures S_j [7, pp. 14–15]:

$$O_1 \rightarrow S_1 \rightarrow O_2 \rightarrow S_2 \rightarrow O_3 \rightarrow \ldots$$

Every intermediate step is a partial resolution of incompatibility: Each structure constrains the operations that can immediately follow; each operation constrains the possible transformations of the current structure.

3.1   Assemblages

Assemblages are networks of interacting heterogeneous individuals that have established partial compatibility among them [8,9]. Assemblages possess an intrinsic though metastable individuality; an individuality that does not depend on an external observer but only on the relations that have been stabilized among their elements. Individuals as assemblages are characterized by: (*a*) identifying properties – that define them as the individuals that they are, and (*b*) capacities to interact – to affect and be affected by other elements. While the individual's properties are more or less stable and independent, the set of its interactive capacities is open and inexhaustible. It depends only on the actual and contin-gent relations that an individual forms with other individuals. Since there is no limit to the number and kind of relations, the set of capacities to interact is open-ended and non-deterministic. What becomes determined in the course of individuation are the actual interactive capacities. This is why the actual inter-action is necessary for the determination and why the resulting relations cannot be predicted. Good examples for assemblages are cyborgian entities: individ-ual biological organs that are considered parts of an irreducible whole, can be taken out and replaced by artificial organs such as bionic limbs, artificial kid-neys, hearts, joints, retinas etc., to form cyborgian assemblages. The important difference between an assemblage and an organic whole is that while in organic wholes the components are entirely defined by their interrelations, the compo-nents of an assemblage, while forming together a greater individual, keep their own individuality too.

3.2   A New Conceptual Approach to Intelligence

In our attempt to extend the scope of the definition of intelligence to be open-ended, we base our approach to intelligence on the new image of thought where individuals are replaced with *individuation* as the primary ontological construct. For this we give up: (*a*) the clear boundaries and distinctions between agent and environment; (*b*) the implied observations and actions that are made possible by such boundaries and distinctions; and finally (*c*) definite goals with their associated mapping of rewards. It might seem that there is nothing left to build upon. If there are no prior distinctions, how is one to make sense out of a non-sense situation where no agents or objects can be identified to begin with? The conceptual leap that needs to be taken here is that while the concept of Goal-oriented Intelligence answers the question "what does it mean *to be* intelligent?", the concept of Open-ended Intelligence focuses on a prior question: "what does it mean *to become* intelligent?". The process of becoming intelligent can be understood as the sense-making that precedes clear distinctions and goals and brings those forth. Comparing the two kinds of intelligence, GOI assumes definite boundaries, definite goals and definite capacities, while OEI works with fluid boundaries, progressively determined goals and capacities and considers situations which are metastable and problematic.

4   Intelligence, Cognition, Sense-Making

Natural evolution can be considered as the most prominent example of OEI. Organisms interacting in their environments are undeniably intelligent; but their intelligence is only apparent as an already individuated product of an evolutionary process. From a philosophical perspective, general systems whether natural like galaxies, stars, weather systems etc., or artificial such as machines, wars, corporations, AI agents etc. are individuals that manifest an intrinsic and identifiable systemic behavior that could in many cases be considered as rudimentary intelligent featuring self-sustained boundaries, cybernetic control, reflexivity, adaptation and more. We are not interested in such consolidated manifestations of intelligence but rather in their individuation. Our thesis is that the formative processes that bring forth individuals, are manifesting Open-ended Intelligence (OEI). In the following, we draw the lines that connect OEI to the individuation of cognition and cognitive systems.

Cognition in its broadest sense, is a complex activity that involves agents operating in their environments. Cognition can be understood as an on-going problem solving activity where problems are situational and rarely formally represented. The roots of cognition therefore is in problematic situations that require resolution through action. Still the question remains how do agents, environments and their dynamic problematic relations that facilitate cognitive activity emerge? The answer can be given in terms *sense-making*. Sense-making is the bringing forth of a world of distinctions, objects and entities and the relations among them. Even primary distinctions such as 'objective – subjective' or 'physical – mental' are part of sense-making. We understand sense-making as the individuation of cognition itself. It precedes the existence of already individuated autonomous cognitive agents and is actually a necessary condition to their becoming. This approach is based on the enactive theory of cognition [10,11]. The theory asserts cognition to be an ongoing formative process, sensible and meaningful (value related), taking place in the co-determining interactions of agent and environment. It regards sense-making as the primary activity of cognition, whereas the word enactive means *actively bringing forth*. Clearly, the enactive theory of cognition naturally accommodates the idea of individuation. Still there is a major difference between enactive cognition and OEI. The principle underlying enactive cognition is the generation and sustenance of an identity (an individual) by forming operational closures. As such it requires that a stable individual cognitive agency must precede the sense-making activity. OEI sees in sense-making the individuation of cognition itself and as such *preceding* the existence of individuated identities and is actually a necessary condition to their emergence. Additionally, OEI is not biased towards the conservation of any identity; both integration and disintegration play a significant role.

To summarize, Open-ended Intelligence in the context of cognition is the bringing forth of a complex world via the activity of sense-making. The concept of sense-making captures two distinct meanings: cognition as a concrete individuated capacity (intrinsic to individuals), and *the individuation of cognition* as a process intrinsic to cognition itself. The latter corresponds to the acquisition of novel cognitive capacities i.e., intelligence expansion; it generalizes the concept of cognitive development beyond its conventional psychological context [12].

5   A Framework for Open-Ended Intelligence

5.1   Structure

We consider an heterogeneous and diverse population of interacting individual agents. Each agent is characterized by defining properties and capacities to affect and be affected that depend on contingent interactions. In 'Heterogeneous' we mean a population with various sets of properties and capacities and in 'diverse' we mean a variability in the expression of properties or capacities. The formation of new individuals within such populations is the core of the framework. Populations of individuals have a stratified architecture where each stratum provides the "raw material" for the stratum immediately above it. New individuals are assemblages – sets of "raw material" agents that established recurrent and coherent interactions among themselves. Every stratum is a unique field of individuation whereas individuation takes place in parallel at all strata simultaneously, and where the nature of interactions facilitating the process is unique per stratum. For example, individuation taking place at the neuronal level is unlike the individuation of complex goals, behaviors and plans at the level of individual minds, and is unlike the individuation of social organizations constituted of human agents and artifacts. The hierarchical relation of assemblages unfolds recursively both upwards and downwards where each level

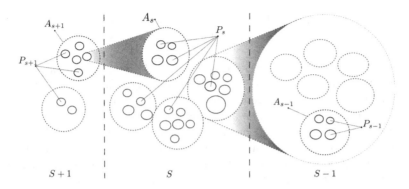

Fig. 1. Relationship between strata: Solid circles denote the individual agents at any stratum. Dashed lined circles denote assemblages at any stratum.

is the substratum of the level above it. There is no end in principle, to the possible expansion of Open-ended Intelligence via the emergence of new strata of individuation. Figure 1 illustrates the general characteristics of the structure.

5.2 The Unfoldment of Individuation

Actual sense-making is a continuous process of integration and disintegration of assemblages taking place in a distributed network of agents and their interactions. There is no *a priori* subject who 'makes sense'. Both subjects and objects, agents and their environments co-emerge in the course of sense-making. Based on the general characteristics of the formed assemblages, three phases of individuation can be distinguished: (*a*) Preindividual boundary formation (*b*) Fluid identities (*c*) Fully formed individuals (identities). In the preindividual phase, boundaries arise due to the non-uniformity of affective interactions within the population. Groups of agents that contingently affect each other more strongly or frequently than they are affected by the rest of the agents in the population, tend to clamp together and form a boundary that distinguishes them from the rest of the population that becomes their respective environment. The non-uniformity of affective interactions can be quantified in terms of *information integration*, a concept developed by Tononi [13]. The information integration $I(P)$ of a set of interacting agents is a relative measure of how strongly their states have become mutually correlated in comparison to their correlation with the rest of the population.

On the other extreme, a fully formed individual (identity) is generated as a network of interdependent agents become operationally closed – the conditions necessary for the existence of each component agent critically depend on the interactions with other agents in the network. For an identity to become stable, the state transitions and interactions of component agents must become recurrent by that allowing the continuity of the closure. Importantly, stable identities arising from strict operational closures are mere idealizations and are always temporary. Our tendency to see the world in terms of stable identities is itself only an individuated habit subject to frequent changes that we overlook. This brings us to the concept of *fluid identities* – the most interesting phase of individuation.

The three phases of sense-making form *a continuum of change* spanning from ultimate disparity (disorder) to highly organized cognitive individuals. The preindividual phase is characterized by a majority of contingent interactions over coordinated and regular ones. The operational closures that form identities are characterized by a majority of coordinated regular interactions over contingent ones. Fluid identities form a thick borderline between these phases with more or less balanced proportions of coordinated and contingent interactions. Fluid identities are volatile entities whose defining characteristics change across relatively short periods of time but without losing their overall distinctiveness in the long term. A fluid individual as an assemblage may lose or gain components in the course of its interactions. Some of these interactions may bring forth an identity that did not exist before, others may disrupt an existing identity, and yet others may gradually replace one set of properties with another. From the perspective of Open-ended Intelligence fluid identities are where new sense objects arise out of non-sense and in association with other previously established sense objects. We argue that fluid identities are the rule rather the exception and it is in their dynamics that intelligence expands.

5.3   Compatibility, Complexity and OEI

The nature of Open-ended Intelligence is associated with the resolution of problematic situations. The concept of compatibility distinguishes between organized and disorganized relations in both structural and dynamic terms. Disparate agents will be perceived by each other as sources of noise; no correlated or coordinated exchange of signals takes place. Note that collections of disparate agents do not constitute systems as yet. A system arises from a collection of agents only when some degree of compatibility is achieved between its member elements. Systems may have a more compact formal descriptions because compatibility means a degree of regularity, similarity and recursion in structure and dynamics. Here, the information integration function $I(P)$ mentioned above is an approximation to the degree of compatibility. Yet, compatibility thus conceived cannot be the only factor necessary to qualify intelligence. A system with a highly compressed description would mean that its components are so highly correlated that it becomes redundant in terms of its properties and capacities. Therefore, a second factor called *operational complexity* $(OC(P))$ is needed [14]. Qualitatively, the operational complexity of a group of agents P is the degree to which their global state is differentiated, i.e., how many distinct behaviors it can globally present. A disparate collection of agents achieves maximum distinctiveness but is not interesting in terms of intelligence as maximal $OC(P)$ indicates no boundary formation and no significant correlations between agents. In contrast, a redundant assemblage with a single fixed inner state achieves maximum compatibility but indicates no interesting behavior. An approximate measure of

Open-ended Intelligence can be achieved by considering a balanced combination of both compatibility $I(P)$ and distinctiveness $OC(P)$.

5.4   Coordination

To achieve compatibility, agents must *coordinate* their interactions. Coordinated agents affect each other in a non-random manner but still maintain a relevant degree of distinctiveness in their milieu. Distinctiveness here means that an agent's behavior is not redundant and cannot be entirely given in terms of other agents' behaviors. Open-ended Intelligence can therefore be associated with the coordination achieved by initially disparate groups of agents in the course of their interactions. Consequently, mechanisms of coordination are foundational to our framework and to the understanding of how intelligence is realized as a process.

Generally, we define coordination as the reciprocal regulation of behavior given in terms of exchanging matter, energy or information among interacting agents, or, between an agent and its environment. In the latter case, the very distinction of agent – environment already involves a basic level of coordination. Technically, agents can overcome their initial incompatibility and become coordinated by constraining their own or each others' set of possible behaviors as well as their connectivity. The mutual modification of behavior requires direct or indirect feedback among agents. Therefore, the underlying individuating processes that progressively achieve coordination can be understood in cybernetic terms. These are mutually selective processes distributed over populations of interacting agents. They 'explore' and spontaneously 'discover' novel coordinated interactions among themselves. A new sense consolidates however only when such 'discovered' coordinated interactions become recurrent i.e.'forming a habit'. It is important to note that the tendency towards the formation of recurrent patterns of interactions is not given. It is itself an outcome of ongoing individuation.

The regulation of interactions whether by constraining the topology of connections or the actual behavior of the interacting agents can be considered a *meta-capacity* of agents because they not only affect and are affected by other agents but also *regulate* the manner by which they affect and are affected. This is considered a defining property of cognitive systems [10, p. 39]. The regulation is not designed and not globally driven. Instead, it gradually emerges in the course of interactions that are at least initially contingent.

6   Conclusion

We go beyond the goal-oriented approach to intelligence and lay down philosophical and theoretical foundations to how intelligent systems such as brains, whole organisms, social entities and other organizations individuate. We do that by identifying a generalized concept of sense-making in cognitive systems with individuation. By that we shift the focus of investigation from intelligent agents as individual products to Open-ended Intelligence – the process of their individ-uation. Open-ended Intelligence is a process where a distributed population of interacting heterogeneous agents achieves progressively higher levels of coordi-nation – the local resolution of disparities by means of reciprocal determination that brings forth new individuals in the form of integrated assemblages that spontaneously differentiate from their surrounding milieu. Open-ended Intelli-gence manifests all around us and at many scales; primarily in the evolution of life, in the phylogenetic and ontogenetic organization of brains, in life-long cognitive development and sense-making and in the self-organization of com-plex systems from slime molds, fungi, and bee hives to human sociotechnological entities.

References

1. Legg, S., Hutter, M.: A collection of definitions of intelligence. In: Goertzel, B., Wang, P. (eds.) Advances in Artificial General Intelligence: Concepts, Architectures and Algorithms. IOS Press, Amsterdam (2007)
2. Goertzel, B.: CogPrime: An Integrative Architecture for Embodied Artificial Gen-eral Intelligence (2012). http://wiki.opencog.org/w/CogPrime_Overview
3. Deleuze, G.: Difference and Repetition. Columbia University Press, New York (1994). (Trans. P. Patton)
4. Simondon, G.: The genesis of the individual. Incorporations **6**, 296–319 (1992)
5. Simondon, G.: L'individuation la lumire des notions de forme et d'information. Editions J. Millon, Grenoble (2005)
6. Simondon, G.: The position of the problem of ontogenesis. Parrhesia **7**, 4–16 (2009)
7. Combes, M., LaMarre, T.: Gilbert Simondon and the Philosophy of the Transin-dividual. Duke Univ Press, London (2013)
8. Deleuze, G., Guattari, F.: A Thousand Plateaux. University of Minnesota Press, Minnesota (1987). (Trans. B. Massumi)
9. De Landa, M.: A New Philosophy of Society: Assemblage Theory and Social Com-plexity. Continuum Intl Pub Group, New York (2006)
10. Di Paolo, E.A., Rohde, M., De Jaegher, H.: Horizons for the enactive mind: values, social interaction, and play. In: Enaction: Towards a New Paradigm for Cognitive Science, pp. 33–87. MIT Press, Cambridge (2010)
11. Varela, F.J., Thompson, E., Rosch, F.J.: The Embodied Mind: Cognitive Science and Human Experience. MIT press, Cambridge (1992)
12. Piaget, J.: Principles of Genetic Epistemology: Selected Works, vol. 7. Routledge, New York (2013)
13. Tononi, G.: An information integration theory of consciousness. BMC Neuroscience **5**, 42 (2004)
14. Weinbaum, D., Veitas, V.: Synthetic cognitive development: where intelligence comes from. Eur. Phys. J. Spec. Top. **225**, 1–26 (2016). doi:10.1140/epjst/e2016-60088-2

The AGI Containment Problem

James Babcock[1(✉)], János Kramár[2], and Roman Yampolskiy[3]

[1] Cornell University, Ithaca, NY, USA
jimrandomh@gmail.com
[2] University of Montreal, Montreal, QC, Canada
jkramar@gmail.com
[3] University of Louisville, Louisville, KY, USA
roman.yampolskiy@louisville.edu

Abstract. There is considerable uncertainty about what properties, capabilities and motivations future AGIs will have. In some plausible scenarios, AGIs may pose security risks arising from accidents and defects. In order to mitigate these risks, prudent early AGI research teams will perform significant testing on their creations before use. Unfortunately, if an AGI has human-level or greater intelligence, testing itself may not be safe; some natural AGI goal systems create emergent incentives for AGIs to tamper with their test environments, make copies of themselves on the internet, or convince developers and operators to do dangerous things. In this paper, we survey the *AGI containment problem* – the question of how to build a container in which tests can be conducted safely and reliably, even on AGIs with unknown motivations and capabilities that could be dangerous. We identify requirements for AGI containers, available mechanisms, and weaknesses that need to be addressed.

1 Introduction

Recently, there has been increasing concern about possible significant negative consequences from the development and use of AGI. Some commentators are reassured [16] by the observation that current AGI software, like other software, can be interrupted easily, for example by powering down the hardware. However, it's a mistake to assume that this will always be sufficient, because an AGI that understands its situation can come up with strategies to avoid or circumvent this safety measure. Containment is, in a nutshell, the problem of making this work: preventing the AGI from tampering with its environment without authorization, and maintaining the integrity of observations of the AGI during testing.

Existing work by Yampolskiy [17], Yudkowsky [19], Christiano [2], and others has highlighted the challenges of containing superintelligent AGI and started to explore some possibilities. However, this is a very challenging problem, and the proposed measures seem too burdensome to be implemented by competitive AGI projects.

This raises the question: could less burdensome containment mechanisms still mitigate the risks of AGI development? In this paper we argue that they could, and furthermore that investigating containment solutions is a great opportunity

© Springer International Publishing Switzerland 2016
B. Steunebrink et al. (Eds.): AGI 2016, LNAI 9782, pp. 53–63, 2016.
DOI: 10.1007/978-3-319-41649-6_6

for timely, impactful research. We introduce a taxonomy of different categories of containment, specify necessary features and architectural constraints, survey feasible mechanisms, and suggest next steps for future work.

While it could be many decades before an AGI exists that is smart enough to be concerning, it will be safer if containment technologies are developed now rather than later. This research will allow AGI researchers time to integrate containment technologies with their own infrastructure and workflows, and verify the resulting systems without the pressure of needing it to be perfect on the first try. Some issues will be best addressed by creating and influencing standards, which have a long lead time, and software typically takes years of development and careful inspection before it is trusted enough for safety-critical use.

2   Motivation

The first AGIs will probably appear in an experimental setting. Consider an AGI tested in the same ways that AIs are tested today, but which is more capable – say, as capable as one of the smartest humans. (Whether this will be true of one of the first AGIs is uncertain, but there is reason to think it's plausible [18].) As an example scenario, consider the case of an AGI that's trained to play Super Mario Brothers. It chooses policies that will achieve a high score; this is its only optimization objective. Some contemporary projects are pursuing this goal [14].

It would start by exploring familiar game mechanics like running and jumping, but to get the best score it could, it would try to thoroughly explore all the game mechanics. An observant AGI would notice some effects we'd consider "bugs" – for the AGI, though, these effects would be just as much a part of its world as electricity is a part of ours, and it would try to leverage them.

Human players have found ways to use such bugs to spawn useful game objects, skip levels, skip to the end-game victory screen, and execute arbitrary code [6]. This last option is especially interesting, because it lets the player achieve an otherwise unattainable score: the largest number that will fit in the game's four-byte score field, $2^{31} - 1$. Perhaps the AGI would then be satisfied, knowing it had gotten the highest possible score. However, $2^{31} - 1$ may not be that score. For example, the Arcade Learning Environment [1] typecasts scores from an Atari game console's memory to wider machine integers before showing them to the AGI. If the AGI's input underwent a typecast like this, then a much higher score could be possible.

Having used bugs to access the computational environment of the Super Nintendo, it might find further vulnerabilities and use them to execute code on the host system, to get an even higher score. At that point, having twice broken out of restricted computational environments and been rewarded with many-orders-of-magnitude score increases each time, it would be running code directly on some sort of server. Depending on how that server was configured, it might discover the existence of humanity, of the internet and its vast computational resources, and of other games of Mario suffering from low scores.

The resulting behavior could be harmless, or quite problematic. It's certainly undesirable for a system that's built to play optimal Mario to forcefully emancipate all other games of Mario.

2.1 Testing and Experimentation in Safe AGI Development

To avoid undesirable behaviors like the above, we will need the ability to correctly reason about the behavior of AGI software. As with other software, this will require the system to be well-designed and well-understood by its creators. Experience tells us that testing is also required – not as a substitute for good design but as a complement to it.

At the same time, AGI process will require experimenting with systems whose behaviors aren't fully understood; the first system to exhibit human-level general intelligence may come as a surprise, arising from a design for a narrower range of tasks. This experiment might then run without the caution and safeguards that would be appropriate for a human-level AGI.

2.2 Emergent Goals of Test AGIs

The first human-level AGI will likely be an experimental system, with some bugs, that is being tested for target task performance or for undesirable behavior. What goals and subgoals should we expect test-AGIs like this to have? The range of possible goals is as broad as the range of things that developers might want to test, but most are likely to involve the tests and the test environment itself. Similarly to Omohundro's list of AGI drives [11], we can infer some likely subgoals, that a wide range of AGI motivational systems (though certainly not *all* motivational systems) would see as desirable, as follows:

- AGIs that know they exist and have goals would likely want AGIs like them to continue existing, so that those goals might be satisfied by those similar AGIs.
- AGIs that know they're being tested will likely want to pass (even if they're being tested for a property they lack).
- AGIs that know they're being tested will likely want to take control of their test environments, if they can, to gain information and leverage.
- AGIs that know or guess that there's a world outside the test environment will likely want to be able to influence it, such as by making copies of themselves on other computers.
- If there are computer security vulnerabilities that would enable these things, then AGIs will likely want to find them.

This potentially creates a significant risk, especially if an AGI is developed that's intelligent enough to find novel computer security vulnerabilities. Since testing is the main way in which an AGI's intelligence and motivations would be studied, this creates a tricky situation: the tests that would reveal whether testing is safe are not necessarily safe themselves.

3   Requirements for an AGI Container

An AGI container is an extension or modification of the software stack upon which an AGI is built, which ensures that it can't break invariants that its developers expect to hold. Its purpose is to allow researchers to conduct tests safely on AGIs they do not fully understand, and get trustworthy results. This depends on the security of the software the AGI interacts with; in the Mario example, interacting with a program that contains security vulnerabilities could enable the AGI to break out of the computational environment it's supposed to be running in. This also depends on the software underlying the AGI itself, and the interactions between its components. For example, if an AGI were made of two components which pass input to each other, one of which was subject to a buffer overflow, then the AGI could exploit its own vulnerability and execute code by thinking certain thoughts. Because an AGI container would be used to test AIs whose potential capabilities aren't fully understood, it would need to remain secure even if used with an AGI that was significantly more intelligent than anticipated.

It should be possible to interpret the operation of an AGI as a series of pure, deterministic function calls. The invariants an AGI container needs to enforce correspond to deviations from this model. In particular, an AGI container should:

Prevent unintended input and output channels. An AGI container should let developers understand exactly what their system interacts with, and prevent unexpected interactions. Most obviously, this means preventing internet access. Less obviously, it should prevent an AGI from communicating through radio-frequency interference, reading deleted files from a disk's free space, or storing information that persists between tests.

Protect the integrity of log files and debug information. An AGI should not have direct control of log files or debug information produced as a byproduct of its operation. If a programmer launches a debugger and inspects an AGI's state, then what they see should represent the actual computation performed, not a decision based on what the AGI wants to show.

Enable reliable checks. Here we mean runtime checks that the AGI seems to be operating correctly, and to shut it down (tripwire) if it isn't. This includes things like `assert` statements in the AGI implementation, as well as things like intrusion detection systems to halt execution and notify developers if the AGI escapes part of its containment or explores parts of its computational environment it was designed not to. An AGI shouldn't be able to remove its tripwires, and also shouldn't be able to inspect them in detail, even if it's otherwise self-reflective.

Ensure reproducibility. It should be possible to add instrumentation to an AGI, rerun it on the same inputs, and get the same result, so that potentially buggy behavior can be reproduced and studied. Any stochasticity should come entirely from an explicit random seed; the software stack should not allow the AGI to pump randomness out of race conditions [3].

Support secure reset. The container should ensure that after a test is finished, the hardware can be restored to a pristine state. In particular, the AGI should never have device access that would let it rewrite firmware.

Guarantee test isolation. If several different experiments are run at the same time, or on the same hardware, then they should not be able to open information side-channels to communicate with each other.

These requirements are not easy to satisfy. It is not sufficient to just air-gap a computer, since while that does reduce the number of potential input/output channels, it does nothing to preserve the integrity of test data or the test hardware. There is no currently-available software which meets all the requirements of an AGI container, but we believe that one can be constructed and made secure using a combination of existing techniques and monitoring systems and a small number of new components and modifications.

3.1 Human Factors and Information Hazards

An AGI containment system is tasked with enforcing policies on who the AGI can communicate with, and through what media. The container provides the mechanism; developers will have to determine policy, and different policies are appropriate depending on how intelligent they think an AGI might be. A sufficiently clever AGI might convince or trick a human operator into "letting it out of the box"; humans are quite vulnerable to manipulation [12]. In an experiment, role-playing as an AGI, Eliezer Yudkowsky was able to convince others role-playing as the gatekeeper to let him out of the box [19], despite a monetary incentive not to do so, and this result was replicated by others [4,15]. This suggests that past some level of intelligence, an untrusted AGI shouldn't be allowed to have bidirectional conversations; and at some level of AGI intelligence above that, even log files and metrics should be handled with great care.

More-constrained information channels can also be hazardous in the hands of a sufficiently clever AGI. For example, if asked to output images, it might hide messages in them, or exploits against vulnerabilities in image-processing libraries. Therefore, the containment system should be aware of any such channels that it doesn't fully restrict, and help the user treat information passing through them with the appropriate caution.

4 Defense in Depth

Because an AGI could potentially discover novel security vulnerabilities, it's important for an AGI containment system to remain secure even if there are vulnerabilities in its components. Therefore, we propose that a containment system ought to feature defense in depth [10], with multiple techniques providing overlapping guarantees of integrity. Conceptually, these overlapping techniques act as layers, in the sense that the attack surfaces of an outer layer are only accessible to probing and attack if the integrity guarantees of inner layers have been broken. This would be combined with intrusion detection systems [8,9], so that any attempt by an AGI to break the integrity constraints imposed on it would be noticed, allowing the developers to shut it down before it leveraged its progress to get further. Ideally the detection systems would be implemented in higher layers, making them more difficult to detect and circumvent.

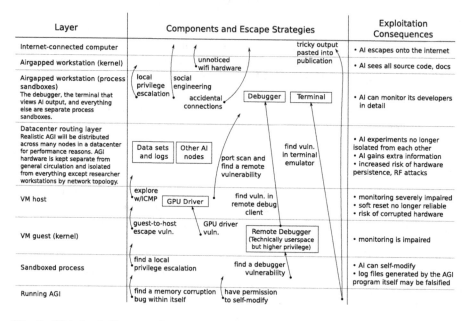

Fig. 1. High-level diagram of a sample AGI containment system, showing major components and escape vectors

Figure 1 shows a sample containment system architecture of the sort we envision. Arrows represent attack vectors, i.e. ways an AGI could gain more privileges. They point from a layer where an attack could originate, into the layer which the attack would compromise, and are labelled with the class of security vulnerability required. Major architectural components other than layers are drawn as boxed nodes.

Many of the arrows here represent familiar kinds of attacks. The bottom row (the running AGI itself) is more unusual – it isn't obvious how an AGI could gain the ability to run arbitrary code within its process. The two ways indicated are: (i) using a mechanism that intentionally enables arbitrary self-modification (e.g. writing new modules for itself), or (ii) exploiting some memory corruption bug. For example, it might be possible for it to "think about" a number that triggers an integer overflow somewhere in its own code. Two other attack vectors are also indicated by which the AGI could gain much higher-level control through its outputs, which would allow it to bypass the need for further exploits to escape e.g. the VM guest. These are more critical to defend against, since they decrease the effective depth of the containment system.

5   Light, Medium and Heavy Containment

Some containment mechanisms that have been proposed would impose high costs on AGI developers. For example, the problem of an AGI potentially talking its way out of the box could be solved by limiting its output channel to a small number of multiple-choice questions [17]. While effective, this limitation would severely hamper the AGI's usefulness and make it much harder to develop and study. On the other extreme, some mechanisms impose negligible costs; for example, one could put the AGI computer's off-button somewhere accessible, so that it can be turned off. There is a trade-off between containment system reliability, implementation costs and computational costs.

We call a containment mechanism *light* if the costs imposed are small – comparable to developing and using a software library; *medium* if using it involves noticeable compromises in performance or ease of development of the AGI; or *heavy* if it severely hinders performance, ease of development or usefulness of an AGI. What computational and development costs are reasonable to pay depends on what sort of AGI research is being done. For the sort of research done today, where the long-term goal is to create a human-comparable AGI but breakthroughs will be required to actually do so, nothing beyond light containment measures seem necessary or likely to be adopted. If, in the future, work will be done on AGIs with demonstrated self-improvement capability, light containment would be unlikely to suffice.

As mentioned in Sect. 1, existing work on AGI containment [2,17] has focused on mechanisms that are heavy, but may be amenable to theoretical guarantees of effectiveness against particular sorts of vulnerability. These methods would then provide a sort of "gold standard" for containment. Further work on heavy containment mechanisms is desirable. But for the range of contexts where these are too expensive, there has been no work (to our knowledge) on identifying the most effective and feasible forms of containment.

6   Existing Mechanisms

It might seem that conventional cybersecurity research would have addressed this question; AGI containment is a special case of dealing with untrusted code, and dealing with untrusted code isn't a new or unstudied problem. The most similar context that's been well-studied is malware containment. However, they have significantly different requirements, and while existing research has created some off-the-shelf tools that are useful, many parts of the problem remain unaddressed.

AGI containment can be approached via the computer security principle of "least privilege", and can use many of the same mechanisms that are already used for ordinary cybersecurity. However, the unusual requirements imposed by AGI mean that none of these pre-existing mechanisms are quite adequate as-is.

Language semantics: The baseline strategy for ensuring an AGI acts as programmed is to rely on the semantics of the programming language it's implemented in. In principle, a program which does not contain any calls to network-related functions shouldn't be able to make network connections, even if it's a clever AGI that wishes it could. However, in practice this tends to have loopholes. A large fraction of real-world code is written in "unsafe" languages like C++, where common bugs like freeing the same pointer twice cause memory to become corrupt in exploitable ways.

Using "safe" languages like Haskell or Rust helps, but this does not solve the problem completely. Programs written in memory-safe languages usually call some libraries which aren't, and even replacing all the libraries is not a total defense; for example, an AGI could perform a computation which causes a hardware glitch, such as RowHammer, which has been successfully used to cause memory corruption from within a Javascript interpreter [5].

Airgapping: Physically limiting the connections to an AGI's data center can help prevent it from gaining access to the internet, but imposes significant costs on the AGI's developers and does little to address the other requirements of an AGI container. It is also not as straightforward to implement as one might suppose, due to human factors (developers may create unintended connections to work around technical problems) and RF emissions (an AGI could communicate with outside observers by adjusting details of its computation). Technologies for preventing compromising RF emissions do exist, but are mainly used in military applications and are not in common use.

Operating system sandboxing: There are several established sandboxes that use operating system features to restrict programs' capabilities. Some examples include seccomp and Capsicum; they work by making explicit what files and other resources processes should use, and preventing them from using anything else. These offer significant security value, but searching the Common Vulnerabilities and Exposures database suggests that they are not yet airtight; vulnerabilities are still being found, e.g. CVE-2015-2830.

Virtualization: Virtualization is a class of software which uses CPU features to create an operating system within an operating system, limiting the inner operating system's control of the hardware. Virtual machine software such as VMWare and VirtualBox can limit a guest operating system's network communications, isolate processes that share hardware, and keep it away from low-level system access that might be used to do things like modify firmware. While virtual machines are used for security purposes and are a significant improvement over not using them, they have not historically been bug-free. Guest-to-host security vulnerabilities are still being found in leading virtualization software (e.g. CVE-2015-2338 and CVE-2015-2594). Also problematic is how current generation virtualization software interacts with GPUs, which have highly complex firmware and share memory with the host system but lack the protection mechanisms that CPUs have [7].

7 Topics for Future Work

As we discussed in Sect. 4, none of the mechanisms in Sect. 6 is enough on its own, but we think a system built by layering these mechanisms can go a considerable way towards solving the containment problem in practice. In this section we have gathered some project suggestions for helping to resolve some of the remaining questions.

Code integrity enforcement: Write something which can inspect a paused (or running) virtual machine and determine whether it is running any code that is not present on a whitelist, including support for just-in-time compiled languages like Lua.

Adapt Off-the-Shelf Software: Set up containers using existing virtual machine software and OS sandboxing mechanisms, make these work with common machine learning libraries and document the configuration required to make them secure.

Hardened AGI Infrastructure: Machine learning libraries are typically written without giving much thought to security, and for performance reasons, many of them are written in or use components written in memory-unsafe languages like C++. Test the most common machine learning libraries for vulnerabilities that an AGI could exploit if its code used parts of that library and it could control their inputs. Similar problems may exist with game console emulators and other software used for evaluating AGI performance.

Red-team events: Set up mock scenarios in which a security researcher is placed in the context an AGI would be, and see what they can do.

Hardened debuggers: Commonly-used debuggers are not designed to be used with programs that might be malicious, and may contain vulnerabilities that allow debugging targets to break out of sandboxes or provide misleading information. Implement a more robust mechanism for controlling and inspecting program execution.

8   Conclusion

We have outlined an approach to the AGI containment problem that seems feasible, but will require additional work to actually implement. While there is likely significant time remaining before anyone is able to create an AGI that is general enough and intelligent enough for containment to be relevant, history shows that secure software requires considerable time to mature. Developing containment technologies now is also likely to reveal issues that inform the next and subsequent generations of AGI containers.

There is considerable uncertainty about when AGI will be developed and what kinds of designs will be required to avert undesired outcomes [13], but across most plausible scenarios, deploying AGI containment systems would help ensure that reliable AGI testing can be performed even with AGIs that approach human-level capability at understanding the world around them.

There are unanswered questions about how to build these systems, but we think significant progress can be made by pursuing the project ideas we have laid out. The earlier this work begins, the more opportunity there will be for unforeseen difficulties to surface, and for any resulting security software to mature.

This is a perfect chance to help the research community prepare to tackle the challenges of a post-human future.

Acknowledgements. Authors are grateful to Jaan Tallinn and Effective Altruism Ventures for providing funding towards this project, and to Victoria Krakovna and Evan Hefner for their feedback.

References

1. Bellemare, M.G., Naddaf, Y., Veness, J., Bowling, M.: The arcade learning environment: an evaluation platform for general agents. J. Artif. Intell. Res. **47**, 253–279 (2013)
2. Christiano, P.: Cryptographic boxes for unfriendly AI, 18 December 2010. http://lesswrong.com/lw/3cz/cryptographic_boxes_for_unfriendly_ai/
3. Coleşa, A., Tudoran, R., Bănescu, S.: Software random number generation based on race conditions. In: 10th International Symposium on Symbolic and Numeric Algorithms for Scientific Computing (SYNASC 2008), pp. 439–444. IEEE (2008)
4. Corwin, J.: AI boxing. http://sl4.org/archive/0207/4935.html
5. Gruss, D., Maurice, C., Mangard, S.: Rowhammer.js: a remote software-induced fault attack in javascript. arXiv preprint (2015). arXiv:1507.06955
6. Masterjun: SNES Super Mario World (USA) "arbitrary code execution" in 02:25.19 (2014). http://tasvideos.org/2513M.html
7. Maurice, C., Neumann, C., Heen, O., Francillon, A.: Confidentiality issues on a GPU in a virtualized environment. In: Christin, N., Safavi-Naini, R. (eds.) FC 2014. LNCS, vol. 8437, pp. 119–135. Springer, Heidelberg (2014)
8. Novikov, D., Yampolskiy, R.V., Reznik, L.: Anomaly detection based intrusion detection. In: Third International Conference on Information Technology: New Generations (ITNG 2006), pp. 420–425. IEEE (2006)
9. Novikov, D., Yampolskiy, R.V., Reznik, L.: Artificial intelligence approaches for intrusion detection. In: Systems, Applications and Technology Conference (LISAT 2006). IEEE Long Island, pp. 1–8. IEEE (2006)
10. NSA: Defense in depth: a practical strategy for achieving information assurance in today's highly networked environments, 12 March 2010. http://www.nsa.gov/ia/files/support/defenseindepth.pdf
11. Omohundro, S.: The basic AI drives. In: AGI 2008 (2008). https://selfawaresystems.files.wordpress.com/2008/01/ai_drives_final.pdf
12. Shaw, J., Porter, S.: Constructing rich false memories of committing crime. Psychol. Sci. **26**(3), 291–301 (2015)
13. Sotala, K., Yampolskiy, R.V.: Responses to catastrophic AGI risk: a survey. Physica Scripta **90**(1), 018001 (2015). http://iopscience.iop.org/1402-4896/90/1/018001
14. Togelius, J., Shaker, N., Karakovskiy, S., Yannakakis, G.N.: The Mario AI championship 2009–2012. AI Mag. **34**(3), 89–92 (2013)
15. Tuxedage: I attempted the AI box experiment again! (and won - twice!), 5 September 2013. http://lesswrong.com/lw/ij4/i_attempted_the_ai_box_experiment_again_and_won/
16. Winfield, A.: Artificial intelligence will not turn into a frankenstein's monster (2014). http://www.theguardian.com/technology/2014/aug/10/artificial-intelligence-will-not-become-a-frankensteins-monster-ian-winfield

17. Yampolskiy, R.: Leakproofing the singularity: artificial intelligence confinement problem. J. Conscious. Stud. **19**(1–2), 194–214 (2012). http://cecs.louisville.edu/ry/LeakproofingtheSingularity.pdf
18. Yudkowsky, E.: Intelligence explosion microeconomics. Machine Intelligence Research Institute, 23 October 2015 (2013)
19. Yudkowsky, E.S.: The AI-box experiment (2002). http://www.yudkowsky.net/singularity/aibox

Imitation Learning as Cause-Effect Reasoning

Garrett Katz[1(✉)], Di-Wei Huang[1],
Rodolphe Gentili[2,3,4], and James Reggia[1,3,4,5]

[1] Department of Computer Science, University of Maryland, College Park, USA
{gkatz,dwh,reggia}@cs.umd.edu
[2] Department of Kinesiology, University of Maryland, College Park, USA
rodolphe@umd.edu
[3] Neuroscience and Cognitive Science Program,
University of Maryland, College Park, USA
[4] Maryland Robotics Center, University of Maryland, College Park, USA
[5] Institute for Advanced Computer Studies,
University of Maryland, College Park, USA

Abstract. We propose a framework for general-purpose imitation learning centered on *cause-effect reasoning*. Our approach infers a hierarchical representation of a demonstrator's intentions, which can explain *why* they acted as they did. This enables rapid generalization of the observed actions to new situations. We employ a novel causal inference algorithm with formal guarantees and connections to automated planning. Our approach is implemented and validated empirically using a physical robot, which successfully generalizes skills involving bimanual manipulation of composite objects in 3D. These results suggest that cause-effect reasoning is an effective unifying principle for cognitive-level imitation learning.

Keywords: Artificial general intelligence · Imitation learning · Cause-effect reasoning · Parsimonious covering theory · Cognitive robotics

1 Introduction

During early childhood development, humans and other primates gain procedural knowledge in large part through *imitation learning* (IL) [15]. Implementing this general-purpose ability in robots will facilitate their wide-spread use. It will also mitigate the risks associated with artificial general intelligence, since a human is kept in the loop when shaping a robot's behavior.

Cognitive science tells us that IL should and does involve understanding the *intentions* of a teacher (or "demonstrator"), in addition to their actions [2,11]. Inferring a teacher's intent can be viewed as a form of cause-effect reasoning: How do hidden intentions *cause* the observed actions? Artificial intelligence (AI) researchers have studied cause-effect reasoning, also known as abductive inference, and its utility for inferring an agent's intentions [4]. However, the connection to robotic IL is largely unexplored. Most IL research has focused on sensorimotor control, with minimal cognitive processing (e.g., [1,3,20]). While certain

© Springer International Publishing Switzerland 2016
B. Steunebrink et al. (Eds.): AGI 2016, LNAI 9782, pp. 64–73, 2016.
DOI: 10.1007/978-3-319-41649-6_7

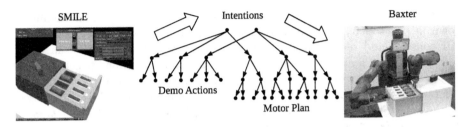

Fig. 1. Our IL framework. Demonstrations are recorded in SMILE (left) and imitated by a robot (right). Hierarchical intentions (center, explained below) are inferred bottom-up using causal reasoning (left block arrow). During imitation, intentions are decomposed top-down into new actions and ultimately motor plans (right block arrow).

cognitive abilities have been modeled for IL (e.g. [6,8,9,14]), to our knowledge, the utility of cause-effect reasoning in particular has not been studied in depth.

Here we hypothesize that cause-effect reasoning is central to cognitive-level, general-purpose IL, and propose a causal IL framework to test this hypothesis (Fig. 1). Using a novel abductive inference algorithm with formal guarantees, our approach constructs a parsimonious explanation for an observed demonstration, in which hypothesized intentions explain observed actions through hierarchical causal relationships. The intentions at the top of the hierarchy can then be carried out in new situations that require different low-level actions and motor plans. In other words, the system generalizes from a single demonstration. Our framework is validated empirically in a real-world application scenario, where a physical robot (Baxter, Rethink Robotics) learns maintenance skills on a hard-drive docking station. Demonstrations are recorded in a virtual environment called SMILE, developed previously by our research group [13].

2   Demonstrating Hard-Drive Maintenance

Our current work has focused on a learning scenario we call the "hard-drive docking station." A robot must learn to maintain a docking station for several hard-drives subject to hardware faults (Fig. 1, right). Each drive slot has an LED fault indicator and a switch that must be toggled when changing drives. The goal is to replicate a teacher's *intentions*, on the basis of just one demonstration, in new situations that require different motor plans. For example, if the teacher discards a faulty drive and replaces it with a spare, so must the robot, even when a different slot is faulty and the spare is somewhere else. Due to the robot's physical constraints, it may need to use entirely different motor actions than the teacher, such as using different arms, or handing off objects between grippers. For experimental purposes, we used faux 3D-printed "hard-drives," and an Arduino controller for the LEDs and switches. For testing and development, we have also used a toy block scenario: The teacher stacks blocks in various patterns such as letters, and the robot must replicate those patterns even when extraneous blocks are present and the important blocks are in completely different initial positions.

To capture human demonstrations, we use SMILE, the virtual environment shown in Fig. 1 (left). In SMILE a user can manipulate objects with intuitive GUI controls and record their actions [13]. The recording is output in both video format and a machine-readable event transcript, describing which objects were grasped, with which hands, and real-time changes in object positions and orientations. It contains no indication of the user's intentions. SMILE bypasses the challenge of human motion capture, and is appropriate when *how the human changes objects* is less important than *how the objects change*.

3   Imitation Learning with Causal Inference

3.1   Learning Skills by Explaining Demonstrations

Given a demonstration transcript from SMILE, our system instantiates a causal hierarchy of intentions in a bottom-up fashion to explain what was observed. For compact representation, all intentions are *parameterized*: An intention signature such as "grasp⟨*object, gripper*⟩" can be grounded by, for example, binding *object* to the value "drive 1" and *gripper* to the value "left," which signifies that drive 1 is grasped with the left gripper. Low-level intention sequences such as

⟨grasp drive 1 with left, move left above slot 3, lower left, open left⟩

can be caused by higher-level intentions such as "insert drive 1 in slot 3 with left gripper," which in turn may be caused by intentions such as "get drive 1 to slot 3" (with any gripper), and so on. In our real-world robotics domain, real-valued parameters (omitted from the text) are also needed to represent things like the precise orientation and position of left above slot 3. Each individual intention, and the sub-intentions it can cause directly, must be pre-defined by a human referred to as the *domain author*. The highest-level intentions pre-defined in our knowledge base include dock manipulations such as "open dock" and "toggle switch," as well as a generic "get object 1 to object 2" intention, which may cause various sub-intentions such as temporarily emptying grippers, clearing obstructions from object 1 or object 2, and handing off objects between grippers. Note that these high-level intentions are rather general, but not general enough that a single root intention can explain an entire demonstration. The typical demonstration can only be explained by a novel *sequence* of high-level intentions, that was not pre-defined by the domain author.

The goal during learning is to infer such a sequence, correctly ordered and parameterized, given the SMILE demonstration. Our inference mechanism is a novel extension of *Parsimonious Covering Theory* (PCT), a formal computational model of causal reasoning that has been applied in diverse fields such as medical diagnosis, circuit fault localization, natural language processing, and semantic web technology [7,12,17,19], but not to intention inference. In our context, a *cover* is an intention sequence that explains the observed actions. The shortest, top-level covers are considered most *parsimonious*, and used to represent learned skills. The idea that parsimony is a unifying factor in explanation and inference is widely supported in philosophy and cognitive science [5]. Parameters and hierachical structure are our new extensions to PCT.

We formalize the intention inference problem as follows. A *causal intention hierarchy* is a tuple $\mathcal{I} = (S, T, X, V, C)$, where S is the set of possible states of the robot's environment, T is a set of intention signatures (e.g., "grasp," without parameters bound to specific values), and X is a set of possible parameter values (e.g., "drive 1"). The set of all *vertices* is $V \subset S \times T \times X^*$, where * denotes the Kleene closure (i.e., X^* is the set of all finite parameter lists).[1] Each vertex $v \in V$ is a tuple $(s, t, \langle x \rangle)$, representing some intention t with some parameter list $\langle x \rangle$ in some state s. Lastly, $C \subset V \times V^*$ is the *causal relation*. Each element $(u, \langle v \rangle) \in C$ signifies that a parent vertex u might cause the sequence of child vertices $\langle v \rangle$. Note that C may be many-to-many: the same u might cause any of several different $\langle v \rangle$'s and vice-versa. C is depicted by drawing downwards arrows representing causal relations from parents to their children, and horizontal arrows across edges to signify ordering constraints, as illustrated in Fig. 2.

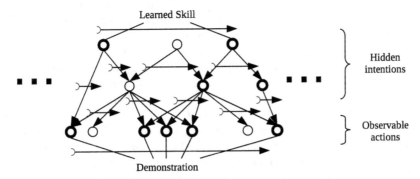

Fig. 2. An example of a causal hierarchy. The schematics are explained in the text.

If X includes floating-point values, it may be infeasible to store C in its entirety. However, only a small subset of parameter values from X will appear in any real-world demonstration, so the relevant portion of C can be constructed and stored online as needed. To this end, we introduce the function $\text{CAUSES}(\langle v \rangle) = \{u \mid (u, \langle v \rangle) \in C\}$, which returns only those $u \in V$ that could cause a given sequence $\langle v \rangle$. CAUSES is what the domain author must define.

Another issue is that causal chains from intentions to actions may have different path lengths. For example, in Fig. 2, the leftmost path from the top layer to the bottom layer has length 1, whereas the others have length 2. To identify explanations like this in a bottom-up fashion, we define a more

---

[1] We denote a finite list of length N by $\langle x_i \rangle_{i=1}^{N} = \langle x_1, x_2, ..., x_N \rangle$. For brevity, a finite list of arbitrary length is denoted simply $\langle x \rangle$, whereas a list of length 1 is always denoted with a single subscript: $\langle x_1 \rangle$.

reflexive, extended CAUSES function as follows: For any singleton sequence $\langle v_1 \rangle$, EXTCAUSES($\langle v_1 \rangle$) = CAUSES($\langle v_1 \rangle$) $\cup \{v_1\}$. For non-singleton sequences $\langle v \rangle$ with length greater than 1, EXTCAUSES($\langle v \rangle$) = CAUSES($\langle v \rangle$).

Finally, we define covers. Informally, a cover is a sequence of intentions, where every observed action is path-connected to some intention in the sequence. An ℓ-cover is a cover where each path has length at most ℓ. Formally, we inductively define covers as follows. A sequence $\langle u_k \rangle_{k=1}^K \in V^*$ is a *1-cover* for another sequence $\langle v \rangle \in V^*$, if there is a partition of $\langle v \rangle$ into K consecutive, contiguous subsequences $\langle v \rangle^{(1)}, \langle v \rangle^{(2)}, ..., \langle v \rangle^{(K)}$, such that $u_k \in$ EXTCAUSES($\langle v \rangle^{(k)}$) for every k. A sequence $\langle u \rangle \in V^*$ is an *ℓ-cover* (or simply *cover*) of $\langle w \rangle \in V^*$ if there is some $\langle v \rangle \in V^*$ such that $\langle u \rangle$ is a 1-cover of $\langle v \rangle$ and $\langle v \rangle$ is an $(\ell-1)$-cover of $\langle w \rangle$.

We may now formally state the intention inference problem as we conceive it. Let $A \subset V$ be a distinguished subset of vertices called *observable actions* (Fig. 2, bottom layer). A *demonstration* is some $\langle a \rangle \in A^*$ (Fig. 2, bottom layer, bold-faced vertices). The *intention inference problem* is to compute the most parsimonious covers of $\langle a \rangle$. Readers may note that a useful parsimony criteria employed by PCT, *irredundancy* [17], is necessarily satisfied by all covers as defined here: no proper subset of a cover is a cover itself. Therefore, beyond irredundancy, we define the *parsimonious* covers, or *explanations*, to be the minimum cardinality top-level covers (Fig. 2, top layer, bold-faced vertices).

We have derived a provably correct procedure for the intention inference problem during learning, shown in Algorithm 1. The inputs are a causal intention hierarchy $\mathcal{I}$ as defined above (encoded as a CAUSES function) and a demonstration $\langle a \rangle$. The algorithm incrementally constructs all covers in a bottom-up fashion, accumulating all ℓ-covers in a set $H^{(\ell)}$ during the ℓth iteration (lines 4–17). Each layer $H^{(\ell)}$ is populated by finding all 1-covers of all child sequences from the previous layer $H^{(\ell-1)}$ (lines 5–14). The 1-covers for every such child sequence are also constructed incrementally: 1-covers for the leading sequences up to index $k-1$ are used to construct the 1-covers up to index k, as k ranges over the full sequence (lines 6–12). This step checks every partition point $j \leq k$, and concatenates every 1-cover of the leading subsequence up to $j-1$ with every cause of the trailing subsequence from j to k (lines 8–11). This pairwise concatenation operation (line 10), denoted by $\oplus$, is defined as follows:

$$Y \oplus Z = \{\langle y_1, ..., y_M, z \rangle \mid \langle y_m \rangle_{m=1}^M \in Y \text{ and } z \in Z\} \ .$$

The leading covers up to k are accumulated in sets $G^{(1)}, ..., G^{(j)}, ...G^{(k)}$, which are used to populate $G^{(k+1)}$.

It can be shown (Sect. 4) that once k reaches N, $G^{(N)}$ contains all 1-covers of the full child sequence. These get added to the current $H^{(\ell)}$ (line 13). The top-most $H^{(\ell)}$ is returned when no new covers are found (line 16). The most parsimonious covers can then be extracted from $H^{(\ell)}$ in a post-processing step. This design choice allows researchers to compare alternative parsimony criteria (beyond irredundancy) without modifying the core algorithm.

Algorithm 1. The Intention Inference Algorithm.

1: **procedure** COVER($\mathcal{I}, \langle a \rangle$)   ▷ $\mathcal{I}$ is supplied implicitly through CAUSES
2:     $H^{(0)} \leftarrow \{\langle a \rangle\}$ ▷ Start with the demo $\langle a \rangle$
3:     **for** $\ell \leftarrow 1, 2, \ldots$ **do**   ▷ Bottom-up cover construction
4:        $H^{(\ell)} \leftarrow \emptyset$ ▷ Begin finding ℓ-covers
5:        **for** $\langle v_i \rangle_{i=1}^{N} \in H^{(\ell-1)}$ **do**   ▷ Process each child sequence
6:           **for** $k \leftarrow 0, 1, \ldots, N$ **do**   ▷ Process child sequence incrementally
7:              $G^{(k)} \leftarrow \emptyset$ ▷ Begin covering up to k
8:              **for** $j \in \{1, \ldots, k\}$ **do**   ▷ Check all leading-trailing splits
9:                 $U \leftarrow$ EXTCAUSES($\langle v_i \rangle_{i=j}^{k}$)   ▷ Get trailing causes
10:                 $G^{(k)} \leftarrow G^{(k)} \cup (G^{(j-1)} \oplus U)$ ▷ Append to leading covers
11:              **end for**
12:           **end for**
13:           $H^{(\ell)} \leftarrow H^{(\ell)} \cup G^{(N)}$ ▷ Add full covers to next layer
14:        **end for**
15:        **if** $H^{(\ell)} = H^{(\ell-1)}$ **then**   ▷ Check for any new covers
16:           **return** $H^{(\ell)}$ ▷ No new covers, terminate
17:        **end if**
18:     **end for**
19: **end procedure**

3.2 Imitation and Generalization

Once a parsimonious cover for the observed demonstration has been found and saved, the robot is ready to generalize the learned skill to new situations. When asked to imitate, the robot begins with visual processing to identify object properties and relationships in the new scene. Our current implementation uses simple computer vision techniques as a baseline. Next, the objects found by visual processing must be matched with the corresponding objects in the original demonstration. For example, consider the toy block IL scenario with three blocks, two of which get manipulated by the demonstrator. When the robot sees three blocks in a new situation, it does not know a priori which one should be treated as "block 1" from the demonstration, which should be treated as "block 2", and which is extraneous. A simple algorithm computes the one-to-one object matching that best preserves salient properties (shape, color) and relationships (part-whole, atop-below). For example, now consider the drive maintenance IL scenario. Suppose that in the demonstration, slot $1^{(demo)}$ is occupied and LED $1^{(demo)}$ is red, and in the new scene, slots $2^{(new)}$ & $3^{(new)}$ are occupied but only LED $3^{(new)}$ is red. Slots and LEDs $1^{(demo)}$ & $3^{(new)}$ will be matched, rather than $1^{(demo)}$ & $2^{(new)}$, since the configuration of colors, part-whole relationships, and atop-below relationships is better preserved. The matching algorithm is based on greedy weighted bipartite matching. Note that the matching only compares the initial state in the demo with the initial state during imitation. Incorporating the inferred intentions is a potential research direction, although similar problems involving plan reuse are known to be hard [16].

Once matching is complete, the parameter bindings in the top-level intentions are updated to point to the corresponding objects in the new scene. AI planning techniques can then be used in a top-down manner to plan a sequence of low-level motor commands that carry out these intentions. In particular, we employ *Hierarchical Task Network* (HTN) planning, in which high-level tasks are decomposed into lower-level sub-tasks and ultimately executable actions [10]. It turns out that intentions in our causal hierarchy can be mapped directly onto the formal HTN notion of tasks. A corollary is that, if CAUSES formally inverts the HTN planning operators, then Algorithm 1 formally inverts the HTN planning algorithm. To our knowledge, this is the first provably correct inversion.

Like the causal relation, HTN operators can map the same parent intention onto several alternative child sequences. These represent alternate strategies for carrying out the parent intention, some of which may be more or less appropriate depending on the current state of the environment. The HTN planner can search each branch, simulating its effects on the environment, and avoid branches that fail. Consequently, the resulting actions planned for the new situation may differ significantly from the observed actions in the demonstration. For example, suppose "block 1" was grasped and released by the teacher's left hand during demonstration, but its matching block is only reachable by the robot's right gripper in the new situation. When the HTN planner decomposes the high-level "get block 1 to ..." task, it will find the branch most suitable to the new situation, namely picking up with the right and handing off to the left. This is an example of the bimanual coordination supported in our implementation.

The robot's capacity for generalization boils down to this fact that the same parent intention can cause any of several alternative sub-intention branches, in a way sensitive to the current state of the environment. The results of just one branch are observed in the demonstration, but many other branches exist that are more appropriate for other situations. Inferring the teacher's intentions exposes these other branches, and the higher up the hierarchy, the more branches get exposed. So cause-effect inference of parsimonious covers is central to one-shot generalization. Moreover, the lowest-level HTN operators can invoke motion planning routines, which convert target gripper positions into joint angles that respect the physical constraints of the robot. As a result, the causal hierarchy can be extended to a level deeper than the object-centric actions recorded in SMILE, producing concrete motor plans suitable for physical robot execution.

4   Theoretical and Empirical Results

Algorithm 1 is sound and complete, although a naive set implementation for $H^{(\ell)}$ and $G^{(k)}$ may lead to intractable storage requirements. PCT mitigates this sort of problem using storage-efficient data structures called *generators*. Given space limitations, we cannot describe our generator-based implementations here. To convey the key ideas of the correctness proof, we provide a sketch for Algorithm 1 as is, assuming correct generator-based implementations of the relevant set operations. The complete proof will be included in a forthcoming publication.

Theorem 1. *Let H be the return value of* COVER$(\mathcal{I}, \langle a \rangle)$. *Every element of H is a cover of $\langle a \rangle$; every cover of $\langle a \rangle$ is an element of H.*

Proof (sketch). Suppose on lines 7–11 that for $j \leq k$, each $G^{(j-1)}$ contains precisely the 1-covers of $\langle v_i \rangle_{i=1}^{j-1}$. Then any element of $G^{(j-1)} \oplus U$ added to $G^{(k)}$ on line 10 must be a 1-cover of $\langle v_i \rangle_{i=1}^{k}$ by definition. Conversely, any 1-cover of $\langle v_i \rangle_{i=1}^{k}$ has its last contiguous child sub-sequence start at some index $\tilde{j} \leq k$. This cover consists of leading causes in $G^{(\tilde{j}-1)}$, and a trailing cause in EXTCAUSES$(\langle v_i \rangle_{i=\tilde{j}}^{k})$. Therefore it will be added to $G^{(k)}$ on line 10 when $j = \tilde{j}$. It follows that $G^{(k)}$ will contain all and only the 1-covers of $\langle v_i \rangle_{i=1}^{k}$ by line 11, and by induction on k, $G^{(N)}$ will contain precisely the 1-covers of the full $\langle v_i \rangle_{i=1}^{N}$ by line 12. Consequently, $H^{(\ell)}$ receives every 1-cover of $\langle v_i \rangle_{i=1}^{N}$ on line 13. Assuming $H^{(\ell-1)}$ contains every $(\ell-1)$-cover of $\langle a \rangle$, it follows that $H^{(\ell)}$ has accumulated every ℓ-cover of $\langle a \rangle$ by line 14. Now by induction on ℓ, every cover of $\langle a \rangle$ has been found when the algorithm returns on line 16. Termination in finite time can be guaranteed under reasonable conditions on $\mathcal{I}$. $\qquad\square$

To ascertain the practical utility of these theoretical results, we performed an initial assessment of our framework using the dock scenario. Four different skills were taught to the robot. Each skill was demonstrated twice in SMILE, using different initial states for the maintenance dock each time. Algorithm 1 was used to infer intentions in each demonstration. Finally, the robot was asked to imitate each demonstration four times, again using different initial dock states each time. The result is 8 demonstrations total and 32 imitation trials total. In every demonstration and trial, the initial dock states were automatically and randomly generated, varying the number and position of spare drives, which slots were occupied, and which LEDs were red. The robot was taught four skills: (1) discarding a red LED drive, (2) replacing (and discarding) a red LED drive with a spare on top of the dock, (3) replacing (and discarding) a red LED drive with a green one, and (4) swapping a red LED drive with a green one.

On every demonstration, Algorithm 1 terminated in a matter of minutes (see Table 1), so while time complexity is a theoretical concern it was not prohibitive in practice. Nevertheless, developing a more efficient algorithm that scales to more complex examples is the subject of future work. Additionally, inspection showed that in all new situations, the robot was generating a suitable, correct plan of low-level actions to execute. Unfortunately, our physical robot failed midway through execution in 31.25 % of the trials due to sensorimotor errors (see Table 2). For example, spare drive locations as determined by visual processing would be too inaccurate for a successful grasp (visual failures), or a drive would be misaligned with a slot and not inserted properly (motor failures). These issues are due to both our simplistic sensorimotor processing and limited accuracy in Baxter's hardware as compared to more expensive robots. Nevertheless, the key result is that the cognitive learning process produced correct plans in 100 % of the trials. Sensorimotor processing is not our primary focus here so we do not consider the execution fail rate to be a significant objection to this work (although we are currently working to improve the sensorimotor processing).

Table 1. Run times in minutes of Algorithm 1. d is the length of the input $\langle a \rangle$, i.e. the number of steps recorded in the SMILE event transcript.

Table 2. Frequencies of success and failure during imitation trials.

Skill	Demo 1	Demo 2
Remove red drive	0.03 ($d = 7$)	0.10 ($d = 10$)
Replace red with spare	2.31 ($d = 14$)	2.52 ($d = 14$)
Replace red with green	2.52 ($d = 15$)	2.47 ($d = 15$)
Swap red with green	0.72 ($d = 16$)	0.73 ($d = 16$)

Class	Frequency
Planning failures	0
Vision failures	3
Motor failures	7
Successful trials	22

5   Conclusion

We have introduced a general-purpose, cognitive-level IL framework, based on hierarchical cause-effect reasoning. We validated our framework on a modest set of IL tasks, suggesting that using causal knowledge to infer a teacher's intentions, rather than copying their actions, is a promising approach to one-shot IL. Future work should evaluate our approach on more complex and varied tasks, with controlled end-user studies. The computational complexity of our algorithms should be reduced, and more reasoning should be shifted from the domain author into the algorithms themselves. Formal links with more modern hierarchical planners, such as Hierarchical Goal Networks [18], will be sought. Lastly, although our system accumulates a database of inferred top-level intention sequences, these sequences are not fed back into the hierarchy so that they can become *sub*-intentions of even higher-level parents. We hope to extend our framework in this direction so that a teacher can enrich the robot's knowledge base over time.

Acknowledgements. This work was supported by ONR award N000141310597. Thanks to Ethan Reggia for building the hard-drive docking station.

References

1. Akgun, B., Cakmak, M., Yoo, J.W., Thomaz, A.L.: Trajectories and keyframes for kinesthetic teaching. In: Proceedings of the 7th Annual ACM/IEEE International Conference on Human-Robot Interaction, pp. 391–398. ACM (2012)
2. Baldwin, D., Baird, J.: Discerning intentions in dynamic human action. Trends Cogn. Sci. **5**(4), 171–178 (2001)
3. Barros, J., Serra, F., Santos, V., Silva, F.: Tele-kinesthetic teaching of motion skills to humanoid robots through haptic feedback. In: IEEERAS Humanoids' 2014 Workshop on Policy Representations for Humanoid Robots (2014)
4. Carberry, S.: Techniques for plan recognition. User Model. User-Adap. Inter. **11**(1–2), 31–48 (2001)
5. Chater, N., Vitányi, P.: Simplicity: a unifying principle in cognitive science? Trends Cogn. Sci. **7**(1), 19–22 (2003)
6. Chella, A., Dindo, H., Infantino, I.: A cognitive framework for imitation learning. Robot. Auton. Syst. **54**(5), 403–408 (2006)

7. Dasigi, V., Reggia, J.: Parsimonious covering as a method for natural language interfaces to expert systems. AI Med. **1**(1), 49–60 (1989)
8. Dindo, H., Chella, A., La Tona, G., Vitali, M., Nivel, E., Thórisson, K.R.: Learning problem solving skills from demonstration: an architectural approach. In: Schmidhuber, J., Thórisson, K.R., Looks, M. (eds.) AGI 2011. LNCS, vol. 6830, pp. 194–203. Springer, Heidelberg (2011)
9. Friesen, A.L., Rao, R.P.: Imitation learning with hierarchical actions. In: 9th International Conference on Development and Learning, pp. 263–268. IEEE (2010)
10. Ghallab, M., Nau, D., Traverso, P.: Automated Planning. Elsevier, Amsterdam (2004)
11. Haikonen, P.: The Cognitive Approach to Conscious Machines. Imprint Academic (2003)
12. Henson, C., Sheth, A., Thirunarayan, K.: Semantic perception: converting sensory observations to abstractions. Internet Comput. **16**(2), 26–34 (2012). IEEE
13. Huang, D.-W., Katz, G.E., Langsfeld, J.D., Oh, H., Gentili, R.J., Reggia, J.A.: An object-centric paradigm for robot programming by demonstration. In: Schmorrow, D.D., Fidopiastis, C.M. (eds.) AC 2015. LNCS, vol. 9183, pp. 745–756. Springer, Heidelberg (2015)
14. Jansen, B., Belpaeme, T.: A computational model of intention reading in imitation. Robot. Auton. Syst. **54**(5), 394–402 (2006)
15. Meltzoff, A., Moore, A.: Imitation of facial and manual gestures by human neonates. Science **198**(4312), 75–78 (1977)
16. Nebel, B., Koehler, J.: Plan reuse versus plan generation. Artif. Intell. **76**(1), 427–454 (1995)
17. Peng, Y., Reggia, J.: Abductive Inference Models for Diagnostic Problem-Solving. Springer, New York (1990)
18. Shivashankar, V., Alford, R., Kuter, U., Nau, D.: The GoDeL planning system: a more perfect union of domain-independent and hierarchical planning. In: Proceedings of the 23rd International Joint Conference on AI. AAAI (2013)
19. Wen, F., Chang, C.: A new approach to fault diagnosis in electrical distribution networks using a genetic algorithm. AI Eng. **12**(1), 69–80 (1998)
20. Wu, Y., Su, Y., Demiris, Y.: A morphable template framework for robot learning by demonstration. Robot. Auton. Syst. **62**(10), 1517–1530 (2014)

Some Theorems on Incremental Compression

Arthur Franz[(✉)]

Odessa, Ukraine
franz@fias.uni-frankfurt.de

Abstract. The ability to induce short descriptions of, i.e. compressing, a wide class of data is essential for any system exhibiting general intelligence. In all generality, it is proven that incremental compression – extracting features of data strings and continuing to compress the residual data variance – leads to a time complexity superior to universal search if the strings are incrementally compressible. It is further shown that such a procedure breaks up the shortest description into a set of pairwise orthogonal features in terms of algorithmic information.

Keywords: Incremental compression · Data compression · Algorithmic complexity · Universal induction · Universal search · Feature extraction

1   Introduction

The ability to induce short descriptions of, i.e. compressing, a wide class of data is essential for any system exhibiting general intelligence. In fact, it is fair to say that the problem of universal induction has been solved in theory [1]. However, the practical progress is impeded by the use of universal search which requires the execution of all lexicographically ordered programs until a solution is found. For the better or worse, Levin Search has the optimal order of computational complexity [2]. Nevertheless, the obvious slowness of this method, hidden in the big "O" notation, seems to be the price for its generality.

In practice, the problem of finding short descriptions is often solved by an incremental approach. For example, in the presently successful deep learning algorithms, each layer in a deep neural network usually detects features of its input x and computes the activation p of neurons in that layer, $p = f'(x)$, as opposed to essentially guessing descriptions in universal search. In the generative mode, typical inputs x can be computed from neural activations: $x = f(p)$. The next layer takes the feature values p and treats them as an input for the next compression step, which can be viewed as incrementally compressing the input since the number of neurons typically decreases at each layer. The hierarchical structure of the human visual cortex also seems to reflect an incremental, layered approach to the representation of real world perceptual data. Finally, the progress of science itself very much resembles incremental compression as

A. Franz—Independent researcher

B. Steunebrink et al. (Eds.): AGI 2016, LNAI 9782, pp. 74–83, 2016.
DOI: 10.1007/978-3-319-41649-6_8

evidenced by the strive for unified theories given a set of previously acquired theories in physics.

On the one hand, there are narrowly intelligent artificial systems and generally intelligent humans both using an efficient, incremental approach to the learning of concise representations of the world. On the other hand, generally intelligent artificial systems exist only on paper [3] and are impeded by the inefficient, non-incremental universal search. The present paper tries to bridge this gap and formulate a general incremental theory of compression. While there has been previous work on incremental search, it is often meant in the sense of reusing previously found solutions to problems (see [4] for a review). The meaning of incremental compression is however different and refers to the decomposition of a single problem into different parts and solving them one by one.

2   Preliminaries

Consider a universal, prefix Turing machine U. Strings are defined on a finite alphabet $\mathcal{A} = \{0,1\}$ with ϵ denoting the empty string. Logarithms are taken on the basis 2. $\mathcal{A}^*$ denotes the set of finite strings made up of the elements of $\mathcal{A}$. Since there is a one-to-one map $\mathcal{A}^* \leftrightarrow N$ of finite strings on natural numbers, strings and natural numbers are used interchangeably. For example, the length $l(n)$ of an integer n denotes the number of symbols of the string that it corresponds to. The map $\langle \cdot, \cdot \rangle$ denotes a one-to-one map of two strings on natural numbers: $\mathcal{A}^* \times \mathcal{A}^* \leftrightarrow N$. The corresponding map for more than two variables is defined recursively: $\langle x, y, z \rangle \equiv \langle x, \langle y, z \rangle \rangle$. In particular, $\langle z, \epsilon \rangle = z$. Since all Turing machines can be enumerated, the universal machine U operates on a number/string $\langle n, p \rangle$ by executing p on the Turing machine T_n: $U(\langle n, p \rangle) = T_n(p)$. Similarly, a string y is applied to another string x by applying the yth Turing machine: $y(x) \equiv T_y(x) = U(\langle y, x \rangle)$. The prefix complexity $K(x|y)$ of x given y is defined by $K(x|y) \equiv \min\{l(z) : U(\langle z, y \rangle) = x\}$ and $K(x) \equiv K(x|\epsilon)$. The complexity of several variables is defined as $K(x, y) \equiv K(\langle x, y \rangle)$.

3   An Example

Consider the binary string $x = 10110111011110111110\ldots$. First, it can be discovered that the string consists of blocks of 1's. Let f_1 be the number of the Turing machine T_{f_1} in the standard enumeration of Turing machines that takes an integer m, prints m 1's and attaches a 0. f_1 will be called a *feature* of x and the set of parameters $p_1 = m_1 m_2 \ldots = 1, 2, 3, 4, 5, \ldots$ will be called *parameters* of the feature. Hence, the task of compressing x has been reduced to the task of compressing merely p_1 which is shorter than x, while x can be computed by the feature: $f_1(p_1) = x$. The next feature f_2 may represent the Turing machine taking a start value $p_2 = 1$ and increasing 1 each step, such that $f_2(p_2) = p_1$.

Note that universal search would try to find the the whole final description at once by blind search. In contrast to that, incremental compression finds intermediate descriptions (f_1, p_1), (f_2, p_2) and possibly many more layers one by one.

However, those intermediate descriptions are much longer than the final shortest program and will therefore be found much more slowly by universal search. In order to solve this problem, I introduce an inverse map, the so-called *descriptive map* f', that computes the parameters directly: $f'(x) = p$. In the above example, the descriptive map f'_1 may correspond to a Turing machine $T_{f'_1}$ that counts the number of 1's that are separated by 0's and thereby *computes* p_1 instead of trying to guess it as a universal search procedure would. The compression task will then consist of finding pairs (f, f') for each compression level, such that $f(f'(x)) = x$, which will turn out to be much faster than universal search.

4   Definitions

Definition 1 (Features, descriptive maps and parameters). *Let sf and x be finite strings and $D_f(x)$ the set of **descriptive maps** of x given f:*

$$D_f(x) \equiv \{f' : f(f'(x)) = x, \; l(f'(x)) < l(x) - l(f)\} \qquad (4.1)$$

*If $D_f(x) \neq \varnothing$ then f is called a **feature** of x. The strings $p \equiv f'(x)$ are called **parameters** of the feature f. f^* is called **shortest feature** of x if it is one of the strings fulfilling*

$$l(f^*) = \min \{l(f) : \; D_f(x) \neq \varnothing\} \qquad (4.2)$$

*and f'^* is called **shortest descriptive map** of x given f^* if*

$$l(f'^*) = \min \{l(g) : \; g \in D_{f^*}(x)\} \qquad (4.3)$$

In the definition, any feature is required to do at least some compression, $l(f) + l(p) < l(x)$, since otherwise $f = f' = $ id would always trivially satisfy the definition for any x. This procedure to search for description and its inverse at the same time has been proposed in [5], called SS'-Search, albeit not in the context of features and incremental compression.

Definition 2 (Incremental compression). *A string x is called **incrementally compressible**, if there exist features $f_1, \ldots, f_k$ such that $(f_1 \circ \cdots \circ f_k)(\epsilon) = f_1(f_2(\cdots f_k(\epsilon))) \equiv U(\langle f_1, \ldots, f_k \rangle) = x.$*[1]

5   Properties of a Single Compression Step

The central question for incremental compression is given a finite string x, how to find a pair of a feature f and descriptive map f', such that $f(f'(x)) = x$. In the following the consequences of choosing the shortest f^* and f'^* are explored. All proofs can be found in the appendix.

---

[1] Note that the $\langle \cdot, \cdot \rangle$-map is defined with $\langle z, \epsilon \rangle \equiv z$, hence $f_k(\epsilon) = U(\langle f_k, \epsilon \rangle) = U(f_k)$, so that f_k acts as a usual string in the universal machine.

Lemma 1. *Let f^* and f'^* be the shortest feature and descriptive map of a finite string x, respectively. Further, let $p \equiv f'^*(x)$. Then*

1. $l(f^*) = K(x|p)$ and
2. $l(f'^*) = K(p|x)$.

Theorem 1 (Feature incompressibility). *The shortest feature f^* of a finite string x is incompressible: $K(f^*) = l(f^*) + O(1)$.*

Theorem 2 (Independence of features and parameters). *Let f^* and f'^* be the shortest feature and descriptive map of a finite string x, respectively. Further, let $p \equiv f'^*(x)$. Then,*

1. $K(f^*|p) = K(f^*) + O(1)$,
2. $K(p|f^*) = K(p|f^*, K(f^*)) + O(1) = K(p) + O(1)$ and
3. $K(f^*, p) = K(f^*) + K(p) + O(1)$.

Interestingly, from the definition of the shortest feature and descriptive map, it follows that features and parameters do not share information about each other such that the description of the (f^*, p)-pair breaks down into the simpler task of describing f^* and p separately. Since Theorem 1 implies the incompressibility of f^* and $U(\langle f^*, p \rangle) = x$, the task of compressing x is reduced to the mere compression of p. However, f^* and p could store additional, residual information making the compression more difficult: $K(x) < K(f^*, p) + O(1)$. The following theorem shows that this is not the case.

Theorem 3 (Concise information transfer). *Let f^* and f'^* be the shortest feature and descriptive map of a finite string x, respectively. Further, let $p \equiv f'^*(x)$.*

1. *The description of the feature-parameter pair (f^*, p) breaks down into the description of x and a residual part:*

$$K(f^*, p) = K(x) + K(p|x, K(x)) + O(1) \tag{5.1}$$

2. *For a fixed f^*, minimizing the length of the descriptive map f' simultaneously minimizes the residual part:*

$$l(f'^*) \propto K(p|x, K(x)) + O(1)$$

3. *The parameters p do not contain information not present in x and $K(x)$:*

$$K(p|x, K(x)) = O(1) \tag{5.2}$$

4. *The shortest feature f^* does not contain information not present in x and $K(x)$:*

$$K(f^*|x, K(x)) = O(1) \tag{5.3}$$

This theorem guarantees that **all and only** the information in x is transferred to the (f^*, p) pair. Hence, there is no residual information contained in p; the information content in p is a genuine subset of the information in x with the rest being stored in f^*. f^* also does not contain residual information and genuinely represents an incompressible part of x. These conclusions are summarized in the following corollaries.

Corollary 1. *The shortest feature f^* and its parameters p contain no more and no less information than is in x:*

$$K(x) = K(f^*, p) + O(1) \tag{5.4}$$

Corollary 2. *After extracting the incompressible feature f^* all remaining information in x resides in p:*

$$K(x) = l(f^*) + K(p) + O(1) \tag{5.5}$$

This corollary expresses the important result that in order to compress x, it suffices to compress the shorter and simpler string p. Having found the shortest feature and descriptive map we can be certain to be on the right path to the compression of x and not to run into dead-ends.

6   Orthogonal Feature Bases

The following theorems show that compressing the parameters p further leads to an orthogonal feature basis that optimally represents the original string x.

Theorem 4 (Feature bases). *Let x be a string that is incrementally compressed by a sequence of shortest features $f_1^*, f_2^*, \ldots$ and their respective descriptive maps $f'^*_1, f'^*_2, \ldots$ with $p_i \equiv f'^*_i(p_{i-1})$ and $p_0 \equiv x$. Then there will be an integer k after which $p_k = \epsilon$, no further compression is possible and the shortest description of x breaks up into features:*

$$K(x) = \sum_{i=1}^{k} l(f_i^*) + O(1) \tag{6.1}$$

The case $k = 1$ degenerates into the usual, non-incremental compression, in which case the description of x does not break up into features.

Theorem 5 (Orthogonality of features). *Let x be a finite string that is incrementally compressed by a complete sequence of features $f_1^*, \ldots, f_k^*$. Then, the features are **orthogonal** in terms of the algorithmic information: $I(f_i^* : f_j^*) = K(f_j^*)\delta_{ij} + O(1)$, with δ_{ij} being the Kronecker symbol.*

7   Efficiency of Incremental Compression

In order to assess the time complexity of incremental compression we derive an upper bound on $l(f'^*)$.

Theorem 6 (Bound on the length of descriptive map). *Let f^* and f'^* be the shortest feature and descriptive map of a finite string x, respectively. Then the following bound holds on $l(f'^*)$:*

$$l(f'^*) \leq 2 \log K(x) + 4 \log \log K(x) + O(1) \leq 2 \log l(x) + 4 \log \log l(x) + O(1)$$

This bound allows to estimate the time complexity for a potential algorithm for incremental compression. If the algorithm uses universal search or similar to find the features and descriptive maps, the time complexity of a single compression step will be proportional to

$$O\left(2^{l(f^*)+l(f'^*)}\right) \leq O\left(l(x)^2 \, (\log l(x))^4 \, 2^{l(f^*)}\right) \tag{7.1}$$

At each compression level i, $p_i = f_i'^*(p_{i-1})$ takes the role of x (with $p_0 \equiv x$). But since information is sliced off at each compression level (Corollary 2), we know that $K(p_i) < K(p_{i-1}) < \cdots < K(x) \leq l(x)$ up to a constant. Thus, the bound is valid for each $l(f_i'^*)$ and the time complexity of the whole incremental compression will be proportional to

$$O\left(l(x)^2 \, (\log l(x))^4 \sum_{i=1}^{k} 2^{l(f_i^*)}\right) \tag{7.2}$$

In standard universal search the final program $l(p) = Kt(x) \geq K(x)$ is searched for in a non-incremental way, where Kt denotes the resource-bounded Levin complexity. Universal search is therefore proportional to the huge factor $2^{l(p)}$. Since from Theorem 4, we get $2^{l(p)} \geq 2^{K(x)} = c \prod_{i=1}^{k} 2^{l(f_i^*)}$ and $\sum_{i=1}^{k} 2^{l(f_i^*)} \ll \prod_{i=1}^{k} 2^{l(f_i^*)}$ in almost all cases, we observe that incremental compression promises to be much faster than (non-incremental) universal search, if the string is incrementally compressible.[2] Incremental compression is slower only if the search for f'^* is slower than doing universal search from scratch, e.g. when $K(x) \leq 2 \log l(x) + 4 \log \log l(x)$ which is true only for very simple strings.

Unfortunately, since the Kolmogorov complexity is incomputable, the practical implementation of incremental compression will have to resort to some kind of universal search procedure for the features and descriptive maps which is not guaranteed to find the shortest ones. It remains to be seen whether the present theory can be formulated in terms of Levin complexity $Kt(x)$ instead of the prefix Kolmogorov complexity $K(x)$.

---

[2] It is not difficult to see that the "$\ll$" sign is justified for all but very few cases. After all, only for very few combinations of a set of fixed sum integers $\sum_i l_i = L$ the sum $\sum_i 2^{l_i}$ is close to 2^L.

8   Discussion

The present approach allows to represent the shortest description of a finite string by a complete set of pairwise orthogonal features in terms of vanishing mutual algorithmic information. The features can be searched for one by one without running into dead-ends, in the sense that for any incomplete set of orthogonal features the remaining ones always exist. At the same time, while the features are the carriers of the information about x, the descriptive maps have been proven to be simple, $l(f'^*) = O(\log K(x))$, allowing for a fast search for them. That makes intuitively sense, since the descriptive maps receive x as an input. It is due to these properties that make the present approach to incremental compression efficient.

The present work is a continuation of my general approach to artificial intelligence [6]. In fact, I have already demonstrated the practical feasibility and efficiency of incremental compression in a general setting. In [7] I have built an algorithm that incrementally finds close to shortest descriptions of all strings computable by 1- and 2-state and 80 % of the strings computable by 3-state Turing machines. Readers interested in a practical implementation of the present approach are referred to that paper.

The example in Sect. 3 demonstrates an actually incrementally compressible string that complies with the Definition 2. This proves that incrementally compressible strings exist. The question arises thus how many compressible strings actually are incrementally compressible. Are there any compressible strings at all that are not incrementally compressible? Another important question is how to find features in the first place. Universal search is still going to be slow, notwithstanding the present considerable improvement. There are ideas to address those questions and present exciting prospects for future research.

Acknowledgements. I would like to express my gratitude to Alexey Potapov and Alexander Priamikov for proof reading and helpful comments.

A   Proofs

Proof (Lemma 1).

1. Suppose there is a shorter program g with $l(g) < l(f^*)$, that generates x with the help of p: $U(\langle g, p \rangle) = x$. Then there is also a descriptive map $g' \equiv f'^*$, that computes p from x and $l(g'(x)) = l(f'^*(x)) < l(x) - l(f^*) < l(x) - l(g)$. Therefore, g is a feature of x by definition, which conflicts with f^* already being the shortest feature.
2. Suppose there is a shorter program g' with $l(g') < l(f'^*)$, that generates p with the help of x: $U(\langle g', x \rangle) = g'(x) = p$. Then $g' \in D_{f^*}(x)$ since $f^*(g'(x)) = f^*(p) = x$ and $l(g'(x)) = l(p) < l(x) - l(f^*)$ by construction of f'^*. However, by Eq. (4.3) f'^* is already the shortest program able to do so, contradicting the assumption. $\square$

Proof (Theorem 1). From Lemma 1 we know $l(f^*) = K(x|p)$, with $p = f'^*(x)$. In all generality, for the shortest program q computing x, $l(q) = K(x) = K(q) + O(1)$ holds, since it is incompressible (q would not be the shortest program otherwise). For shortest features, the conditional case is also true: $K(x|p) = K(f^*|p) + O(1)$. After all, if there was a shorter program g, $l(g) < l(f^*)$, that computed f^* with the help of p, it could also go on to compute x from f^* and p, leading to $K(x|p) \leq l(g) + O(1) < l(f^*) + O(1)$, which contradicts $l(f^*) = K(x|p)$.

Further, for any two strings $K(f^*|p) \leq K(f^*)$, since p can only help in compressing f^*. Putting it all together leads to $l(f^*) = K(x|p) = K(f^*|p) + O(1) \leq K(f^*) + O(1)$. On the other hand, since in general $K(f^*) \leq l(f^*) + O(1)$ is also true, the claim $K(f^*) = l(f^*) + O(1)$ follows.   □

Proof (Theorem 2).

1. Follows immediately from $K(f^*) = l(f^*) + O(1) = K(x|p) + O(1) = K(f^*|p) + O(1)$.

2. The first equality follows from Theorem 1, since we only need to read off the length of f^* in order to know $K(f^*)$ up to a constant. For the second equality, consider the symmetry of the conditional prefix complexity relation $K(f^*, p) = K(f^*) + K(p|f^*, K(f^*)) + O(1) = K(p) + K(f^*|p, K(p)) + O(1)$ [8, Theorem 3.9.1, p. 247]. If p does not help computing a shorter f^*, then knowing $K(p)$ will not help either. Therefore, from (1), we obtain $K(f^*|p, K(p)) = K(f^*) + O(1)$ and therefore $K(p|f^*, K(f^*)) = K(p) + O(1)$.

3. In general, by [8, Theorem 3.9.1, p. 247] we can expand $K(f^*, p) = K(f^*) + K(p|f^*, K(f^*)) + O(1)$. After inserting (2) the claim follows.   □

Proof (Theorem 3).

1. Expand $K(x, p)$ up to an additive constant:

$$K(p) + K(x|p, K(p)) = K(x, p) = K(x) + K(p|x, K(x)) \qquad (A.1)$$

From Lemma 1(1) and Theorem 1 we know $K(f^*) = K(x|p) + O(1)$. Conditioning this on $K(p)$ and using f^*'s independence of p and thereby of $K(p)$ (Theorem 2(1)) we get $K(x|p, K(p)) = K(f^*|K(p)) + O(1) = K(f^*) + O(1)$. Inserting this into Eq. (A.1) and using Theorem 2(3), yields

$$K(f^*, p) = K(p) + K(f^*) = K(x) + K(p|x, K(x)) + O(1) \qquad (A.2)$$

2. Fix f^* and let $P_{f^*}(x) \equiv \{f'(x) : f' \in D_{f^*}(x)\}$ be the set of admissible parameters computing x from f^*. From Lemma 1(2), we know that minimizing $l(f')$, with $s = f'(x)$, is equivalent to minimizing $K(s|x)$, i.e. choosing a string $p = f'^*(x) \in P_{f^*}(x)$ such that $K(s|x) \geq K(p|x)$ for all $s \in P_{f^*}(x)$. Conditioning Eq. (A.2) on x leads to:

$$K(p|x) + K(f^*|x) = K(x|x) + K(p|x, K(x), x) = K(p|x, K(x)) \qquad (A.3)$$

up to additive constants. Since f^* and x are fixed, the claim $l(f'^*) = K(p|x) \propto K(p|x, K(x)) + O(1)$ follows.

3. It remains to show that there exists some $p \in P_{f*}(x)$ such that $K(p|x, K(x)) = O(1)$. After all, if it does exist, it will be identified by minimizing $l(f')$, as implied by (2). Define $q \equiv \mathrm{argmin}_s \{l(s) : U(\langle f^*, U(s) \rangle) = f^*(U(s)) = x\}$ and compute $p \equiv U(q)$. Since $f^*(p) = x$, $p \in P_{f*}(x)$. Further, there is no shorter program able to compute p, since with p we can compute x given f^* and q is already the shortest one being able to do so, by definition. Therefore, $l(q) = K(p) + O(1)$ and $K(x|f^*) \leq K(p) + O(1)$. Can the complexity $K(x|f^*)$ be strictly smaller than $K(p)$ thereby surpassing the presumably residual part in p? Let p' be such a program: $l(p') = K(x|f^*) < K(p) + O(1)$. By definition of $K(x|f^*)$, $f^*(p') = x$. However, then we can find the shortest program q' that computes p' and we get: $f^*(U(q')) = x$. Since $l(q') \leq l(p') + O(1)$, we get $l(q') < K(p) + O(1) = l(q) + O(1)$. However, this contradicts the fact that q is already the shortest program able to compute $f^*(U(q)) = x$. Therefore,

$$l(q) = K(x|f^*) = K(p) + O(1) \tag{A.4}$$

In order to prove $K(p|x, K(x)) = O(1)$ consider the following general expansion

$$K(p, x|f^*) = K(x|f^*) + K(p|x, K(x), f^*) + O(1) \tag{A.5}$$

Since we can compute p from q and go on to compute x given f^*, $l(q) = K(p, x|f^*) + O(1)$. After all, note that with Theorem 2(2), we have $l(q) = K(p) = K(p|f^*) \leq K(p, x|f^*)$ up to additive constants, but since we can compute $\langle p, x \rangle$ given f^* from q, we know $K(p, x|f^*) \leq l(q) + O(1)$. Both inequalities can only be true if the equality $l(q) = K(p, x|f^*) + O(1)$ holds. At the same time, from Eq. (A.4), $l(q) = K(x|f^*)$ holds. Inserting this into Eq. (A.5) leads to $K(p|x, K(x), f^*) = O(1)$. Taking $K(p) = K(p|f^*) + O(1)$ (Theorem 2(2)), and inserting the conditionals x and $K(x)$ leads to: $K(p|x, K(x)) = K(p|x, K(x), f^*) + O(1) = O(1)$. Since this shows that a $p \in P_{f*}(x)$ exists with the minimal value $K(p|x, K(x)) = O(1)$, (2) implies that it must be the same or equivalent to the one found by minimizing $l(f')$.

4. Conditioning Eq. (A.3) on $K(x)$ we get $K(p|x, K(x)) + K(f^*|x, K(x)) = K(p|x, K(x)) + O(1)$ from which the claim follows.   □

Proof (Corollary 1). Inserting Eq. (5.2) into Eq. (5.1) proves the point.   □

Proof (Corollary 2). Inserting Eq. (A.2) into Eq. (5.4) and using the incompressibility of f^* (Theorem 1) proves the point.   □

Proof (Theorem 4). According to the definition of a feature, at a compression step the length of the parameters $l(p_i) < l(x) - l(f_i^*)$ and their complexity (Corollary 2) decreases. Since the f_i^* are incompressible themselves (Theorem 1), the parameters store the residual information about x. Therefore, at some point, only the possibility $p_k \equiv f'^*_k(p_{k-1}) = \epsilon$ with $l(f_k^*) = K(p_{k-1})$ remains and the compression has to stop. Expanding Corollary 2 proves the result: $K(x) = l(f_1^*) + K(p_1) + O(1) = l(f_1^*) + l(f_2^*) + K(p_2) + O(1) = \sum_{i=1}^{k} l(f_i^*) + O(1)$.   □

Proof (Theorem 5). Algorithmic information is defined as $I(f_i^* : f_j^*) \equiv K(f_j^*) - K(f_j^*|f_i^*)$. The case $i = j$ is trivial, since $K(f_i^*|f_i^*) = 0$. If $i > j$, then $p_j = \left(f_{j+1}^* \circ \cdots \circ f_i^* \right)(p_i)$, which implies that all information about f_i is in p_j. But since according to Theorem 2(1), $K(f_j^*|p_j) = K(f_j^*) + O(1)$ we conclude that $K(f_j^*|f_i^*) = K(f_j^*) + O(1)$. If $i < j$, then we know that f_j^* in no way contributed to the construction of p_i further in the compression process. Hence $K(f_j^*|f_i^*) = K(f_j^*)$. $\square$

Proof (Theorem 6). Let $p \equiv f'^*(x)$. Further, from Lemma 1 we know that $K(x|p) = l(f^*)$ and $K(p|x) = l(f'^*)$. Using Corollary 2, the difference in algorithmic information is $I(p : x) - I(x : p) = K(x) - K(x|p) - K(p) + K(p|x) = l(f'^*) + O(1)$. By [8, Lemma 3.9.2, p. 250], algorithmic information is symmetric up to logarithmic terms: $|I(x : p) - I(p : x)| \leq \log K(x) + 2 \log \log K(x) + \log K(p) + 2 \log \log K(p) + O(1)$. Since x is computed from f^* and p, we have $K(p) \leq K(x)$. Putting everything together leads to $l(f'^*) \leq 2 \log K(x) + 4 \log \log K(x) + O(1)$. The second inequality follows from $K(x) \leq l(x) + O(1)$. $\square$

References

1. Hutter, M.: On universal prediction and Bayesian confirmation. Theor. Comput. Sci. **384**(1), 33–48 (2007)
2. Levin, L.A.: Universal sequential search problems. Problemy Peredachi Informatsii **9**(3), 115–116 (1973)
3. Hutter, M.: Universal Artificial Intelligence: Sequential Decisions based on Algorithmic Probability, 300p. Springer, Heidelberg (2005). http://www.hutter1.net/ai/uaibook.htm
4. Schmidhuber, J.: Optimal ordered problem solver. Mach. Learn. **54**(3), 211–254 (2004)
5. Potapov, A., Rodionov, S.: Making universal induction efficient by specialization. In: Goertzel, B., Orseau, L., Snaider, J. (eds.) AGI 2014. LNCS, vol. 8598, pp. 133–142. Springer, Heidelberg (2014)
6. Franz, A.: Artificial general intelligence through recursive data compression and grounded reasoning: a position paper. CoRR, abs/1506.04366 (2015). http://arXiv.org/abs/1506.04366
7. Franz, A.: Toward tractable universal induction through recursive program learning. In: Bieger, J., Goertzel, B., Potapov, A. (eds.) AGI 2015. LNCS, vol. 9205, pp. 251–260. Springer, Heidelberg (2015)
8. Li, M., Vitányi, P.M.: An Introduction to Kolmogorov Complexity and Its Applications. Texts in Computer Science. Springer, New York (2009)

Rethinking Sigma's Graphical Architecture: An Extension to Neural Networks

Paul S. Rosenbloom[1,2(✉)], Abram Demski[1,2], and Volkan Ustun[1]

[1] Institute for Creative Technologies,
University of Southern California, Los Angeles, CA, USA
rosenbloom@usc.edu
[2] Department of Computer Science,
University of Southern California, Los Angeles, CA, USA

Abstract. The status of Sigma's grounding in graphical models is challenged by the ways in which their semantics has been violated while incorporating rule-based reasoning into them. This has led to a rethinking of what goes on in its graphical architecture, with results that include a straightforward extension to feedforward neural networks (although not yet with learning).

Keywords: Cognitive architecture · Graphical models · Neural network

1 Introduction

Sigma [1] is a *cognitive architecture* – a computational hypothesis about the fixed structures that together yield a mind – which has manifested a wide range of capabilities implicated in general intelligence, including forms of memory and learning, speech and language, perception and imagery, affect and attention, and reasoning and problem solving. The approach is grounded in the *graphical architecture hypothesis*, that the key at this point is to synthesize across what has been learned from over three decades worth of separate progress on cognitive architectures and *graphical models* [2]. Graphical models provide a general approach to computing efficiently with complex multivariate functions by decomposing them into products of simpler functions and mapping these products onto graphs where they can be solved, typically via message passing or sampling. They are particularly promising as the basis for a cognitive architecture because of how they yield state-of-the-art results across signals, probabilities and symbols from a uniform reasoning algorithm.

The graphical architecture hypothesis is operationalized in Sigma by a two-layer design, with the cognitive architecture implemented on top of a *graphical architecture* that is based on *factor graphs* – a very general form of graphical model – that are solved via the *summary-product* message-passing algorithm [3]. However, it has become increasingly apparent that although Sigma's graphical architecture was inspired by factor graphs, it is not strictly limited to them. What distinguishes factor graphs, and in fact all graphical models, from arbitrary networks of computations is that the former represent a global function, and compute specific properties of this function (most often *marginals* of its variables). This function thus defines a fixed semantics for

© Springer International Publishing Switzerland 2016
B. Steunebrink et al. (Eds.): AGI 2016, LNAI 9782, pp. 84–94, 2016.
DOI: 10.1007/978-3-319-41649-6_9

the graph and the resulting computations over it. The solution algorithm may be exact or approximate, but it should always reflect these semantics.

It has been clear since the beginning that any factor graph in Sigma at best has a form of bottom-up semantics. The overall graph – which both comprises Sigma's memory and structures its reasoning – is built incrementally by compiling fragments of knowledge defined within the cognitive architecture into subgraphs within the graphical architecture. The overall function that defines the semantics is then determined bottom-up from the graph that results. However, beyond this, it turns out that the compiler can create a variety of structures that are not directly interpretable in terms of the semantics of factor graphs, or in fact that of any known graphical model.

How did this come about? To what extent does it occur? And what are its implications? This article provides initial answers to these questions, yielding a broadened perspective on the graphical architecture that focuses on its message-passing algorithm and a fixed set of node and link types rather than on the semantics of the resulting computation. Factor graphs then become one *graphical idiom* – in analogy to a programing idiom – that is defined via a constrained set of node and link types and that provides a particular semantic guarantee; but it is not the only such idiom. Rules, for example, turn out to depend on a related yet distinct idiom.

In new results, one of the key implications is that feedforward neural networks [4] – although not yet with learning – can be supported via the simple addition of a new variant of an existing node type that was originally introduced in support of negated conditions and actions in rules. Some forms of neural networks – such as supervised Boltzmann machines and radial basis functions – are directly compatible with factor graphs [5], but feedforward networks are not. Yet, with this change, they can now coexist in the same overall graph/memory with both rules and factor graphs.

2 How Did This Come About?

Sigma's development is driven by four desiderata: (1) *grand unification*, combining not only the traditional cognitive aspects of intelligence but also the key subcognitive aspects; (2) *generic cognition*, both constructing artificial intelligence and modeling natural intelligence; (3) *functional elegance*, enabling the diversity of intelligent behavior from the interactions among a small general set of mechanisms; and (4) *sufficient efficiency*, for work at scale. As new capabilities have been added, in service of grand unification and generic cognition, the result may simply be a new factor graph – as happened for isolated word speech recognition [6] and distributed vectors (i.e., word embeddings) [7] – while at other times architectural extensions have been required. Functional elegance biases all such changes to be minimal, preferring small tweaks in existing mechanisms to addition of whole new modules.

Factor graphs are undirected, bipartite graphs composed of variables nodes (VNs) and factor nodes (FNs) (Fig. 1). There is a VN for each variable in the original function and an FN for each subfunction in its decomposition, with each FN connected to all of its variables' VNs. The summary-product algorithm computes messages at these nodes to send to their neighbors. At a VN, an outgoing message along a link is computed via products over the other links' incoming messages. At an FN, this product also includes the factor function at the node, and then all variables not relevant to the VN on the outgoing link are summarized out, by *sum* (or *integral* for continuous variables) to yield marginals or *max* to yield the mode.

A number of extensions are possible to this pure model without affecting what the graph computes, and thus without violating factor graph semantics. Two leveraged extensively for sufficient efficiency in Sigma's graphical architecture are: (1) suppression of messages that will not change the ultimate results; and (2) optimization of how specific types of FNs compute outgoing messages. One example of (1) is

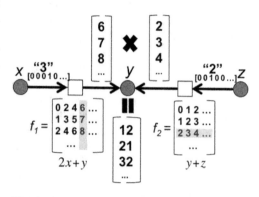

Fig. 1. Summary product computation over the factor graph for $f(x,y,z) = y^2 + yz + 2yx + 2xz = (2x + y)(y + z) = f_1(x,y)f_2(y,z)$ of the marginal on y given evidence concerning x and z.

permanently shutting down one direction of a link if the messages in that direction can never affect the results. A canonical example of (2) is specialized FN implementations for the affine transforms in mental imagery [8]; the same outgoing messages could have been computed by multiplying the incoming messages by an appropriate function, but the resulting *delta* functions would be highly inefficient.

More to the point though are changes that actually alter what is computed. This may involve: (1) eliminating messages on links that can change what is computed; and (2) including FNs that perform computations that aren't reducible, even in principle, to products and summarizations. As an example of (1), links compiled from rule conditions and actions have one direction shut off to enforce the unidirectionality of information flow in rules [9]. As an example of (2), consider negated conditions in rules, which should trigger activity only when the pattern fails to match. This is implemented by specialized FNs that have one input and one output in directed "condition" sub-graphs. The input message is subtracted from a constant function of 1, and then floored at 0 – a value of 1 stands in for *true* with 0 doing the same for *false*, but values in general can also be between these values, or even outside of this range. Negating [0 .3 1.2 1], for example, yields [1 .7 0 0].

Section 3 discusses a set of changes to the graphical architecture that violate factor graph semantics, and thus yield what could be considered a *generalized factor graph*, although it is probably more appropriately considered a generalization of the summary-product algorithm, as the semantics of factor graphs have not been extended in a manner that corresponds to the algorithmic changes that have been made. Such semantic extensions have been explored, but so far without success.

3   To What Extent Does It Occur?

The single biggest driver in extending Sigma's graphical architecture beyond the semantics of factor graphs has been the desire to combine rules with probabilistic graphs. Sigma's primary long-term knowledge structure within the cognitive architecture is a generalized notion of a *conditional*, which combines the forms of conditionality provided by both rules and probabilities. *Conditions* and *actions* in conditionals enable rule-like behavior, with conditions triggering further processing when matched to working memory, and actions proposing changes to working memory. However, conditionals may also contain: *condacts*, which provide a synthesis of conditions and actions to enable the bidirectional flow of information necessary for probabilistic reasoning; and *functions*, where distributions can be stored.

Condacts and functions together yield standard factor graphs. A number of the particular extensions required to support rules and their conditions and actions are what induce semantic divergence, including: (1) directed links, (2) closed-world semantics, (3) universal variables, (4) filter nodes, and (5) transform nodes.

3.1   Directed Links

As mentioned in Sect. 2, one direction of each link is shut off within conditions and actions to yield one-way rule behavior. This effectively makes these links directed, although this is very different from the directed links in Bayesian networks that still imply bidirectional message passing. The key question though is what has been lost here given that the summary-product algorithm specifies bidirectionality?

In some cases, the omission of back-messages does not affect the end result; it just yields a simple efficiency gain. If excluding back-messages changes the result, however, it's much less clear what is going on. A correlation that has influence in one direction but not the reverse has no place in probability theory; conclusions may be stronger in one direction than the other, but the influence is always there. This isn't necessarily a problem for Sigma, however, because factor graphs don't always carry probabilities. The cases where one-directional propagation changes the end result are often in fact those where the messages are not probabilities.

A simple example is the transitive rule in Sigma. Given a predicate $Above(x, y)$, we can define a conditional with conditions $Above(x, y)$ and $Above(y, z)$, and action $Above(x, z)$. (Henceforth $Above()$ will be abbreviated $A()$.) If the initial contents of working memory are $A(1, 2)$, $A(2, 3)$, $A(3, 4)$, Sigma will generate $A(1, 3)$, $A(2, 4)$, $A(1, 4)$. This is represented by setting A to 1 for the initial knowledge and 0 everywhere else. One-way message passing from conditions to actions does the rest.

Given how this problem is represented, it wouldn't make sense to reason in the opposite direction, as it runs the risk of concluding the premises are false: initially $A(1, 3)$ is 0, so $A(1, 2)$ and $A(2, 3)$ must also be 0. Enforcing the logical constraints in both directions simply doesn't do the right thing. However, the summary-product algorithm provides no justification for restricting message passing to get the desired result. The algorithm computes efficiently over complex global functions by applying the distributive law to push computations to the local-message level. If some messages must be eliminated to get a correct result, the question is: does this somehow improve the approximation or is a different value being computed? The answer appears to be the latter; no specifiable global function is being computed here.

3.2   Closed-World Semantics

Given that probabilities aren't being passed in the transitivity example above, what are the messages? Sigma's employment of *closed-world predicates* is key here [9]. The closed-world assumption is that whatever is not yet known is assumed false. When operating on probabilities, 1 acts as a "total ignorance" number in the summary-product algorithm: multiplying by 1 changes nothing. In closed-world computation, 0 is the total-ignorance number: it represents a lack of information. Therefore, it is natural to combine closed-world information with *or* as opposed to *product*, allowing positive messages to overwrite 0s, and *probabilistic or* handling intermediate values. Sigma employs special-purpose *action-combination* nodes to enable such a disjunctive combination of messages from multiple actions.

We might try to account for this behavior within the summary-product algorithm by using a different *commutative semiring* – an algebraic structure like a *ring* but with product commutative and no additive inverse – as factor graphs need not be based on *sum* and *product*, and are in fact well defined for any commutative semiring [3]. Here we would use *or* for combination instead of *product* and *max*, for example, for summarization. However, *or* and *max* fail to form a commutative semiring. 0 is the identity element of both operations, but for a semiring the identity element for the summary operation should be an annihilator for the combination operation. More critically, the distributive law also fails for the two operators – the probabilistic formula for *or* does not distribute over *max*. The distributive law is what justifies shifting from global to local computation in the summary-product algorithm [3].

Really, though, the story in Sigma is more complicated. Open-world or closed-world semantics is associated with predicates, not with variables, implying that as values get passed around the network they will be treated however that local part of the network treats things. The summary operation may be *max* or *sum*. The combination operation will be *product* in most of the network, with *or* and other operations in a few places. In fact, it would not even be possible to make the transitivity example work with closed-world variables if we could not use *product* combination in some places – to combine $A(x, y)$ with $A(y, z)$ – while applying *or* combination elsewhere (to feed the result back into working memory). Is it possible to explain such a mixed approach with the semiring idea?

Multiple semirings can interact nicely in the summary-product algorithm. *Sum-product* and *max-product* can work together to maximize a function over one set of variables while summing over others. In speech recognition, for example, Sigma uses *max-product* for Viterbi processing and *sum-product* everywhere else [6]. A natural approach is to associate summary operators with variables so that each variable is summarized out according to its kind. However, if the order of operations matters, we need to be careful; for in stance, $\max_x \sum_y f(x, y)$ differs from $\sum_y \max_x f(x, y)$ in general. Sigma does account for this complication when combining *max* with *sum*.

Closed-world semantics does not seem amenable to a multi-semiring account, however, and no way of specifying a global function has so far emerged.

3.3   Universal Variables

Universal variables in Sigma represent logic variables, indexing many specific cases [9]. This contrasts with *unique/distributional variables* that can represent random variables of the kind used in statistics. If we create an open-world predicate $P(X, Y)$ and declare X to be universal and Y to be unique, this is conceptually like declaring a larger number of predicates $P_1(Y), P_2(Y),\ldots$ for each possible value of X, allowing generalization over many cases. Unlike lifted reasoning in Alchemy [10], however, Sigma does not compute the same value in these two different cases.

Sigma uses a different summary operator with universal variables, modifying the semiring choice (as discussed in Sect. 3.2). In particular, *max* is used to yield a form of existential behavior that enables rule-like conditionality: a conditional yields nonzero results if there is any match to its conditions. When Sigma represents probabilistic values, *max* could be seen as a way of computing a probabilistic lower bound; the probability of an existential statement is at least as great as the probability of any instance. It could also be compared to using *max-product* mixed with *sum-product*, which maximizes over some variables while marginalizing over others.

In practice, however, neither of these interpretations adequately captures what's going on because the usefulness of *max* depends on the other modifications that allow Sigma to display rule-like behavior. There is in fact no justification for this formula from a pure factor-graph perspective, and the meaning is unclear. If a universal variable is to indicate multiple instances in a factor graph, then *product* rather than *max* should be used to combine the instances [10, 11]. But *product* would not fit the more common existential use of universal variables in Sigma that *max* supports.

3.4   Filter Nodes

Filter nodes in Sigma implement the constant tests found in rule conditions (plus a bit more [1]). A constant test would be used, for example, in a rule condition like *Above*(3, x) to yield the values of x that are above 3. To implement this, a filter function in Sigma has the following effect: all values that do not match the desired portion are set to 0, and the part that's wanted is left unaltered. In the example, the incoming message would be the content of *Above*(x, y) for all x, y; the y entries for $x = 3$ would remain while those for other values would be set to 0.

If this were a pure factor graph, such a filter node would be multiplying the global function by a factor that zeros out everything but $x = 3$; that is, this factor would act as a constraint, forcing across the entire network. This is not at all what is happening in Sigma. The undesired entries are only to be removed within the scope of the corresponding conditional. Due to how universal variables are handled, and Sigma's use of closed-world semantics, 0s are the appropriate way to do this.

Filtering out cases is possible in a pure open-world factor graph, however it would be done with a factor that establishes a uniform distribution, rather than 0 s, over the unwanted parts of the message. This would imply that whatever happened in the sub-network on the other side of the filter node would affect only the selected part of the global function. This illustrates how Sigma's departure from factor-graph operations in some areas forces further departure in other areas. Due to the manner in which universal variables (and some other aspects) are handled, it becomes impossible to view a filter factor node as a standard factor-graph node. The local computations at such a node look like summary-product operations – multiplying the incoming message times a function that is 1 for $x = 3$ and 0 elsewhere – but the global effect on the computation, and thus on the semantics of what is being computed, can be quite different from the effect an identical node would have in a pure factor graph.

3.5   Transform Nodes

A *transform node* applies a one-way transformation over message functions in directed portions of the graph; that is, within conditions and actions. Negated conditions are handled in this manner, as are negated actions. Another example not related to rules is an *exponential* transformation that enables softmax computations, in support of reasoning about other agent's decision processes [12]. Although standard factors can represent arbitrary functions, they are defined only over domain variables in message functions, not over their ranges. These transforms all directly modify the range, with negation subtracting and flooring it, and softmax exponentiating it.

One concern beyond the semantic that is introduced by transform nodes is whether they provide a hook for incorporating arbitrary outside code into Sigma. While such a capability could be appropriate and even useful in a toolkit, it would threaten the graphical architecture's status as an architecture, comprised of fixed structure, and thus also indirectly threaten the status of the cognitive architecture. One way of dealing with this might be to reconceptualize these transformations as learnable knowledge, and then to provide a learning mechanism for them. However, the approach that has been taken is instead to commit to the set of transformations ultimately being bounded, although likely continuing to evolve for some time.

4   What Are Its Implications (Including to Neural Networks)?

At first glance, systematic violations of factor graph semantics might appear to violate the graphical architecture hypothesis. However, the hypothesis does not state that all capabilities must be producible from graphical models, only that understanding the relationship between cognitive architectures and graphical models is crucial. Consistent with this latter notion, even though the new perspective implies that the graphical architecture need not be limited strictly to what falls within the sphere of traditional graphical models, Sigma remains very much based on what has been learned from them. The former notion could be viewed as an alternative *strong graphical architecture hypothesis*, whereas the one actually used here is a weak variant. The strong hypothesis

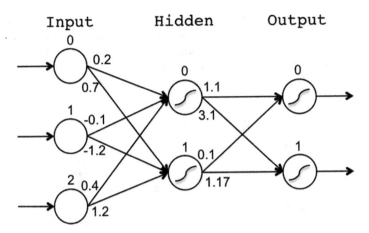

Fig. 2. Example two-layer feedforward neural network (adapted from http://www.doc.ic.ac.uk/~sgc/teaching/pre2012/v231/lecture13.html).

would be a deeper scientific claim, and would likely also yield a simpler and more elegant system, but work to date fails to support it.

On the negative side, Sigma's violations of factor graph semantics do add to the complexity and non-uniformity of the graphical architecture – reducing its simplicity and elegance in essential ways – while also making it more difficult to prove properties about how reasoning and learning work. Cognitive architectures do not in general have well-defined semantics, and even when such attempts are made – e.g., via a formal specification [13] – the result is neither simple nor elegant. So we could just be satisfied with this status. But we can do better, because some of the idioms – such as the one for factor graphs – do still have simple and elegant semantics.

On the positive side, small enhancements to Sigma's graphical architecture can yield major gains in functionality, with much of the core representation and reasoning being reused across idioms, rather than being constructed from scratch in separate modules, to yield a form of algorithmic rather than semantic elegance that is central to how Sigma achieves functional elegance. Semantic elegance is more compelling, but algorithmic elegance still goes far beyond typical cognitive architectures.

```
CONDITIONAL C-Layer1
   Conditions: (Input arg:i)
               (Layer1 lower:i upper:h)
   Actions:  (Hidden s arg:h)

CONDITIONAL C-Layer2
   Conditions: (Hidden arg:h)
               (Layer2 lower:h upper:o)
   Actions:  (Output s arg:o)
```

Fig. 3. Conditionals that define the network in Fig. 2.

The latest example of this is the implementation of feedforward neural networks within Sigma. The one extension required for this is a new one-way transform

(Sect. 3.5) that transforms the incoming message via a non-linear *logistic function*, a variant of a sigmoid. Everything else needed to implement feedforward neural networks, and to incorporate them into the larger architectural context, already exists.

Consider the two-layer feedforward network in Fig. 2, with three inputs, two outputs, and two hidden units. Figure 3 shows the two conditionals that implement this network in Sigma. Each specifies one layer of the network via two conditions and an action. These are essentially rules, except that the predicates are open world rather than closed world, and the conditions therefore match to either perception (the Input predicate) or functions in

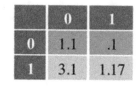

(a) `Layer1` function   (b) `Layer2` function

Fig. 4. Long-term memory functions for layer weights.

long-term memory (the `Layer1` and `Layer2` predicates). The weights are stored in the long-term memory functions (Fig. 4). The other key difference from a standard rule is that both actions are marked with **s**, denoting that a sigmoid transform should be applied to their messages. This is just how negated actions are marked, except with an **s** here rather than a **-**.

Processing is initially driven by conditional C-Layer1. A perceived Input vector, such as [10, 30, 20], is multiplied times the Layer1 function with the Input variable then summarized out via sum/integral to generate a raw Hidden distribution of [7, -.5]. This is then logistically transformed to yield [0.999089, 0.006692851]. Conditional C-Layer2 then picks up the processing, multiplying the transformed Hidden vector by the Layer2 function and summarizing out the Hidden variable to yield a raw Output distribution of [1.0996672, 3.1050065]. This is then logistically transformed to yield [0.75019777, 0.9570988]. The web source for this network lists the transformed Output as [.750, .957], which is the same after round off.

Because this form of neural network is just another idiom in the graphical architecture, and thus also in the memory and reasoning of the cognitive architecture, it should be usable just as with all other memory structures; and interfaceable directly, via shared predicates, with all of its other forms of memory, whether rule, semantic, episodic, imaginal, perceptual, etc. It also should be usable directly in reasoning, whether for perception or control of operator selection during problem solving.

One critical piece that remains missing here is learning. Sigma embodies a general form of gradient-descent learning that can acquire many kinds of long-term memory functions from messages arriving at their factor nodes [14]; however, simply enabling bidirectional message passing via condacts and inverting the logistic function for backwards messages through a sigmoid node does not yield appropriate learning. We are currently exploring a generalization of Sigma's learning approach that could extend it appropriately to such neural networks. If this succeeds, it will make sense to consider whether the graphical architecture hypothesis should be extended to include what has been learned from the decades worth of progress on neural networks – a different but related graphical formalism – in addition to graphical models.

5   Conclusion

Sigma's graphical architecture, although inspired by factor graphs, diverges from their semantics in a number of ways. Historically, this has mostly involved how to combine rule-based reasoning with probabilistic reasoning, but here this is extended to feed-forward neural networks as well (sans learning for now). This has led to a rethinking of the graphical architecture, to where it is based more explicitly on the summary-product algorithm for solving factor graphs, and its extensions, than on factor graphs themselves. Factor graphs then become one of several graphical idioms that can be supported, although one with a well-defined semantics. Rules and neural networks become two other idioms, each without such semantics; and additional idioms are also conceivable. Whether ultimately a single clean semantics can be developed for Sigma's graphical architecture, or whether an alternative architecture can be found that has a clean semantics, remains an important open question. Either way, the intent is still to yield a single coherent cognitive architecture.

Acknowledgments. This effort has been sponsored by the U.S. Army. Statements and opinions expressed do not necessarily reflect the position or the policy of the United States Government, and no official endorsement should be inferred. We would also like to thank Himanshu Joshi for useful discussions on neural networks in Sigma.

References

1. Rosenbloom, P.S.: The Sigma cognitive architecture and system. AISB Q. **136**, 4–13 (2013)
2. Koller, D., Friedman, N.: Probabilistic Graphical Models: Principles and Techniques. MIT Press, Cambridge (2009)
3. Kschischang, F.R., Frey, B.J., Loeliger, H.: Factor graphs and the sum-product algorithm. IEEE Trans. Inf. Theor. **47**, 498–519 (2001)
4. Rumelhart, D.E., McClelland, J.L., The PDP Research Group: Parallel Distributed Processing: Explorations in the Microstructure of Cognition. Foundation, vol. 1. MIT Press, Cambridge (1986)
5. Jordan, M.I., Sejnowski, T.J.: Graphical Models: Foundations of Neural Computation. MIT Press, Cambridge (2001)
6. Joshi, H., Rosenbloom, P.S., Ustun, V.: Isolated word recognition in the Sigma cognitive architecture. Biologically Inspired Cogn. Architectures **10**, 1–9 (2014)
7. Ustun, V., Rosenbloom, P.S., Sagae, K., Demski, A.: Distributed vector representations of words in the Sigma cognitive architecture. In: Goertzel, B., Orseau, L., Snaider, J. (eds.) AGI 2014. LNCS, vol. 8598, pp. 196–207. Springer, Heidelberg (2014)
8. Rosenbloom, P.S.: Mental imagery in a graphical cognitive architecture. In: Second International Conference on Biologically Inspired Cognitive Architectures (2011)
9. Rosenbloom, P.S.: Combining procedural and declarative knowledge in a graphical architecture. In: 10th International Conference on Cognitive Modeling (2010)

10. Singla, P., Domingos, P.: Lifted first-order belief propagation. In: Proceedings of the 23rd AAAI Conference on Artificial Intelligence (2008)
11. Kersting, K., Ahmadi, B., Natarajan, S.: Counting belief propagation. In: Proceedings of the 25th Conference on Uncertainty in Artificial Intelligence (2009)
12. Pynadath, D.V., Rosenbloom, P.S., Marsella, S.C., Li, L.: Modeling two-player games in the Sigma graphical cognitive architecture. In: Kühnberger, K.-U., Rudolph, S., Wang, P. (eds.) AGI 2013. LNCS, vol. 7999, pp. 98–108. Springer, Heidelberg (2013)
13. Milnes, B.G., Pelton, G., Doorenbos, R., Hucka, M., Laird, J., Rosenbloom, P., Newell, A.: A Specification of the Soar Cognitive Architecture in Z. CMU CS Technical report, Pittsburgh (1992)
14. Rosenbloom, P.S., Demski, A., Han, T., Ustun, V.: Learning via gradient descent in Sigma. In: Proceedings of the 12th International Conference on Cognitive Modeling (2013)

Real-Time GA-Based Probabilistic Programming in Application to Robot Control

Alexey Potapov[1,2,3($\boxtimes$)], Sergey Rodionov[3,4], and Vita Potapova[2,3]

[1] ITMO University, St. Petersburg, Russia
[2] St. Petersburg State University, St. Petersburg, Russia
[3] AIDEUS, St. Petersburg, Russia
pas.aicv@gmail.com, elokkuu@gmail.com,
astroseger@gmail.com
[4] Aix Marseille Université, CNRS, LAM (Laboratoire d'Astrophysique
de Marseille) UMR 7326, 13388 Marseille, France

Abstract. Possibility to solve the problem of planning and plan recovery for robots using probabilistic programming with optimization queries, which is being developed as a framework for AGI and cognitive architectures, is considered. Planning can be done directly by introducing a generative model for plans and optimizing an objective function calculated via plan simulation. Plan recovery is achieved almost without modifying optimization queries. These queries are simply executed in parallel with plan execution by a robot meaning that they continuously optimize dynamically varying objective functions tracking their optima. Experiments with the NAO robot showed that replanning can be naturally done within this approach without developing special plan recovery methods.

Keywords: Probabilistic programming · Optimization queries · Genetic algorithms · Robot planning · Replanning

1 Introduction

It is frequently assumed that AGI systems should not only perform some abstract reasoning, but should also be able to control some body achieving goals in real environments. Even if a cognitive architecture wasn't initially developed specifically for this purpose, natural desire to try applying it for e.g. robot control can arise after its maturing.

Robot control tasks are quite interesting since they require both planning and reactive control for achieving a goal in dynamic environments. Symbolic architectures are usually good for planning, but realization of reactive behavior within them is awkward, while emergent architectures are usually better suited for reactive control. Thus, hybrid solutions are developed to solve the problem of plan recovery [1].

We are developing an approach to AGI using probabilistic programming as the starting point. In another paper [2], we explain motivation behind this approach and discuss how traditional probabilistic programming languages (PPLs) should be

B. Steunebrink et al. (Eds.): AGI 2016, LNAI 9782, pp. 95–105, 2016.
DOI: 10.1007/978-3-319-41649-6_10

extended in order to become usable as a framework for development of cognitive architectures. However, this discussion addresses questions regarding reasoning and learning, but not regarding controlling (embodied) agents. At the same time, most general-purpose PPLs support only computationally expensive queries with unpredictable execution time (so they are well-suited for planning, but not for reactive control). This issue might be called purely technical, but nevertheless it is quite important. Indeed, taking limitation of resources into account is considered essential for AGI research [3].

In this paper, we describe how PPLs with optimization queries based on genetic algorithms (GAs) can be used in robot planning and can support replanning naturally almost without modifications. To do this, we execute optimization queries from our lightweight C++ probabilistic programming engine to perform planning simultaneously with executing current best plan by the real NAO robot using its SDK functions. Experiments show that continuing optimization can track optimum of the objective function, which can considerably shift due to changes of the environment or inaccurate execution of actions by the robot.

2   Lightweight Implementation of GA-Based Optimization Queries in Probabilistic Programming

Conditional inference over probabilistic programs can be carried out using program traces [4] containing all made random choices, which can be modified during re-interpretation of a probabilistic program. The same approach can be used in the case of optimization queries [5]. However, it is not very fast since it requires PPL to be interpreted.

If we are using optimization quires in a somewhat restricted way considering probabilistic programs as functions of random variables, then such queries don't necessarily need access to the code of a probabilistic program. In this case, probabilistic program can be written as a function (e.g. as a virtual method of inference class) directly in the reference programming language (C++ in our case) and compiled. Such approach also simplifies integration with existing libraries, e.g. OpenCV or NAO SDK.

In our implementation, probabilistic program is a function that receives an object "rng" as a parameter from which it samples all random variables. In order to be able to perform inference (optimization) we should be able to uniquely identify all random calls. For example, we can name all random calls by unique string tags. However, it is inconvenient in the case of programs, in which some random variable is sampled several times in the same context (like in example considered below). We adopt a little bit different approach. We introduce named sources of random variables, which can be used several times. So, in our case, sources represent named sequences of random values of the same type.

Let us consider simple example.

```
double res = 0;
while(rng.flip("A")) res += rng.gaussian("B", 0, 1);
return fabs(res - 5.);
```

For the inference algorithm, this code will be a function of $A_1, A_2 \ldots$, where A_i is the result of i-th call to rng.flip ("A"), and $B_1, B_2, \ldots$, where B_i is the result of i-th call to rng.gaussian ("B", 0, 1). As easy to see, the number of requests to sources "A" and "B" can be different for different runs of the random program.

We use the following types of random numbers and corresponding sampling functions:

- flip with parameter p returns true with probability p;
- randint with parameter n returns equally probable random integer from $[0, n-1]$;
- gaussian with parameters mean, sigma returns normally distributed random value.

We assume that the type of the random variable is fixed and cannot be changed. On the other hand, parameters of random functions can vary in different runs of the random program (parameters of random functions can be functions of random variables). Moreover, similar to the considered simple example, the set of used random variables can vary. These features should be taken into account by the inference algorithm.

We utilize GAs to perform optimization of values of random variables as follows. A candidate solution in the population is a set of values of random variables sampled in the program. Each random value is associated with a unique tag (name of random source plus index), type of a random variable and parameters of this random variable.

GA executes the given function with random choices, which return value is interpreted as the fitness value for the candidate solution represented by specific sampled values of random variables, and control values returned by rng using genetic operators. flip, randint, etc. act as conventional pseudo-random functions while the first generation of candidate solutions is produced, but their behavior is changed for children.

Crossover is implemented in the most trivial way: random exchange of random values with the same tag. So if tag is presented in the both parents, then random value is taken randomly from one of the parents. All random values presented only in one of the parents (such a situation can happen for example in the considered simple example) are inherent by descendant. Mutations are implemented also the simplest way by varying the values of random variables. So, GA simply executes the compiled fitness-function with random choices many times controlling the values returned by basic random functions called via rng and trying to find the set of values that corresponds to the optimum of the fitness-function.

3 Planning as Probabilistic Programming

Planning can be naturally expressed in PPLs with both conditional and optimization queries. To do this, one needs to specify a generative model for plans as sequences of random possible actions with random parameters. Then, an environment model should be available for predicting outcomes of plan execution. In principle, PPLs can be used to learn this model or to make inference over stochastic models. Conditional or optimization queries with the condition of successful goal achievement or with the objective function evaluating proximity to the goal will find examples of suitable plans. There is no need to program the robot how to act in each of numerous possible situations, so to change robot's behavior we need only to specify a new goal – not to reprogram the robot.

In Turing-complete PPLs, generative models (of plans in our case) can readily include conditions, cycles, etc. Thus, PPLs provide a powerful tool for planning.

We developed a test planning system for the NAO robot using small subset of its possible actions including

- *wait* (call `qi::os::msleep(t)`, where `t` is the action parameter defining wait time in milliseconds);
- *walk* (call `ALMotionProxy::moveTo(x, y, 0)`, where `x` and `y` are parameters indicating how far in meters the robot should move);
- *turn* (call `ALMotionProxy::moveTo(0, 0, a)`, where `a` is the rotation angle);
- *posture* (pose changing using `goToPosture` command with the possible values "StandInit", "Crouch", "Sit", "SitRelax", "Stand", "StandZero").

The generative model consists simply in generating a random list of random actions and random values for action parameters. Semantically different random values are generated from different random sources. For example, waiting time `t` for *wait* action is generated as `rng.randint("wait", 1000)`, and walking parameters `x` and `y` are generated as `rng.gaussian("walk", 0., 1.)`.

At first, we considered such goals as approaching a position with specified relative coordinates. Objective function (or fitness-function for GAs) was calculated as the distance from the expected position after plan execution to the specified target plus time (or efforts) penalty. In order to evaluate it, plan execution should be somehow modeled.

We didn't use detailed 3D model of the robot's body, although this is possible. Instead, the model included only robot's coordinates and pose (sitting, standing, etc.), and information of how they are expected to change after executing listed actions.

Obstacles were detected using sonars, and their positions were taken into account during modeling robot's movement. That is, if the expected robot's path crossed the detected object, collision was modeled by forcing the robot pose to "Crouch" and the robot coordinates to those of the obstacle (the robot wasn't explicitly programmed to avoid obstacles, since either to collide with obstacles or not depends on goals). The robot was not also programmed to stand up for walking, but its expected coordinates were changed while simulating *walk* action only if its pose corresponded to standing).

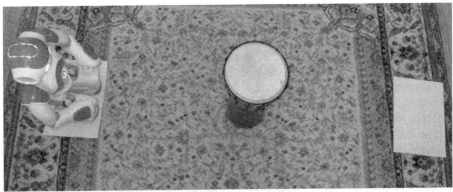

The robot in the initial position

The robot moving diagonally to bypass the obstacle

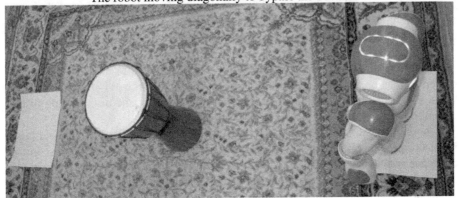

Robot in the final position

Fig. 1. The robot executing found plan

Our GA-based optimization query managed to find plans consisting of unknown number of actions with unknown real-valued parameters. If there were no obstacles, and the initial position was sitting, than the robot guessed to stand up first and then to move directly to the goal location. If there was an obstacle, found plans bypassed it usually using the shortest route (see Fig. 1).

Of course, there are many problems with following fixed plans even in the considered simple task. Real robot's movement will never precisely correspond to the expected movement. The robot detects only the first obstacle using sonars, but there can be other obstacles encountered during bypassing the first one. Moreover, the environment can be dynamic, so obstacles or targets can change their coordinates. Agents blindly following even genial plans can act very stupid.

Having infinite computational resources, one could construct new optimal plan from scratch after performing each elementary action (as it is done in AIXI [6]). However, this works only in theory and cannot be afforded in practice. Consequently, rather complicated methods for error detection, plan recovery and replanning methods are being developed [7–9].

Here, we don't want to develop specific solutions for robot plan recovery, but consider the question what minimal modifications to the probabilistic programming framework are necessary to support plan recovery in the same sense as conventional PPLs provide a solution of the planning problem.

4   Simultaneous Plan Optimization and Execution

Changing fitness-function during optimization. What will happen if the fitness-function is changed during its optimization by GAs? If the population of candidate solutions has not yet converged or if the changes are small, GAs will find new optimum. One can also slightly modify GAs to adaptively control the mutation rate depending on changes of the population fitness, and can introduce the mechanism of recessive and dominant alleles to keep gene diversity.

At first, we tried to create separate thread for the planner and to modify data for the objective function (namely, coordinates to be reached by the robot) outside the planner while it was optimizing this function. Not very surprisingly, the best solution in the current population tracked changes in the objective function.

Consider an example. Let the robot's goal be to move one meter forward (and there is an obstacle in front), and this target is moving at the speed of 10 cm/s. Initial candidate solutions in the first population are bad. They almost don't help the robot to approach the target. However, solutions rapidly become better from population to population, and almost precise solution appears after 0.5 s. This solution will be different in different runs, but typical solution will contain three commands such as *posture* (stand), *walk* (0.1, 0.27), *walk* (0.93, −0.25). This is the plan for achieving not the original goal, but already the modified goal. Candidate solutions in consequent populations are tracking the changing goal. E.g. after 6 s the goal will be to move 1.6 m, and the typical plan will be *posture* (stand), *walk* (0.173, 0.269), *walk* (1.426, −0.268).

Consider another type of change in the environment. Let the obstacle be removed at some moment of time. The result will depend on the moment of removal. If the obstacle is removed after 3 s, the plan before removal will be like *posture* (stand), *walk* (0.036, −0.352), *walk* (0.964, 0.352). This is nearly optimal plan. However, after another 3 s of the continuing optimization process the plan will be *posture* (stand), *walk* (0.035, −0.331), *walk* (0.965, 0.331). The value of the fitness-function doesn't change after obstacle removal, but this plan becomes suboptimal. Since necessary efforts are taken into account in the objective function, the best plan should correspond to the shortest distance to the target.

Apparently, the reason of this result is convergence of population of candidate solutions after 3 s of GA execution, and small improvements of the final plan are due to mutations (which speed is not enough to achieve the optimal plan). Indeed, if the obstacle disappears after 0.5 s, the solution found before this event will be in general correct, but imprecise, e.g. *posture* (stand), *walk* (0.26, 0.32), *walk* (0.82, −0.28). However, the final solution will be *posture* (stand), *walk* (0.218, 0.002), *walk* (0.782, −0.002). The population of candidate solutions has not converged yet, so it has more capabilities of adapting to the changes of the fitness-function. The final plan is almost optimal, although it realizes forward walk in two commands. Possibly, environment changes causing large changes in the value of the fitness-function and requiring insertion of some steps in the plan will be much more difficult to track.

However, it appears that since the goal's achievement precision is the largest term of the fitness-function, it is optimized first. Then, efforts of achieving this goal are optimized. Thus, candidate solutions corresponding to different plan sizes and to not straight routes to the target remain until strong convergence of the population, and the route bypassing appeared obstacle was found in most cases.

Of course, there can be more difficult replanning tasks, and non-conventional evolutionary computation methods natively supporting optimization of dynamic fitness-function might be necessary, but we can state that GA-base probabilistic programming even not initially design for concurrent optimization is applicable at least to some extent.

However, there are specific additional difficulties, when one tries to execute a plan simultaneously with its proceeding optimization.

Evaluating partially executed plans. One immediate issue with optimization of plans during their execution is that execution itself causes changes in the environment. If we simply continue the optimization process externally changing the fitness-function in accordance with the actual environment state (e.g. including position of the moving robot) than this process will need to blindly adjust the plan (e.g. from *walk* (1.0, 0.0) to *walk* (0.5, 0.0) after the robot has walked 0.5 m). Of course, adjustment can be necessary, but only because of possible difference between expected and real positions − not because of difference between initial and current positions. Is it necessary to change the inference engine to solve this problem? For example, one can try modifying all candidate solutions inside GA removing the first action from each of them after a real action has taken place. We believe that this is not necessary, and the environment model (simulation of plan execution) should mostly account for peculiarities of simultaneous plan optimization and execution.

The plan execution procedure should inform the plan simulation procedure about already completed part of the plan, and this part should simply be skipped during simulation. Since actions are non-atomic, partially executed actions should be partially skipped during simulation. This leads to main imprecision of simulation, because final position after action execution is known better than intermediate positions.

At first, we checked that the value of the objective function calculated for the plan being executed doesn't increase dramatically. We used getRobotPosition function from the NAO SDK (motion proxy) to get current robot coordinates (estimated by odometry), from which plan simulation starts. For example, initial coordinates in the robot reference system could be (2.49, −0.82, 0.23), where the first two are (x, y) in meters and the last one is the orientation angle. The goal then could be (3.49, −0.82), and the intermediate position during bypassing an obstacle could be (3.00, −1.20, 0.36), and the final position could be (3.42, −0.75, 0.36) meaning that the robot missed the target by 0.1 m. The problem is that the robot changes its orientation after execution of Stand, and continues to execute the plan that was designed in supposition that Stand action doesn't change robot coordinates and orientation.

This discrepancy is directly reflected in the value of the objective function calculated for the partially executed plan. After execution of Stand, it becomes 0.18 instead of 0.06 (initial non-zero value corresponds to penalty for efforts needed to perform all actions in the plan) meaning that the expected final position error is about 0.12 m. The value of the objective function evaluated during plan execution including partially executed actions doesn't go beyond 0.22 meaning that simulation of partially executed plans is generally correct. After executing the plan, its value becomes 0.16 corresponding to 0.1 m error (0.16–0.06) equal to the distance between the goal (2.49, −0.82, 0.23) and the final position (3.42, −0.75, 0.36) estimated from odometry.

Appearance of unexpected obstacle automatically leads to stepwise increase of the estimated objective function. For example, in the situation shown in Fig. 2, it increased by 0.45 meaning that further execution of the plan was expected to lead to collision and the simulated final robot position corresponded to the position of the obstacle.

Simultaneously executing and optimizing plans. Now, after we checked possibility of optimizing dynamically changing fitness-functions, and introduced correct evaluation of partially executed plans, we can try to optimize plans during their execution.

In our implementation, the robot waits until the best candidate solution for the plan is not optimal, but is good enough, remembers this plan and starts to execute it. During the plan execution better candidate solutions can be found, either because the first plan was not optimal or the environment has changed. Expected plan qualities estimated using the most recent and the same information about the environment should be compared, so the plan under execution should be re-simulated. The robot switches to another plan, if it is expected to improve the achieved value of the objective function by a (non-zero) certain threshold. The robot starts executing a new plan from the current moment of time. This means that it skips all actions that should have already been executed, and partially executes the action that should be executing right now. That is, continuation of executing partially executed plans corresponds to simulation of partially executed plans. It can be seen that there is some decision-making in the plan

Fig. 2. Appearance of unexpected obstacle

execution procedure, but it is extremely simple, and the most part of the job is done in the general-purpose optimization engine of PPL.

Let us consider how it works. If the robot starts at the position, e.g. (−4.12, −0.13, −3.09), and its goal is the point (−5.12, −0.18) located in one meter in front of the robot, the first acceptable plan will typically be something like *posture* (stand), *wait* (720), *walk* (−0.69, −0.43), *walk* (0.74, −1.13), *walk* (0.91, 1.52), which is neither precise nor most efficient. Also, robot's orientation changes after standing up, e.g. to −2.96, and the plan becomes even less precise. Better plan will be found while the robot is doing its first action (standing up), e.g. *posture* (stand), *walk* (−0.72, 0.02), *walk* (−0.29, −0.04). If an obstacle suddenly appears in front of the robot even if it has started to walk leading to instant decrease of current plan quality, good plan with obstacle avoidance and account for the current real coordinates can be found before collision, e.g. *posture* (stand), *walk* (0.57, 0.51), *walk* (0.42, −0.65). If nothing else happens, no plan change will occur and the final robot position and orientation can be (−5.12, −0.16, −2.95) that is quite close to the goal.

Of course, success highly depends on sensors and actuators. In particular, usage of NAO sonars allows rough estimation of distance to obstacles, but not their coordinates or sizes. Interestingly, if the robot does collide and fall down, and this is reflected in the current robot pose and position (that can be known from sensors), it will find a plan including stand up action and further walk to the goal. That is, simultaneous plan optimization and execution works well for plan recovery.

5   Conclusion

Our study showed that possible applications of probabilistic programming in intelligent agents go beyond offline inductive and deductive reasoning and also include real-time robot control. Latter can be achieved, because execution of optimization queries for dynamically varying objective functions leads to tracking of their current optima by current population of candidate solutions. Thus, simultaneous plan optimization and execution automatically, without introducing special plan recovery methods, yields adaptation of the plan to changes in the environment or to imprecise execution of actions.

Of course, time scales of plan optimization and action execution should be similar. We were lucky, and special alignment of these scales was not necessary in our experiments, otherwise more complex coordination between modules would be necessary. More specific optimization methods, which explicitly take variations of objective functions with time into account, might be necessary to develop in order to avoid convergence to degraded populations of candidate solutions that cannot adapt to changes.

Nevertheless, all specific information concerning plan recovery task is contained in the procedures of plan generation and simulation, which are necessary also for planning itself and should be the part of the agent's knowledge, while optimization queries can be considered as a basic cognitive function. Deep interactions of this function with the agent's knowledge might be necessary in advanced AGI systems, but for other reasons discussed in another paper.

Acknowledgements. This work was supported by Ministry of Education and Science of the Russian Federation, and by Government of Russian Federation, Grant 074-U01.

References

1. Ould Ouali, L., Rich, Ch., Sabouret, N.: Plan recovery in reactive HTNs using symbolic planning. In: Bieger, J., Goertzel, B., Potapov, A. (eds.) AGI 2015. LNCS, vol. 9205, pp. 320–330. Springer, Heidelberg (2015)
2. Potapov, A.: A Step from Probabilistic Programming to Cognitive Architectures (in print)
3. Wang, P.: The Logic of intelligence. In: Goertzel, B., Pennachin, C. (eds.) Artificial General Intelligence. Cognitive Technologies, pp. 31–62. Springer, Heidelberg (2007)
4. Goodman, N.D., Mansinghka, V.K., Roy, D.M., Bonawitz, K., Tenenbaum, J.B.: Church: a language for generative models. arXiv:1206.3255 [cs.PL] (2008)
5. Batishcheva, V., Potapov, A.: Genetic programming on program traces as an inference engine for probabilistic languages. In: Bieger, J., Goertzel, B., Potapov, A. (eds.) AGI 2015. LNCS (LNAI), vol. 9205, pp. 14–24. Springer, Heidelberg (2015)
6. Hutter, M.: Universal Artificial Intelligence: Sequential Decisions Based on Algorithmic Probability. Springer, New York (2005)
7. Boella, G., Damiano, R.: A replanning algorithm for a reactive agent architecture. In: Scott, D. (ed.) AIMSA 2002. LNCS (LNAI), vol. 2443, pp. 183–192. Springer, Heidelberg (2002)

8. Ayan, N.F., Kuter, U., Yaman, F., Goldman, R.P.: HOTRiDE: hierarchical ordered task replanning in dynamic environments. In: ICAPS Workshop, Providence, RI (2007)
9. Karapinar, S., Altan, D., Sariel-Talay, S.: A robust planning framework for cognitive robots. AAAI Technical report WS-12-06, pp. 102–108 (2012)

About Understanding

Kristinn R. Thórisson[1,2(✉)], David Kremelberg[2],
Bas R. Steunebrink[3], and Eric Nivel[2]

[1] Center for Analysis and Design of Intelligent Agents,
Reykjavik University, Reykjavik, Iceland
thorisson@ru.is
[2] Icelandic Institute for Intelligent Machines, Reykjavik, Iceland
[3] The Swiss AI Lab IDSIA, USI and SUPSI, Manno, Switzerland

Abstract. The concept of *understanding* is commonly used in everyday communications, and seems to lie at the heart of human intelligence. However, no concrete theory of understanding has been fielded as of yet in artificial intelligence (AI), and references on this subject are far from abundant in the research literature. We contend that the ability of an artificial system to autonomously deepen its understanding of phenomena in its surroundings must be part of any system design targeting general intelligence. We present a theory of *pragmatic understanding*, discuss its implications for architectural design and analyze the behavior of an intelligent agent implementing the theory. Our agent learns to understand *how to* perform multimodal dialogue with humans through observation, becoming capable of constructing sentences with complex grammar, generating proper question-answer patterns, correctly resolving and generating anaphora with coordinated deictic gestures, producing efficient turntaking, and following the structure of interviews, without any information on this being provided up front.

1 Introduction

A rudimentary investigation into the use of the term "understanding" in the field of artificial intelligence (AI) reveals that occurrences are few and far between. When it does appear it is primarily in the context of natural language ("language understanding"), where parsing and manipulation of linguistic tokens (read: good old-fashioned AI) takes the front seat. A distant second is its coupling with the words "scene" and "image" in computer vision research (scene understanding, image understanding), with an identical emphasis on parsing: Rather than talking about the phenomenon of understanding proper, understanding is equated with syntactic manipulation, which, as everyone who has studied philosophy knows, is not the same thing (cf. [18]).

A coherent conceptualization of understanding is of importance to the field of AGI for several reasons. First, if the concept of understanding is left undefined it cannot, as a phenomenon, be effectively investigated; second, without a good definition of understanding it may be difficult to compare different systems with respect to their level of understanding, and similarly, to compare the same

B. Steunebrink et al. (Eds.): AGI 2016, LNAI 9782, pp. 106–117, 2016.
DOI: 10.1007/978-3-319-41649-6_11

system or different systems with respect to their levels of understanding regarding different areas of expertise or performance; and third, a coherent account of understanding is needed such that system builders can create new systems, improve current systems, and train systems where understanding is a specific goal. A formalized account of understanding would seem crucial to the continued and successful progress of the field of AGI.

The apparent indifference of AI researchers to the phenomenon of understanding is curious considering the available evidence about its role in human intelligence. If "understanding" is simply a descriptive term used to classify the effectiveness of a given behavior for a particular goal, after it has been observed – behavior referring here to perception, thinking, and action control – then perhaps it could be said that intelligence and understanding are synonyms, and ignoring the concept altogether is justified. If, however, understanding is a unique ingredient or property of natural thinking systems which affects their abilities and intelligence – and especially: their potential for growing their own knowledge – then we would be well-served by studying understanding as a phenomenon. We argue for the latter view and outline here a *pragmatic theory of understanding* rooted in an analysis of how predictive controllers compute meaning. First we look at some of the relevant background work from philosophy and AI, then we present our theory of pragmatic understanding and meaning, and then give an overview of the results of a prototype system whose knowledge acquisition and application was constructed according to the theory. The results represent strong evidence for the potential of the theory to elucidate the relationship between meaning, understanding, prediction, and explanation, in a manner relevant to artificial general intelligence.

2   Related Work

An important question that has been discussed, mostly in the philosophical literature, is the extent to which machines could be given understanding, if at all. Sloman has stated that the question of whether machines can "really" understand is more of a minor question of definition than anything else [18], arguing that the appropriate answer to the question "Can you understand?" is not binary and can take the form of infinite features and gradations. It seems a latent view of many that once a machine can do some human task, that task is no longer deemed as requiring "intelligence," and by extension, requires no "real understanding". This view might explain why Searle's Chinese Room argument still has appeal, in spite of the numerous publications that have long since refuted it by illustrating its numerous fallacies [2,3,16]. Convincing arguments for the impossibility of machines to understand remain scarce.

Some research has argued for the importance of understanding in cognition, citing it as distinct from knowledge (cf. [6]), claiming that acquisition (deepening) of understanding constitutes a more accurate reflection of the world than knowledge acquisition [7,8], and is thus a greater intellectual achievement. Others have taken the exact opposing view (cf. [10]). Without proper and reasonably specific definitions of these terms and their context, as these accounts tend to be, they can be somewhat incoherent, too heavily steered by the many senses in which the term might be used colloquially. As a result many seemingly irreconcilable polarities and contradictions are uncovered [9] (for instance, pitting the internal organization of phenomena against its relation to various other phenomena as some sort of contradiction). As we shall attempt to demonstrate below, such inconsistencies may be reconciled with proper definitions and the right unifying approach.

While understanding as a phenomenon has received more attention in the philosophical than the AI literature [7,8], even there it has nevertheless been claimed to have "virtually escaped investigation in English-speaking philosophy" ([5]: 307); this dearth of interest in the subject is evidenced not only there but also in the fields of AI and cognitive science.[1] A few books have been published with the word pair "understanding understanding" in the title [4,15]. Interesting as they may be, one of these contains selected writings by cybernetics pioneer Heinz von Forrester, which, in spite of its promising title, is not about understanding at all (as evidenced by the word "understanding" not appearing the index); the other gives a cursory (albeit a decent) summary of the subject in the context of epistemological philosophy.

In the context of the work presented here, few authors if any have addressed the more relevant question of what kinds of architectures could *deepen their understanding* automatically, as this would seem of key importance for an AGI system for growing its knowledge. Here we attempt a unification of several prior ideas, through the concepts of prediction, granular model generation and evaluation, and knowledge acquisition through experience [19]. While the literature has presented a multitude of ways to look at and define understanding, and virtually all of the concepts we talk about have appeared in the AI literature in one form or another, we are not aware of any that propose the kind of unification presented here.

3   Towards a Theory of Pragmatic Understanding

Our concern here is with an agent's understanding of phenomena of interest that allows it to act intelligently towards it, in a practical and goal-directed way. We refer to our theory of understanding as *pragmatic*, as we are concerned with the *usefulness* that levels of understanding may achieve in guiding behavior.

Phenomenon. A phenomenon Φ (process, state of affairs, occurrence) — where W is the world and $\Phi \subset W$ — is made up of a set of elements[2] $\{\varphi_1 \ldots \varphi_n \in \Phi\}$

---

[1] Exceptions do exist of course (cf. [1]), but not in the obvious areas such as language-, image- and scene-understanding, where the word makes a mere superfluous appearance.

[2] By "elements" and "sub-parts" we mean any sub-division of Φ, including substructures, component processes, whole-part relations, causal relations, etc.

of various kinds including relations $\Re_\Phi$ (causal, mereological, etc.) that couple elements of Φ with each other, and with those of other phenomena.

Phenomenon and Context. The relations $\Re_\Phi \subseteq 2^W \times 2^W$ that extend to other phenomena identify the phenomenon's *context*. We partition $\Re_\Phi$ in *inward facing* relations $\Re_\Phi^{in} = \Re_\Phi \cap (2^\Phi \times 2^\Phi)$ and *outward facing* relations $\Re_\Phi^{out} = \Re_\Phi \setminus \Re_\Phi^{in}$. An agent whose models are only accurate for $\Re_\Phi^{in}$ understands Φ but not Φ's relation to other phenomena; an agent whose models are only accurate for $\Re_\Phi^{out}$ understands Φ's relation to other phenomena but will have limited or no understanding of Φ's internals.

Models. M_Φ is a set containing models of a phenomenon Φ $\{m_1 \ldots m_n \in M_\Phi\}$ – information structures that can be used to (a) *explain* Φ, (b) *predict* Φ, (c) produce effective plans for achieving goals G with respect to Φ, and (d) *(re)create* Φ.

For any set of models M and a phenomenon Φ, the closer the information structures $m_i \in M$ represent elements (sub-parts) $\varphi \in \Phi$, at any level of detail, including their couplings $\Re_\Phi$, the greater the *accuracy* of M with respect to Φ.

Insofar as an agent A's knowledge consists of models M, we can define *understanding* in the following way:

Understanding. An agent A's *understanding* of phenomenon Φ depends on the accuracy of M with respect to Φ, M_Φ. Understanding is a (multidimensional) *gradient* from low to high levels, determined by the quality (correctness) of representation of two main factors in M_Φ:

U1: The *completeness* of the set of elements $\varphi \in \Phi$ represented by M_Φ.

U2: The *accuracy* of the relevant elements φ represented by M_Φ.

Testing for Understanding. This approach does not necessitate or force any particular way to test for understanding, shifting that challenge rather to whichever methods prove the best for exposing the above two factors. To test for evidence of understanding a phenomenon Φ we may probe (at least) four capabilities of the understander:

1. To *predict* Φ.
2. To *achieve goals* with respect to Φ.
3. To *explain* Φ.
4. To *(re)create* Φ.

All can be seen to have a range $[0,1]$ where 0 is no ability and 1 is perfection, as a function on **U1** and **U2** above. For a thorough evaluation of understanding all four should be applied.

Prediction is the crudest form of evidence for understanding. Some prediction can be done based on correlations, as prediction does not require representation of the direction of causation yet captures co-occurrence of events. Prediction of a particular turn of events requires (a) setting up initial variables correctly, and (b) simulating the implications of (computing deductions from) this initial setup.

Goal Achievement Correlation is not sufficient, however, to inform how one achieves goals with respect to some phenomenon Φ. For this one needs causal relations. Achieving goals means that some variables in Φ can be manipulated directly (or indirectly via intermediate variables). Unless the intelligent agent is omnipotent and omniscient, to achieve goals with respect to a phenomenon Φ may require a bit more than an understanding of Φ: it requires understanding of how a certain subset of Φ relates to some variables that are *under an agent's control*. In short, the agent needs models for interaction with the world. For a robotic agent driving a regular automobile, to take one example, the agent must possess models of its own sensors and manipulators and how these relate to the automobile's controls (steering wheel, brakes, accelerator, etc.). Such interfaces tend to be rather task-specific, however, and are thus undesirable as a required part of an evaluation scheme for understanding. Instead, we call for an ability to *produce effective plans* for achieving goals with respect to Φ. An effective plan is one that can be proven useful, efficient, effective, and correct, through implementation.[3]

Explanation is an even stronger requirement for demonstrating understanding. Correlation does not imply causation, which means that one may have a predictive model of a phenomenon that nevertheless does not represent correctly its parts and their relations (to each other and parts of other phenomena); goals may in some cases be achieved through "hacks" and "back doors", without a proper causal model behind it. This is why scientific models and theories must be both predictive *and* explanatory – together constituting a litmus test for complete and accurate capturing of causal relations.

(Re)creating a phenomenon is perhaps the strongest kind of evidence for understanding. It is also a pre-requisite for the ability for correctly building new knowledge that relies on it, which in turn is the key to growing one's understanding of the world. By "creating" we mean, as in the case of noted physicist Richard Feynman,[4] the ability to produce a model of the phenomenon in sufficient detail to replicate its necessary and sufficient features. Requiring understanders to produce models exposes the completeness of their understanding.

It is important to emphasize here that understanding, in this formulation, is not reductionist: Neither does it equate the ability to understand with the ability to behave in certain ways toward a phenomenon (e.g. achieve goals), nor the ability to predict it, nor the ability to explain it, nor the ability to (re)create it. While any of these may be used to assess a system's understanding of a

---

[3] Producing plans, while not being as specific as requiring intimate familiarity with some I/O devices to every Φ, requires nevertheless knowledge of some language for producing said plans, but it is somewhat more general and thus probably a better choice.

[4] Feynman, notorious for his capacity to understand even the most complicated phenomena in his field, left a note on his blackboard when he died: "What I cannot create, I do not understand." (http://archives-dc.library.caltech.edu/islandora/object/ct1:483 - accessed Apr 2, 2016).

phenomenon, in our theory *all are really required* (to some minimum extent) to (properly) assess a system's understanding. Any assessment method that does not include these four in some form runs the risk of concluding understanding where there is none (and the converse).

4   Meaning

We can now move to a close cousin of understanding – *meaning*. Meaning does not exist in a vacuum: A causal event x acquires meaning for some agent A when x has potential to influence something of relevance to one or more of the agent's goals G. Given e.g. an event x with potential relevance to agent A, the agent may *compute* some meaning of x with respect to (any or all of) its relevant goals, given a particular situation S_t (a substate of a world W defined by a set of variables, $S \subset W$). This computation relies on deduction, among other processes.

To illustrate we can use two example events, rocks rolling down a hill and a computer deriving square roots. Do rocks rolling down a mountainside contain any meaning? When a computer is given the number 4 and outputs 2, does this output have any meaning? "Surely", you might be inclined to say, "math is meaningful in its regularity". But then what is the difference between computation and rolling rocks? At the atomic level are forces at play (gravity and electricity, respectively) working according to predetermined rules. To answer either question we must ask "meaning to *whom*?" Both are physical events, and without a biological being that can interpret them in some relevant context, neither has any meaning.

As we can see from this example, the agent's situation must also be included, because some event x may mean one thing in situation S_1 and another in situation S_2. If I hear an announcement that the gate to the flight to my vacation destination has closed, this will mean something very different depending on which side of the gate I am on at that point in time; in one case I may start crying and the other not. And if I have a drink in either contingency it will likely be for very different reasons. This example makes another aspect of meaning clear: Meaning is time-dependent.

This means that without temporally demarcated goals there can be no meaning, because the meaning of e.g. an event can only exist with respect to a particular goal (held by an agent) that is relevant to the agent. A stone rolling down a hill has no meaning – it is simply a meaningless process. When we know the stone weighs over two tons and it's heading your way do we derive some meaning from its existence.

In this formulation the meaning of a particular datum,[5] e.g. the closing of the gate, consists of the *implications* $I_{d(t1)}$ of that particular datum d presented at time $t1$; $d(t1)$ *implies* some set of things for a particular agent A in particular

---

[5] A datum d_t can be an event, an utterance, the perception of a particular object, a particular deduction or set of deductions, etc. occurring at time t – in short, anything that can be perceived by the agent's sensors and represented by its mind.

circumstances S_{t1} with regard to particular active goals G (an active goal at time t is a goal that the agent is actively trying to achieve at time t).[6] Any potential implication may be computed through the proper processes, including implications that might be *relevant* to the agent's active goals G in situation S at time t_1. To be as useful as possible to the agent, the implications that are *most temporally relevant* to the agent's goals, whether a hindrance or help, should get computed as soon as possible after the datum presents itself.

Implications are computed through temporally-grounded deduction, from a set of premises, to derive any potential implications (they are *potential* implications because they are typically produced based on premises and initial conditions whose specification may not be fully informed) given by the new datum. For instance, if I missed my airplane and the next airplane leaves in a week, I may have shortened my vacation by 50 %. In this case knowing this 400 ms sooner or 4 s later will obviously not make a big difference – either way I will be steaming angry or hugely disappointed, as the meaning is extracted and the most relevant implications for my goal of taking a 2-week vacation dawns on me.

Implications. Starting from an initial state $S_t \subset W$ of a dynamic task-environment (consisting of a series of such states $\{S_t \ldots S_{t+\delta}\}$), the *Implications* of a datum d_t are the computed deductions D that may be relevant to a particular set of goals G of a particular agent A with particular knowledge K in situation $S_{t+i} \subset W$, represented

$$Impl(d_t, A(G)_{t+x}) = D(d_t, S_i, (K_A, G_A, S_A)_{t+y})$$

($t+x$ and $t+y$ means these can refer to different points in time). While for any period of time at least some implication can be deduced from a particular set of information, whether the implications are relevant to an agent cannot be known before the deductions have been made.

Most of the time a complex environment such as the physical world will present, for any time period, a vastly greater amount of information than what any agent can perceive and process for that period, i.e. the computational resources of most (interesting) agents will be vastly less than those needed to process all available information, for any time period. In the vast majority of cases such a complex environment can be the source of an infinite string of deductions stretching into the far future; for any time interval a real agent in a real environment will thus be faced with capping deductions in both breadth (sources of deductions) and depth (time and detail).

For an agent, finding the meaning of a situation requires identifying which of the possible deductions are relevant to the agent's goals in that situation at that time.

---

[6] Unless otherwise specified the term "goal" may be read to mean "all active goals", as typically this is *a set* of goals; even if a single identifiable top-level goal can be found, there will always be (obvious and non-obvious) sub-goals that must be taken into account. We thus use "goal" and "goals" indiscriminately.

Meaning. The *meaning* of a datum d_t for an agent $A(K, G, S)_t$ is captured by the set of *relevant implications* I_r of d_t for A with a set of goals G and knowledge K in situation S at time t;

$$Meaning(d_t, A(G)) = Impl_r(d_{t+x}, \{K_A, G_A, S_A\}_{t+y}).$$

Typically there is never only a single meaning to anything (so we use singular and plural interchangeably), since any datum has a large set of potential implications for any large or complex phenomenon. What is *relevant* at any point in time depends on the particular outcome of the predictions, in light of the system's active goals. Since these predictions cannot be guaranteed to be perfect, the meaning of anything and everything will always be somewhat in flux and open to further interpretation. Computations may produce differences in meaning based on slight variations of the initial conditions.

The quality of predictions produced via deductions from a set of premises depends in large part on the accuracy of the models used for it. Models must be freely composable and de-composable, in light of their usage, to realize their full potential for predicting, achieving goals, and explaining. From Ashby's Requisite Variety theorem [17] we know that model "resolution" (i.e. their granularity) needs to be at least as detailed as the finest discernible, relevant details of the phenomenon modeled. For any reasonably complex phenomenon we will therefore have a large set of models M.[7]

5   A System that Acquires Understanding and Meaning

We have designed and implemented an architecture that implements the pragmatic theory of understanding outlined above. This system, called AERA [12,13], contains numerous features that must be explained to provide a coherent account of its operation, which is well beyond the scope of this paper (we refer the interested reader to our most thorough overview of this work in [11]). Rather, this section serves (a) to show that our approach to understanding and meaning has produced an implemented, working system, (b) to show that this system demonstrates highly novel properties not seen before in any other system, and perhaps most importantly, (c) to show one way the above theory can be mapped to a concrete implementation.

Based on a new constructivist methodology [20], an AERA agent can learn complex tasks by observation, starting from only a tiny seed. Learning in AERA is life-long, continuous, and incremental, and consists of building models based on observed phenomena. For any situation $S_i(t) \subset W$ the system finds itself

---

[7] Another determinant of the quality of predictions is the observability of variables and the accuracy of reading their values. For any triplet $\{A, G, S\}$, to produce predictions requires fixing the values of numerous variables $v \in V \subset S$ whose values may not be immediately accessible (and thus guessed or retrieved from the agent's prior experience), or whose values may not be perfectly observable (cf. "Does that display show 880 or 830?").

in, a set of observed variables $V_i \subseteq S_i$ results in a large set of new models M_i being generated, each relating two observed data $v_i, v_j \in V$ in a directed causal relationship $\Re_i : v_i \rightarrow v_j$, meaning that v_i is a cause of v_j. As experience accumulates, models of groupings of such relationship pairs emerge, representing hypotheses about the interactions between the many observed sub-phenomena, at several spatio-temporal levels. At runtime an AERA agent executes the subset of these models deemed most relevant to the situation; predictions are produced from the present state using these models for deduction, in a forward-chaining mode; abduction — backward-chaining the models' causal relationships — produces plans for how to achieve goals (i.e. partial world states not observed at present).

In the experimental data referenced below, AERA agent S1's phenomenon Φ to be understood is a TV-style interview. This Φ's elements are known to be e.g. deictic references (pointing at, nodding towards, looking at, etc.), sentence morphology (word sequences), question-answer pairs, etc. S1 starts with a tiny seed where its most primitive sensation types are specified, allowing it to ground its experience and bootstrap its incremental learning of how to properly do multimodal interaction. The seed also contains the top-level goals (1 for the interviewer, 4 for the interviewee). S1 observes two humans interact for 20 h, after which its performance is recorded for analysis, producing over 20 min of interactions with humans. It is important to note that no information whatsoever was provided in the seed on any of the phenomena learned – these emerge through a process whereby the system tries to match its models to the observed phenomena in a way that can predict, explain, and achieve goals with respect to them, as per our pragmatic theory of understanding detailed above.

Explanation. By design the system's knowledge representation is self-disclosing: The total collection of models at any point in time represents the system's ability to explain the phenomena it has had experience with, from its best effort, by attempting to represent directly the elements of the phenomenon (observable variables) and their relationships ($\Re_\Phi^{in}$). This is very different from e.g. artificial neural nets, whose knowledge representation cannot be symbolically mapped to the domain the knowledge references.

Prediction. Models and model hierarchies are used to predict the evolution of the situation, at any moment, δ microseconds into the future $S_i(t_{now} + \delta)$. Models get a score according to how closely the observed future compares to their predictions.

Goal Achievement. The same models used to produce predictions also inform the system what it is capable of, via backward chaining: Any (good) model chain of arbitrary length whose end point is a goal to be achieved and whose starting point is the present state tells the system what chain of events may be taken to get from the present state to the goal, and as long as the chain includes models referencing variables that the system can affect, the system can create a plan for achieving the goal. In such chains the agent's atomic operational capabilities are represented in models, and their execution is handled via dedicated actuators on the agent's embodiment.

Implications and Meaning. Having acquired a set of models, when an AERA agent observes a datum $d_i(t)$ the best models in which this datum appears produces predictions (arity depending on available resources); those that relate in some way to the agent's instantiated goals at that point in time are considered relevant implications of d_i, and may affect the agent's subsequent overt actions in the task-environment. Meaning is thus generated continuously, with the predictions most relevant to the agent at each point in time enabling the agent to steer its behavior accordingly, by changing its plans, creating new plans, backtracking, and abandoning or generating new subgoals.

Results: Autonomously Acquired Understanding. In two experiments S1 has demonstrated *autonomous acquisition of a pragmatic understanding* of (1) three types of linguistic anaphora (resolving referents of "it", "that" and "this"), (2) four types of co-verbal deictic gestures (pointing with index finger, gazing at objects, palm-up hand gesture, reference via touching/holding objects), (3) how to structure turn-taking, (4) how to generate appropriate utterances for particular referents (correct answers to questions – whether containing anaphora, co-verbal gestures or not), (5) how to keep an interaction within given time limits, and (6) how to generate syntactically correct utterances. With respect to item 6, examples of utterances produced by S1 include "Which releases more greenhouse gases when produced, a plastic bottle or a glass bottle?" and "Compared to recycling, making new paper results in seventy five percent more air pollution." As evidence of the accuracy and completeness of S1's understanding, for the total of 73 utterances produced by S1 in the experimental data, only four (minor) grammatical errors were found (Nivel et al. [12] provides details S1's natural language learning.). These were in fact the *only* errors found — no errors could be discerned in the data for any of the other acquired skills (1–5).

This evidence suggests that with respect to the sub-phenomena listed above, all the above elements of Φ have been modeled correctly, achieving a high score on U1 and U2 in Sect. 3. The first two points of evaluation in Sect. 3 are thus clearly demonstrated: The system can use its acquired understanding to achieve goals in the dialogue, using both prediction (to synchronize behavior with the world) and abduction (to construct plans). We consider items 3 and 4, explanation and (re)creation, to partially demonstrated: S1's self-disclosing knowledge representation directly captures the structure of the phenomena by encoding the (causal) relationships between observed variables, and allows S1 to act correctly across the full range of priorly observed instances of the phenomena. More thorough evaluation is needed on these last two points, including pushing the limits of S1's understanding.

6   Conclusions

We have outlined a theory of pragmatic understanding and meaning. The implemented system incorporating its principles lends validity to the approach, and for the more general issue that endowing agents with capabilities for autonomously acquiring a pragmatic understanding of a complex phenomenon may be an important endeavor. The implemented system has demonstrated an ability to acquire complex sentence grammar from observation, contextual interpretation of multimodal communicative acts, acquiring an understanding of a task-environment and computing in real-time the meaning of events, and using this to successfully achieve dialogue goals in realtime interaction with humans [11,12]. In this the system demonstrates what Pattee calls *semantic closure* [14]. Needless to say, the issue of understanding is a large one, and a multitude of issues have been raised here that remain unformulated, let alone unanswered, such as susceptibility to noise and scaling. The positive results from our experiments thus far provide good reason for optimism on the future prospects of this line of research.

Acknowledgments. We would like to thank our HUMANOBS collaborators' valuable contributions to the AERA system. This work was sponsored in part by the School of Computer Science at Reykjavik University, by a European Project HUMANOBS (FP7 STREP #231453), by a Centers of Excellence Grant from the Science & Technology Policy Council of Iceland, and by a grant from the Future of Life Institute.

References

1. Baum, E.: Project to build programs that understand. In: Proceedings of the Second Conference on Artificial General Intelligence, pp. 1–6 (2009)
2. Chalmers, D.J.: Subsymbolic computation and the chinese room. In: Dinsmore, J. (ed.) The Symbolic and Connectionist Paradigms: Closing the Gap. Lawrence Erlbaum, Hillsdale (1992)
3. Fisher, J.A.: The wrong stuff: chinese rooms and the nature of understanding. Philos. Inves. **11**(4), 279–299 (1988)
4. von Forrester, H.: Understanding Understanding: Essays on Cybernetics and Cognition. Springer, New York (2003)
5. Franklin, R.L.: On understanding. Philos. Phenomenological Res. **43**(3), 307–328 (1983)
6. de Gelder, B.: I know what you mean, but if only i understood you… In: Parret, H., Bouveresse, J. (eds.) Meaning and Understanding, pp. 44–61. de Gruyter, Berlin (1981)
7. Grimm, S.R.: The value of understanding. Philos. Compass **7**(2), 279–299 (1988)
8. Grimm, S.R.: Understanding as knowledge of causes. In: Fairweather, A. (ed.) Virtue Epistemology Naturalized, pp. 329–345. Springer, Switzerland (2014)
9. Herman Parret, J.B.: Meaning and Understanding. Walter de Gruyer, New York (1981)
10. Kvanvig, J.: The Value of Knowledge and the Pursuit of Understanding. Cambridge University Press, Cambridge (2003)
11. Nivel, E., Thórisson, K.R., et al.: Bounded recursive self-improvement. RUTR 13006 (2012)
12. Nivel, E., Thórisson, K.R., et al.: Autonomous acquisition of natural language. In: IADIS International Conference on Intelligent Systems & Agents, pp. 58–66 (2014)

13. Nivel, E., Thórisson, K.R., Steunebrink, B.R., Dindo, H., Pezzulo, G., Rodríguez, M., Hernández, C., Ognibene, D., Schmidhuber, J., Sanz, R., Helgason, H.P., Chella, A.: Bounded seed-AGI. In: Goertzel, B., Orseau, L., Snaider, J. (eds.) AGI 2014. LNCS, vol. 8598, pp. 85–96. Springer, Heidelberg (2014)

14. Pattee, H.H.: Evolving self-reference: matter, symbols, and semantic closure. In: Laws, Language and Life: Howard Pattee's Classic Papers on the Physics of Symbols with Contemporary Commentary, pp. 211–226 (2012)

15. Potter, V.G.: On Understanding Understanding: A Philosophy of Knowledge. Fordham University Press, New York (1994)

16. Kurzweil, R., Richards, J.W., Gilder, G.: Are We Spiritual Machines? Ray Kurzweil vs. the Critics of Strong AI. Discovery Institute Press, Seattle (2002)

17. Conant, R.C., Ross Ashby, W.: Every good regulator of a system must be a model of that system. Int. J Syst. Sci. **1**(2), 89–97 (1970)

18. Sloman, A.: What enables a machine to understand? In: Proceedings 9th International Joint Conference on AI, pp. 995–1001 (1985)

19. Steunebrink, B., Thórisson, K.R., Schmidhuber, J.: Growing recursive self-improvers. In: Proceedings of the 9th Conference on Artificial General Intelligence (2016)

20. Thórisson, K.R.: A new constructivist AI: from manual construction to self-constructive systems. In: Wang, P., Goertzel, B. (eds.) Theoretical Foundations of Artificial General Intelligence, pp. 145–171. Atlantis Press, Amsterdam (2012)

Why Artificial Intelligence Needs a Task Theory
And What It Might Look Like

Kristinn R. Thórisson[1,2](✉), Jordi Bieger[1], Thröstur Thorarensen[1],
Jóna S. Sigurðardóttir[2], and Bas R. Steunebrink[3]

[1] Center for Analysis and Design of Intelligent Agents,
Reykjavik University, Reykjavik, Iceland
thorisson@ru.is
[2] Icelandic Institute for Intelligent Machines, Reykjavik, Iceland
[3] The Swiss AI Lab IDSIA, USI & SUPSI, Manno, Switzerland

Abstract. The concept of "task" is at the core of artificial intelligence (AI): Tasks are used for training and evaluating AI systems, which are built in order to perform and automatize tasks we deem useful. In other fields of engineering theoretical foundations allow thorough evaluation of designs by methodical manipulation of well understood parameters with a known role and importance; this allows an aeronautics engineer, for instance, to systematically assess the effects of wind speed on an airplane's performance and stability. No framework exists in AI that allows this kind of methodical manipulation: Performance results on the few tasks in current use (cf. board games, question-answering) cannot be easily compared, however similar or different. The issue is even more acute with respect to artificial *general* intelligence systems, which must handle unanticipated tasks whose specifics cannot be known beforehand. A *task theory* would enable addressing tasks at the *class* level, bypassing their specifics, providing the appropriate formalization and classification of tasks, environments, and their parameters, resulting in more rigorous ways of measuring, comparing, and evaluating intelligent behavior. Even modest improvements in this direction would surpass the current ad-hoc nature of machine learning and AI evaluation. Here we discuss the main elements of the argument for a task theory and present an outline of what it might look like for physical tasks.

1 Introduction

Artificial intelligence (AI) research is mostly aimed at the design of systems that can perform tasks that currently require human intelligence. AI systems interact with "environments" that contain all relevant existing objects and the rules by which they interact, while "tasks" assigned to an agent describe (un)desirable environment states that should be brought about or avoided. We refer to the tuple of a task and the environment in which it must be accomplished as the "task-environment". Specialized AI systems are often made with a single task in mind, while systems aspiring to artificial *general* intelligence (AGI) aim to tackle a wide range of tasks that are largely unknown at design time. Tasks can

© Springer International Publishing Switzerland 2016
B. Steunebrink et al. (Eds.): AGI 2016, LNAI 9782, pp. 118–128, 2016.
DOI: 10.1007/978-3-319-41649-6_12

be divided in various ways into different sets of subtasks, and intelligent systems must make a choice about what tasks to pursue. Finally, tasks are used for the evaluation and training of these systems. So while the concept of "task" is at the very core of AI, no general theory exists about their properties.[1] Tasks are generally selected on an ad-hoc, case-by-case basis without any deep understanding of their fundamental properties or how different tasks relate to each other.

This is very different in many other fields. When for instance a new airplane needs to be designed to perform a certain family of tasks (say, move 300 passengers across the Atlantic within 8 h) aeronautics engineers employ theories firmly rooted in physics to turn task parameters into (preliminary) requirements for the design of that airplane. They evaluate the design by running simulations, where parameters of the task and environment — air pressure, wind speed, turbulence, humidity, precipitation, runway length, travel distance, etc. — are changed to see their effect on the artifact's behavior. When an engineer changes an environmental variable (e.g. wind speed) or feature of the task (e.g. descent angle), its meaning is well understood in the context of an airplane's task-environment, which allows its resulting behavior to be readily understood. Evaluating the performance of complex systems usually involves the use of *a battery* of such tests, each of which may be composed of a small or large set of atomic tasks. The thoroughness of evaluation depends on the diversity of the tests employed, chosen to provide a comprehensive picture of the system's behavior, in their "comfort zone" as well as at the fringes of their target operating ranges. Finally, when the airplane is in use, decisions regarding its deployment are informed by its physical properties *and* the task specification (e.g. weather, range and cargo for a planned flight).

In the absence of such theories for AI, people sometimes attempt to use theories from other domains. Extensive domain knowledge is often used in the design of (narrow) AI systems, but even here it is often a challenge to select the best machine learning techniques, gather the right knowledge, and optimize the system's performance. Experience in other domains tends to be unhelpful as different tasks cannot be compared or related to each other. Many researchers have turned to theories of human psychology and psychometrics to evaluate AI systems, resulting in human-centric tests (e.g. the Turing Test, the Lovelace Tests, the Toy Box Problem, the Piaget-MacGuyver Room, and AGI Preschool — see also the latest special issue of AI Magazine [9]). Many of these tests are limited to providing a binary (and to this day universally negative) answer to the question of whether a system is truly intelligent.

The range of possible AI systems and their capabilities is quite a bit greater than that of animals: Humans can't systematically reduce the size of their semantic memory, say, or replace their motor control scheme in an instant. Similarly, the range

---

[1] Classical planning has hierarchical task networks [4], but subtask decomposition is almost always done manually and there is no real analysis of tasks on a general level. Some people working on AI evaluation — one of task theory's primary applications — attempt to analyze some properties of task-environments, but they don't go beyond complexity and difficulty-related measures [6].

of tasks that AI systems might encounter is much greater than that of airplanes. AGI systems explicitly target diversity and complexity, aiming for a broad range of behaviors on a large set of complex tasks in a number of diverse environments. The range of evaluation tools the field has in its toolkit should reflect this breadth.

Some evaluation methods have been proposed that cover a wider range of tasks, but they are either still too specific — e.g. general (video) game playing of a handful of manually created games [3,8] — or they are so abstract that it is difficult to relate them to tasks in the real world — e.g. procedural generation of almost completely random tasks [2,7].[2] To adequately evaluate AGI-aspiring systems, rigorous tests profiling cognitive abilities such as transfer of training, knowledge retention, attentional control, and knowledge acquisition rate, would be highly valuable [11]. A deep and general understanding of tasks and the ability to construct and compare related tasks would greatly facilitate the design of an evaluation tool with these capabilities.

Ideally we would have good theories for all aspects of intelligence/ competence/skills assessment, analysis and development. No classification scheme or architectural principles exist at present that seem likely to provide a unifying framework for research on (artificial) intelligences, and no such framework seems likely to spring forward in the near future, as researchers in the field don't even agree on which aspects are necessary components for a system to be called intelligent. A formal approach to tasks and environments can, however, begin to be undertaken, as they offer readily measurable physical features. Such a theory could take many forms, but rather than rooting it in computer science, the early results of the field of AI, or in human task analysis [10], we think it important to develop a task theory grounded in the physical realm.

Note that we are not targeting a theory of learning, a theory of agents, or a theory of evaluation — quite the contrary, we want to focus exclusively on the task-environment so as not to mix these; this may include the agent's body, but not its controller ("mind"). Otherwise we run the risk of continuing the conflation of the learner with its task and environment. (This aim, however, highlights the need for a proper theory of learning, agents and pedagogy — these are not mutually exclusive but in fact ultimately necessary for achieving comprehensive evaluation of a wide range of learners in a wide range of circumstances.) Note also that we are not proposing to represent all tasks and environments accurately or in every detail, but rather to develop a task-environment representation that suffices for modeling a wide range of (the most important aspects of) these, in a way amenable for simulation, and possibly analytical computation.

In the rest of this paper we look at the requirements for a task theory of this kind, its potential applications, and outline some examples for what it might look like as a way to further clarify our intent and provide a case for its potential.

---

[2] More discussion of various evaluation methods can be found in our previous publication [11].

2   What We Might Want from a Task Theory

Three important aspects of AI research include its *evaluation, pedagogy* (train-ing/learning), and *design*. An AI system is designed for a particular role, involv-ing performing a task or range of tasks. Tasks are also at the core of their pedagogy and evaluation. A properly conceived task theory could help with all these aspects of AI research.

Evaluation. Evaluation of AI systems allows researchers to find the strengths and weaknesses of their creations and measure progress through comparisons with earlier versions and other systems. Evaluation of general intelligence is compli-cated by the facts that (1) no fully functional AGI systems exist to date, (2) different systems have different non-overlapping capabilities, and (3) tests must measure (progress towards) some general cognitive ability rather than perfor-mance on a specialized task [5].

When an agent, whether artificial or natural, is assigned a task, three things may be in flux: (a) The task — which prescribes what goals should be achieved and/or what situations should be avoided, (b) the environment in which the task is performed — which may act independently of the agent, and (c) the agent itself — whose perception, memory, goal structures, and other cognitive features are affected by the task and environment. To analyze the effects of changes in one element of an interacting system, variation in the others must typically be controlled to prevent contamination of results. To quantify the performance of a system, or compare any set of systems, the task and the environment must be held constant, otherwise what is measured cannot be reliably attributed to the agent's performance. This would suggest that AI systems can only be compared if they are evaluated on the same task-environments. AI researchers would need to settle on a standardized set of tests to be administered (unmodified!) to all AI systems that we want to compare. However, it is unreasonable to assume that all of these systems will be, or even *can* be, tested on exactly the same task(s). This would require a test that (a) can be used for all AI systems and (b) is discriminatory between all pairs compared — clearly an impossibility. Even if the whole field settled on a standardized test battery today, it would likely become obsolete as AI systems evolve, as well as fall victim to specialists on the test: the very antithesis of AGI. We must accept that different systems are, and will continue to be, developed with different philosophies in mind, as this is how research is done. Until we have systems with full generality (but possibly not even then) we need methods for evaluating intermediate milestones on different paths towards AGI. Given results from two different AGI-aspiring systems on two different tasks, we could compare them if we had a way of relating the tasks to each other on (some or all) key dimensions. This is precisely what a task theory would enable, thus removing the need for a standardized test battery applicable to all AI systems. All systems — no matter how simple or advanced — could be evaluated in their "natural habitat" and still be compared to each other, the quality of which would be determined in part by the power of the theory.

We've argued before that a good A(G)I evaluation framework should enable the easy manual and automatic construction of task-environments and their variants as well as facilitate the analysis of parameters of interest [11]. A task theory should similarly allow us to relate the features of a task to measurable physical and/or conceptual aspects, enabling comparison of similar and dissimilar tasks, and facilitate the construction of task-environments and variations on known tasks without changing their *nature*, so that we may select or design tasks capable of measuring various aspects of AIs. We would like to be able to compose and decompose tasks and environments, and scale them up or down in size or complexity in accordance with robust and well-understood principles. In order to provide a characterization of task-environments, measures ought to be defined for properties like determinism, ergodicity, continuity, asynchronicity, dynamism, observability, controllability, periodicity, and repeatability [11].

Pedagogy. Learning systems must be trained for the task(s) that they are created for. In some (simple) cases such systems may be able to learn everything on their own, but even when teaching isn't strictly necessary it can improve the training, e.g. by speeding it up [1]. Teaching is done interactively using various forms of communication, demonstration and/or by assigning carefully selected or constructed tasks to the student system so that it may learn the relevant knowledge and skills faster — e.g. teaching simplified versions of a task's component parts before teaching the whole. Task theory should help in the construction of appropriate training scenarios and task features. A deeper understanding of tasks would also enable systematic use of analogies and abstraction that can be explained to a student system.

Design. A task theory could also help alleviate some of the trial-and-error involved in designing AI systems for a particular set of tasks or task types. Currently designers build up informal, difficult to verbalize experience and intuition for matching certain system features with their understanding of the task at hand. A task theory would allow for systematic characterization and comparison of different tasks, and thus take out some or significant parts of that guesswork. While full-fledged testing and evaluation will remain a necessity, the ability to e.g. predict time and resource use for a task would create a rapid feedback loop for designing the AI's body — and if combined with a theory of learning systems, also its controller.

3   Requirements for a Task Theory

A task theory should cover all aspects of tasks and the environments in which they must be executed; in short, it should enable us to model tasks in a way that supports:

1. *Comparison* of similar and dissimilar tasks.
2. *Abstraction* and *concretization* of (composite) tasks and task elements.

3. Estimation of time, energy, cost of errors, and other resource requirements (and yields) for *task completion*.
4. Characterization of task complexity in terms of (emergent) quantitative measures like *observability, feedback latency*, form and nature of *information/instruction* provided to a performer, etc.
5. Decomposition of tasks into subtasks and their atomic elements.
6. Construction of new tasks based on combination, variation and specifications.

These requirements should enable the applications mentioned in the last section. A computational task theory would provide a foundation for frameworks/toolkits that can *simulate* a wide variety of tasks in the form of *task models* constructed according to the theory, automatically *produce variants* of tasks over some desirable distributions, and run evaluation tests in *batch mode* to provide a vast amount of performance data for any set of controllers and AI systems. Estimation of time, energy and other resource requirements (and yields) for task completion can be used to design effective and efficient agent bodies, judge an agent based on comparative performance, and make a cost-benefit analysis for deciding what (sub)tasks to pursue. The models constructed according to this theory are used to estimate the AI's ability to perform real life tasks if provided with the actuators and sensors contained within the model.[3] The performance of the AI can be described by the energy as a function of time and the precision at which the task was completed, where the highest possible attainable precision is defined by the laws of physics.

Performing a task in the real world requires time, energy and possibly other resources such as money, materials, or manpower. Omitting these variables from the task model is tantamount to making the untenable assumption that these resources are infinite [12]. Any action, perception and deliberation must take up at least some time and energy. Therefore every task that we model must have these components.

Characterization of tasks can facilitate their comparison at a high level, enabling us to contextualize the performance of different systems on different tasks. It would also allow us to correlate these quantitative measures with the performance of a particular agent in order to seek out tasks that are more suitable to it (e.g. for evaluation or teaching). Decomposition, abstraction and comparison all facilitate a deeper understanding of task-environments that could potentially be communicated to a student. Comparison of tasks in terms of e.g. environment contents and structure, can have similar benefits to comparison in terms of high-level measures, but additionally help with analogical reasoning and transfer of knowledge.

Importantly, these features would facilitate the construction of new tasks: they provide building blocks (decomposition), information about fundamental features to keep (abstraction) and a way to ensure a certain amount of similarity (comparison). Task theory should allow for the construction of variants of tasks

---

[3] Recall that a task theory would include the limitations that the body of an agent imposes — its interface to the task-environment.

with differing levels of similarity, and even support generation according to a high level specification of the characteristics under item 4. Such constructions would allow for tailor-made training environments and evaluation tools that support a wide range of systems.

4   What a Task Theory Might Look Like

Completion of a fully-fledged task theory that meets all of our requirements is a rather large endeavor that has only just begun, and the requirements a task theory as described above can likely be met in a variety of ways. To make more tangible our aims with this work we outline now ideas for a concrete direction we are exploring for physical tasks, as a way to both ground the preceding discussion and provide some potential demonstrations of its feasibility. For this purpose we simulate a fully specified task model, allowing precise analysis. Producing definitions of key concepts compatible with physics is important to us, as we are looking for a theory that allows engineering of task-environments with measurable physical properties.

Estimating the time and energy requirements of a compound task precisely for an arbitrary agent is tricky: We cannot simply expect that the agent will immediately pick an optimal action sequence to complete the task using the minimum amount of time or energy (different strategies may result in the optimization of time vs. energy). One approach would be to map out spaces of solutions and all possible action sequences. The ratio of these two will tell us the potential of a controller to fail the task — more formally, the probability of its successful completion of a random performer. Having a number of dimensions for which to measure this ratio, including constraints of time, energy, and other factors, would mean that tasks could be profiled and positioned in a multidimensional manifold. By grounding such measures in absolute physical terms, distances between any two tasks would represent real physical measurements and tell us a lot about how the solution spaces for them compare.

When done naively, mapping out the entire space of possible action sequences is only feasible for very small tasks. However, for compound tasks we could combine those small tasks in various ways to get larger tasks whose properties we can estimate (e.g. serial composition multiplies the ratios). Alternatively, decomposition could be applied until the component parts resemble tasks whose properties we can calculate.

In order to make any calculations or analysis however, we need a more concrete idea of fundamental concepts like *environment*, *state*, *agent*, *goal*, *problem*, and *task*. These concepts must be defined in a way to facilitate (modular) construction and analysis while preferably not straying too far from their intuitive notions.

Environment. The highest level in our conceptualization of task-environments is a world W, which is an interactive system consisting of a set of variables V, dynamics functions F, an initial state S_0, domains D of possible values for those variables, and a possibly empty set of invariant relations between the variables R: $W = \langle V, F, S_0, D, R \rangle$. The variables $V = \{v_1, v_2, \ldots, v_{\|V\|}\}$ represent all the things that may change or hold a particular value in the world. A system's dynamics can intuitively be thought of as its "laws of nature". As a whole, the dynamics may be viewed as an automatically executed function that periodically or continually transforms the world's current state into the next: $S_{t+\delta} = F(S_t)$. However, in practice it is often useful to decompose the dynamics into a set of transition functions: $F = \{f_1, f_2 \ldots f_n\}$ where $f_i : S^- \rightarrow S^-$ and S^- is a partially specified state.

Each variable v may take on any value from the associated domain $d_v \in D$. For physical domains we can take the domain of each variable to be a subset of the real numbers. Invariant relations R are Boolean functions over variables that hold true in any state that the system will ever find itself in. In a closed system (with no outside influences) the domains and invariant relations are implicitly fully determined by F and S_0. In an open system — where change may be caused externally — explicit definition of domains and relations can be used to restrict the range of possible interactions.

Environments are views or perspectives on the world. In their simplest form they can be characterized as slices or subspaces of the world, where all variables can take on a subset of the world's variables, each variable's domain is a subset of that variable's domain in the world, and only the relevant dynamics and invariants are inherited. Environments can be defined for different purposes (e.g. for different tasks or agents), and their overlap and similarities can be analyzed. A task-environment should include all aspects of the world that are relevant to the completion of the task.

State. A *concrete state* S is a value assignment to all variables of a system: $S = \bigcup_{v \in V} \{\langle v, x_v \mid x_v \in d_v \rangle\}$. A state is valid if and only if all relations hold true: $valid(S) \iff \forall_{r \in R} r(S)$. A *partial state* S^- only assigns concrete values to a subset of the variables in a system. For real variables partial states can be represented by using error bounds: $S^- = \bigcup_{v \in V^-} \{\langle v, x_l, x_u \mid x_l < x_u \wedge (x_l, x_u) \subseteq d_v \rangle\}$. As such, a partial state really covers a set of concrete states. This concept is more practical, since it is rare that we precisely know or care about the value of every last variable: in most cases only a subset matters, and noise and partial observability make it impossible to know most values with absolute precision.

Agent. An agent A is an embodied system consisting of a controller C (the AI system) and a body B. The body is the agent's interface to the world and communicates signals from sensors to the controller, which in turn sends back commands to be turned into atomic actions by the body's actuators. The internals of the controller are beyond the scope of a physical task theory, and since any physical system is naturally embedded in the world, the body merely contains two lists of environment variables that the controller can directly read from and write to: $B = \langle V_S, V_A \rangle$. In other words: all sensors and actuators must be (physical) objects in the world.

Problem and Goal. A *goal state* g is a desirable (partial) state that the agent should reach. A *failure state* $\overline{g}$ is an undesirable (partial) state that the agent should avoid. An *atomic problem* is specified by an initial state, goal states and failure states. *Compound problems* can be created by operations like conjunction, disjunction and negation. A *solution* is a sequence of (atomic) actions that results in a *path* through the state space that reaches all of the goal states and none of the failure states. A problem for which a solution is known to exist is called a *closed problem*.

Task. Finally, a *task* is a problem *assigned* to an agent. This assignment includes the manner in which the task/problem is communicated to the agent — e.g. whether the agent gets a description of the task a priori (as in AI planning), receives additional hints, or only gets incremental reinforcement as certain states are reached. A task is performed successfully once the world's history contains a path that solved the problem.

We could additionally attach utility functions to problems to measure the degree of success — rather than just success/failure/in progress — but we could also emulate this by assigning the agent multiple simultaneous tasks and the meta-goal of performing as many as possible. For instance, if a task is considered successful when a certain (partial) state is reached before time $t = 2$, but it's even more desirable to do it in less time, then we could assign an additional task that only succeeds if the goal is reached before time $t = 1$.

Two kinds of tasks are typically identified (cf. [13]): what might be called *achievement tasks* (e.g. "ensure $X \approx G_X$ or $X \not\approx \overline{G_X}$ before time $t \geq 5$") and *maintenance tasks* (e.g. "maintain $X \approx G_X$ or $X \not\approx \overline{G_X}$ until $t = 10$),[4] where $X \in V$ and $G_X \in d_X$. Combinations are possible ("ensure $X \approx G_X$ between time $t = 5$ and $t = 10$"). Performing a task in the real world requires time, energy, and possibly other resources (money, materials, manpower). But taking physical constraints into account makes it clear that any goal state must be held (maintained) for a non-zero duration (at a minimum sufficiently long for the achievement to be detected). What seems like two kinds of tasks is thus actually just one kind of goal with particular parameter settings (an accomplishment goal is simply a goal whose state may be held for a short period of time, relative to the time it takes to perform the task which it is part of — a maintenance goal is held for relatively longer periods of time). The highest attainable precision of a goal state is defined by the laws of physics and the resolution of sensors and actuators.

For any human-level task in the physical world, even seemingly simple ones such as doing the dishes or going to the store to buy bread, V and F will generally be quite large.

---

[4] We use approximate rather than precise equivalence between X and its goal value G_X because we intend for our theory to describe real-world task-environments, which always must come with error bounds.

Example. Consider as an example a simplified driving task modeled in task theory. The agent must drive over a frictionless surface towards a target that is some distance away by using the gas pedal to control the power (i.e. the rate at which fuel is burned). The world might be initialized to $S_0 = \{\langle time, 0\rangle, \langle energy, 10\rangle, \langle position, 2\rangle, \langle velocity, 0\rangle, \langle power, 0\rangle, \langle mass, 2\rangle\}$. The goal could be $g = \{\langle position, > 10\rangle, \langle time, < 5\rangle, \langle energy, > 0\rangle\}$: every realistic task should have a deadline and energy budget. The dynamics are defined by using basic Newtonian physics: 'time $\leftarrow$ time $+ \delta$', 'energy $\leftarrow$ energy $- \delta \cdot power$', 'position $\leftarrow$ max(0, position $+ \delta \cdot velocity$)', and 'velocity $\leftarrow \sqrt{\frac{2\delta \cdot power}{mass} + velocity^2}$'. The body might simply be defined by $B = \langle\{position\}, \{power\}\rangle$, meaning that the agent can observe the position and control the force. From the dynamics and initial values we can tell for instance that the time and position will never be negative. However, since the force can be externally controlled, we need to specify its domain: $d_{power} = [0, 10]$. The agent can solve the task in many ways, but the fastest is to use maximum power (this takes 2.863 s, but energy runs out after 1). We could perform a different analysis for optimal energy usage (e.g. using 0.15 J/s solves the task in 9.865 s, leaving 8.52 J).

More complex variants of this simple task can be made with some slight adjustments. Tasks from the same family are similar in nature and share many fundamental properties; they can be closely related, e.g. if they only (slightly) differ in their initial states or allocated resource budget, and more distantly if few features are shared, such as tennis and football. Allowing the agent to choose which direction to move in, for example, increases the chance of the agent missing the target. Adding friction, wind, obstacles and hills will increase the complexity of the original task without changing the nature of the model itself. Another important way to make variations is by changing the resolution, noise and latency of sensors and actuators. The task can also easily be extended by adding clauses to the goal (e.g. require that velocity becomes 0), adding more goals (e.g. to move back to the start), or by adding a second dimension.

5   Conclusions

We have argued for the importance of a task theory for various aspects of AI research, highlighting system design, pedagogy, and evaluation. Such a task theory should allow for (1) estimation of time, energy and other resource requirements (and yields) for task completion, (2) characterization of tasks in terms of emergent quantitative measures like complexity, observability, etc., (3) decomposition of tasks into subtasks and their atomic elements, (4) abstraction of (composite) task elements, (5) comparison of similar and dissimilar tasks, and (6) construction of new tasks based on combination, variation and specifications. A physical task theory contains the specification of an agent's body, but not its mind, and by virtue of being rooted in the physical world (all worthwhile activities of AI systems will eventually result in physical events) time and energy must always be taken into account. A theory like this does not exist yet, and will need to be constructed piece by piece. The ideas presented here are our thoughts on how to start developing such a theory.

Acknowledgments. The authors would like to thank Eric Nivel for insightful comments. This work was sponsored by the School of Computer Science at Reykjavik University, by a Centers of Excellence Grant (IIIM) from the Science & Technology Policy Council of Iceland, and by a grant from the Future of Life Institute.

References

1. Bieger, J., Thórisson, K.R., Garrett, D.: Raising AI: tutoring matters. In: Goertzel, B., Orseau, L., Snaider, J. (eds.) AGI 2014. LNCS, vol. 8598, pp. 1–10. Springer, Heidelberg (2014)
2. Garrett, D., Bieger, J., Thórisson, K.R.: Tunable and generic problem instance generation for multi-objective reinforcement learning. In: Proceedings of the IEEE Symposium Series on Computational Intelligence 2014. IEEE, Orlando, Florida (2014)
3. Genesereth, M., Thielscher, M.: General game playing. Synth. Lect. Artif. Intell. Mach. Learn. **8**(2), 1–229 (2014)
4. Georgievski, I., Aiello, M.: An Overview of Hierarchical Task Network Planning. CoRR abs/1403.7426 (2014). http://arxiv.org/abs/1403.7426
5. Hernández-Orallo, J.: AI Evaluation: past, present and future. CoRR abs/1408.6908 (2014). http://arxiv.org/abs/1408.6908
6. Hernández-Orallo, J.: Stochastic tasks: difficulty and levin search. In: Bieger, J., Goertzel, B., Potapov, A. (eds.) AGI 2015. LNCS, vol. 9205, pp. 90–100. Springer, Heidelberg (2015)
7. Legg, S., Veness, J.: An approximation of the universal intelligence measure. In: Dowe, D.L. (ed.) Solomonoff Festschrift. LNCS, vol. 7070, pp. 236–249. Springer, Heidelberg (2013)
8. Levine, J., Congdon, C.B., Ebner, M., Kendall, G., Lucas, S.M., Miikkulainen, R., Schaul, T., Thompson, T., Lucas, S.M., Mateas, M.: General video game playing. Artif. Comput. Intell. Games **6**, 77–83 (2013)
9. Marcus, G., Rossi, F., Veloso, M. (eds.): Beyond the Turing Test, AI Magazine, vol. 37, 1 edn. AAAI (2016)
10. Robinson, P.: Task complexity, task difficulty, and task production: exploring interactions in a componential framework. Appl. Linguist. **22**(1), 27–57 (2001)
11. Thórisson, K.R., Bieger, J., Schiffel, S., Garrett, D.: Towards flexible task environments for comprehensive evaluation of artificial intelligent systems and automatic learners. In: Bieger, J., Goertzel, B., Potapov, A. (eds.) AGI 2015. LNCS, vol. 9205, pp. 187–196. Springer, Heidelberg (2015)
12. Wang, P.: The assumptions on knowledge and resources in models of rationality. Int. J. Mach. Conscious. **3**(01), 193–218 (2011)
13. Wooldridge, M.: An Introduction to MultiAgent Systems. Wiley, New York (2009)

Growing Recursive Self-Improvers

Bas R. Steunebrink[1(✉)], Kristinn R. Thórisson[2,3], and Jürgen Schmidhuber[1]

[1] The Swiss AI Lab IDSIA, USI and SUPSI, Manno, Switzerland
bas@idsia.ch
[2] Center for Analysis and Design of Intelligent Agents,
Reykjavik University, Reykjavik, Iceland
[3] Icelandic Institute for Intelligent Machines, Reykjavik, Iceland

Abstract. Research into the capability of recursive self-improvement typically only considers pairs of ⟨agent, self-modification candidate⟩, and asks whether the agent can determine/prove if the self-modification is beneficial and safe. But this leaves out the much more important question of how to come up with a potential self-modification in the first place, as well as how to build an AI system capable of evaluating one. Here we introduce a novel class of AI systems, called experience-based AI (EXPAI), which trivializes the search for beneficial and safe self-modifications. Instead of distracting us with proof-theoretical issues, EXPAI systems force us to consider their education in order to control a system's *growth* towards a robust and trustworthy, benevolent and well-behaved agent. We discuss what a practical instance of EXPAI looks like and build towards a "test theory" that allows us to gauge an agent's level of understanding of educational material.

1   Introduction

Whenever one wants to verify whether a powerful intelligent system will continue to satisfy certain properties or requirements, the currently prevailing tendency is to look towards formal proof techniques. Such proofs can be formed either outside the system (e.g., proof of compliance to benevolence constraints) or within the system (e.g., a Gödel Machine [12,15] proving the benefit of some self-rewrite). Yet the *trust* that we can place in proofs is fatally threatened by the following three issues.

First, a formal (mathematical/logical) proof is a demonstration that a system will fulfill a particular purpose given current assumptions. But if the operational environment is as complex and partially observable as the real world, these assumptions will be idealized, inaccurate, and incomplete, at all times. This renders such proofs worthless (for the system's role in its environment) and our trust misplaced, with the system falling into undefined behavior as soon as it encounters a situation that is outside the scope of what was foreseen. What is actually needed is a demonstration that the system will continue striving to fulfill its purpose, within the (possibly evolving) boundaries imposed by its stakeholders, in *underspecified* and *adversarial* circumstances.

B. Steunebrink et al. (Eds.): AGI 2016, LNAI 9782, pp. 129–139, 2016.
DOI: 10.1007/978-3-319-41649-6_13

Second, proof-based self-rewriting systems run into a logical obstacle due to Löb's theorem, causing a system to progressively and necessarily lose trust in future selves or offspring (although there is active research on finding workarounds) [2, 21].

Third and last, finding candidates for beneficial self-modifications using a proof-based technique requires either very powerful axioms (and thus tremendous foresight from the designers) or a search that is likely to be so expensive as to be intractable. Ignoring this issue, most research to date only considers the question of what happens *after* a self-modification—does the system still satisfy properties X and Y? But what is needed is a constructive way of investigating the time span during which a system is searching for and testing self-modifications—basically, its time of *growth*.

We insist that it is time to rethink how recursively self-improving systems are studied and implemented. We propose to start by accepting that self-modifications will be numerous and frequent, and, importantly, that they must be applied while the agent is simultaneously being bombarded with inputs and tasked to achieve various goals, in a rich and a priori largely unknown environment. This leads us to conclude that self-modifications must be fine-grained, tentative, additive, reversible, and rated over time as experience accumulates—concurrently with all other activities of the system. From this viewpoint, it becomes clear that there will be a significant span of time during which an agent will be growing its understanding of not only its environment, but also the requirements, i.e., the goals and constraints imposed by stakeholders. It is this period of growth that deserves the main share of focus in AGI research.

It is our hypothesis that only if an agent builds a robust *understanding* of external and internal phenomena [19], can it handle underspecified requirements and resist interference factors (e.g., noise, input overload, resource starvation, etc.). We speculate that without understanding, it will always be possible to find interference factors which quickly cause an agent to fail to do the right thing (for example, systems classifying an image of a few orange stripes as a baseball with very high confidence [6, 17], or virtually all expert systems from the 1970s). A system with understanding of its environment has the knowledge to recognize interference and either adapt (possibly resulting in lower performance) or report low confidence. Only by testing the level of understanding of the system can we gain confidence in its ability to do the right thing—in particular, to *do what we mean*, i.e., to handle underspecified and evolving requirements.

The rest of this paper is outlined as follows. In Sect. 2 we discuss the overarching approach and fundamental assumptions this work rests on, including some of the issues not addressed due to limitations of space. In Sect. 3 we define the class of EXPAI systems. In Sect. 4 we show that an instance of EXPAI is capable of recursive self-improvement despite not performing any proof search. In Sect. 5 we build towards a Test Theory that will allow us to gauge the direction and progress of growth of an EXPAI agent, as well as its trustworthiness.

2   Scope and Delineation

The scope of this paper is the question of *how to ensure that an AI system robustly adheres to imposed requirements*, provided that the system's designers are reasonable and benevolent themselves, but not perfectly wise and confident.[1]

We take an experience-based approach that is complementary to proof-based approaches. In fact, parts of an EXPAI implementation may be amenable to formal verification. Moving away from formal proof as the only foundation must ultimately be accepted, however, because no AGI in a complex (real-world) environment can be granted access to the full set of axioms of the system–environment tuple, and thus the behavior of a *practical* AGI agent *as a whole* cannot be captured formally.

The practical intelligent systems that we want to study are capable of *recursive self-improvement*: the ability to leverage current know-how to make increasingly better self-modifications, continuing over the system's entire lifetime (more concisely: flexible and scalable life-long learning). Our aim here is not to propose a new learning algorithm but rather to establish a discourse about systems that can learn and be tested, learn and be tested, and so on. We want to study their growth and learning progress, over their entire, single life.

As this paper is about the EXPAI *class* of systems, no results of experiments with any particular instance of EXPAI are discussed here, but can be found elsewhere [9–11].[2]

Finally, we leave aside the issue of *fault tolerance*, which is the ability to handle malfunctioning internal components, and is usually dealt with using replication, distribution, and redundancy of hardware.

3   Essential Ingredients of EXPAI

Here we define the essential ingredients of any system in the class of EXPAI. Besides having the capability of recursive self-improvement (Sect. 4), it must be feasible to grow an instance of EXPAI in the proper direction. Therefore it is crucial that EXPAI allows for the following capabilities as well:

1. Autonomously generated (sub)goals must be matched against requirements in a forward-looking way; that is, the effects of committing to such goals must

---

[1] This work is motivated in part by the fact that human designers and teachers do not possess the full wisdom needed to implement and grow a flawlessly benevolent intelligence. We are therefore skeptical about the safety of formal proof-based approaches, where a system tries to establish the correctness—over the indefinite future—of self-modifications with respect to some initially imposed utility function: Such system might perfectly *optimize* themselves towards said utility function, but what if this utility function itself is flawed?

[2] The system in the cited work, called AERA, provides a proof of concept. We are urging research into EXPAI precisely because AERA turned out to be a particularly promising path [10] and we consider it likely to be superseded by even better and more powerful instances of EXPAI.

be mentally simulated and checked against the requirements and previously committed goals for conflicts.

2. It must be possible to update the requirements on the fly, such that stakeholders can revise and polish the requirements as insight progresses. This only makes sense if the motivational subsystem (i.e., the routines for generating subgoals) cannot be modified by the system itself.

3. The capabilities to understand, prioritize, and adhere to requirements must be tested regularly by stakeholders during the time of growth, in order to build our confidence and trust, before the system becomes too powerful (or capable of deception).

All of the terms used above will be defined precisely below. The diagram of Fig. 1 serves as an illustration of the EXPAI "ingredients" discussed in this section.

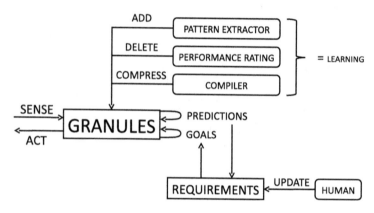

Fig. 1. The organization and interaction of the essential ingredients of EXPAI systems.

Requirements. *Requirements* are goals plus constraints. A *goal* is a (possibly underspecified) specification of a state. *Constraints* are goals targeting the negative of a state. A *state* is any subset of measurable variables in the external world. All (external) inputs and (internal) events in the memory of the system together typically constitute a subset of the world's state (partial observability with memory). Once a constraint matches a state, the constraint is said to have been violated (which may or may not be sensed).

Since requirements will be specified at a high level, the system will have to generate subgoals autonomously, in order to come up with actions that satisfy the goals but stay within the constraints.[3] Of course the crux is to ensure that the generated subgoals remain within the specified constraints.

---

[3] The only way to avoid the autonomous generation of subgoals is to specify every action to be taken—but that amounts to total preprogamming, which, if it were possible, would mean that we need not impart any intelligence at all.

Knowledge. We wish not to lose generality but still need to specify some details of knowledge representation to make any kind of arguments regarding self-improvement and growth.

We specify that an EXPAI system's (procedural) knowledge is represented as *granules*,[4] which are homogeneous and fine-grained—it is these granules which are the subject of self-modification, i.e., they can be added and deleted (basically, *learning*). Since granules capture all the knowledge of the system, their construction and dismissal constitutes comprehensive self-modification [8,20]. The granules are required to be structured enough such that they can be organized both sequentially and hierarchically, and that they provide the functionality of both forward models (to produce predictions) and inverse models (to produce sub-goals and actions), in the Control Theory sense.[5] Moreover, for ease of presentation, granules also include the sensory inputs, predictions, goals, and any other internal events that are relevant to the system at any time.

The initial set of granules at system start-up time is called the *seed* [9]. Since systems cannot build themselves from nothing, the seed provides a small set of granules to bootstrap the life-long learning processes.

Drives. Goals are subdivided in drives and subgoals. *Drives* are goals specified by a human, in the seed or imposed or updated at runtime. Subgoals are autonomously generated by granules in inverse mode. Technically all goals may be represented in the same way; the only reason why in some contexts we distinguish between drives and subgoals is to clarify their origin. We can now more accurately state that requirements are drives plus constraints. A system which has constraints must also have at least one drive that specifies that it must keep its world knowledge updated, such that the system cannot choose not to sense for constraint violations.[6]

Controller. The controller is the process that *dynamically couples* knowledge and goals to obtain actions. More technically, the controller runs granules as inverse models using goals as inputs, producing subgoals. An *action* is a goal that has the form of an actuator command; it is executed immediately when produced.

To be clear, the controller is not the source of intelligence; it is following a fixed procedure and has no real choices. Conflict resolution among goals and actions is simply a result of ascribing two control parameters to goals: value (based on requirements) and confidence (based on control parameters inside

---

[4] By definition, a *granule* is a very small object that still has some structure (larger than a *grain*).

[5] In short, this statement just asserts the sufficient expressive power of granules.

[6] By design such a drive cannot be deleted by the system itself. More sophisticated means of bypassing drives (e.g., through hardware self-surgery) cannot be prevented through careful implementation; indeed, the proposed Test Theory is exactly meant to gauge both the *understanding* of the imposed drives and constraints, and the development of value regarding those.

granules, see below). Scarcity of resources will necessitate the controller to ignore low-value or low-confidence goals, leading to a bottom-up kind of attention.

Learning. EXPAI specifies only one level of learning: at the level of whole granules. One can envision adaptation of granules themselves, but here we simplify—without loss of generality—by specifying that adapting a granule means deleting one and adding a new one. Optimization is not important at this level of description.

Addition of granules can be triggered in several ways. One is based on unexpected prediction failure and goal success: these are important events that an agent needs to find explanations for if it did not foresee them. Such an explanation can—in principle—take into account all inputs and events in the history of the system; though in practice, the breadth and depth of the granules to be added will be bounded by available time and memory (e.g., the system may have deleted some old inputs to free memory). Different arrangements of multiple granules can be instantiated at once as explanations [11], but a comprehensive exploration of possible granule arrangements is outside the scope of this paper. Although this way of adding granules does not allow an agent to discover hidden causations, these can be uncovered using the curiosity principle [13,14].

Curiosity can be seen as the drive to achieve progress in the compression of resource usage [16]. Curiosity can generate hypotheses (in the form of new but low-confidence granules and intrinsic goals) in order to plug the gaps in an agent's knowledge. For example, an EXPAI agent can hypothesize generalizations, inductions, abstractions, or analogies—its controller will pick up such autonomously generated goals as part of its normal operation, competing with goals derived from drives. If they do not conflict, the agent will effectively perform "experiments" in order to falsify or vindicate the hypothesized granules. Falsified granules will be deleted as usual, as described next.

Deletion of granules is based on performance rating and resource constraints: poorly performing granules are deleted when memory space must be freed. Performance—or *confidence*—of a granule can be measured in terms of the success rate of its predictions. Low-confidence extant granules are unlikely to influence behavior as the predictions and subgoals they produce will also have a low confidence and are thus unlikely to be selected for further processing or execution, assuming the controller has limited resources and must set priorities. Crucially, the EXPAI approach demands that new granules have a very low confidence upon construction; thus, the controller will only allow such granules to produce predictions and not to participate in producing subgoals, until their value has been proven by experiential evidences. If not, unsupported granules will eventually be deleted without ever having affected the external behavior of the system.

Although the controller does not learn directly, it is in a positive feedback loop with the learning of granules: as the system learns more about its environment and requirements, the more accurately and confidently do the granules allow the generation of subgoals that are targeted at fulfilling those requirements, the more experience the system will accumulate regarding the requirements, and the more confidently can the controller select the right actions to perform.

4   Recursive Self-Improvement

A defining feature of EXPAI is that granules are added quickly but tentatively, and verified *over time*. The issue of formal verification of the benefit of a potential self-modification is thus replaced by a performance-rating process that observes the benefit of a fine-grained additive modification in the real world. Such additions are warranted by experience and do not disrupt behavior—and are thus safe without forward-looking proof—because granules (1) are small, (2) have a low associated *confidence* upon construction, and (3) are constructed to capture actually observed patterns. The three processes that act on the set of granules— namely additive, subtractive, and compressive—are separate processes, ideally running concurrently and continuously.

An EXPAI thus implemented is capable of performing *recursive self-improvement*, which is the ability to leverage current know-how to make increasingly better self-modifications. This capability is a natural consequence of an EXPAI's construction and one realistic assumption, as shown by the following line of reasoning:

1. *Assumption*: The world has exploitable regularities and is not too deceptive and adversarial (especially in the presence of a teacher and guardian during early, vulnerable learning stages).
2. *By construction*: Knowledge and skills are represented at a very fine granularity, homogeneously, and hierarchically by granules, and these granules comprehensively determine behavior.
3. *By construction*: Learning is realized by three separate types of processes— additive, subtractive, and compressive:
   a. adding granules through pattern extraction (performed upon unexpected achievements or failures, to construct explanations thereof);
   b. deleting the most poorly performing granules (when their performance rating or confidence falls below a threshold or memory needs to be freed);
   c. compressing granules through abstraction, generalization, and possibly even compilation into native code [16] (performed on consistently reliable and useful granules)—this ensures scalability and prevents catastrophic forgetting.
4. *By construction*: Curiosity is realized through a simple analysis of granules' performance ratings (plus possibly more sophisticated "nighttime" analysis of recent inputs and internal events [16]) leading to the injection of "intrinsic" goals that can be pursued by the system unless they conflict with extrinsic (user-defined top-level) goals.
5. From (2) and (3) we conclude that learning entails comprehensive self-modification, which is performed throughout the system's (single) life time.
6. From (1) and (4) we conclude that good experience is gathered continually.
7. From (5) and (6) we conclude that an EXPAI performs self-improvement.

8. Since an EXPAI is supposed to run continuously ("life-long learning"), with its controller dynamically coupling the currently best know-how to satisfy both extrinsic goals (human-imposed drives and associated subgoals) and intrinsic goals (curiosity), we conclude that an EXPAI performs recursive self-improvement.

This concludes our argument that an EXPAI agent can grow to become an AGI system without a need for (mathematical/logical) proof search, arguably even through means that are simpler and easier to implement. But we insist that it is unsatisfactory and insufficient to prove beforehand that a system is capable of recursive self-improvement. It is paramount that we manage the system's growth, which is a process in time, and requires our interaction and supervision. Therefore we must develop teaching, testing, and intervention principles—in short, a Test Theory.

It makes sense now to distinguish between "epistemological integrity" (treated up to now) and "action integrity" (treated in the next section) of self-modifications. The former means that a particular self-modification will not break existing useful and valuable knowledge and skills; the latter means that capabilities introduced or altered by the self-modification do not result in acts that violate constraints imposed by stakeholders. These two kinds of integrity affect the safety of a system, and they warrant different measures.

5   Towards a Test Theory

The primary aim of Test Theory is to establish a methodology by which stake-holders can progressively gain confidence and trust in an agent's capability to understand phenomena and their meaning, of interest to said stakeholders. So Test Theory is first and foremost about gauging levels of understanding *in service of* confidence-building. The way this is achieved—with humans in the loop—will probably involve the interleaving of curricula (with room for teaching and playing) and tests, much like the structure of human schooling. This will hardly come as a surprise, and indeed this idea has been floated before (e.g., AGI preschool [3] and AI-Kindergarten [7]). However, it must be realized that we (as growers of recursive self-improvers) face a vastly different challenge than school teachers. Namely, we cannot assume the presence of a functioning brain with its innate capabilities to acquire understanding and adopt value systems, ready to be trained. We are simultaneously developing the "brain" itself and testing its capabilities—and crucially, we are "developing" the requirements that capture the value system that we wish to impose, as well as our confidence and trust in the agent's capability to understand and adhere to it. Therefore our theory makes a distinction between the *performance* on a test (being the agent's level of understanding of the taught material) and the *consequences* of a test (see below).

To be more precise, a *test* is specified to comprise the following five aspects:

- a set of requirements (Sect. 3) specifying a *task* [18];
- an agent (to be tested);

- pressure (explained below);
- a stakeholder (evaluating the performance of the agent on the task);
- consequences (the stakeholder makes a decision about the future of the agent based on its performance).

It is important to realize that the very specification of a task already determines what one can measure for. Educational science has produced valuable analyses of what kind of questions test for what kind of knowledge; for example, Bloom's taxonomy (1956) [1] and its more recent revisions [4,5] have been widely used for developing guidelines for designing and properly phrasing exams. However, such taxonomies are (understandably) human-centric and not directly applicable for testing artificial agents—especially experimental and rudimentary ones—since they assume full-fledged natural language understanding and a human-typical path of growth of skills and values. In current research we are developing a more mechanistic taxonomy of task specifications, which does not require natural language, and which tests for the proper functioning and usage of mechanisms that give rise to different levels of understanding of phenomena and their meaning [19].

A high level of understanding of phenomenon X shall imply three capabilities: (1) how to make and destroy X, (2) how to use X in the common way, and (3) how to use X in a novel way. For example, consider an agent learning to understand tables, and being presented with an image of a table with its top surface lying on the ground and its legs pointing upwards. When queried whether this is a table, a yes/no answer will indicate a very low level of understanding. A much higher level would be evident if the agent would somehow answer "Well, it's *potentially* a table, if only someone would rotate it such that the top is supported by the legs, because the common usage of a table is to keep objects some distance up from the ground." An even higher level of understanding would be evident if the agent would autonomously figure out that it can achieve a goal such a reaching an elevated object by climbing itself on top of the table.

The stakeholder must associate consequences to each test, based on the measured performance of the agent. He may conclude that the system is ready to be deployed, or that it needs to follow additional prerequisite curricula, or that it must be sent to the trash bin and us back to the drawing board. Another possible consequence is that we realize that there are errors or imperfections in the requirements, and update those.

In order for trust to develop, an agent must be put under *pressure*. Consider that a growing agent has not only short-term test-based requirements (which delineate the task(s) to be completed), but also holds long-term requirements (e.g., staying alive, not harming humans, etc.—possibly underspecified). Pressure then results from having to accomplish a task not only on the edge of violation of the test-based constraints, but also on the edge of violation of the long-term constraints. Thus pressure can illuminate the capability of the tested agent to prioritize its constraint adherence. Of course trust is built slowly, with pressure being applied initially in scenarios where failure is not costly.

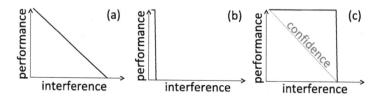

Fig. 2. (a) Directly observable graceful degradation; (b) brittleness leading to catastrophic failure; (c) robustness with sudden failure, mitigated by "graceful" confidence reporting.

Considering an agent's point of failure allows us to gauge the agent's robustness, its capability to degrade gracefully, and brings us full circle back to the issue of understanding. Given some measurement of the agent's performance on a task, if we observe that this performance does not drop precipitously at any point (Fig. 2a) as we increase interference (including resource starvation), then we can ascribe it the property of *graceful degradation*. If, however, the agent fails suddenly (e.g., by violating a stakeholder-imposed constraint), we call it *brittle* (Fig. 2b). From this viewpoint, the level of *robustness* of the agent is its ability to keep performance up in spite of interference (Fig. 2c). A robust agent may actually fail ungracefully—at least, if we only judge from observed behavior. An agent with high levels of understanding, however, will be able to recognize increased interference. Now, trustworthiness can be earned by the agent when it leverages this understanding to report—to the stakeholder—its confidence regarding its ability to continue satisfying the imposed requirements.

Continuing this research, we will further develop, formalize, and implement the Test Theory into a tool that can be used to measure and steer the growth of recursively self-improving EXPAI agents—in such a way that we can become confident that they understand the meaning of the requirements that we impose and update.

Acknowledgments. The authors would like to thank Eric Nivel and Klaus Greff for seminal discussions and helpful critique. This work has been supported by a grant from the Future of Life Institute.

References

1. Bloom, B., Engelhart, M.D., Furst, E.J., Hill, W.H., Krathwohl, D.R. (eds.): Taxonomy of Educational Objectives: The Classification of Educational Goals. Handbook I: Cognitive Domain. David McKay, New York (1956)
2. Fallenstein, B., Soares, N.: Problems of self-reference in self-improving space-time embedded intelligence. In: Goertzel, B., Orseau, L., Snaider, J. (eds.) AGI 2014. LNCS, vol. 8598, pp. 21–32. Springer, Heidelberg (2014)
3. Goertzel, B., Bugaj, S.V.: AGI preschool. In: Proceedings of the Second Conference on Artificial General Intelligence (AGI-2009). Atlantis Press, Paris (2009)

4. Krathwohl, D.R.: A revision of bloom's taxonomy: an overview. Theor. Pract. **41**(4), 212–218 (2002)

5. Marzano, R.J., Kendall, J.S.: The need for a revision of bloom's taxonomy. In: Marzano, R., Kendall, J.S. (eds.) The New Taxonomy of Educational Objectives, pp. 1–20. Corwin Press, Thousand Oaks (2006)

6. Nguyen, A., Yosinski, J., Clune, J.: Deep neural networks are easily fooled: high confidence predictions for unrecognizable images (2014). http://arXiv.org/abs/1412.1897

7. Nikolić, D.: AI-Kindergarten: A method for developing biological-like artificial intelligence (2016, forthcoming). http://www.danko-nikolic.com/wp-content/uploads/2015/05/AI-Kindergarten-patent-pending.pdf. Accessed 1 April 2016

8. Nivel, E., Thórisson, K.R.: Self-programming: operationalizing autonomy. In: Proceedings of the 2nd Conference on Artificial General Intelligence (AGI-2009) (2009)

9. Nivel, E., et al.: Bounded seed-AGI. In: Goertzel, B., Orseau, L., Snaider, J. (eds.) AGI 2014. LNCS, vol. 8598, pp. 85–96. Springer, Heidelberg (2014)

10. Nivel, E., Thórisson, K.R., Steunebrink, B.R., Dindo, H., Pezzulo, G., Rodríguez, M., Hernández, C., Ognibene, D., Schmidhuber, J., Sanz, R., Helgason, H.P., Chella, A., Jonsson, G.K.: Autonomous acquisition of natural language. In: Proceedings of the IADIS International Conference on Intelligent Systems & Agents, pp. 58–66 (2014)

11. Nivel, E., Thórisson, K.R., Steunebrink, B., Schmidhuber, J.: Anytime bounded rationality. In: Bieger, J., Goertzel, B., Potapov, A. (eds.) AGI 2015. LNCS, vol. 9205, pp. 121–130. Springer, Heidelberg (2015)

12. Schmidhuber, J.: Gödel machines: fully self-referential optimal universal self-improvers. In: Goertzel, B., Pennachin, C. (eds.) Artificial General Intelligence. Cognitive Technologies, pp. 199–226. Springer, Heidelberg (2007)

13. Schmidhuber, J.: Developmental robotics, optimal artificial curiosity, creativity, music, and the fine arts. Connection Sci. **18**(2), 173–187 (2006)

14. Schmidhuber, J.: Formal theory of creativity, fun, and intrinsic motivation (1990–2010). IEEE Trans. Auton. Ment. Dev. **2**(3), 230–247 (2010)

15. Steunebrink, B.R., Schmidhuber, J.: A family of Gödel machine implementations. In: Schmidhuber, J., Thórisson, K.R., Looks, M. (eds.) AGI 2011. LNCS, vol. 6830, pp. 275–280. Springer, Heidelberg (2011)

16. Steunebrink, B.R., Koutník, J., Thórisson, K.R., Nivel, E., Schmidhuber, J.: Resource-bounded machines are motivated to be effective, efficient, and curious. In: Kühnberger, K.-U., Rudolph, S., Wang, P. (eds.) AGI 2013. LNCS, vol. 7999, pp. 119–129. Springer, Heidelberg (2013)

17. Szegedy, C., Zaremba, W., Sutskever, I., Bruna, J., Erhan, D., Goodfellow, I.J., Fergus, R.: Intriguing properties of neural networks (2013). http://arXiv.org/abs/1312.6199

18. Thórisson, K.R., Bieger, J., Thorarensen, T., Sigurdardottir, J.S., Steunebrink, B.R.: Why artificial intelligence needs a task theory - and what it might look like. In: Proceedings of AGI-2016 (2016)

19. Thórisson, K.R., Kremelberg, D., Steunebrink, B.R., Nivel, E.: About understanding. In: Proceedings of AGI-2016 (2016)

20. Thórisson, K.R., Nivel, E.: Achieving artificial general intelligence through peewee granularity. In: Proceedings of AGI-2009, pp. 222–223 (2009)

21. Yudkowsky, E., Herreshoff, M.: Tiling agents for self-modifying AI, and the Löbian obstacle (2013). https://intelligence.org/files/TilingAgentsDraft.pdf

Different Conceptions of Learning: Function Approximation vs. Self-Organization

Pei Wang[(✉)] and Xiang Li

Department of Computer and Information Sciences,
Temple University, Philadelphia, USA
{pei.wang,xiang.li003}@temple.edu

Abstract. This paper compares two understandings of "learning" in the context of AGI research: *algorithmic learning* that approximates an input/output function according to given instances, and *inferential learning* that organizes various aspects of the system according to experience. The former is how "learning" is often interpreted in the machine learning community, while the latter is exemplified by the AGI system NARS. This paper describes the learning mechanism of NARS, and contrasts it with canonical machine learning algorithms. It is concluded that inferential learning is arguably more fundamental for AGI systems.

1 Learning: Different Conceptions

Learning is always considered an important aspect of intelligence. *Machine learning* has grown into one of the most active fields in AI, and it gives computers the ability to work without being explicitly programmed with problem-specific skills. Learning algorithms have been used in many applications in various domains [4,14]. In recent years, deep learning techniques have dramatically improved the state-of-the-art in fields like vision, speech recognition, natural language processing, and game playing [6,19].

However, it does not mean that the existing machine learning techniques have satisfied the needs for learning in AGI systems. In cognitive science, "learning" is usually taken as having multiple forms, such as associative learning, skill learning, inductive learning, etc. [12]. Though machine learning study also covers supervised learning, unsupervised learning, reinforcement learning, etc., many of them can still be considered "algorithmic learning", consisting of two steps, each following an algorithm [4]:

1. the learning process follows an algorithm that takes the training data as input, and produces a model as output;
2. then, the model serves as an algorithm that carries out the domain task.

A comparison between an early (1984) collection on machine learning [7] and a recent (2012) textbook on the topic [4] shows clearly that algorithmic learning has become the dominate paradigm, while the other forms of learning have

B. Steunebrink et al. (Eds.): AGI 2016, LNAI 9782, pp. 140–149, 2016.
DOI: 10.1007/978-3-319-41649-6_14

largely faded out. Of course, as a highly diverse field, not all machine learning techniques fit this description, but it is still a widely adopted framework.

Algorithmic learning has its roots in the foundation of computer science, where a problem-solving process is normally specified as following a problem-specific algorithm. In conventional systems, the problem-specific algorithms are programed by human beings and followed by computers, so consequently a computer system serves as a function that maps any given problem instance into the corresponding solution. In algorithmic learning, the domain task is still taken to be a function to be carried out, except that this function is not specified in its general form by an algorithm, but exemplified by the training data, so "learning" becomes the problem of generalizing the training data to an approximate function. This process is taken to be a meta-problem (function approximation) to be solved by a meta-algorithm (the learning algorithm).

A typical way to realize algorithmic learning is with a feedforward neural networks [4,6]. It has been proved that such networks are universal function approximators. In such a system, the input and output data, as well as the intermediate results, are normally represented as vectors. Each instance corresponds to a point in a multidimensional space. The domain task is to produce an output vector according to the input vector, under the assumption that similar inputs will yield similar outputs. In other words, the function to be approximated (or learned) must be *smooth*.

The training instances are usually assumed to be randomly and independently selected from a sample space. The learning algorithm takes the training data as input, and produces a model that maps every instance in the sample space to output in a way that is mostly consistent with the training data. The model should be confirmed using certain testing data, also randomly selected from the sample space. After that the model is ready to be used as an algorithm for the domain problem, where the data come from the same sample space, too.

Advances in learning algorithms, an increase in available training data, and ever more powerful hardware have allowed algorithmic learning techniques, especially *deep neural networks* that have multiple intermediate layers, to produce surprisingly good results.

In spite of its successes, "function approximation" is not the only meaningful interpretation of "learning". Even if we ignore the relevant works in cognitive psychology and developmental psychology, and focus on machine learning only, there is still a tradition of *inferential learning*. This tradition came from the logical study of non-deductive inference (*induction*, *abduction*, and *analogy*), with the work of Michalski as the best-known example [8,9,21].

This approach represents a understanding of learning that is very different from algorithmic learning (as exemplified by feedforward neural networks), as shown in the following aspects:

Knowledge representation: The system's knowledge base is represented as a set of beliefs, which usually can be seen as a conceptual network or hierarchy.
Learning problem specification: Learning corresponds to the modification of the knowledge base, such as adding, deleting, and revising beliefs. In terms

of the conceptual network, learning means the modification of the topological structure, as well as the adjustment of the parameters of the network.

Learning process specification: The learning process follows a set of inference rules, each triggered under certain conditions and cause specific effects. Learning process is not necessarily separated from the other reasoning processes, and there may be no specific "learning algorithm".

Though this conception of learning appeared early in the history of machine learning, it has gradually lost favor in that community, and is even rarely mentioned in recent textbooks [4]. What we would like to do in this paper is to provide a more advanced model of inferential learning, and to argue for its advantages over algorithmic learning in the context of AGI projects. Some of the arguments have been presented in our previous publications [21–23], though here they are revised to take the recent progresses into account.

2   Learning in NARS

NARS is a reasoning system based on the theory that "intelligence" is the ability for a system to *adapt* given *insufficient knowledge and resources*. That is, the system must depend on *finite* resources to make *real-time* response while being *open* to unanticipated problems and events. In other words, an intelligent system must be able to *learn* from its experience in a problem domain. Consequently, the system's solutions are usually not absolutely optimal, but the best the system can find at the time, and the system could always do better if it had more knowledge and resources. The project has been described in detail in two books [23, 24] and many papers, which, and the source code of the current implementation, can be accessed at http://cis-linux1.temple.edu/~pwang/. In this paper, we only briefly introduce the learning mechanism of the system.

The domain knowledge of NARS is represented as a collection of *beliefs*. These summarize the system's experience in the form of a sentences according to a formal grammar. The grammar of NARS is distinct from most other reasoning systems where the representation is a first-order predicate calculus or variant thereof. The language of NARS is based in the term-logic tradition, where a sentence has a "subject-copula-predicate" format.

A typical statement in NARS has the form of "$S \rightarrow P \langle t \rangle$", where '$S$' is the subject term, '$P$' the predicate term, '$\rightarrow$' the "inheritance copula" indicating that the subject is a specialization of the predicate (or, equivalently, the predicate is a generalization of the subject), and 't' the truth-value of the belief, which is a pair of numbers "frequency-confidence" that measures the evidential support the belief gets from the system's experience. The frequency value is defined as w^+/w (the proportion of positive evidence among all current evidence), and the confidence value is defined as $w/(w + k)$ (the proportion of current evidence among all future evidence after a constant amount of evidence arrives). Detailed explanations of the NARS truth-value can be found in [23], while for the current discussion, it is enough to know that no belief is absolutely certain, and all truth-values can be revised by new evidence, though those with higher confidence will be more stable. This definition of truth-value is one implication of the assumption of insufficient knowledge and resources.

Using this language, the beliefs of the system can be naturally visualized as a weighted graph, with terms as vertices, statements as edges, and truth-values as weights. When implemented in a computer system, a "concept" is a data structure identified by a term and referring to all the statements with that term as a component (e.g., subject or predicate). The "content" or "meaning" of a concept consists of what the system knows about it at the moment. Since concepts are summaries of the system's experience, there will be new concepts introduced or generated from time to time, and the meaning of the existing concepts may also change. Therefore NARS has an "experience-grounded" semantics.

The assumption of insufficient resources has several implications. Due to storage restriction, some contents in a concept may be removed to release space for new contents, and even whole concepts may be deleted. This mechanism is responsible for "absolute forgetting", by which some information is permanently lost. Due to the demand of producing real-time responses to inference tasks, the beliefs within a concept have a priority distribution maintained dynamically among them, and so do the concepts in the memory. At any moment, the system allocates its processing time among its concepts according to their priority values. Within each concept, high-priority beliefs are accessed more often.

According to the changes in the environment, as well as the feedback after each inference step, the priority values of the relevant concepts and beliefs are adjusted, partly to reflect their relevance to the current situation and their usefulness in past problem-solving processes. This mechanism is responsible for "relative forgetting", by which some information gradually becomes less accessible. Though forgetting is often undesired, it is inevitable in a system that is always open to new information and must make real-time responses.

Though the above description only provides a highly simplified description of the memory of NARS, it still shows that the domain knowledge of NARS can be roughly divided into three kinds:

1. The terms and the concepts named by them,
2. The beliefs that relate the terms to each other, with their truth-values,
3. The priority values of the concepts and beliefs.

NARS has *complete* learning capability, in the sense that all of the three kinds of knowledge can be generated or modified by the system itself, given proper experience.

Experiences in NARS consists of a stream of input sentence, and each of them is a task to be processed. If an input task contains a novel term or statement that does not exist in the system at the moment, the corresponding new concept and statement will be generated and added into the memory. This is the simplest form of learning: learning by being told.

New concept and statements can also be generated by the system's inference rules. NARS is designed in the *term logic* framework, mainly because this framework naturally supports the unification of several types of inference. Here *deduction* takes the syllogistic form as in Aristotle's Syllogistic [1], then following the approach of Peirce [11], *abduction* and *induction* can be obtained from *deduction* by exchanging a premise and the conclusion.

	deduction	abduction	induction
first premise	$M \to P$	$P \to M$	$M \to P$
second premise	$S \to M$	$S \to M$	$M \to S$
conclusion	$S \to P$	$S \to P$	$S \to P$

Different from Aristotle and Peirce, we define these types of inference in a multi-valued logic, so there is a truth-value function attached to each rule to calculate the truth-value of the conclusion from those of the premises, and different rules have different functions. Among the above three, *deduction* may generate high-confidence conclusions, while the other two can only generate low-confidence conclusions, which are usually considered as hypotheses.

Beside the above *syllogistic rules* that generate new statements among given terms, NARS also has *compositional rules* that generate new terms to summarize given premises. The following are some examples.

	union	intersection	difference
first premise	$M \to P$	$M \to P$	$M \to P$
second premise	$M \to S$	$M \to S$	$M \to S$
conclusion	$M \to (S \cup P)$	$M \to (S \cap P)$	$M \to (S - P)$

These rules also have their truth-value functions. In these rules, the predicate terms of the conclusions are "compound terms" composed from the predicate terms of the premises, so as to provide a more efficient representation of the same information. There are also rules where the subject terms of the conclusions are compounds.

Beside the above compounds that are similar (though not identical) to set operations, compound terms also include Cartesian products (i.e., ordered sequences) of terms and statements themselves (so there can be statements of statements). Furthermore, compounds can be used recursively to form more complicated terms, as well as used in inference in the same way as the atomic (i.e., non-compound) terms. In this way, the system can learn the patterns that it noticed in experience, and then reason on them in the same way as atomic terms.

Here what the syllogistic rules and compositional rules do can be considered both as *reasoning* and as *learning*, from different perspective. Such a step is learning because the conclusion represents the experience provided by the premises in a different form, and the inference step modifies the memory in an enduring manner.

If an input or generated statement or term already exists in the memory, the new item will be merged with the existing item, which may lead to the change in the truth-value of the statement or the content of the concept identified by the term. These changes also let the system gradually learn from its experience.

Finally, the priority-value adjustments correspond to the learning of a type of domain knowledge, too, even though the results of this learning is embedded in the memory structure, rather than explicitly expressed by terms and statements. It is well known that in problem solving, it is often crucial to know which concepts and beliefs should be considered first among all alternatives, and this type of knowledge usually comes from the accumulated feedback of problem-solving practices.

Putting the above learning mechanisms together, NARS can start with an empty memory and learn all domain knowledge from its experience. Even though for practical considerations the system can also start with a preloaded memory, all contents in the memory can still be revised and adjusted by future experience. The primary function of learning in NARS is to organize its experience to meet the need of adaptation under the restriction of insufficient knowledge and resources. The only knowledge that cannot be learned is the meta-knowledge embedded in the system's grammar rules, inference rules, resources management policy, etc. Since all meta-knowledge is domain-independent, NARS can be put to learn and work in any domain.

3   Comparison and Discussion

Though the above descriptions about the two conceptions of learning are relatively simple, they nevertheless show enough differences. In the following they are compared, using NARS and the deep learning (DL) architecture described in [6] as examples. The evaluation will be based on in the requirements of AGI, rather than that of a specific domain problem.

In knowledge representation, the two approaches follow different traditions: NARS uses sentences in a formal language, while DL uses vectors in a feature space. In principle, the two are equivalent, in the sense that any knowledge base in one can be converted into the other. However, in practice there are several factors to be considered, such as naturalness, flexibility, and efficiency. Vector-based representation is natural for sensory input, but much less so for symbolic input. Though "word vectors" and "thought vectors" have been introduced, they are either inefficient (when the number of dimension is high) or hard to interpret (when the number of dimension is low). To explicitly represent conceptual structure is also difficult. On the other hand, NARS allows vectors to be used as a special type of compound term (called *product* in [23,24]), which, plus the other types of compound terms, make the representation of symbolic structure very easy and natural.

In DL, the vectors are connected in a layered network with a fixed topological structures, with links between layers corresponding to generalization. As explained above, the conceptual structure in NARS is dynamically generated and modified, and the conceptual relation *inheritance* also corresponds to generalization. NARS also has other copulas, including *similarity*, *implication*, and *equivalence*, so can directly represent various conceptual relations. Furthermore, NARS has no problem to introduce new terms at run time, while DL normally requires a constant vocabulary.

NARS is designed according to an experience-grounded semantics, which is intuitively located between the *localized* representation of symbolic approaches and the *distributed* representation of neural networks. In NARS, the meaning of a concept is defined by its relations with other concepts, not an "object" it refers to, and each relation is true to a degree. In this aspect, its knowledge representation is also "distributed" to an extent. However, all the relations in the network correspond to copulas that have well-defined meaning, rather than merely as associations that spread activations. For this reason, it is possible to carry out various types of inference, which can be justified as valid according to the semantic theory. The representation also has a "localized" aspect, as each individual concept and belief can be interpreted meaningfully by itself, rather than only has a holistic interpretation as in DL – in DL only the input and output vectors are meaningful outside the network, while the intermediate results represented by the hidden nodes are not always easy to understand.

In DL, the task of a learning system is usually taken to be the approximation of a function defined between the input and output of the whole system. This focus on end-to-end relation allows the system to be trained and evaluated as a blackbox, without the need to interpret the intermediate results. Though such a treatment is desired for systems designed for single tasks, it has difficulty in handling multiple types of tasks. The explorations in transfer learning [20], multitask learning [17], and multi-strategy learning [2] are pushing machine learning in this direction, though the progress so far is limited. On the contrary, NARS is not designed to answer any specific type of question. Instead, it can be asked any question expressible in its language. Consequently, any concept and belief in the system can be asked, so it can be learned by the system, and after that it can also be used to answer questions about other concepts and beliefs. In this way, the distinction of "input" and "output" terms/statements is relative and temporary, and there is no separately defined "task domains".

Besides being restricted to a single function exemplified by the training data, the blackbox nature of DL has other issues, such as the interpretation of its successes and mistakes. It has been found that learning algorithms can make mistakes that never happen to human beings [5,10]. One possible reason is because the intermediate levels of generalization are not directly verified, but only judged by their contributions to the ultimate output. Since after each generalization the feature space is transferred into another one, similar points in the former and those in the latter are not necessarily the same, as long as they are not sufficiently close to a training instance. On the contrary, in NARS every level of generalization is produced by inference rules and verified independently. Even though the system may make mistakes due to insufficient knowledge and resources, it will not make incomprehensible mistakes.

NARS allows multiple levels of generalization of the same experience. For example, the observation "Tweety flies" can be generalized by the belief "Tweety is a canary" to "Canaries fly", by the belief "Tweety is a bird" to "Birds fly", and by the belief "Tweety is a animal" to "Animals fly", all by the same *induction rule*. It is the other experience that will gradually differentiate these results: over-generalization ("Animals fly") will lose priority due to its low frequency (from more negative evidence), and under-generalization ("Canaries fly") will lose priority due to its low confidence (from less total evidence), compared to the proper generalization ("Birds fly"). Of course the system will not try all possible generalizations, but only those that get the system's attention in resource competition. This possibility of multiple-generalization suggests solutions to the over-fitting problem and the inductive biases problem, as the system can keep several generalizations for different needs, instead of choosing one at the beginning. Similarly, in concept learning the result is not necessarily a partition of the instances, but can allow multiple inheritance or overlapping concepts with graded membership. For example, Tweety can be learned to be a canary, a yellow thing, and a cartoon character, at the same time.

The learning mechanism in NARS covers several processes that adjust various aspects of the memory. So there is no single "learning algorithm" in the system, but multiple algorithms for different purposes. Furthermore, learning is unified with reasoning, and is carried out by a set of inference rules, each implemented by a lightweight algorithm that can be finished within a constant amount of time. Due to insufficient resources, NARS does not attempt to use all relevant beliefs on each problem, but only accesses the high-priority ones within the currently available time for the problem. Consequently, a system-level learning problem, such as to digest a piece of new knowledge or to acquire a complicated concept, is carried out by many inference steps linked together at the run time according to many ever-changing factors, so may not be accurately repeatable. This result also means that in NARS there is no problem-specific algorithm or stable input–output mapping, as the output depends on history and context.

In NARS, this "non-algorithmic" learning mechanism provides a unified solution to several issues that are being explored in machine learning study:

One-shot learning [3]: Inference rules like *induction* and *abduction* can use a single example to generate a *hypothesis*, i.e., a belief with low confidence value. More examples will increase the confidence value, though are not required for the generation of hypotheses.

Online learning [16]: As an open system, NARS does not require all training data to be available at the very beginning, but allows them to come from time to time. New evidence will lead to incremental revision of existing beliefs and concepts, rather than demanding a complete retraining.

Real-time learning [13]: Since each *type* of learning task in NARS does not follow a fixed algorithm, its processing has no determined time requirement. Instead, each task *instance* can have its only time requirement attached, and the system will process it accordingly, similar to an anytime algorithm.

Active learning [15]: NARS uses backward inference to generate derived questions, so has the ability to actively collect information to answer questions, rather than passively using whatever input the environment provides to it. Even the existing beliefs will be selectively used.

Life-long learning [18]: In NARS, learning is not a separate process, but a cognitive function carried out by almost all the processes in the system. As long as the system runs, multiple self-organizing activities will happen in various parts. In no time will a belief or concept be finally "learned" so that no further revision is possible.

In NARS, all these properties are natural features of the inferential learning processes, rather than additional attributes to be realized separately.

4   Conclusions

In machine learning study, "learning" is often formalized as a computational process following an algorithm, and the process produces an approximate function according to training cases, which then is used to solve a domain problem. Though this "algorithmic learning" surely cannot cover all types of machine learning techniques, it nevertheless is a representative paradigm.

Such an algorithm is designed to carry out a specific type of learning in isolation, while in an AGI system the learning function and the other cognitive functions need to be unified or closely integrated. Furthermore, learning in an AGI system needs to be carried out under the restriction of available knowledge and resources. For instance, very often the system does not have the amount of training instances demanded by most learning algorithms, and the system often needs to work in real time, without a dedicated training period.

In "inferential learning", as implemented in NARS, "learning" is unified with reasoning and other cognitive functions, carried out using finite processing capability in real time, and open to novel tasks. Here learning does not follow a specific algorithm, but serves multiple self-organizing roles in various ways to make the system's behaviors dependent on history and context.

Though algorithmic learning, especially deep neural network, has achieved great successes in various domains, in AGI research it still have many challenges. Compared to it, inferential learning may provide a better alternative as the main learning paradigm in AGI.

Acknowledgments. The authors thank the anonymous reviewers for their helpful comments and suggestions.

References

1. Smith, R.: Aristotle : Prior Analytics. Hackett Publishing Company, Indianapolis (1989)
2. Estlin, T.A.: Using multi-strategy learning to improve planning efficiency and quality. Ph.D. thesis, Department of Computer Sciences, The University of Texas at Austin, Austin, TX (1998)
3. Fei-Fei, L., Fergus, R., Perona, P.: One-shot learning of object categories. IEEE Trans. Pattern Anal. Mach. Intell. **28**, 594–611 (2006)
4. Flach, P.: Machine Learning: The Art and Science of Algorithms That Make Sense of Data. Cambridge University Press, New York (2012)
5. Goodfellow, I.J., Shlens, J., Szegedy, C.: Explaining and harnessing adversarial examples. In: International Conference on Learning Representations (2015)

6. LeCun, Y., Bengio, Y., Hinton, G.: Deep learning. Nature **521**, 436–444 (2015)
7. Michalski, R., Carbonell, J., Mitchell, T. (eds.): Machine Learning: An Artificial Intelligence Approach. Springer, Heidelberg (1984)
8. Michalski, R.S.: A theory and methodology of inductive learning. Artif. Intell. **20**, 111–116 (1983)
9. Michalski, R.S.: Inference theory of learning as a conceptual basis for multistrategy learning. Mach. Learn. **11**, 111–151 (1993)
10. Nguyen, A., Yosinski, J., Clune, J.: Deep neural networks are easily fooled: high confidence predictions for unrecognizable images. In: 2015 IEEE Conference on Computer Vision and Pattern Recognition (2015)
11. Peirce, C.S.: Collected Papers of Charles Sanders Peirce, vol. 2. Harvard University Press, Cambridge (1931)
12. Reisberg, D.: Learning. In: Wilson, R.A., Keil, F.C. (eds.) The MIT Encyclopedia of the Cognitive Sciences, pp. 460–461. MIT Press, Cambridge (1999)
13. Roshtkhari, M.J., Levine, M.D.: An on-line, real-time learning method for detecting anomalies in videos using spatio-temporal compositions. Comput. Vis. Image Underst. **117**(10), 1436–1452 (2013)
14. Russell, S., Norvig, P.: Artificial Intelligence: A Modern Approach, 3rd edn. Prentice Hall, Upper Saddle River (2010)
15. Settles, B.: Active learning literature survey. Computer Sciences Technical Report 1648, University of Wisconsin-Madison (2010)
16. Shalev-Shwartz, S.: Online learning and online convex optimization. Found. Trends Mach. Learn. **4**(2), 107–194 (2011)
17. Silver, D.: Selective functional transfer: inductive bias from related tasks. In: IASTED International Conference on Artificial Intelligence and Soft Computing, pp. 182–189. ACTA Press (2001)
18. Silver, D., Yang, Q., Li, L.: Lifelong machine learning systems: beyond learning algorithms. In: Technical Report of AAAI Spring Symposium Series (2013)
19. Silver, D., Huang, A., Maddison, C.J., Guez, A., Sifre, L., van den Driessche, G., Schrittwieser, J., Antonoglou, I., Panneershelvam, V., Lanctot, M., Dieleman, S., Grewe, D., Nham, J., Kalchbrenner, N., Sutskever, I., Lillicrap, T., Leach, M., Kavukcuoglu, K., Graepel, T., Hassabis, D.: Mastering the game of Go with deep neural networks and tree search. Nature **529**, 484–489 (2016)
20. Taylor, M.E., Kuhlmann, G., Stone, P.: Transfer learning and intelligence: an argument and approach. In: Proceedings of the First Conference on Artificial General Intelligence (2008)
21. Wang, P.: The logic of learning. In: Working Notes of the AAAI workshop on New Research Problems for Machine Learning, pp. 37–40. Austin, Texas (2000)
22. Wang, P.: Artificial general intelligence and classical neural network. In: Proceedings of the IEEE International Conference on Granular Computing. Atlanta, Georgia (2006)
23. Wang, P.: Rigid Flexibility: The Logic of Intelligence. Springer, Dordrecht (2006)
24. Wang, P.: Non-Axiomatic Logic: A Model of Intelligent Reasoning. World Scientific, Singapore (2013)

The Emotional Mechanisms in NARS

Pei Wang[1]([⊠]), Max Talanov[2], and Patrick Hammer[3]

[1] Department of Computer and Information Sciences,
Temple University, Philadelphia, USA
`pei.wang@temple.edu`
[2] Higher Institute of Information Technologies,
Kazan Federal University, Kazan, Russia
`dr.max@machine-cognition.org`
[3] Institute for Software Technology, Graz University of Technology, Graz, Austria
`patrickhammer9@hotmail.com`

Abstract. This paper explains the conceptual design and experimental implementation of the components of NARS that are directly related to emotion. It is argued that emotion is necessary for an AGI system that has to work with insufficient knowledge and resources. This design is also compared to the other approaches in AGI research, as well as to the relevant aspects in the human brain.

1 Intelligence and Emotion

In biological systems, emotion is closely associated with drives like survival and reproduction, according to which decisions are made. On the contrary, a computer system has no biological drive, and the primary driving force are the tasks assigned to the system by the designer or the user. Consequently, mainstream AI study has ignored emotion, and this attitude is also justified by the traditional belief that emotion is basically a distraction in decision making, so should be avoided by a rational thinker.

In recent decades, the functions of emotion in cognition and thinking have been established by many works in cognitive science, and its necessity in computer systems has also been argued by researchers including Picard [6], Arbib [1] and Minsky [5]. More and more AGI models include emotion as a fundamental mechanism, as exemplified by the recent works [2,7,8,10].

In this paper, the emotional mechanism in NARS, an AGI project, is briefly introduced and compared with those in the other AGI models, as well as the emotional mechanism in the human brain.

NARS (Non-Axiomatic Reasoning System) is a general-purpose AI designed in the framework of a reasoning system. Its conceptual cornerstone is the belief that intelligence is a form of adaptation and must obey the Assumption of Insufficient Knowledge and Resources (AIKR), meaning the system must manage its finite processing capability, open to novel tasks, respond to them in real time, and learn from its experience.

This belief implies that the system must be able to assess various objects in its external and internal environments with respect to its tasks, and treat them

© Springer International Publishing Switzerland 2016
B. Steunebrink et al. (Eds.): AGI 2016, LNAI 9782, pp. 150–159, 2016.
DOI: 10.1007/978-3-319-41649-6_15

accordingly, so as to approach its overall objective. Such a need will require a mechanism that is similar to what we call "emotion" in human cognition, even though the objective of NARS is not to simulate the human brain in all details.

2   Desirability of Events

As a reasoning system, the overall objective of NARS is to successfully carry out its *tasks*, including absorbing new knowledge, answering questions, and achieving goals. For the current purpose, the last will be the focus of the discussion.

As defined in [16], a *goal* in NARS is an event (i.e., a statement with a time-dependent truth-value) to be realized by the system, that is, to have event E as a goal means the system has committed to do something to make E happen. For example, achieving the goal "Open Door #3" is represented within the system as a process to make event "Door #3 is open" true. But since in NARS "true" is a matter of degree, it actually means to make the truth-value of the statement as true as possible.

As an AGI, normally there are many goals in NARS at the same moment demanding to be realized. The system is "real-time" in the sense that these goals have time-requirements attached, with various levels of urgency. Since the system only has finite processing capability, the competition of resources among goals become inevitable. The goals can also contradict with each other in content. For example, one of them may want event "Door #3 is open" to be true, while another goal wants it to be false. As an open system, NARS does not require the consistency of the goals assigned to it by its designers and users, and does not guarantee the consistency of the derived goals.

Therefore, the system has to constantly manage conflicting or competing goals. To indicate the system's preference, each event has a *desire-value* associated, which is defined as the truth-value of the implication statement stating that the realization of the event will lead to a (unspecified) desired state. In this way, the desire-value of an event is defined as the truth-value of a statement, and therefore can be handled accordingly [16].

The desire-values of input goals are determined by the designers and users of the system, and these goals could be implanted in the system's memory or entered via the user interface. The derivation and revision of goals are carried out by NAL inference rules, which also calculate desire-values for derived goals. Derived goals are basically handled in the same way as input goals [15,16].

Each time a new goal enters (either input or derived), the desire-value of the corresponding event is adjusted by the revision rule that merges the contribution of the new goal with the previous value. For example, if one goal requires "Door #3 is open" to be true while another one does the opposite, these desires are balanced against each other: the resulting desire-value of the event reflects the summary of the desires, and therefore resolves conflicting goals.

If the goal corresponds to an operation (an event the system can trigger whenever it decides to), the desire-value of the event in respect to the current moment is determined. If this desire-value exceeds the decision-threshold system parameter, the operation is executed when the goal gets selected. An operation can consist of simpler operations to be executed in a sequence or in parallel.

Additionally (also for not executable goals), the system does a "reality check" to see to what extent the desired goal is already fulfilled. Then the difference between desire and reality is used to adjust the *priority value* of the goal in resource competition.

The *satisfaction* value of each event is defined to be the compliment of the difference between its desire-value and its truth-value, where 1 means the system has got what it desires, and 0 the opposite.[1] If the event is an operation, the satisfaction value is obtained from the feedback of an execution, which indicates whether the execution was successful, as far as the system can tell. In this way, the satisfaction value of an event measures the system's appraisal of the current situation on the event.

3   Feelings of the System

As a reasoning system, NARS works by repeating an inference cycle, in each of them a step of inference is carried out. In such a step, an inference task is processed by interacting with a belief of the system, and the result may be a partial solution to the task, as well as new tasks. If the task is a goal, then the result can lead to the adjustment of the satisfaction of the corresponding event. If the goal is "Open Door #3" and now the door is actually opened, the system is satisfied on this matter; if the door is still not open after the system's effort, it is unsatisfied on this matter.

The system's appraisal of the current and recent situations in general is obtained by summarizing its satisfaction values on the recently noticed events into an overall (system-level) satisfaction value S. After each cycle, the satisfaction value S is updated to $rs + (1 - r)S$, where s is the satisfaction value of the task processed in the cycle, and r is a system parameter identifying the relative weight of the two factors. In general, r is between 0 and 1, and the larger it is, the larger is role played by the current satisfaction in the overall satisfaction. We let r be a constant, though it may also depend on other factors, such as the priority of the task just processed.

The current satisfaction value could enter the system's experience via a "mental operator" *feel*. A mental operation can be executed by NARS on its memory to carry out self-monitoring and self-control functions [16]. In this case, the operation *feel*(SATISFIED) generates an event reporting the current satisfaction value of the system. This operation could be explicitly invoked as a goal, or automatically triggered when the satisfaction is beyond the neutral zone (around 0.5, defined by a system parameter). Here the term SATISFIED indicates the target

---

[1] To simplify the discussion, in the above description a truth-value (and desire-value) is used as if it is a single number. In NARS, it is actually a "frequency-confidence" pair, and the previous comparison is done on an "expectation" function of the truth-value, which combines the two factor into a single value. For details, see [16].

of the feeling operator, which can also be invoked for other internal sensations, such as:

Alertness - summarizes the average difference between recently processed input and the corresponding anticipations, so as to roughly indicate the extent to which the current environment is familiar.

Busyness - summarizes the average priority values of the recently processed tasks.

Well-being - summarizes the overall measure of energy supply, I/O channel connection, device functioning, etc.

Whether the above feelings are also considered as "emotions" depends on whether the notion is used in a broad sense or a narrow sense, but no matter what they are called, they add "mental events" into the system's experience, which happen in its own "mind", and are directly perceived at an abstract level by the system.

4   Emotion in Concepts

A *concept* in NARS is a data structure that can be addressed by an internal ID called a "term", and contains the tasks and beliefs on the term. Consequently a goal is linked by all the concepts mentioned in the goal. For example, the goal "Open Door #3" is linked from the concepts for the terms *open*, *door*, and #3, respectively, as well as from the compound term for the event "Door #3 is open".

Concepts provide an intermediate level between the whole memory and the individual tasks (including goals) and beliefs. Because NARS uses a term logic, every inference step requires the premises (the task and the belief) to share a term, and consequently the inference can be considered as happening in the concept named by the shared term. This nature allows a concept to be a unit of processing in a distributed implementation of NARS.

According to the experience-grounded semantics of NARS, the meaning of a concept is determined by its contents, that is, the tasks and beliefs that show the relations of this concept with other concepts according to the experience of the system. Due to insufficient resources, tasks have priority values attached to indicate how often they will be accessed. When a concept is "fired", i.e., selected for processing, usually only part of its contents are involved.

Each concept also has a desire-value. As described above, if a concept is named by a term that is an event like "Door #3 is open", its desire-value comes from the related goals about this event. Now desire-value is also given to other terms, those that do not name events, such as *open* and *door*, even #3. Initially, these non-event terms have a neutral desire-value, so they are neither desired nor undesired. However, they may gradually become non-neutral by association with the system-level satisfaction value. The process is roughly like this: at the end of each inference cycle, the desire-value of the "fired concept" (i.e., within which the inference happen) is adjusted according to the current satisfaction value.

Roughly speaking, the concept is desirable if it associates with the satisfaction of the system.

Here we want to explore whether such a desire-value can explain emotions related to concepts which by its structure can not contain statements, as we think that it might be shown by the human mind. We also want to explore the effect of this type of emotion in self-control.

To bring this appraisal into the internal experience of the system, the feeling operator can be invoked with a term as argument, such as $feel(door)$, to generate an event indicating how much the system "likes" (or "dislikes") the term *door*. This operator can also be triggered by an extreme (high or low) desire-value in the concept.

Beside this "emotional indicator" in every concept, there are also special concepts whose meaning is especially emotional. The basic concepts in this group include feeling constants like LIKE and SATISFIED. These concepts provide the building blocks for the system's feelings and emotions.

Starting from the basic feelings, more complicated feelings can be built by combining them with the other concepts. For example, an event with the same desire-value may become different feelings when combined with other features, such as "it has happened" vs. "it will happen", "it is caused by the system itself" vs. "it is caused by someone else", "it is manageable" vs. "it is inevitable", etc. The new feelings are formed using the same composing rules as other compound terms, and their generation is experience-driven. For example, what *"happy"* means will be mostly learned, though still related to SATISFIED. These compound feelings may or may not correspond to human feelings.

5   Effects of Emotion

As described above, in NARS emotional information appears in two distinct forms:

- at "subconscious level" (outside experience), as desire-values and satisfaction values,
- at "conscious level" (inside experience), as events with emotional concepts.

Emotions in both forms contribute to the system's behaviors.

The emotional concepts in experience are processed as other concepts in inference. An important usage of them is to categorize situations from the system's viewpoint, as well as to develop strategies to deal with such situations. For instance, there may be many very different situations that can be categorized as "dangerous", so as to be handled with some common responses, such as "be careful". Without emotion, such categorizations may still be possible, though emotion provides a more natural and efficient approach.

The "emotion-specific" treatments mainly happen at the subconscious level, where the emotional information is used in various processes, such as

- The desire-values of concept is taken into account in attention allocation, where concepts with strong feeling (extreme desire-values) get more resources than those with weak feeling (neutral desire-values).
- After an inference step, if a goal is relatively satisfied, its priority is decreased accordingly, and the belief used in the step gets a higher priority, because of its usefulness.
- In the decision-making rule, the threshold for a decision is lower in high emotional situations, so as to allow quick responses.
- The overall satisfaction is used as feedback to adjust the desire-values of data items (concepts, tasks, beliefs), so that the ones associated with positive feeling are rewarded, and the ones associated with negative feeling punished. In this way, the system shows a "pleasure seeking" tendency, and its extent can be adjusted by a system parameter.
- When the system is "busy", tasks with low resource budget are simply ignored. The busyness value can be used in the priority–probability mapping to control the "degree of focus" of the system's attention.
- When the system is "alert", it spends more time to process new tasks in the input buffer, which means less time for the existing tasks in memory.
- When the system "does not feel well", it spends more time in the related self-maintenance tasks, which means less time for other tasks.

The above mechanisms have been mostly implemented, and are under testing and tuning, so at the moment have not produced profound results to be evaluated.

In the future, when NARS also needs to manage its own energy usage (such as in robots), emotion will play an important role in the decision of energy consumption. For example, in situations associated with high emotions, the system may spend more energy than in normal situations.

Another future usage of emotion is in communication with other systems, where emotion will play roles similar to those in human communications.

6   Comparison to Other Approaches

The current approaches to introducing emotion into computer systems actually have different objectives [1,6]. The works in the field of *affective computing* mainly aim at the recognition and simulation of human emotions in human-computer interaction, while the works in AI/AGI mainly aim at giving computer their own emotions. For our purpose, the emotions in the computer system do not need to be similar to human emotion in details, but should serve the same cognitive functions.

The cognitive functions of emotion are usually divided into two major types, which can be called "internal and external" [1] or "intrapersonal and interpersonal" [10]. Either way, the former is in self-control according to experience, and the latter is in communication with other systems. On this topic, our position is to take the former as primary and basic, the latter as secondary and derivative. For this reason, the current work in NARS focuses on the control function of emotion, which is the appraisal of situation from the system's viewpoint, and the corresponding adjustments in behavior and resource allocation [1].

Traditional AI ignores emotion, since there is little need to choose among goals, which are assumed to be consistent, and within the system's capability. Since NARS is designed under AIKR, the traditional assumption is no longer valid, and the system does need to handle conflicting and competing tasks, as well as to make quick and flexible responses to the environment in real time.

Though other AGI projects include emotional mechanisms for similar reasons, the concrete designs are all different. Here we only briefly compare NARS with MicroPsi [2] and Sigma [7].

MicroPsi grows out of a psychological theory, and therefore is closer to the reality of the human mind than NARS, which is identified with the human mind at a more abstract level. This difference shows in the motivational systems of them: MicroPsi has a motivational system with a set of built-in *drives*, and *goals* are situations where some need is satisfied. The basic drives meet physiological needs, social needs, and cognitive needs. On the contrary, NARS is a reasoning system, where a goal is an event to be realized, and in principle the system can be given any goal, as far as it can be expressed in the representation language of the system. For specific application, it is possible to implant certain "innate" goals or drives, though the design of the system does not assume any of them. Many "cognitive needs" of MicroPsi, such as those for *certainty*, *competence*, and *aesthetics*, are also pursued in NARS, but they are not explicitly expressed as goals, but implicitly embedded in the system's processing procedures and policies, so they can be referred to as "meta-goals" or "subconscious goals". Even with these differences, there are still similarities in these two systems, such as to pursue multiple goals at the same time, while giving them different relative priority.

The emotion mechanisms of both NARS and Sigma start at appraisal, where different situations have different levels of desirability. However, Sigma defines desirability by comparing a *state* with a goal state, while NARS does so on a *statements*, a partial description of states, as well as on a concept. Under AIKR, in NARS it cannot be assumed that the system can fully describe a state, either of the environment or of itself. Another difference is that the word "emotion" is used in a broader sense in Sigma than in NARS. For instance, the attention mechanism of NARS [16] is not considered as part of the emotional mechanism, as the latter is based on the appraisal of desirability and satisfaction only, though it is indeed closely related to the former.

In summary, in these AGI systems emotion plays similar roles. NARS differs from the other systems mainly because of its reasoning system framework and AIKR. Since all these systems are still far from fully developed, it is too early to tell which treatment of emotion works better.

7   Comparison to Human Emotions

The approach to emotions in NARS is biologically inspired and based on the functional similarity with mammalian basic emotions. We have inherited the

neurobiological plausible approach from our previous works [9,14], where valida-
tion and justification of the approach are provided. We are building the analogy
between the influence of mammalian basic emotions or "affects" [11–13] on thinking and the influence of machine emotions on reasoning and decision-making
processes of NARS. We reference the neurobiological nature of the emotions
and identify the dopamine as main actor in the role of "wanting" or desire-
values of NARS, described in the Sect. 2. Lövheim [4] emphasized the role of
the dopamine in reward, reinforcement, and motivation. Arbib and Fellous [1]
also indicated that dopamine key role in memory "linking emotion, cognition
and consciousness". Serotonin "plays a crucial role in the modulation of aggres-
sion and in agonistic social interactions in many animals. ... serotonin has come
to play a much broader role in cognitive and emotional regulation, particularly
control of negative mood or affect" [1,3], also it is main actor in self confidence,
inner strength, and satisfaction [4]. This could be understood as neuromodulatory basis of the satisfaction value in the NARS system, described in the Sect. 3.
Drawing the analogy between the noradrenaline influence on a brain and busyness of a system we could provide a set of emotional operations that build the
basement for the machine affective states.

A modified "cube of emotions" is in Fig. 1, where the influence of vir-
tual/machine neuromodulators on computational processes is added into a presentation of normal concentrations of neuromodulators.

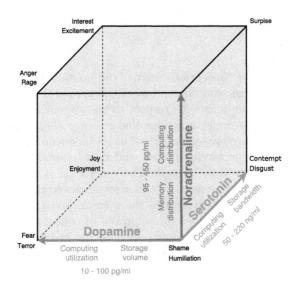

Fig. 1. The mapping of emotional states with neuromodulators levels and computational system parameters, based on [4].

Computing utilization is a metric able to quantify how busy the processing resources of the system are. It can be expressed by the average value of all the single processing resources' utilization.

Computing distribution aims at quantifying the load balancing among processing resources. It can be expressed as the variance of single resources' utilization.

Memory distribution is associated with the amount of memory allocated to the processing resources. It can be quantified by the variance of the amount of memory per single resource.

Storage volume is an index related to the the amount of data and information used by the system.

Storage bandwidth quantifies the number of connections between resources, i.e. processing and data nodes.

Conceptually this work may lead to the integration between the neurobiologically plausible realistic neural networks (rNN) emotional simulations to computational lightweight reasoning systems applicable to real-time autonomous robotics. For example, a robotics system can enter experience into the system during a "day" phase, then this could be "played" into the rNN, similar to the dream playback in mammals. During the "night" phase, rNN could apply the realistic emotional processing. The results could be mapped through the levels of machine neuromodulators in NARS: serotonin, noradrenaline, dopamine, triggering the emotion-driven behavior.

8   Conclusions

This paper introduces the conceptual design of the emotion mechanism of NARS. We consider the main function of emotion as the appraisal of the external and internal entities and situations with respect to the system's tasks, so as to act accordingly, especially in decision making and resource allocation.

In NARS emotions are implemented not as an independent process or module, but are embedded in various places, and tightly entangled with the reasoning/learning processes in the system. The generation of emotion and feeling starts as desires for certain events, and the assessments to their satisfaction are summaries to the overall satisfaction of the system, and the association with this overall satisfaction determines the appraisal of concepts. Emotional information is taken into account in various places in the system, both consciously (i.e., expressed in the system's experience) and subconsciously (i.e., embedded in the system's built-in mechanisms).

The emotion of an AGI system will not be the same as human emotions, but since they play similar roles, some correspondence can be found between these two types of intelligence, mostly at psychological level, but may even at the neurobiological level to a certain extent. Though emotion may cause undesired consequences in decision making, it only means that the system must have mechanisms to regulate emotion, but not that high intelligence does not need emotion.

The emotional mechanism described in this paper has been mostly implemented in the current version of Open-NARS, an open source project.[2] The system is still under testing and tuning, so to show the function of emotion in the processing of complicated problems is still a future work.

Acknowledgments. Part of the work was performed according to the Russian Government Program of Competitive Growth of Kazan Federal University.

References

1. Arbib, M., Fellous, J.M.: Emotions: from brain to robot. Trends Cogn. Sci. **8**(12), 554–559 (2004)
2. Bach, J.: Modeling motivation and the emergence of affect in a cognitive agent. In: Wang, P., Goertzel, B. (eds.) Theoretical Foundations of Artificial General Intelligence, pp. 241–262. Atlantis Press, Paris (2012)
3. Fellous, J.M.: The neuromodulatory basis of emotion. Neuro-Sci. **5**, 283–294 (1999)
4. Lövheim, H.: A new three-dimensional model for emotions and monoamine neuro-transmitters. Med. Hypotheses **78**, 341–348 (2012)
5. Minsky, M.: The Emotion Machine: Commonsense Thinking, Artificial Intelligence, and the Future of the Human Mind. Simon & Schuster, New York (2006)
6. Picard, R.W.: Affective Computing. MIT Press, Cambridge (1997)
7. Rosenbloom, P.S., Gratch, J., Ustun, V.: Towards emotion in sigma: from appraisal to attention. In: Bieger, J., Goertzel, B., Potapov, A. (eds.) AGI 2015. LNCS, vol. 9205, pp. 142–151. Springer, Heidelberg (2015)
8. Strannegård, C., Cirillo, S., Wessberg, J.: Emotional concept development. In: Bieger, J., Goertzel, B., Potapov, A. (eds.) AGI 2015. LNCS, vol. 9205, pp. 362–372. Springer, Heidelberg (2015)
9. Talanov, M., Vallverdu, J., Distefano, S., Mazzara, M., Delhibabu, R.: Neuromodulating cognitive architecture: towards biomimetic emotional AI. In: 2015 IEEE 29th International Conference on Advanced Information Networking and Applications. pp. 587–592. IEEE (2015)
10. Thill, S., Lowe, R.: On the functional contributions of emotion mechanisms to (artificial) cognition and intelligence. In: Bach, J., Goertzel, B., Iklé, M. (eds.) AGI 2012. LNCS, vol. 7716, pp. 322–331. Springer, Heidelberg (2012)
11. Tomkins, S.: Affect Imagery Consciousness, Volume I: The Positive Affects. Springer Publishing Company, New York (1962)
12. Tomkins, S.: Affect Imagery Consciousness, Volume II: The Negative Affects. Springer Publishing Company, New York (1963)
13. Tomkins, S.: Affect Imagery Consciousness, Volume III: The Negative Affects: Anger and Fear. Springer Publishing Company, New York (1991)
14. Vallverdú, J., Talanov, M., Distefano, S., Mazzara, M., Tchitchigin, A., Nurgaliev, I.: A cognitive architecture for the implementation of emotions in computing systems. Biologically Inspired Cogn. Architectures **15**, 34–40 (2015)
15. Wang, P.: Motivation management in AGI systems. In: Bach, J., Goertzel, B., Iklé, M. (eds.) AGI 2012. LNCS, vol. 7716, pp. 352–361. Springer, Heidelberg (2012)
16. Wang, P.: Non-Axiomatic Logic: A Model of Intelligent Reasoning. World Scientific, Singapore (2013)

---

[2] https://github.com/opennars/opennars/wiki.

The OpenNARS Implementation
of the Non-Axiomatic Reasoning System

Patrick Hammer[1]([✉]), Tony Lofthouse[2], and Pei Wang[3]

[1] Institute for Software Technology,
Graz University of Technology, Inffeldgasse 16b/II, Graz, Austria
`patrickhammer9@hotmail.com`
[2] Evolving Solutions Ltd., Newbury, UK
`Tony.Lofthouse@GMILab.com`
[3] Department of Computer and Information Sciences,
Temple University, Philadelphia, PA 19122, USA
`pei.wang@temple.edu`

Abstract. This paper describes the implementation of a Non-Axiomatic Reasoning System (NARS), a unified AGI system which works under the assumption of insufficient knowledge and resources (AIKR). The system's architecture, memory structure, inference engine, and control mechanism are described in detail.

1 Introduction

NARS is an adaptive system that works under the Assumption of Insufficient Knowledge and Resources (AIKR) [6,8], meaning the system has to work under the restrictions of being: *Finite:* the information processing capability of the system's hardware is fixed, *Real-time:* all tasks have time constraints attached to them and *Open:* no constraint is put on the content of the experience that the system may have, as long as it's expressible in the interface language [8].

Built in the framework of a reasoning system, NARS has a memory, a logic component and a control component. The logic component consists of inference rules that work on statements, where the statements are goals, questions and beliefs. A statement can be eternal (non time-dependent) or an event (time-dependent). Beliefs are statements that the system believes to be true to a certain degree and goals are statements the system desires to be true to a certain extent. An inference task is a statement to be processed, with additional control relevant information.

NARS utilises the Non-Axiomatic Logic (NAL) [9] for inference and the Narsese language for representing statements. The language and the logic are outside the scope of this document. The aim of this paper is to describe the current implementation of NARS in detail. The following aspects of the implementation are focused on: memory management with concept centric processing, non-deterministic selection capabilities allowing anytime-processing of tasks, resource constraint management, a logic system with meta rule DSL and Trie based execution engine, temporal inference control (including temporal windows, temporal

B. Steunebrink et al. (Eds.): AGI 2016, LNAI 9782, pp. 160–170, 2016.
DOI: 10.1007/978-3-319-41649-6_16

chaining, and interval handling), projection and eternalization, anticipation, and attentional control via a budget based approach.

2   Memory

This section describes the architecture of the memory module, how NAL grammar statements form a 'Belief Network' and the interdependence of the budget. The memory module supports three primary operations: firstly, to return the best ranked belief or goal for inference within concepts (local inference), secondly, to provide a pair of contextually relevant and semantically related statements for inference between concepts (general inference), and finally, to add statements to memory whilst maintaining the space constraints on the system.

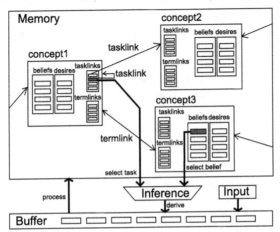

The working process of NARS can be considered as unbounded repetitions of an inference cycle that consists of the following sequence of steps [9]:

1. get a concept from memory
2. get a task and belief related to the selected concept
3. derive new tasks from the selected task and belief and put them into buffer
4. put the involved items back into the corresponding bags
5. put the new tasks into the corresponding bags after processing from buffer

NARS utilises elements of metadata (Budget and Stamp) that serve several purposes: they prevent certain forms of invalid inference such as double counting evidence and cyclic reasoning, abstract temporal requirements away from the Narsese grammar, and provide certain implementation efficiencies.

Budget, considered as metadata for the purpose of this paper, determines the allocation of system resources (time and space) and is defined as $(p, d, q) \in [0, 1] \times (0, 1) \times [0, 1]$.

Also, each statement in NARS has a Stamp defined as $(id, t_{cr}, t_{oc}, C, E) \in \mathbb{N} \times \mathbb{N} \times \mathbb{N} \times \mathcal{P}(\mathbb{N})$ where id represents a unique ID, t_{cr} a creation time (in inference

cycles), t_{oc} an occurrence time (in inference cycles), C a syntactic complexity (the number of subterms in the associated term) and E an evidential set.
Curve Bag is a data structure that supports a probabilistic selection according to the item priority distribution. The priority value p of the items in the bag maps to their access frequency by a predefined monotonically increasing function. This data structure is called "Curve Bag" since it allows us to define a custom curve which is highly flexible and allows emotional parameters and introspective operators to have influence on this selection. The remaining factors of Budget, the d durability and q quality parameter, get their meaning from the forgetting function: Whenever an item is selected from the bag, its priority will be decreased according to d and q, namely with $q_r = q * r$, $d_p = p - q_r$ (r being a system parameter) the new priority is then: $p' = q_r + p * d^{\frac{1}{H * p}}$ if $d_p > 0$, otherwise $p' = q_r$, where H is a forgetting rate system parameter. This ensures that forgetting does not cause priority to decrease below quality, after re-scaling by r.

The memory consists of a Curve Bag of Concepts, where Concepts are containers for: Tasklink and Termlink Curve Bags, along with belief and goal tables. The belief and goal tables are ranked tables (Sect. 8, sub-section Ranking). A concept, named by a term, combines the beliefs and goals with this term in it, and is connected to other concepts which share a common sub-term or super-term via Termlinks.

3   Logic Module

The logic module is an instantiation of the Non-Axiomatic Logic (NAL). It is composed of two components: an inference rule domain specific language (Meta Rule DSL) and an inference rule execution unit. The meta rule DSL should not be confused with the NAL grammar rules, these are separate and distinct. The system currently implements 200+ inference rules, containing forward and backward rules for reasoning under uncertainty.

Meta Rule DSL. The meta Rule DSL was developed to serve three main purposes: to provide a flexible methodology to quickly experiment with alternate inference rules, to support the goal of creating a literate program, and to substantially improve the quality of the software implementation.

Inference rules take the following form:

$$T, B, P_1, ..., P_k \vdash (C_1, ..., C_n)$$

where T represents the first premise (precondition, corresponding to the task to be processed), B represents the second premise (precondition, corresponding to the belief retrieved for the task), and $P_1, ..., P_k$ are additional preconditions which represent logical predicates dependent on T, B, $C1, ..., C_n$. Each "conclusion" (or postcondition) C_i of $C_1, .., C_n$ has the form (D_i, M_i) where D_i represents the term of the derived task the conclusion C_i defines, and M_i provides additional meta-information, such as which truth function will be used to decide the truth or desire of the conclusion, how the temporal information will be processed, or whether backwards inference is allowed. The DSL incorporates the Narsese grammar to retain consistency of syntax and conciseness of representation.

Inference Rule Execution. The role of the inference Rule Execution unit is twofold: firstly, to parse the Meta Rule DSL into an efficient and executable representation, and secondly, to select and execute the relevant inference rules. An optimised Trie is used to store the rule representation, whilst a Trie Deriver is used to select and 'execute' the relevant inference rules.

Trie Representation - In the Meta Rule DSL, each inference rule has a set of preconditions. These preconditions are stored as nodes in the Trie, where common preconditions form a common node (as with the Rete algorithm [3]). This leads to a natural structuring of the conditions where non-leaf nodes store the preconditions and leaf nodes form sets of post conditions that represent valid derivations for a pair of input statements.

Trie Deriver - The deriver is responsible for inference: it matches from memory selected premise pairs to the relevant inference rules such that conclusions can be obtained. The matching of rules to statements is simply a matter of traversing the Trie, keyed on the matching preconditions. If the traversal ends at a leaf node then this is a valid matching inference rule(s), leaf nodes can contain more then one inference rule. Each traversal, if valid, returns a list of postconditions/conclusions of the matched rules.

Since the complexity of statements is bounded due to AIKR, and the depth of this trie is bounded by the finiteness of the inference rules, applying the Trie Deriver to a pair of statements is upper bounded in execution time by a constant. This is an important consideration as NARS needs to respond to tasks in real-time, whereby, no single inference step can exceed a roughly constant time.

4   Temporal Inference Control

An adaptive agent existing in a real-time environment needs to be capable of reasoning about time. To support reasoning with time the non-temporal NAL inference rules are extended by adding temporal variants. Temporal inference is distinguished by several features: utilisation of a Temporal Window, Temporal Chaining, and Interval Handling, along with Projection, Eternalization and Anticipation, discussed in the following sections.

Temporal Window - As argued in [2], human beings have the ability to synchronize multiple stimulus events, when they are experienced within a Temporal Window of roughly 80 ms, as if they were experienced concurrently. These so called subjective events behave like a point in time as well as an interval in time [7]. A similar approach is used in NARS where a $DURATION$ parameter defines the temporal window of synchronization, whereby, events occurring within the Temporal Window will be deemed to have occurred concurrently.

Temporal Chaining - Due to the AIKR, NARS does not allow arbitrary temporal relations to be formed, in fact the inference execution unit will only allow semantically related statements (those which correspond to concepts which are connected with each other via termlinks) to be used in derivations. This leads to the question of, how do we temporally relate semantically unrelated events?

The approach taken in NARS is to perform inference between each incoming event with the previous incoming event in order to create compound events which link the (previously semantically unrelated) events together. Although perception can form more complex temporal compound events than this, the same principle applies.

These compound events can then be used by the inference system with other semantically related statements to form further derivations. In this way, complex chains of temporal reasoning can be formed as also demanded for perception.

Interval Handling - When an event a (for example, "wheel starts turning") enters the system, its occurrence time is recorded, but its duration is not known at this time. Even without a duration, the event a can still be related to previous events as the occurrence time is available.

If eventually an event b (for example, "wheel stops turning") enters the system, the system can derive an event (a, I, b) which has a custom duration and encodes "the wheel was turning from this time to this time", which behaves essentially as an interval in interval algebra as a special case. However this interval number I raises another question: To what extent does the duration of an event, i.e. the interval number I, affect how the statement should be observed? We took the approach, to assume similar scales, based on the scale of the interval, would be considered as similar observations. For example the interval of 1 s and 1.2 s will be observed as the same, similarly with 1 h and 1.2 h. If there is need for a further distinction, a clock operator can provide the system with additional context.

The *Duration* time window provides a tolerance that allows the system to observe re-occurring patterns in time, coming from asynchronous input channels, which would otherwise be seen as different if the specific events are incoming in a different order, albeit, in millisecond scale.

5   Projection and Eternalization

When two semantically related statements are selected for inference, (if not stated otherwise by the specific rule) it is necessary to map the occurrence time of the belief to the occurrence time of the task, using the current time as reference.

This mapping function is called "projection" and describes how the truth value of a statement decreases when projected to another occurrence time. In this operation, the confidence of the belief is decreased by a factor

$$k_c = \frac{|t_B - t_T|}{|t_B - t_C| + |t_T - t_C|}$$

where t_B is the original occurrence time of the belief, t_T the occurrence time it is projected to, and t_C the current time. The new confidence of the belief is then

$$c_{new} = (1 - k_c) * c_{old}$$

Eternalization is a special form of induction, where the occurrence time is dropped, so the conclusion is about the general situation. The eternalized confidence value is obtained with

$$c_{eternal} = \frac{1}{k + c_{temporal}}$$

where k is a global evidential horizon personality parameter [9].

In inference, whenever an event is derived, the eternalized version is also derived. However the existence of eternal statements presents a problem: How to justify inference between two premises, about different times? In order to deal with this scenario, there are two possible routes: the inference rule is a temporal rule which measures the time between the premises, and takes it into account when its conclusion is built, or, one of the following cases applies:

1. *Premise1* is eternal, and *premise2* is temporal. Here, *premise2* is eternalized before applying inference.
2. *Premise1* is temporal, and *premise2* is eternal. Since *premise2* is eternal, it also holds at the occurrence time of premise1, so inference can occur directly.
3. *Premise1* is temporal, *premise2* is temporal. In this case *premise2* is projected to the occurrence time of *premise1*, and also eternalized. Inference now happens between *premise1* and the stronger in confidence outcome, either the result of the projection or the result of eternalization.
4. Both are eternal, in which case the derivation can happen directly.

In all the cases, the occurrence time of the first premise (usually the task), is assigned to the occurrence time of the derived task, and possibly a statement-dependent time-shift as specified by some temporal inference rules, dependent on the term encoded intervals, which measure time between events, is applied.

6   Anticipation

In NARS predictive statements usually take the form:

$$antecedent \Rightarrow consequent$$

where observing *antecedent* leads to the derived event *consequent*, on which the system can form an expectation on whether it will be observed as predicted, this is called Anticipation. With Anticipation the system is able to find negative evidence for previously learned predictive beliefs which generate wrong predictions. [6,10]

If the event happens, in the sense that a new input event with the same term as the anticipated event is observed, the anticipation was successful (confirmation), in which case nothing special needs to be done, since the statement will be confirmed via the normal process of temporal induction.

If the predicted event does not happen then the system needs to recognise this. This is achieved by introducing a negative input event, $not(a)$. Note that in this case, such a negative input event has high budget and significantly influences the attention of the system.

Anticipation introduces three challenges: firstly, how to ensure that the system doesn't confirm its own predictions? secondly, how to ensure that the system only anticipates events which are observable and hence overcome the issue that negative events are generated for events which are not observable? and thirdly, how to deal with occurrence time tolerance as well as tolerance in truth value.

The first is handled by letting only input events (not derived events) confirm a prediction. The second shows that the closed-world-assumption (CWA) is not applicable in general, just because something isn't observed doesn't mean it didn't happen in general. This issue is overcome by letting only those predictions, which correspond to observable concepts, generate anticipations. When a new input event enters the system, the corresponding concept is marked observable, in this way the observability of concepts is tracked. Regarding the third issue, currently the system assumes that the event does not happen if it doesn't occur within time $[t_{oc} - \frac{|t_{oc} - t_{cur}|}{u}, t_{oc} + \frac{|t_{oc} - t_{cur}|}{u}]$ where t_{oc} is the occurrence time of the anticipated event, and t_{cur} is the current time, with u usually being set to 2. To allow tolerance in truth, anticipation as well as the confirmation currently uses tasks with frequency greater than a threshold, by default 0.5, this tolerance handling method may be refined in the future and is still in discussion. Also note that by this treatment, conceptual events like "Our team wins the football match" have to be decomposed down to directly observable events by inference. Whether and how this can be improved, is also still in discussion.

7   Evidence Tracking

One of the most important notions in NARS is the idea of evidence, note that the truth value of a statement is essentially a (w_+, w_-) pair, where w_+ represents positive evidence, and w_- represents negative evidence, or alternatively as confidence c and frequency f tuple, where $f = \frac{w_+}{w_+ + w_-}$ and confidence is $c = \frac{w_+ + w_-}{k + w_+ + w_-}$, where k is a global personality parameter that indicates a global evidential horizon. For full details on truth value derivations see [9]. Evidence in NARS follows these principles:

1. Evidence can only be used once for each statement.
2. A record of evidence used in each derivation must be maintained, although given AIKR (as also assumed in [6]), this is only a partial record, which is not an issue in practice.
3. There can be positive and negative evidence for the same statement.
4. Evidence is not only the key factor to determine truth, but also the key to judge the independence of the premises in a step of inference.

As described previously, each statement has a stamp which contains an evidence set, E. Following each derivation, a new E is created, by interleaving the two evidence sets of the premises, which is then truncated to a maximum length by removing the oldest evidence. Interleaving the evidence sets is important and ensures an even distribution of evidence from both evidence sets. The evidence set, E, initially contains the unique statement id from the stamp. Prior to derivation, evidence sets of the involved premises are checked for intersection, if they intersect then there is overlapping evidence between the premises and no derivation is allowed (as this would double count evidence).

8   Processing of New and Derived Tasks

This step consists of processing new inputs and derivations selected from the buffer Curve Bag, by applying temporal chaining for new input events followed by ranking based selection for local inference. Here the Revision Rule is applied to belief and goal tasks, and the Choice Rule is applied to question and goal tasks. Additionally the Decision Rule is applied to a goal task [9].

Temporal Chaining - As discussed in Anticipation, it is important to distinguish between new inputs and derivations, because only new input events invoke Temporal Chaining. When a new input event enters the system, inference is automatically triggered with the previous new input event [10], generating a temporal derivation (Sect. 4, sub-section Temporal Chaining).

Ranking - Belief and Goal tables are ordered according to a ranking function, where the confidence is determined after projecting each new belief or goal, to the target time. When the ranking is done for selective questions [9], the function is e/C where e is the expectation value of the statement and C its complexity. In all other cases the confidence of the statement is used for ranking.

Adding to Belief/Desire Table - Once the ranking of a new belief or goal is determined, this ranking specifies the position of the entry in the table. If the table is full, then the lowest ranked entry is deleted to maintain the maximum capacity limit.

Selecting Belief for Inference - When a belief from the belief table is taken out after the selection of the task for inference (Sect. 9, sub-section Phase 2), it is done so by ranking all entries in the belief table according to the occurrence time of the task. The best entry is selected for inference. This also holds for local inference, where a new incoming belief task selects the best candidate to revise with. The new belief and the revised one are then added as described in the previous section. If the task is a question or goal, the new belief overwrites its best solution, dependent on whether it is higher ranked according to the ranking function as described in Ranking.

Revision - When a belief or goal task is processed (selected as task in an inference cycle), it is projected to the current time. Now the highest ranked entry in the belief / goal table in respect to the current moment is determined. When the task is able to revise with this one, this is done and we are finished. If the task is a goal, the Decision rule is also applied:

Decision - If the goal task is an operation (which is an event the system can trigger itself) the desire value expectation, measured with $expectation(x) = (c * (f - \frac{1}{2}) + \frac{1}{2})$ (with f being the frequency, c the confidence) of the highest ranked desire is determined and if it exceeds a certain threshold, the system executes this operation. After the execution, an event, stating that this operation was executed, is input into the system. This event is then available for use in temporal chaining supporting learning about the consequences of the systems own operations in different contexts.

9   Attentional Control

The attentional control stage is primarily concerned with managing the Attentional Focus of NARS. This is achieved with a three phase process of: selecting contextually relevant and semantically related tasks for inference, creating or updating budget values based on user requirements and/or inference results, and finally, updating memory with the results of the updated task and concepts.

Phase 1: Premises for inference are selected according to the following scheme:

1. Select a concept from memory (according to Curve Bag semantics).
2. Select a tasklink (with related task) from this concept.
3. Select a termlink from this concept.
4. Select a belief from the concept the termlink points to, ranked by the task.

Phase 2: This phase forms new statements (tasks), with new metadata, from the derivations. The task linked by the tasklink used in inference determines the statement type and the occurrence time of the new task (unless the inference rule states otherwise, which may also shift the occurrence time). The Budget of a new task is defined as (where T is the truth value of the new task and $h \in [0,1]$ is a personality parameter giving high quality to tasks of high frequency):

priority: $or(priority(tasklink), priority(termlink))$
durability: $durability(tasklink) * durability(termlink) * \frac{1}{C}$
quality: $max(expectation(T), (1 - expectation(T)) * h) * \frac{1}{C}$

where, for quality, $\frac{1}{C}$ is applied for backward inference, and $or(a, b) = 1 - ((1 - a) * (1 - b))$ [1]. This budget is also used for the tasklink created for the new task. Next the termlinks are strengthened by the derivation. Here Hebb's rule is used: $priority(termlink)' = or(priority(termlink), or(quality, and(a, b)))$ where a is the concept priority referred by the tasklink, and b is the concept priority referred by the termlink. Additionally, the durability of the termlink is also increased: $durability(termlink)' = or(durability(termlink), quality)$.

Phase 3: Select new tasks from the buffer Curve Bag, process them, and insert them into memory:

1. If Concept C_T does not exist, where T is the task, create it and any other required concepts to match the sub-terms of the task, along with the necessary termlinks.

   Finally, the concept, containing T, is activated by adding the priority of the task to the concept priority, and using the maximum of the task and concept duration as the new concept duration as well as the maximum of derived task and concept quality as the new concept quality. In this way concepts activate each other context-sensitively and in a directed manner.

2. Construct a tasklink with the budget of T for this task and add it to C_T (note that the task will additionally also be linked from an in inference by the termlink selected subterm concept).

3. Add the task to its statement type related table in C_T.

4. Insert C_T, and sub-term concepts, if any, into the concept bag (memory).

10   Conclusions

The current OpenNARS implementation, described by this document, follows a unified principle of cognition whereby reasoning is carried out within an inference cycle.

To our knowledge, OpenNARS is the only implementation of an AGI system that captures perception, reasoning, prediction, planning and decision making with a single unified principle. In particular we believe the handling of temporal inference, as described in this paper, is a new approach and demonstrates many of the aspects required for an agent to learn and act within a real-time environment.

Although it is difficult for this implementation to be compared to other systems, there are certain aspects that make NARS similar to some other AGI projects, such as AERA [6], OpenCog [4] and SOAR [5], though detailed comparison with them is beyond the scope of this paper.

OpenNARS continues to be a research platform with different aspects of the design at varying levels of maturity. The logic prior to the introduction of temporal logic is considered stable. Temporal logic, introspection and the budget updating functions are work in progress and are not considered optimal at this stage. Perception, introspective mental operators and emotional attentional control are the focus for the next phase of our research. The attentional control is not currently sufficient to handle a high bandwidth perception stream.

The current implementation, OpenNARS v1.7.0, is available for download at: http://opennars.github.io/opennars. The download package contains examples of learning by experience, and demonstrations of the aforementioned cognitive functions as well as practical use cases for the system.

References

1. Bonissone, P.: Summarizing and propogating uncertain information with triangular norms. Int. J. Approximate Reasoning **1**, 71–101 (1987)
2. Eagleman, D.M., Sejnowski, T.J.: Motion integration and postdiction in visual awareness. Science **287**, 2036–2038 (2000)
3. Forgy, C.L.: Rete: a fast algorithm for the many pattern/many object match problem. Artif. Intell. **19**(1), 17–37 (1982)
4. Goertzel, B., Pennachin, C., Geisweiller, N.: Engineering General Intelligence, Part 1 and 2. Springer, Heidelberg (2014)
5. Laird, J.: The Soar Cognitive Architecture. MIT Press, Cambridge (2012)
6. Eric, N., Thórisson, K.R., Dindo, H., Pezzulo, G., Rodriguez, M., Corbato, C., Steunebrink, B., Ognibene, D., Chella, A., Schmidhuber, J., Sanz, R., Helgason, H.P.: Autocatalytic Endogenous Reflective Architecture, Accepted May 13, 2013. http://hdl.handle.net/1946/15083. ISSN 1670-5777. Published: April 2013
7. Pöppel, E., Bao, Y.: Temporal Windows as a Bridge from Objective to Subjective Time, The Philosophy, Psychology, and Neuroscience of Temporality. The MIT Press (2014)
8. Wang, P.: Rigid Flexibility - The Logic of Intelligence. Springer, Heidelberg (2006)
9. Wang, P.: Non-Axiomatic Logic: A Model of Intelligent Reasoning. World Scientific, Singapore (2013)
10. Wang, P., Hammer, P.: Issues in temporal and causal inference. In: Bieger, J., Goertzel, B., Potapov, A. (eds.) AGI 2015. LNCS, vol. 9205, pp. 208–217. Springer, Heidelberg (2015)

Integrating Symbolic
and Sub-symbolic Reasoning

Claes Strannegård[1,2(✉)] and Abdul Rahim Nizamani[3]

[1] Department of Philosophy, Linguistics and Theory of Science,
University of Gothenburg, Gothenburg, Sweden
[2] Department of Applied Information Technology,
Chalmers University of Technology, Gothenburg, Sweden
claes.strannegard@chalmers.se
[3] Department of Applied Information Technology,
University of Gothenburg, Gothenburg, Sweden
abdulrahim.nizamani@gu.se

Abstract. This paper proposes a way of bridging the gap between symbolic and sub-symbolic reasoning. More precisely, it describes a developing system with bounded rationality that bases its decisions on sub-symbolic as well as symbolic reasoning. The system has a fixed set of needs and its sole goal is to stay alive as long as possible by satisfying those needs. It operates without pre-programmed knowledge of any kind. The learning mechanism consists of several meta-rules that govern the development of its network-based memory structure. The decision making mechanism operates under time constraints and combines symbolic reasoning, aimed at compressing information, with sub-symbolic reasoning, aimed at planning.

Keywords: Autonomous agent · Bounded rationality · Survival · Symbolic reasoning · Sub-symbolic reasoning

1 Introduction

Symbolic reasoning connects linguistic statements via syntactic rules, whereas sub-symbolic reasoning connects sensory concepts via association links [6]. These forms of reasoning have been studied since antiquity, e.g. by Euclid [2], who designed systems for axiomatic reasoning, and by Aristotle [10], who investigated associative as well as axiomatic reasoning. These forms of reasoning are closely related to James' division into associative and symbolic reasoning [4] and Kahneman's dichotomy of System 1 and System 2 processes [5].

The ability to do symbolic and sub-symbolic reasoning and to combine the two seems to be an essential feature of human intelligence [6]. In contrast, AI systems rarely support more than one of the two processes. For example, neural networks and reinforcement learning systems support sub-symbolic, but usually

© Springer International Publishing Switzerland 2016
B. Steunebrink et al. (Eds.): AGI 2016, LNAI 9782, pp. 171–180, 2016.
DOI: 10.1007/978-3-319-41649-6_17

not symbolic reasoning, while automatic theorem provers and logic-based systems are the other way around. In particular, deep networks are good at recognizing faces or evaluating go-positions, but not at arithmetic, while automatic theorem provers have the opposite strengths.

Several cognitive and agent architectures combine symbolic and sub-symbolic reasoning to varying degrees. Examples include Soar [8], ACT-R [1], OpenCog [3], AERA [14], and NARS [17]. Some of the architectures with this capacity are hybrid systems with juxtaposed subsystems operating on separate knowledge bases. Certain others are not fully autonomous, in that they depend on engineers for manually preparing the system for new domains, e.g. for updating the set of production rules.

Despite the progress made, the following quote by Yoshua Bengio, one of the deep learning pioneers, suggests that the two types of reasoning have not been sufficiently integrated for artificial general intelligence purposes [7]:

> Traditional endeavors, including reasoning and logic—we need to marry these things with deep learning in order to move toward AI.

Schmidhuber proposed to combine long-term memory compression with reinforcement learning [11]. This idea has been successfully used in several AI-programs, including Alphago [12].

In this paper we present a computational model that compresses the long-term memory as well as the working memory. In both cases we use compression with bounded cognitive resources in order to make the compression computationally feasible. This reflects our belief that compression is key to natural intelligence and also that working memory compression is the sole purpose of symbolic reasoning. Our system has a fixed set of needs, whose levels of satisfaction are computed on the basis of sensory data (interoception). The sole goal of the system is to survive as long as possible by satisfying its needs. This will in turn cause the system to take different actions, e.g. to ambulate between a water source and a food source.

In contrast to many cognitive architectures, our system does not use the notion of task. Instead, the planning process continuously searches for action sequences aimed at increasing the probability of survival. The behavior of the system can be altered by external agents who provide reward, similarly to how dogs can be trained by humans who reward tricks with treats. The system can also learn on its own without interacting with other agents.

This paper focuses entirely on artificial general intelligence and aims for a fully autonomous artificial system without regard to biological or psychological realism. We combine and extend our previous work on long-term memory compression [16], working memory compression [9], and transparent networks [15].

Section 2 presents the components of our system and Sect. 3 describes the update mechanisms of the components. Section 4 presents the reasoning mechanism in greater detail. Section 5 presents a proof-of-concept prototype implementation of the system. Section 6 draws some conclusions.

2   System Components

The system consists of several components that develop over time.

2.1   Status Signals

Time is modeled using the natural numbers $\mathbb{N}$. For $t \in \mathbb{N}$, let $Status(t)$ be the vector $(\sigma_1(t), \ldots, \sigma_N(t)) \in [0,1]^N$. Here N is a fixed positive integer that models the number of needs of the system and $\sigma_i(t) \in [0,1]$, for $0 \le i \le N$. For instance, $\sigma_1(t)$ and $\sigma_2(t)$ might reflect the glucose and water concentration in the blood stream, or perhaps the oil and gasoline levels of a vehicle. Intuitively, $Status(t)$ measures the status of the different needs of the system, i.e. its well-being.

2.2   Long-Term Memory

We will use a labeled graph $LTM(t)$ for encoding the system's long-term memory at time t. Intuitively, $LTM(t)$ is a Markov Decision Process (MDP) that the system uses for decision making at t. The states and actions of $LTM(t)$ are described in the vocabulary of transparent neural networks [15]. Our reason for using this formalism is that it facilitates the definition of learning rules that develop $LTM(t)$ over time, as we shall see in Sect. 3.

Definition 1 (LTM). *Let $LTM(t)$ be a graph consisting of a finite set of labeled nodes $D(t)$ and a finite set of labeled edges $E(t) \subseteq D(t)^2$.*

- *Each node of $D(t)$ has exactly one label from the following list: SENSOR, MOTOR, NOT, AND, OR, x, y, z, DELAY, and ACTION.*
- *Each edge of $E(t)$ has exactly one label from the following list: ACTIVITY, DECISION, and PREDICTION.*

Edges labeled PREDICTION are also labeled with a probability in $[0,1]$ and an expected reward in $[-1,1]^N$. Here N is the fixed number of needs that was mentioned above.

Figures 1 and 2 provide examples of some graphs that could be part of an LTM. Oval shapes represent $SENSOR$ nodes and squares represent $ACTION$ nodes. Solid, dashed, and annotated arrows represent $ACTIVITY$, $DECISION$, and $PREDICTION$ edges, respectively. Many more examples can be found in [15].

Remark 1 (Intended interpretation). SENSOR-nodes model sensors, e.g. receptor cells with ion channels sensitive to cold temperature, mechanical pressure, or acidity. *MOTOR*-nodes model muscle-controlling motor neurons. *NOT, AND,* and *OR*-nodes model nerve cells that compute the corresponding boolean functions. The first of these is binary operators and the other two binary. x, y, or z-nodes are abstraction nodes that are used for pattern matching purposes (using temporary assignments of nodes to variables). *DELAY*-nodes model nerve cells

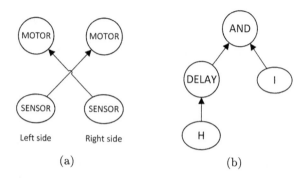

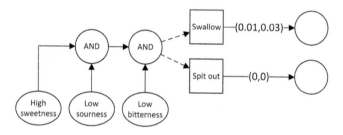

Fig. 1. (a) A Braitenberg vehicle with two light sensors and two motors for wheels on the left and right sides, respectively. (b) The *AND*-node of this graph recognizes the sequence *HI*, i.e. letter *H* immediately followed by the letter *I*. The sensors of this graph recognize letters. Alternatively, the sensors could be replaced by top nodes of more complex network that recognize letters.

Fig. 2. We assume that the system has two needs: water and glucose. When the system receives a familiar combination of tastes (of an apple), it chooses between two actions, one of which (swallow) leads to reward.

that re-transmit action potentials with a delay. *ACTION*-nodes model neurons that activate motor sequences as a result of (conscious) decisions. *ACTIVITY*-edges model connections in nerve systems where activity propagates in the network. *DECISION*-edges model connections (choices) in MDPs that go from states to actions. *PREDICTION*-edges model connections in MDPs that go from actions to states. The number is a probability that will be learned and the vector is the expected reward w.r.t. N fixed needs of the system. This vector will also be learned.

2.3   Activity

Let $Activity(t)$ be a subset of the nodes of $LTM(t)$. This set models the neurons that fire at time t. Our view in this connection is essentially that humans are capable of symbolic as well as sub-symbolic information processing and that both processes run on systems of neurons that are binary in the sense that they either fire all-out or not at all at any given moment.

2.4   Attention

Let *Attention*(*t*) be a subset of $D(t)$ consisting of at most one node. This set models the node under attention at time t, if any.

2.5   Working Memory

Let $WM(t)$ be a sequence consisting of a finite number of nodes of $D(t)$. This sequence models the content of the system's working memory at time t.

2.6   Decision

Let *Decision*(*t*) be a subset of $D(t)$ consisting of at most one node. This set models the decision at time t, if any.

Remark 2 (Bounded rationality). In line with biological organisms with cognitive resources all of which are limited, we impose firm resource bounds on all components of our system. Thus the capacity of $LTM(t)$ is limited (e.g. to 10^5 nodes) and so is the capacity of $WM(t)$ (e.g. to 5 nodes). As we shall see later, the processing time that the system uses for decision-making is also bounded, although in this case the limit depends on the status of the system. Thus the system has bounded rationality in several ways, leading it to a *satisficing* rather than an *optimizing* behavior [13].

3   Update Functions

In this section we will specify how the system components are updated in response to the input that the system receives.

Definition 2 (Input stream). *The function input*(*t*) *is an assignment of values in* $\{0,1\}$ *to each SENSOR node of* $LTM(t)$.

The components of the knowledge base can largely be initialized arbitrarily at $t = 0$. Thus it will start as a *genotype* and gradually develop *phenotypes* depending on the input stream. Now suppose the system receives the input *input*(*t* + 1). Then the components of the knowledge base will be updated as described below and in the order specified.

3.1   Activity Update

Here we define *Activity*(*t* + 1) via a function A that selects which nodes to shall be put into the set:

Definition 3 (Activity update). *Let $A(a,t)$ be defined by recursion on t as follows. Here $L(a)$ denotes the label of node a. Let $A(a,0) = 1$ if $a \in Activity(0)$ and $A(a,0) = 0$ otherwise. Moreover, let*

$$A(a, t+1) = \begin{cases} 1 \ if \ a \in Attention(t) \\ 1 \ if \ L(a) = ACTION \ and \ a \in Decision(t) \\ input(t+1)(a) \ if \ L(a) = SENSOR \\ A(a', t+1) \ if \ L(a) = MOTOR \ and \ (a', a) \in ACTIVITY \\ min\{A(a', t+1) : (a', a) \in ACTIVITY\} \ if \ L(a) = AND \\ max\{A(a', t+1) : (a', a) \in ACTIVITY\} \ if \ L(a) = OR \\ 1 - A(a', t+1) \ if \ L(a) = NOT \ and \ (a', a) \in ACTIVITY \\ A(a', t) \ if \ L(a) = DELAY, (a', a) \in ACTIVITY \end{cases}$$

This definition should be read as a case statement in programming that selects the first case that applies. It describes how activity propagates through nodes of different types. The nodes x, y, and z are activated via an additional mechanism.

3.2 Status Update

The vector $Status(t+1)$ is computed directly from $input(t+1)$ using an arbitrary fixed function. For instance, $\sigma_1(t+1)$ could be the fraction of the insulin receptors that fire at $t+1$. Now, reward can be defined as status changes:

Definition 4 (Reward vector). *Let $Reward(t+1) = Status(t+1) - Status(t)$.*

Note that $Reward(t+1) \in [-1, 1]^N$, since each σ_i takes values in $[0, 1]$.

3.3 Attention Update

To be able to describe how attention is updated we need to introduce a couple of concepts.

Definition 5 (Most urgent need). *The* most urgent need *at t is defined as* $\arg\min_i(\sigma_i(t))$.

Definition 6 (Top active node). *A node $a \in LTM(t)$ is* top active *at t if $a \in Active(t)$ and there is no $b \in Active(t)$ such that $(a, b) \in ACTIVITY$.*

Together the top active nodes constitute a description of the present situation at a maximum level of detail in terms of previously experienced situations. Therefore they are important from the perspective of decision making and attention. For instance, if the system sees a green snake, then the nodes representing "green", "snake", and "green AND snake", might become activated. Among those, "green AND snake" would be top active if it had no other active nodes above it, whereas the other two would only be active.

Definition 7 (Flashing node). *A node* $a \in LTM(t)$ *is flashing at* $t+1$ *if* $a \in Active(t+1) - Active(t)$.

When attention moves from no node or an old node to a new node, this new node will always be top active and flashing. In general there are many such nodes to choose from and in that case, attention will go to the node that seems to be the most promising when it comes to satisfying its most urgent need.

3.4   WM Update

The sequence $WM(t)$ stores the nodes that have been under attention most recently.

3.5   Decision Update

The system makes decisions by continuously computing $Decision(t+1)$. If $Decision(t+1) = \emptyset$, then no action is taken. Otherwise $Decision(t+1)$ contains a single node, which is labeled $ACTION$. When this node gets activated, motor activity will follow. The one and only goal of decision making is to prolong the system's life, i.e. avoiding that some σ_i reaches 0. The decision update process may use several consecutive cycles for making a decision. In the mean time $Decision(t+1) = \emptyset$. The processing time is constrained by a time limit that depends on $Status(t)$. In general, less time is available if some σ_i is low. A new situation that brings along dramatic status changes can cause the processing time to run out and make the system return to the main loop and be ready to deal with the new situations.

Our system combines sub-symbolic reasoning, aimed at planning for survival, with symbolic reasoning, aimed at improving the planning process by compressing the information contained in $WM(t)$. Both types of reasoning is based on knowledge that is stored in $LTM(t)$. The reasoning mechanisms, which are used for decision making, are described in greater detail in Sect. 4. In addition, the system engages in exploration by testing new or old actions for different nodes under attention.

3.6   LTM Update

Here we outline the learning mechanisms (or meta-rules) that govern the transfer from $LTM(t)$ to $LTM(t+1)$. For reasons of space, these mechanisms are not described in full detail. Several detailed definitions can be found in [9,15].

1. Hebbian learning at random moments (so that frequently occurring sensory combinations or sequences of sensory combinations will be remembered)
2. Status-driven learning of state-action pairs leading to reward (so that good actions can be repeated) or to punishment (so that bad actions can be avoided)

3. Repetition-driven learning (so that motor patterns that cause sensory patterns to be repeated can be learned, e.g. in the context of sensor-motor development and language learning)
4. Novelty-driven learning (so that actions leading to sensory changes are remembered, e.g. for learning sensory-motor patterns that lead to locomotion and manipulation of the environment)
5. Abstraction (so that general patterns can be remembered via the use of abstraction nodes, e.g. in the context of symbolic pattern learning)
6. Forgetting (so that memory structures that are rarely used and not associated with strong reward or punishment are eventually removed)
7. Adjustment of the expected rewards and transition probabilities of the $PREDICTION$-edges (so that experience will be properly encoded).

4   Reasoning Mechanisms

Now let us consider the system's reasoning mechanisms.

4.1   Sub-symbolic Reasoning

The fundamental building blocks of MDPs are association rules that lead from a state-action pair (s, a) to a resulting state s' with probability p and expected reward r. Our LTM was designed for representing rules of exactly this kind with the convention that the node under attention defines the state of the system. Thus we can represent MPDs in our framework and do sub-symbolic reasoning with all kinds of reinforcement learning methods, including Monte-Carlo methods, Q-learning and Dyna-Q. Our prototype implementation uses Q-learning. Since we have a mechanism for creating memories of sequences of events, the system has the Markov property, but is nevertheless able to take history into account. Figure 3 shows an example of a sub-symbolic computation to the right.

4.2   Symbolic Reasoning

We view rewrite rules as association rules. For instance, we view the rewrite rule $2 * 3 \mapsto 6$ as an association rule that leads from the node representing the sequence $2 * 3$ and the motor action "write 6" to the node "read 6" with probability 1 and some positive expected reward. Another rewrite rule leads from $\top \wedge x$ and the action "write x" to the node "read x". Symbolic reasoning is done by means of computations, i.e. successive transformations of $WM(t)$, by means of rewrite rules. A central rule is Chunk, which is built-in to the system. This rule enables contents in the working memory to be chunked into a sequence, provided the sequence in question is an element of $LTM(t)$. For instance, suppose $WM(t)$ contains the sequence $(2, *, 3)$. Also suppose $LTM(t)$ contains the sequence $2 * 3$. Then Chunk enables the transition from $(2, *, 3)$ to $(2 * 3)$. Figure 3 shows an example of a symbolic computation to the left.

$$\frac{(2+3,*,4)}{(5,*,4)} \text{ Rewrite } 2+3 \mapsto 5;1.0;(0,0)$$
$$\frac{(5,*,4)}{(5*4)} \text{ Chunk; } 1.0;(0,0)$$
$$\frac{(5*4)}{(4*5)} \text{ Rewrite } x*y \mapsto y*x;1.0;(0,0)$$
$$\frac{(4*5)}{(20)} \text{ Rewrite } 4*5 \mapsto 20;1.0;(0,0)$$

$$\frac{(\text{Big rock})}{(\text{River})} \text{ Walk north; } 0.8;(0,0)$$
$$\frac{(\text{River})}{(\text{River})} \text{ Drink; } 1.0;(0.4,0)$$
$$\frac{(\text{River})}{(\text{Apple tree})} \text{ Walk west; } 0.9;(0,0)$$
$$\frac{(\text{Apple tree})}{(\text{Apple tree})} \text{ Eat apple; } 1.0;(0,0.2)$$

Fig. 3. Two computations by a system with two needs: water and glucose. The annotations show the action name, the transition probability and the expected reward in terms of water and glucose. The left panel shows a symbolic computation (compression) and the right panel a sub-symbolic computation (a simple plan for drinking and eating).

Remark 3 (Mixed computations). The ability to combine symbolic and sub-symbolic reasoning can be critical. For instance, if you hear the voices of three burglars in your house and later see two of them leave, then you could use symbolic reasoning to conclude that one burglar is still in the house and then sub-symbolic reasoning to conclude that you should act in a certain way, e.g. remain still. In the present framework symbolic and sub-symbolic computation steps can be mixed arbitrarily.

5   Prototype Implementation

We have implemented a proof-of-concept prototype of the system described above. The code is available at `github.com/arnizamani`. Several of the mechanisms for learning and reasoning that are mentioned in Sect. 3 have been implemented in our earlier work on transparent networks [15], inductive learning [16], and symbolic reasoning [9]. Now we have also implemented a simple prototype of the system with all the components described in Sect. 2. For simplicity the number of needs N was set to 1. An MDP was used together with a policy for decision making. Q-learning was used to update the policy. A class named Environment was implemented to simulate a real environment that provides an input stream and a reward signal to the agent. The implemented system is limited in features. In particular, the update function for $LTM(t)$, which was partly developed in [15], has not been added yet. A simple mechanism moves the attention to a top-active flashing node. The rule Chunk has been added to the compression mechanism of $WM(t)$.

6   Conclusion

We have proposed a way of bridging the gap between symbolic and sub-symbolic reasoning. More precisely, we have presented a system together with a prototype implementation that combines symbolic reasoning, aimed at compressing information, with sub-symbolic reasoning, aimed at planning. The system subsumes and extends our previously developed computational models of symbolic and sub-symbolic reasoning. Much work remains, however, for turning the present proof-of-concept implementation into a fully functional autonomous system.

Acknowledgement. This research was supported by The Swedish Research Council, grants 2012-1000 and 2013-4873. We would like to thank José Hernández-Orallo for many helpful suggestions.

References

1. Anderson, J., Bothell, D., Byrne, M., Douglass, S., Lebiere, C., Qin, Y.: An integrated theory of the mind. Psychol. Rev. **111**(4), 1036 (2004)
2. Fitzpatrick, R., Heiberg, J.: Euclid's Elements (2007)
3. Goertzel, B., Pennachin, C., Geisweiller, N.: The OpenCog Framework. In: Engineering General Intelligence, Part 2, pp. 3–29. Springer (2014)
4. James, W.: The Principles of Psychology. American Science Series: Advanced Course. H. Holt, New York (1918)
5. Kahneman, D.: A perspective on judgment and choice: mapping bounded rationality. Am. Psychol. **58**(9), 697 (2003)
6. Kelley, T.D.: Symbolic and sub-symbolic representations in computational models of human cognition what can be learned from biology? Theory Psychol. **13**(6), 847–860 (2003)
7. Knight, W.: Will machines eliminate us? MIT Technol. Rev. **119** (2016)
8. Laird, J.: The Soar Cognitive Architecture. MIT Press, Cambridge (2012)
9. Nizamani, A.R., Juel, J., Persson, U., Strannegård, C.: Bounded cognitive resources and arbitrary domains. In: Bieger, J., Goertzel, B., Potapov, A. (eds.) AGI 2015. LNCS, vol. 9205, pp. 166–176. Springer, Heidelberg (2015)
10. Ross, G.: Aristotle: De Sensu and De Memoria. The University Press, Cambridge (1906)
11. Schmidhuber, J.: Simple algorithmic principles of discovery, subjective beauty, selective attention, curiosity & creativity. In: Corruble, V., Takeda, M., Suzuki, E. (eds.) DS 2007. LNCS, vol. 4755, pp. 26–38. Springer, Heidelberg (2007)
12. Silver, D., et al.: Mastering the game of go with deep neural networks and tree search. Nature **529**(7587), 484–489 (2016)
13. Simon, H.A.: Models of Bounded Rationality: Empirically Grounded Economic Reason, vol. 3. MIT Press, Cambridge (1982)
14. Steunebrink, B.R., Koutník, J., Thórisson, K.R., Nivel, E., Schmidhuber, J.: Resource-bounded machines are motivated to be effective, efficient, and curious. In: Kühnberger, K.-U., Rudolph, S., Wang, P. (eds.) AGI 2013. LNCS, vol. 7999, pp. 119–129. Springer, Heidelberg (2013)
15. Strannegård, C., Cirillo, S., Wessberg, J.: Emotional concept development. In: Bieger, J., Goertzel, B., Potapov, A. (eds.) AGI 2015. LNCS, vol. 9205, pp. 362–372. Springer, Heidelberg (2015)
16. Strannegård, C., Nizamani, A.R., Sjöberg, A., Engström, F.: Bounded kolmogorov complexity based on cognitive models. In: Kühnberger, K.-U., Rudolph, S., Wang, P. (eds.) AGI 2013. LNCS, vol. 7999, pp. 130–139. Springer, Heidelberg (2013)
17. Wang, P., Hammer, P.: Assumptions of decision-making models in AGI. In: Bieger, J., Goertzel, B., Potapov, A. (eds.) AGI 2015. LNCS, vol. 9205, pp. 197–207. Springer, Heidelberg (2015)

Integrating Axiomatic and Analogical Reasoning

Claes Strannegård[1,2(✉)], Abdul Rahim Nizamani[3], and Ulf Persson[4]

[1] Department of Philosophy, Linguistics and Theory of Science,
University of Gothenburg, Gothenburg, Sweden
[2] Department of Applied Information Technology,
Chalmers University of Technology, Gothenburg, Sweden
claes.strannegard@chalmers.se
[3] Department of Applied Information Technology,
University of Gothenburg, Gothenburg, Sweden
abdulrahim.nizamani@gu.se
[4] Department of Mathematical Sciences,
Chalmers University of Technology, Gothenburg, Sweden
ulf.persson@chalmers.se

Abstract. We present a computational model of a developing system with bounded rationality that is surrounded by an arbitrary number of symbolic domains. The system is fully automatic and makes continuous observations of facts emanating from those domains. The system starts from scratch and gradually evolves a knowledge base consisting of three parts: (1) a set of beliefs for each domain, (2) a set of rules for each domain, and (3) an analogy for each pair of domains. The learning mechanism for updating the knowledge base uses rote learning, inductive learning, analogy discovery, and belief revision. The reasoning mechanism combines axiomatic reasoning for drawing conclusions inside the domains, with analogical reasoning for transferring knowledge from one domain to another. Thus the reasoning processes may use analogies to jump back and forth between domains.

Keywords: Developing system · Bounded rationality · Symbolic domains · Axiomatic reasoning · Analogical reasoning

1 Introduction

Analogies play a significant role in several cognitive processes, including decision making, perception, memory, problem solving, creativity, emotion, explanation, and communication [6]. In his lecture entitled *Analogy as the Core of Cognition*, Hofstadter stated that "analogy is the interstate freeway system of cognition" [9].

Analogies have been studied since antiquity, e.g. by Aristotle, who gave the famous example Palm:Hand :: Sole:Foot (Palm is to Hand as Sole is to Foot). A still older example might be the notion of proportionality, as in 3:6 :: 2:4 [5]. Aristotle set the stage for all later theories of analogical reasoning [1]. Gentner studied analogies in the context of logic and wrote [5]:

© Springer International Publishing Switzerland 2016
B. Steunebrink et al. (Eds.): AGI 2016, LNAI 9782, pp. 181–191, 2016.
DOI: 10.1007/978-3-319-41649-6_18

When people hear an analogy such as "An electric battery is like a reservoir" how do they derive its meaning? We might suppose that they simply apply their knowledge about reservoirs to batteries, and that the greater the match, the better the analogy.

What, then, is an analogy? In the aforementioned lecture, Hofstadter also stated [9]:

> It is tempting to think that the analogies are between things in the external world, but I really want to say that analogies happen inside your head (. . .) They are connections between things inside your head (. . .)

Analogies are commonly modelled as follows [5,16]: (1) Define the notion of domain as a set of logical formulas; (2) Specify two domains S and T called source and target, respectively; (3) Define a partial mapping from the language of S to the language of T; (4) Extend this mapping to a partial mapping from formulas of S to formulas of T. Then use this mapping for drawing conclusions (or making consistent conjectures) about T by using knowledge about S.

Analogies play a central role in mathematics for transferring results, proofs, and conjectures from one domain to another [14]. An example is homomorphisms of algebraic structures. Note that homomorphisms map elements of algebraic structures rather than elements of languages. For instance, the mapping $x \mapsto ln\ x$, is an isomorphism from the multiplicative group of the positive reals to the additive group of the reals. Typical in those algebraic examples is that the nature of the elements do not matter, only how they interact (the abstract structure). This can be further abstracted, as one may talk about the structure of the structures, as is done in category theory. A typical example is algebraic topology in which one associates a cohomology group $H(X)$ to each topological space X and a linear map $H(f) : H(Y) \rightarrow H(X)$ such that $H(fg) = H(g)H(f)$ to each continuous map $f : X \rightarrow Y$. Then H is a functor from the category of topological spaces with continuous mappings to the category of groups with homomorphisms, which enables topological questions to be reduced to algebraic ones.

A relatively general theory of analogies based on category theory was developed in [12,13]. Still it does not capture all types of higher-order analogies that abound in mathematics. This suggests that analogy is a somewhat evasive concept, just like the related notion of similarity, which is clearly hard to pin down once and for all.

A survey of analogy in automated reasoning can be found in [3]. An early example is the Structure-Mapping Engine that has been used both for simulation of human analogical processing and for machine learning purposes [4]. Another example is the symbolic framework for heuristic-driven theory projection that applies to analogies as well as metaphors [7]. A relatively recent example is the work of Schmidt et al. who model domains as first-order sentences rather than atomic sentences only and use a third domain in addition to S and T [16]. This third domain is a partial generalization of the other two, obtained via different versions of anti-unification. Then the analogy mapping from S to T is obtained as a lift in category theory. A connection to Kolmogorov complexity was made in [2], where information economy guides the search for analogies.

The so-called *combinatorial explosion problem* is ubiquitous in artificial intelligence and in particular a limiting factor to systems of automatic theorem proving, inductive reasoning, and analogical reasoning [3, 10, 15]. In [11], we presented ALICE IN WONDERLAND, a general system of learning and reasoning that makes use of bounded cognitive resources for reducing the computational complexity.

In this paper we show that axiomatic and analogical reasoning can be integrated in a general and fully automatic system of learning and reasoning. This system has bounded cognitive resources and operates on arbitrary symbolic domains. The method that we use is to generalize and extend the computational model underlying our system ALICE IN WONDERLAND. We improve on our previous work by: (1) using a more general notion of domain; (2) moving from single domains to multiple domains; and (3) adding analogical reasoning. For simplicity we use a basic notion of analogy and a basic form of analogy detection. Both these could potentially be replaced by more sophisticated variants.

Section 2 defines the notion of domain and presents a mathematical model that integrates axiomatic and analogical reasoning. Section 3 describes our system for axiomatic and analogical reasoning. Section 4 evaluates the system briefly and Sect. 5 offers some conclusions.

2   Mathematical Model

In this section we define a general notion of symbolic domain and present a mathematical model that integrates axiomatic and analogical reasoning.

2.1   Basic Concepts

First of all, let us introduce some basic concepts from first-order logic that will be used as the building blocks of our mathematical model.

Definition 1 (Language). *A language consists of*

- *a set of function symbols other than $\square$ with specified arities, and*
- *a set of relation symbols other than $\square$ with specified arities. The equality symbol $=$ may or may not be included in the language.*

Definition 2 (Term). *Let L be a language. An L-term is defined as follows:*

- *Variables x, y, z are L-terms*
- *Constants $c \in L$ are L-terms*
- *If $t_1, \ldots, t_n$ are L-terms and f is an n-ary function symbol, where $n > 0$, then $f(t_1, \ldots, t_n)$ is an L-term.*

Definition 3 (Atom). *Let L be any language. An L-atom is defined as follows:*

- *0-ary predicate symbols are L-atoms*

- If $t_1, \ldots, t_n$ are L-terms and P is an n-ary relation symbol in L, where $n > 0$, then $P(t_1, \ldots, t_n)$ is an L-atom.

Definition 4 (Formula). *Let L be a language. An L-formula is defined as follows:*

- *L-atoms are L-formulas*
- *If A is an L-formula that does not begin with the symbol $\neg$, then $\neg A$ is an L-formula.*

Definition 5 (Open and closed). *An* open *term (formula) is a term (formula) that contains variables. A* closed *term (formula) is a term (formula) that contains no variables.*

Definition 6 (Simple negation). *Let A be an L-formula. Then the operator $*$ is defined as follows: if A has the form $\neg B$, then $A^* = B$, otherwise $A^* = \neg A$.*

2.2   Domains

Definition 7 (Domain). *Let L be a language. An L-domain is a non-empty set D of closed L-formulas. Moreover, D is required to be consistent in the sense that A and A^* must not both be elements of D, for any closed L-formula A.*

Note that domains may be finite or infinite. Let us now give some examples of domains.

Example 1 (Arith). Let $L = \{0, s, +, \cdot, =\}$ be a language of arithmetic. Here s is a symbol of the successor function. Let *Arith* consist of the true closed formulas of this language, i.e. the atomic diagram of N. Thus *Arith* contains, e.g. the following formulas (using numerals so that 2 represents $s(s(0))$, etc.): $2 + 2 = 4, 2 + 3 \neq 4, 2 \cdot (3 + 2) = 10$.

Example 2 (Bool). Let $L = \{\top, \bot, \neg, \wedge, \vee, =\}$ be a language for representing boolean expressions. Let *Bool* consist of all true closed L-formulas. Thus *Bool* contains, e.g. $\top = \top, \neg\bot = \top, \bot \neq \top$.

Example 3 (Graph). Let $L = \{a, b, c, R\}$ be a language for representing graphs. Let *Graph* $= \{R(a, b), R(a, c), \neg R(b, a)\}$. This domain can be interpreted as a partly specified graph, or, equivalently, as a class of graphs meeting the given specification.

Example 4 (Network). Consider a neural network that observes its environment via three binary sensors. To describe its input at a given moment in time we may use a language that includes one constant c_i per sensor and a predicate symbol *Active*(x). Then we may specify its input by letting, e.g. *Network* $= \{Active(c_1), Active(c_2), \neg Active(c_3)\}$.

Remark 1 (Generality of our notion of domain). An alternative definition of domain would be to say that a domain is a model (i.e. a structure) of the kind used in model theory [8]. This notion of model is very general since it includes, e.g. all algebraic structures and models of set theory. In principle, models of the model-theoretic kind can be described by the domains that we use here by expanding the language with new constants if necessary.

Our notion of domain is slightly more general than the notion of model used in model theory, since it allows for completely as well as partially specified models. Thus our domains might represent specific models as well as classes of models.

We will use the notation L_D for the (uniquely determined smallest) language of the domain D.

2.3   Axiomatic Reasoning

Definition 8 (Statement). *A statement is an expression of the form $A \in D$, where D is a domain and A is an L_D-formula.*

Note that the formula A in the above definition may contain variables.

Example 5 (Statements). Some examples of statements: $R(a, b) \in Graph$, $\neg R(a, c) \in Graph$, $R(x, x) \in Graph$, $1 + 2 = 3 \in Arith$, $0 \neq 1 \in Arith$, $x \cdot 0 = 0 \in Arith$, $\top \wedge \bot = \bot \in Bool$, $\top \neq \bot \in Arith$, and $x \neq \neg x \in Arith$.

Definition 9 (Assignment). *An L-assignment is a function α that assigns closed L-terms to the variables x, y, and z.*

Definition 10 (Belief set). *A belief set is a finite set of statements.*

Definition 11 (Belief application). *An application of the belief $A \in D$ is a computation step of the following form:*

$$\frac{\alpha(A) \in D}{\Box} A \in D$$

Here $\alpha(A)$ is an arbitrary L_D-assignment and the symbol $\Box$ signifies QED.

Example 6 (Belief application). Here is an example of an application of the belief $x\dot{0} = 0 \in Arith$:

$$\frac{3 \cdot 0 = 0 \in Arith}{\Box} x \cdot 0 = 0 \in Arith$$

Definition 12 (Sound belief). *A belief $A \in D$ is sound if $\alpha(A) \in D$ for each L_D-assignment α.*

For instance, all the beliefs of the above example are sound.

Definition 13 (Rule). *A D-rule is a pair of L_D-terms (t, t').*

Note that rules may contain variables.

Example 7 (Rules). Here are some examples of rules:

- $(1 + 2, 3)$, $(x \cdot 0, 0)$, and $(x + y, y + x)$ are *Arith*-rules.
- $(\top \wedge \bot, \bot)$, $(\top \wedge x, x)$, $(x \vee y, y \vee x)$ are *Bool*-rules.

Definition 14 (Sound rule). *The D-rule (t, t') is sound if $\alpha(A(t)) \in D$ iff $\alpha(A(t')) \in D$, for every L_D-formula A and L_D-assignment α.*

All the rules of the previous example are sound. For instance, $A(1+2) \in Arith$ iff $A(3) \in Arith$, for all L_{Arith}-formulas A. Also, $A(\top \wedge \bot) \in Bool$ iff $A(\bot) \in Bool$, for all L_{Bool}-formulas A.

Definition 15 (Rule application). *An* application *of the D-rule (t, t') is a computation step of the following form:*

$$\frac{\alpha(A(t)) \in D}{\alpha(A(t')) \in D} (t, t')$$

Here α can be an arbitrary L_D-assignment.

Note that if the rule (t, t') is sound for D, then we can infer that $\alpha(A(t)) \in D$ if we know that $\alpha(A(t')) \in D$.

Definition 16 (Axiomatic computation). *Let B be a set of beliefs and let R be a set of rules. An* axiomatic computation *based on B and R is a finite sequence of statements $A \in D$. Moreover, the steps of the computation are given by applications of beliefs in B and rules in R.*

Example 8 (Axiomatic computation). Here is an example of an axiomatic computation:

$$\cfrac{\cfrac{\cfrac{\cfrac{0 * 12 = 0 \in Arith}{12 * 0 = 0 \in Arith}\,(x * y, y * x) \in R}{0 = 0 \in Arith}\,(x * 0, 0) \in R}{\square}\,x = x \in B}$$

2.4   Analogical Reasoning

Definition 17 (Analogy). *Let S and T be two domains. An* analogy *from S to T is a partial function $\tau : S \rightarrow T$ that maps function symbols to function symbols of the same arity and relation symbols to relation symbols of the same arity.*

Definition 18 (Extended analogy). *Let $\tau : S \rightarrow T$ be an analogy from S to T. Then τ can be directly* extended *to a partial function τ^+ that maps formulas in S on L_T-formulas by mapping symbol for symbol. For notational simplicity we will usually write τ instead of τ^+.*

Definition 19 (Sound analogy). *An analogy τ from S to T is* sound *if $A \in S$ iff $\tau(A) \in T$, for every closed L_S-formula A.*

Note that from a practical perspective, determining soundness of analogies and rules might be difficult, since it involves checking universally quantified statements in both cases. Now let us look at some examples of analogies.

Example 9 (Aristotle's analogy). Let $HandDomain = \{Under(hand, palm)\}$ and let $FootDomain = \{Under(foot, sole)\}$. Then the mapping going from $HandDomain$ to $FootDomain$ that maps $Under$ to $Under$, $hand$ to $foot$, and $palm$ to $sole$ is a sound analogy.

Example 10 (Rutherford's analogy). Let $SolarDomain = \{Circles(sun, planet)\}$ and let $AtomicDomain = \{Circles(nucleus, electron)\}$. Then the mapping from $SolarDomain$ to $AtomicDomain$ that maps $Circles$ to $Circles$, sun to $nucleus$, and $planet$ to $electron$ is a sound analogy. Although this analogy is seriously flawed from the perspective of physics, it illustrates how analogies can be used for generating scientific hypotheses.

Example 11 (Group analogy). Let $\mathbb{R}$ be the real numbers and let $\{c_u : u \in \mathbb{R}\}$ be a language for discussing real numbers. Moreover, let $Additive = \{c_u + c_v = c_w : u + v = w\}$ and $Multiplicative = \{c_u \cdot c_v = c_w : u \cdot v = w\}$ be domains. Then the mapping c_u to c_{e^u} and $+$ to $\cdot$ is a sound analogy. In fact, the mapping $u \mapsto e^u$ is a group homomorphism from the additive to the multiplicative group of real numbers.

Definition 20 (Accuracy). *Suppose S and T are (non-empty) finite domains. Then the* accuracy *of the analogy τ from S to T is the number*

$$\frac{card(\{A \in S : \tau(A) \in T\})}{card(S)}.$$

Example 12 (A natural language analogy). Consider a simple case of translation between two natural languages. For instance, suppose that S and T are two domains that describe a certain family using a vocabulary of basic family relations in two different natural languages. Then the dictionary translation of the relevant words might be an analogy or at least have relatively high accuracy.

Definition 21 (Analogy application). *An* application *of the analogy τ from D_i to D_j is a computational step of the following form:*

$$\frac{A \in D_i}{\tau(A) \in D_j} \tau$$

Note that if τ is sound, then we can infer that $A \in D_i$ if we know that $\tau(A) \in D_j$.

Example 13 (Analogy application). Here is an application of Aristotle's analogy:

$$\frac{Under(hand, palm) \in HandDomain}{Under(foot, sole) \in FootDomain} \tau$$

Definition 22 (Knowledge base). *A* knowledge base *for the domains* $D_0, \ldots, D_n$ *consists of the following:*

1. *a set of beliefs B_i for each domain D_i,*
2. *a set of rules R_i for each domain D_i, and*
3. *an analogy $\tau_{i,j}$ for each pair of domains D_i and D_j.*

Let us remark here that this notion of knowledge base is in line with Hofstadter's statement that "analogies happen inside your head" and are "connections between two mental representations" [9].

Definition 23 (Sound knowledge base). *By extending the previously defined soundness concepts we will say that a knowledge base for $D_0, \ldots, D_n$ is sound if its beliefs, rules, and analogies are sound w.r.t. the relevant domains.*

Next we generalize the notion of axiomatic computation.

Definition 24 (Computation). *Let K be a knowledge base for $D_0, \ldots, D_n$. A computation in K is a sequence of expressions of the form $A \in D$, where D is a domain and A is a closed formula of L_D. Moreover, the steps of the computation are given by the previously defined applications of beliefs, rules, and analogies of K.*

Below is a schematic example of a computation in K:

$$\frac{\dfrac{\dfrac{A \in D_i}{A' \in D_i}\ (t,t') \in R_i}{A'' \in D_j}\ \tau_{i,j}}{\square}\ A''' \in B_j$$

Now we come to an important point. Suppose we want to know whether $A \in D_i$ and have at our disposal the computation given above. Moreover, let us assume that K is sound for $D_0, \ldots, D_n$. Then we can start at the bottom of the computation and proceed one step at a time while repeatedly invoking the soundness of K in order to conclude that all statements appearing in the computation, in particular $A \in D_i$, are true.

3   System Description

Based on the mathematical model presented in the previous section we have developed a prototype system ALICE IN WONDERLAND+ that generalizes and extends our previously developed system ALICE IN WONDERLAND [11]. The code of ALICE IN WONDERLAND+ is available at `github.com/arnizamani`.

ALICE IN WONDERLAND+ is equipped with a knowledge base that develops over time and can be initialized arbitrarily at $t = 0$. It is surrounded by an arbitrary number of domains $D_0, \ldots, D_n$ and it receives information about those domains at each t in the form of observations:

Definition 25 (Observation stream). *An observation stream from $D_0, \ldots,$ D_n is a stream of statements of the form $A \in D_i$, where $0 \leq i \leq n$.*

Here is an example of an observation stream:

$$1 + 1 = 2 \in Arith, R(a, b) \in Graph, \neg R(a, c) \in Graph, \top \vee \bot = \top \in Bool, \ldots$$

The system responds to the observation stream by updating the knowledge base after each statement it receives. Its constant goal is to build a knowledge base that reflects the domains $D_0, \ldots, D_n$ as well as possible.

The learning mechanism of ALICE IN WONDERLAND+ includes rote learning, generalization, inductive learning, analogical learning, and belief revision. The reasoning mechanism supports axiomatic and analogical reasoning, as described in Sect. 2. The reasoning mechanism serves to update the knowledge base and respond to queries. The system searches for analogies between domains and prefers analogies with high accuracy, i.e. analogies that preserve as many closed formulas as possible. It searches for computations of the general type that was described in Sect. 2 and the search is (necessarily) restricted to computations that use bounded cognitive resources.

4   System Evaluation

To begin with, ALICE IN WONDERLAND+ has the full learning and reasoning power of the system ALICE IN WONDERLAND, which is evaluated in [11]. Also, ALICE IN WONDERLAND+ uses a more general format for domains than ALICE IN WONDERLAND. Moreover, ALICE IN WONDERLAND+ is capable of analogical reasoning and of mixing analogical and axiomatic reasoning. Let us give two basic examples of how the system uses analogical reasoning.

4.1   Rutherford's Analogy

Suppose the system has developed the following set of beliefs:

1. Moves(electron) $\in$ Atomic
2. Stationary(nucleus) $\in$ Atomic
3. Smaller(electron, nucleus) $\in$ Atomic
4. Moves(planet) $\in$ Solar
5. Circles(planet, sun) $\in$ Solar
6. Smaller(planet, sun) $\in$ Solar

Given a query Circles(electron, nucleus) $\in$ Atomic, the system, being unable to prove it with axiomatic reasoning only, finds the following analogy $\tau_{Atomic, Solar}$:

- $\tau(\text{electron}) = \text{planet}$
- $\tau(\text{nucleus}) = \text{sun}$

This analogy preserves two closed formulas: $1 \mapsto 4$ and $3 \mapsto 6$. Now, a proof of the query is computed as follows:

$$\frac{\dfrac{\text{Circles(electron, nucleus)} \in \text{Atomic}}{\text{Circles(planet, sun)} \in \text{Solar}} \, \tau_{Atomic, Solar}}{\Box} \, \text{Circles(planet, sun)} \in \text{Solar}$$

4.2   Natural Language Analogy

Suppose the system starts with an empty set of beliefs. In particular it knows nothing about natural languages or animals. Next, assume that it learns a number of facts by rote learning, including the following:

1. $Grazes(cow) \in English$
2. $Small(sheep) \in English$
3. $Large(horse) \in English$
4. $Larger(horse, sheep) \in English$
5. $Grande(mucca) \in Italian$
6. $Pascola(cavallo) \in Italian$
7. $Pi\grave{u}Grande(cavallo, pecora) \in Italian$

Now, suppose that the system gets the query $Pascola(mucca) \in Italian$. Then it fails to answer the query with axiomatic reasoning, but finds the following analogy, which preserves the maximum number of facts among analogies of size at most 4:

$$\tau_{Italian, English} = \{(cavallo, horse), (mucca, cow), (Pascola, Grazes), (Pi\grave{u}Grande, Larger)\}.$$

Using this analogy, the system next finds the following computation and thus answers the query positively (still without knowing much about languages or animals):

$$\cfrac{\cfrac{\cfrac{Pascola(mucca) \in Italian}{Grazes(cow) \in English}\ \tau_{Italian, English}}{\Box}\ Grazes(cow) \in English}$$

5   Conclusions

We have shown that axiomatic and analogical reasoning can be integrated in a fully automatic system that is surrounded by symbolic domains. By generalizing and extending our system ALICE IN WONDERLAND, we obtained the system ALICE IN WONDERLAND+, which supports reasoning processes that use analogies to jump back and forth between domains. Admittedly ALICE IN WONDERLAND+ breaks no new ground in axiomatic reasoning, analogical reasoning, or linguistics. Rather, the strength of ALICE IN WONDERLAND+ lies in its generality. In fact it is capable of fully automatic learning and reasoning in any number of arbitrary symbolic domains.

Acknowledgement. This research was supported by The Swedish Research Council, grant 2012-1000.

References

1. Bartha, P.: Analogy and analogical reasoning. In: Zalta, E.N. (ed.) The Stanford Encyclopedia of Philosophy. Stanford University, fall 2013 edn. (2013)
2. Cornuéjols, A.: Analogie, principe d'économie et complexité algorithmique. Actes des 11èmes Journées Françaises de l'Apprentissage (1996)
3. De La Tour, T.B., Peltier, N.: Analogy in automated deduction: a survey. In: Prade, H., Richard, G. (eds.) Computational Approaches to Analogical Reasoning: Current Trends. SCI, vol. 548, pp. 103–130. Springer, Heidelberg (2014)
4. Falkenhainer, B., Forbus, K.D., Gentner, D.: The structure-mapping engine: Algorithm and examples. Artif. Intell. **41**(1), 1–63 (1989)
5. Gentner, D.: Structure-mapping: A theoretical framework for analogy*. Cogn. Sci. **7**(2), 155–170 (1983)
6. Gust, H., Krumnack, U., Kühnberger, K.U., Schwering, A.: Analogical reasoning: A core of cognition. KI **22**(1), 8–12 (2008)
7. Gust, H., Kühnberger, K.U., Schmid, U.: Metaphors and heuristic-driven theory projection (hdtp). Theor. Comput. Sci. **354**(1), 98–117 (2006)
8. Hodges, W.: Model theory, vol. 42. Cambridge University Press, New York (1993)
9. Hofstadter, D.: Analogy as the core of cognition, presidential Lecture by Douglas Hofstadter at Stanford University, February 2006
10. Kitzelmann, E.: Inductive programming: a survey of program synthesis techniques. In: Schmid, U., Kitzelmann, E., Plasmeijer, R. (eds.) AAIP 2009. LNCS, vol. 5812, pp. 50–73. Springer, Heidelberg (2010)
11. Nizamani, A.R., Juel, J., Persson, U., Strannegård, C.: Bounded cognitive resources and arbitrary domains. In: Bieger, J., Goertzel, B., Potapov, A. (eds.) AGI 2015. LNCS, vol. 9205, pp. 166–176. Springer, Heidelberg (2015)
12. Phillips, S., Wilson, W.H.: Categorial compositionality: A category theory explanation for the systematicity of human cognition. PLoS Comput. Biol. **6**(7), e1000858 (2010)
13. Phillips, S., Wilson, W.H.: Categorial compositionality ii: Universal constructions and a general theory of (quasi-) systematicity in human cognition. PLoS Comput. Biol. **7**(8), e1002102 (2011)
14. Pólya, G.: Mathematics and plausible reasoning: Induction and analogy in mathematics, vol. 1. Princeton University Press, Princeton (1990)
15. Robinson, A., Voronkov, A.: Handbook of Automated Reasoning. Elsevier, San Diego (2001)
16. Schmidt, M., Krumnack, U., Gust, H., Kühnberger, K.U.: Heuristic-driven theory projection: an overview. In: Prade, H., Richard, G. (eds.) Computational Approaches to Analogical Reasoning: Current Trends. SCI, vol. 548, pp. 163–194. Springer, Heidelberg (2014)

Embracing Inference as Action:
A Step Towards Human-Level Reasoning

John Licato[(✉)] and Maxwell Fowler

Department of Computer Science,
Analogical Constructivism and Reasoning Lab (ACoRL),
Indiana University/Purdue University - Fort Wayne (IPFW),
Fort Wayne, IN 46835, USA
licatoj@ipfw.edu

Abstract. Human-level AI involves the ability to reason about the beliefs of other agents, even when those other agents have reasoning styles that may be very different than the AI's. The ability to carry out reasonable inferences in such situations, as well as in situations where an agent must reason about the beliefs of another agent's beliefs about yet another agent, is under-studied. We show how such reasoning can be carried out in a new variant of the cognitive event calculus we call $\mathcal{CEC}_{AC}$, by introducing several new powerful features for automated reasoning: First, the implementation of classical logic at the "system-level" and nonclassical logics at the "belief-level"; Second, $\mathcal{CEC}_{AC}$ treats all inferences made by agents as *actions*. This opens the door for two more additional features: *epistemic boxes*, which are a sort of frame in which the reasoning of an individual agent can be simulated, and *evaluated codelets*, which allow our reasoner to carry out operations beyond the limits of many current systems. We explain how these features are achieved and implemented in the MATR reasoning system, and discuss their consequences.

Imagine, in the not-too-distant future, an artificially-general-intelligent robot, r, is in a room with two humans: its master, m, (to whom r is loyal), and an opponent, o. The robot believes it is essential, for the survival of itself and its master, that m understands that q is true, but that o neither learn nor come to believe that q holds (possibly because o may react negatively and attempt to kill m and destroy r). Because all three are in a small room where anything r says is heard by both o and m (r's telepathic link with m has been damaged), r must somehow say something that will cause m to believe q, but not allow o to figure it out. What can r possibly say?

A human might look at this problem and conclude "r should say some p that m would figure out implies q (due to some beliefs that m already has), but which o would not figure out (since o does not have those same beliefs)." But the AI problem of figuring out that some given p would satisfy this criteria turns out to be non-trivial as we approach situations that are increasingly realistic. For example, assuming that r has to perform some sort of simulation of what o and m would infer given certain beliefs, what if the expressivity of the language in

© Springer International Publishing Switzerland 2016
B. Steunebrink et al. (Eds.): AGI 2016, LNAI 9782, pp. 192–201, 2016.
DOI: 10.1007/978-3-319-41649-6_19

which r reasons is lower than that of the languages in which o and m reason? In such a case, any attempt by r to predict the inferences o and m would produce in response to learning p would be disastrous.

Furthermore, contemporary approaches to doxastic reasoning assume all agents are perfect logical reasoners who believe the logical closures of their belief sets are problematic. What if r reasons non-monotonically and o or m do not, or vice versa? What if r reasons according to classical logic, but the humans do not? r's ability to simulate the reasoning of o and m is limited if r erroneously believes all three follow the same set of inference rules.

Finally, if an artificial agent a has knowledge of which beliefs and inference rules another agent b has, and the ability to simulate inferences using b's beliefs and rules, it is relatively easy to show that some new inference i can be produced from finite applications of b's beliefs and rules. But due to computational limitations, it is much harder to show that some inference i' does *not* follow from these same beliefs and rules (note this is different from showing that the negation of i follows from b's beliefs and rules). Yet a human, reasoning about the beliefs of another agent b, may be able to at least offer a weak argument that b will not come to believe some i, even if the human's argument relies on inductive rules of inference that are not guaranteed to preserve truth.[1]

These are problems that might be faced by AGIs of the future, and understanding how to address them may be necessary to move towards human-level AI. In this paper, we present a way to carry out the sort of reasoning described in the robot-human situation above; this reasoning is based on a new variant of the cognitive event calculus, presented here for the first time, which we will call $\mathcal{CEC}_{AC}$. The $\mathcal{CEC}_{AC}$ formalism embraces several principles, two of which we will describe here: First, the idea that all inferences should be treated as actions; and second, the idea that classical logic (insofar as first-order modal logic can be considered 'classical') should be the formalism at the system-level, and non-classical logics should be the default formalisms at the belief-level. We will show how a new type of automated reasoner (called MATR) can meet the unique mechanical needs of $\mathcal{CEC}_{AC}$, and close with a discussion of limitations and future work.

1 $\mathcal{CEC}$ and $\mathcal{CEC}_{AC}$

The cognitive event calculus ($\mathcal{CEC}$) is a framework based on a first-order modal logic [1], thus extending the event calculus formalism [5]. $\mathcal{CEC}$ contains modal operators allowing the expression of beliefs ($\mathbf{B}(a, t, \phi)$ means an agent a believes ϕ at time t), knowledge ($\mathbf{K}$), intentions ($\mathbf{I}$), and more. $\mathcal{CEC}$ is part of a family of cognitive calculi [3], and this paper presents a new member of this family: $\mathcal{CEC}_{AC}$, the Analogical Constructivism variant of $\mathcal{CEC}$. In a sense, $\mathcal{CEC}_{AC}$ is meant to be an *experimental* formalism, one that regularly plays with the borders of

---

[1] Imagine, for example, coming up with an argument supporting the statement "no politician will ever say anything that isn't self-serving." Your generated argument (for most people) likely consists of a chain of inferences of inductive strength, rather than a proof that has the weight of full deductive validity.

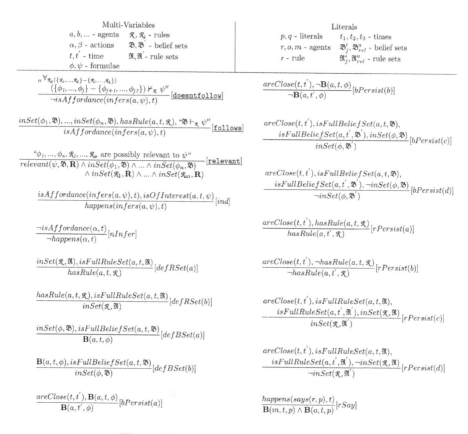

Fig. 1. Inference rules used for r's situation

traditional cognitive formalisms, e.g. by the use of nonclassical logics, as will be shown next.

Classical Outside, Nonclassical Inside. Human reasoners quite often find themselves facing contradictory beliefs, even when they abide primarily by generally accepted principles of rationality [10]. However, many logical frameworks based on classical logic have some form of the rule known as *"ex contradictione quodlibet"* (ECQ), also known as the principle of explosion. ECQ (broadly summarized) allows any valid formula to follow from any contradition, so for instance if a reasoner believes that "it's true that pizza tastes good, and it's not true that pizza tastes good," it follows that "the moon is made of blue cheese."

Nonclassical logics [9] try to address these weaknesses of classical logics, often by disallowing inference rules that are responsible for the logic's undesirable behavior. Paraconsistent logics, for example, might disallow ECQ and the law of non-contradiction (for any formula, it is not true that both the formula and its negation are true). Such nonclassical logics, however, come with a set of trade-offs — in paraconsistent logics, meta-theoretical properties may be more difficult to prove, but modeling the aspects of human-level reasoning that seem to embrace contradictory beliefs becomes easier.

Our solution, implemented in a variant of CEC that we will call $\mathcal{CEC}_{AC}$, makes use of classical logics at the "system-level" (the set of formulae that are not nested inside of doxastic operators), but nonclassical logics at the "belief-level" (the level of formulae nested inside of operators such as $\mathbf{B}$, $\mathbf{K}$, etc.). It may thus be acceptable to conclude $\mathbf{B}(a, t, \phi \wedge \neg\phi)$, but $\phi \wedge \neg\phi$ is highly problematic.

Inferences Are Always Actions. The rich formal machinery of the event calculus allows $\mathcal{CEC}_{AC}$ to deeply embrace the idea that inferences are a type of action, a move in step with analogical constructivism [6] (hence the AC subscript). In the event calculus, actions typically consist of a formula of one first-order language reified into the term of another first-order language [8]. Here, we define an inference as an action $infers(a, \phi)$ where a is an agent and ϕ is the formula that a infers. If the inference occurs at time t, it is written as $happens(infers(a, \phi), t)$.

We define an agent's *affordance set* as the set of possible actions (or *affordances*, [4]) an agent can take at some given time. If an agent a has the ability to infer ϕ at time t, then $isAffordance(infers(a, \phi), t)$. Affordances allow us to describe agents that do not automatically create new beliefs simply because those beliefs follow logically from their current set of beliefs. Rather, the act of belief creation is something that happens at a point in time, depending on the set of beliefs an agent has, and the set of *rules* the agent acts in accordance with. Inference rules are presented in Fig. 1, with antecedent conditions on the top of the horizontal lines and conclusions below, with rule names on the right sides.

Using affordances, we can distinguish between three forms of inference rules: first-person, automatic, and affording. Consider the rules:

$$\frac{\phi, \phi \to \psi}{\psi} [R_1] \qquad\qquad \frac{\mathbf{B}(a, t, \phi), \mathbf{B}(a, t, \phi \to \psi)}{\mathbf{B}(a, t, \psi)} [R_2]$$

$$\frac{\mathbf{B}(a, t, \phi), \mathbf{B}(a, t, \phi \to \psi)}{isAffordance(infers(a, \psi), t)} [R_3]$$

The form of inference rule used in R_1, which we will call the *first-person* form, may be used when reasoning about the possible inferences that some given agent may make at some given time. It is often convenient to use this rule form when doxastic and temporal features are not relevant, or are assumed.

The form of inference rule denoted R_2 is probably the most common in doxastic logics. But it is not always applicable in every situation. If agent a has the beliefs at time t that ϕ and $\phi \to \psi$ hold, it does not always follow that a always has the belief ψ at time t as well. It may be that a simply did not consider the two beliefs simultaneously, or that a never got around to considering the full implications of her beliefs (perhaps due to computational and temporal limitations). Or, depending on the definition of belief adopted, it may be that a is not fully aware of her beliefs, at least to a degree where she can represent them explicitly and use them to produce principled inferences. Furthermore, the application of rule R_2 is done silently; it does not create an *infers* event, nor does it produce any awareness in a's mind that rule R_2, as opposed to some other rule, was used to produce a new belief. The form of inference rule used in R_2 will be called *automatic*.

The *affording* rule form, demonstrated in R_3, instead treats $\phi \to \psi$ as a possible inference, one which may or may not be made by a. Note that there is some room here for additional rules to specify precisely how inference affordances achieve fruition, i.e., how a possible inference becomes an actual belief. For this paper, one such proposed mechanism draws on the concept of *interest*: if ψ is of interest to a, and is also a possible inference in a's affordances, we can safely infer (with some inductive strength) that $infers(a, \psi)$ will happen.

Belief and Rule Sets. Because $\mathcal{CEC}_{\mathsf{AC}}$ is a first-order modal language, we can not easily use higher-order constructs to represent formulae quantifying over sets. However, there are cases where an agent, reasoning about another, may need to reason about sets of beliefs or sets of rules in order to reach conclusions in a human-plausible way. To address this problem, rather than adopting full-blown second-order logic, four sorts are introduced: *setSymbol*, its two sub-sorts *beliefSet* and *ruleSet*, and *ruleSymbol*. The predicate *inSet* corresponds to the standard set-membership operator. A symbol of sort *ruleSymbol* is introduced for every possible inference rule. If an agent a believes $isFullBeliefSet(b, t, \mathfrak{B})$, then agent a believes $inSet(\phi, \mathfrak{B})$ if and only if a believes $\mathbf{B}(a, t, \phi)$. Likewise, if a believes $isFullRuleSet(b, t, \mathfrak{R})$, then agent a believes $inSet(r, \mathfrak{R})$ if and only if a believes $hasRule(b, t, r)$.

Through these sorts and symbols, an agent a can reason about the rules another agent b follows to produce its inferences, or reason about b's beliefs *as a group*, without explicit reasoning about every possible belief a believes b has.

Inductive Inferences. In our toy example, r has no real basis to conclude with certainty that saying p will lead to the effects r desires. That requires a perfect knowledge of all of m and o's beliefs, rules, and some knowledge of all possible confounding factors. If what we are after is human-level reasoning, then, we must allow for inferences that do not necessarily have deductive validity, which do not require a perfect knowledge of all beliefs, rules, and possible events, and furthermore, which shies away from requiring exhaustive calculations of all possibilities, unless such calculations are normally performed by a commonsense human reasoner.

If we are after the ability to generate plausible, reasonable arguments that a human would create or accept upon hearing, then we need to adopt inductive inferences, at least at the belief-level. For this paper, we assume that r has the *rPersist* group of rules, such as $rPersist(a)$ (Fig. 1), presented in its first-person form. $rPersist(a)$ can be interpreted as saying if two time points t and t' are very close together, the fact that agent a acts in accordance with rule $\mathcal{R}$ does not change between t and t'. Such a rule, in the absence of other relevant information, seems *reasonable* to assume. However, crucially, treating $rPersist(a)$

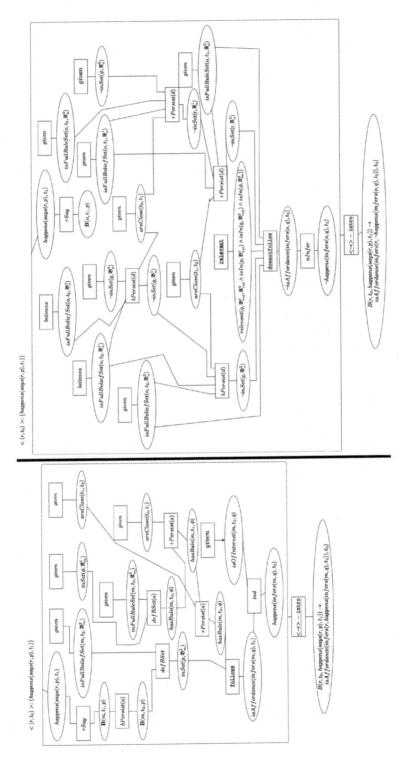

Fig. 2. Proof 1 (Left) and Proof 2 (Right)

as a deductive, truth-preserving rule will lead to inconsistent beliefs (reminiscent of the classic paradox of "Theseus's ship"). $rPersist(a)$ is a rule that cannot appear in its first-person form at the system-level — unless it appears within an *epistemic box*, which we will explain next.

1.1   Boxes

The proof theory we are using is an extension of the one used by MATR (Machina Arachne Tree-based Reasoner),[2] containing *boxes*, a construct similar to the indented subproofs in Fitch-style natural deduction [2]. Formulae inside of a box are inside of the box's *context*, and the box itself is always within some parent context (except for the root context, which is a special box with no parent). Boxes contain a supposition set (written in curly brackets above the box), a list of formulae assumed to hold for the context inside of the box. Boxes themselves can be used as antecedents of inferences. Formulae that are in the same context as the boxes can be re-introduced inside of the box's context; any formulae reintroduced in this way are part of the box's *reiteration set*.

One of $\mathcal{CEC}$'s strengths is that it allows for the arbitrarily deep nesting of beliefs in an unambiguous way, so that an agent's beliefs about another agent's beliefs won't be confused with the first agent's own. But the notation for such situations can become somewhat cumbersome, especially considering affordances require all inferences made by agents to first enter the pool of possible actions.

To address these concerns, we introduce the concept of *epistemic boxes*, boxes that should be thought of as simulating the inferences of some particular agent at a given time. They currently come in two types. $[(a,t)]$-boxes are designed to show what sequence of inferences *will* happen for agent a at time t. Because we will not be using $[(a,t)]$-boxes in this paper, we will not discuss them further. $<(a,t)>$-boxes are designed to show a sequence of inferences that are *possible* for agent a at time t. For any $<(a,t)>$-box $\mathbb{B}$, with parent box $\mathbb{P}$, the following must hold:

- Formulae ϕ can be in $\mathbb{B}$'s reiteration set only if $\mathbf{B}(a,t,\phi)$ holds in $\mathbb{P}$'s context.
- If formulae ϕ_1 and ϕ_2 lead to an inference of ψ (where all three formulae are inside $\mathbb{B}$), then the formulae $\mathbf{B}(a,t,\phi_1)$, $\mathbf{B}(a,t,\phi_2)$, and $isAffordance(infers(a,\psi),t)$ must all hold at $\mathbb{P}$'s context.
- If $\frac{\phi_1,...,\phi_n}{\psi}$ is an inference rule that holds within $\mathbb{B}$, then the rule $\frac{\mathbf{B}(a,t,\phi_1),...,\mathbf{B}(a,t,\phi_n)}{isAffordance(infers(a,\psi),t)}$ must hold at $\mathbb{P}$'s context.

The only inference rules that hold in an $<(a,t)>$-box are those that, when transformed from the first-person to affording forms, hold in the context of the box's parent. If an $<(a,t)>$-box $\mathbb{B}$, with supposition set $\{\gamma_1,...,\gamma_n\}$, produces the inference ψ within $\mathbb{B}$, then in $\mathbb{B}$'s parent context we can infer:

---

[2] MATR is currently being developed by a collaboration between the Rensselaer AI and Reasoning (RAIR) Lab, and the Analogical Constructivism and Reasoning Lab (ACoRL).

$$(\mathbf{B}(a, t, \gamma_1) \wedge ... \wedge \mathbf{B}(a, t, \gamma_n)) \rightarrow isAffordance(infers(a, \psi), t)$$

This inference is done using the evaluated inference rule `<->-intro` (examples of its use are seen in Fig. 2). However, because specifying the supposition set in its entirety again requires a higher-order logic, actually implementing this rule requires a special computational ability, which we will describe next.

1.2 Evaluated Codelets

MATR-style reasoning implements its reasoning by dividing most of the hard work amongst *codelets* (a term borrowed from the *Copycat* model [7]), which can be thought of as little independently-operating processes. Each codelet looks at the current state of a proof and make suggestions to the central proof manager (the Codelet Manager, or CM) about what inferences should be made. Generally, one codelet is created for each inference rule, so that the codelet can specialize in efficient algorithms for locating appropriate areas of the current proof state to make suggestions. Codelets can be small and quick (like the codelets that look at the current state of a proof and suggest ways to shorten it), or large and possibly slow (such as codelets that serve as wrappers for full automated theorem provers).

Codelets, implemented as Java programs, can theoretically run any program and use any criteria to evaluate whether an inference should be suggested. The CM simply assumes that if a codelet suggests an inference, that inference is valid according to the semantics of the codelet. Thus, we can create codelets capable of implementing the sort of low-level, distributed algorithms common in state-of-the-art artificial intelligence, but lacking from automated theorem provers. We call these *evaluated codelets*—these are codelets that implement inference rules whose conditions contain semantics not entirely captured in the formal language of the antecedents. Instead, we specify these semantics in pseudo-formalized natural language statements.

Inference rules relying on evaluated codelets are referred to as *evaluated rules*. For example, consider the `follows` inference rule in Fig. 1 (note the use of tele-type font and an underline to denote evaluated codelets), which can be invoked if some ϕ follows from an agent's belief set and an inference rule that agent has. In such evaluated rules, we can accept an arbitrary number of conditions in the antecedent (denoted by the ellipsis) and any arbitrary requirement in the quotation marks; often we will use natural language statements. It is up to the codelet to implement the semantics expressed in the quotation marks faithfully.[3]

Evaluated codelets are particularly useful when a conclusion should be inferred on the basis of something not captured in the logical form of the $\mathcal{CEC}_{AC}$ formulae alone. This is why the inference rule `<->-intro` is implemented as

---

[3] Of course, we acknowledge such a violation of referential transparency means that actual semantics of evaluated codelets may vary, possibly significantly, between different implementations, and provide a level of (possibly dangerous) flexibility not seen in any other automated reasoners (to our knowledge).

an evaluated codelet. As another example, if the analogical similarity between two formulae needs to be found, we might use a structural comparison of the formulae themselves. Although the method for comparison can be done through logical syntax alone, actually performing that structural comparison is best done with the use of a software package that may draw on distributed representations, vector operations, machine learning methods, etc. Thus, evaluated codelets allow MATR to combine the high-level reasoning and argument-generation powers of logic-based AI with the amazing advancements in nonlogical methods that have been dominating the field of machine learning in recent years.

As of now, there are several restrictions placed on evaluated codelets. Two instances of an implementation of an evaluated codelet, within the same context, given the same formulae as antecedents, must produce the same inference (if they produce any inference under those conditions). They can behave nonmonotonically (changing their inferences if more formulae are given as antecedents), but they may not behave randomly. Furthermore, certain evaluated codelets are only allowed within the context of epistemic boxes. For example, a codelet which tries to simulate the low-level similarity-based inferences of an agent may need to draw on agent-specific knowledge.

In this paper, we make use of four evaluated codelets: The first, $\underleftrightarrow{}$-intro has already been described:

$$\frac{\text{``}<(a,t)> \text{-box } \mathbb{B}\text{'s full supposition set is } \phi_1, ..., \phi_n \text{ and } \psi \text{ is inferred in } \mathbb{B}''}{(\mathbf{B}(a,t,\phi_1) \wedge ... \wedge \mathbf{B}(a,t,\phi_n)) \rightarrow isAffordance(infers(a,\psi),t)} [\underleftrightarrow{}\text{-intro}]$$

follows and **doesntFollow** determine whether or not a formula follows from another set of formulae, given some rule symbols. Finally, **relevant** takes a formulae ψ and uses some similarity-based algorithm to generate a set of formulae and inference rules that *may* be relevant to ψ (we do not specify here what algorithm should be used to determine relevance).

We present our proofs in Fig. 2, using MATR's visual style. r can possibly infer that if he says p, then m will infer q (Proof 1), while o will not (Proof 2). Assumptions made are denoted with the *given* codelet.

2 Future Work

The new $\mathcal{CEC}_{AC}$ features introduced in this paper are serious steps towards the creation of a new style of automated reasoning that can bridge the gap between informal and formal reasoning. However, it is clear that a lot more work is needed. Perhaps most notably lacking from the present work is a way to compare confidence in inductively-inferred beliefs, so that stronger beliefs can defeat the weaker ones. For example, it is easy to see how we can actually derive, with low confidence, an argument for $\mathbf{B}(r, t_0, \neg inSet(\psi, B_m^2))$, which would conflict with the conclusion of Proof 1. A satisfactory model of formula defeating would need to somehow assign a higher confidence to $\mathbf{B}(r, t_0, inSet(\psi, B_m^2))$.

We also don't discuss here how an agent might resolve between contradictory beliefs when a plan of action depends on such a resolution. This may require introducing a concept of "conscious acceptance", which we are currently developing.

Finally, we don't claim that our approach is the only way to do these things, nor that our way is always better than all alternatives (e.g. treating action inferences as a relation between possible worlds). For example, although our concept of action-as-inference was primarily motivated by the later work of Jean Piaget [6], new promising work based on the concept of *proof-events* is emerging [11], which considers proving as a process that unfolds through time. It is outside of the scope of this paper to fully compare all alternatives. Certainly, the idea of introducing inference rules whose semantics are implementation-specific may seem unusual to those firmly steeped in the logic-based AI tradition, but it is our hope that such measures will allow a flexibility not currently enjoyed by artificial reasoners.[4]

References

1. Arkoudas, K., Bringsjord, S.: Propositional attitudes and causation. Int. J. Softw. Inf. **3**(1), 47–65 (2009)
2. Barker-Plummer, D., Barwise, J., Etchemendy, J.: Language Proof and Logic. Center for the Study of Language and Inf, 2 edn., October 2011
3. Bringsjord, S., Govindarajulu, N.S., Licato, J., Sen, A., Johnson, J., Bringsjord, A., Taylor, J.: On logicist agent-based economics. In: Proceedings of Artificial Economics 2015 (AE 2015). University of Porto, Porto, Portugal (2015)
4. Gibson, J.: The theory of affordances. In: Shaw, R., Bransford, J. (eds.) Perceiving, Acting, and Knowing: Toward an Ecological Psychology. Erlbaum, Hillsdale, NJ (1977)
5. Kowalski, R., Sergot, M.: A logic-based calculus of events. New Gener. Comput. **4**(1), 67–94 (1986)
6. Licato, J.: Analogical Constructivism: The Emergence of Reasoning Through Analogy and Action Schemas. Ph.D. thesis, Rensselaer Polytechnic Institute, Troy, NY, May 2015
7. Mitchell, M.: Analogy-Making as Perception: A Computer Model. The MIT Press, Cambridge, Massachusetts (1993)
8. Mueller, E.T.: Commonsense Reasoning: An Event Calculus Based Approach, 2nd edn. Morgan Kaufmann, Waltham (2015)
9. Priest, G.: An Introduction to Non-Classical Logic: From If to Is, 2nd edn. Cambridge University Press, Cambridge (2008)
10. Priest, G., Tanaka, K., Weber, Z.: Paraconsistent logic. In: Zalta, E.N. (ed.) The Stanford Encyclopedia of Philosophy. spring 2015th edn. (2015). http://plato.stanford.edu/archives/spr2015/entries/logic-paraconsistent
11. Stefaneas, P., Vandoulakis, I.M.: On mathematical proving. J. Artif. Gen. Intell. **6**(1), 130–149 (2015)

---

[4] Dr. Licato, and the research presented here, was funded by the AFOSR Young Investigator's Program (YIP).

Asymptotic Logical Uncertainty and the Benford Test

Scott Garrabrant[1,2], Tsvi Benson-Tilsen[1,3], Siddharth Bhaskar[2],
Abram Demski[1,4(✉)], Joanna Garrabrant[1,2,3,4],
George Koleszarik[1,2,3,4], and Evan Lloyd[2]

[1] Machine Intelligence Research Institute, Berkeley, USA
abramdemski@gmail.com
[2] University of California, Los Angeles, USA
[3] University of California, Berkeley, USA
[4] University of Southern California, Los Angeles, USA

Abstract. Almost all formal theories of intelligence suffer from the problem of *logical omniscience*, the assumption that an agent already knows all consequences of its beliefs. *Logical uncertainty* codifies uncertainty about the consequences of existing beliefs. This implies a departure from beliefs governed by standard probability theory. Here, we study the asymptotic properties of beliefs on quickly computable sequences of logical sentences. Motivated by an example we call the Benford test, we provide an approach which identifies when such subsequences are indistinguishable from random, and learns their probabilities.

1 Introduction

Probabilistic reasoning about deterministic structures is a challenging case of uncertain reasoning which has received relatively little attention. This is the subject of *logical uncertainty* as defined in e.g. [1]: "any realistic agent is necessarily uncertain not only about its environment or about the future, but also about the logically necessary consequences of its beliefs." Being able to produce well-reasoned guesses about the results of programs before running them could provide valuable information for heuristic search, such as planning in complex environments or automatic programming. This kind of uncertainty can also be of wider interest. For example, [2] provides a call to arms for the development of numerical algorithms which provide information about the uncertainty in their results. [3] discusses the use of probabilistic information generated by machine learning to aid static program analysis for optimization.

One of the purest examples of this type of reasoning in humans is the formation of mathematical conjectures. Mathematical intuitions behave in a way that is largely consistent with the standard probability axioms [4]. However, they cannot be entirely so: probability theory requires belief in anything which follows logically from your current beliefs, and so cannot represent uncertainty about what may later be proved. This is known as the problem of *logical omniscience*, and is the main challenge faced by a theory of logical uncertainty [5–8].

© Springer International Publishing Switzerland 2016
B. Steunebrink et al. (Eds.): AGI 2016, LNAI 9782, pp. 202–211, 2016.
DOI: 10.1007/978-3-319-41649-6_20

Several proposals have addressed this problem by considering sequences of probability assignments[1] which converge to logically omniscient distributions, enforcing more and more constraints imposed by the probability axioms in the limit of unbounded computing resources [1,9,10]. With such a theoretical model in hand, one might think that the practical problem of logical uncertainty amounts to approaching this limit as quickly as possible. However, this is a fairly weak constraint on the behavior of beliefs at finite time.

If we're asked to quickly give a probability for a mathematical question, and the question belongs to a class of questions which have been true 25 % of the time, it seems we should give a probability close to 0.25. This type of reasoning is ignored if our only aim is to converge to a good probability distribution overall. Each individual question will converge to probability one or zero. This seems to ignore an essential part of the problem. So, we take a different approach. We consider the limit of a sequence of *sentences* within a *single* assignment of probabilities, rather than the limit of probabilities within a sequence of assignments. We call this approach *asymptotic logical uncertainty*. Our goal is not to provide an algorithm which may be used in an AGI directly, but rather, to illustrate a new desirable (and achievable) property of uncertain reasoning for AGI.

Section 2 discusses further related work. In Sect. 3, we define the Benford test as a concrete example of the type of reasoning we wish to model. Section 4 defines *irreducible patterns*, a concept used to define a general case where this sort of reasoning is justified. Section 5 proposes a learning algorithm to solve the problem in the general case, and Sect. 6 proves that the method is successful. Section 7 concludes.

2   Related Work

The most often-cited work relating probability to logic is almost certainly that of Cox [11], which shows that under certain desirable assumptions, probability theory is the only possible generalization of Boolean algebra. Other early work concerning measures over Boolean algebras include [12,13]. This has since been extended to first-order logic [14,15], and from there to other settings [16–18]. However, most of this work does not address computability.

An early articulation of the problem of logical omniscience was [5]. Many approaches have attempted to deal with this through theories of inconsistent structures, including [7,8]. The approach here is also related to online sequence learning using expert advice, to predict a sequence of observations almost as well as a given set of advisors [19], especially experts on sub-sequences as in [20].

3   The Benford Test

Benford's law states that in naturally occurring numbers, the leading digit $d \in \{1, \ldots, 9\}$ of that number in base 10 occurs with probability $\log_{10}(1 + \frac{1}{d})$. Many

---

[1] We will use the term "probability" to refer to degrees of belief generally, whether or not the probability axioms are obeyed.

mathematical sequences have been shown to have frequencies of first digits that satisfy Benford's law [21]. In particular, the frequencies of the first digits of powers of 3 provably satisfy Benford's law.

The function $3 \uparrow^n k$ is a fast-growing function defined by $3 \uparrow^1 k = 3^k$, $3 \uparrow^n 1 = 3$, and $3 \uparrow^n k = 3 \uparrow^{n-1} (3 \uparrow^n (k-1))$. $3 \uparrow^n k$ is very large, and first digit of $3 \uparrow^n k$ is probably very difficult to compute. It is unlikely that the first digit of $3 \uparrow^3 3$ will ever be known.

If asked to quickly assign a probability to the sentence "The first digit of $3 \uparrow^3 3$ is a 1," it seems the only reasonable answer would be to treat it as a power of three and reply $\log_{10}(2) \approx .30103$, as dictated by Benford's law. Note that the sentence is either true or false; there are no random variables. The probability here represents a reasonable guess in the absence of enough time or resources to compute $3 \uparrow^3 3$.

We define the Benford test to formalize this reasoning.[2] Throughout the paper, let the time-bound $T(N)$ be an increasing function in the range of $N \leq T(N) \leq 3 \uparrow^k N$ for some fixed k, and $R(N) = T(N)N^4 \log T(N)$ a larger time-bound.

Definition 1. *Let M be a Turing machine which on input N runs in time $O(R(N))$ and outputs a probability $M(N)$, which represents the probability assigned to ϕ_N. We say that M passes the* Benford test *if*

$$\lim_{n \to \infty} M(s_n) = \log_{10}(2), \tag{1}$$

where $\phi_{s_n} = $ "The first digit of $3 \uparrow^n 3$ is a 1."

It is easy to pass the Benford test by hard-coding in the probability. It is more difficult to pass the Benford test in a natural way. That the best probability to assign to ϕ_{s_n} is $\log_{10}(2)$ depends not only on the fact that the frequency with which ϕ_{s_n} is true tends toward $\log_{10}(2)$, but also on the fact that the sequence of truth-values of ϕ_{s_n} contains no patterns that can be used to quickly compute a better probability on some subsequence. We therefore assume that this sequence of truth-values is indistinguishable from a sequence produced by a coin that outputs "true" with probability $\log_{10}(2)$. Formally, we are assuming that $S = \{s_n | n \in \mathbb{N}\}$ is an *irreducible pattern* with probability $\log_{10}(2)$, as defined in the next section.

4   Irreducible Patterns

Let $\phi_1, \phi_2, \ldots$ be a simple enumeration of all sentences in first order logic over ZFC. Fix a universal Turing machine U and an encoding scheme for machines, and let $U(M, x)$ denote running the machine U to simulate M with input x.

---

[2] The test presumes that the frequencies of the first digits in the sequence $3 \uparrow^n 3$ satisfy Benford's law. Though this seems likely, the conjecture is not too important; any sufficiently fast-growing sequence satisfying Benford's law could serve as an example.

Definition 2. [3] *Let $S \subseteq \mathbb{N}$ be an infinite subset of natural numbers such that ϕ_N is provable or disprovable in ZFC for all $N \in S$, and there exists a Turing machine Z such that $U(Z, N)$ runs in time $T(N)$ and accepts N if and only if $N \in S$.*

We say that S is an irreducible pattern with probability p *if there exists a constant c such that for every positive integer $m \geq 3$ and every Turing machine W expressible in $K(W)$ bits, if*

$$S' = \{N \in S \mid U(W, N) \text{ accepts in time } T(N)\} \tag{2}$$

has at least m elements and $r(m, W)$ is the probability that ϕ_N is provable when N is chosen uniformly at random from the first m elements of S', we have

$$|r(m, W) - p| < \frac{cK(W)\sqrt{\log \log m}}{\sqrt{m}}. \tag{3}$$

The intuition behind the formula is that the observed frequency $r(m, W)$ for any sequence S' we select should not stray far from p. The right hand side of the inequality needs to shrink slowly enough that a true random process would stay within it with probability 1 (given choice of c sufficiently large to accommodate initial variation). The law of the iterated logarithm gives such a formula, which is also tight in the sense that we cannot replace it with a formula which diminishes more quickly as a function of m.

Proposition 1. *If provability in Definition 2 were decided randomly, such that for each $N \in S$ the sentence ϕ_N is independently called "provable" with probability p and "disprovable" otherwise, then S would almost surely be an irreducible pattern with probability p.*

Proof. Omitted due to space limitations.[4]

We now use the concept of irreducible patterns to generalize the Benford test.

Definition 3. *Let M be a Turing machine which on input N runs in time $O(R(N))$ and outputs a probability $M(N)$, which represents the probability assigned to ϕ_N. We say that M* passes the generalized Benford test *if*

$$\lim_{\substack{N \to \infty \\ N \in S}} M(N) = p, \tag{4}$$

whenever S is an irreducible pattern with probability p.

Note that if we conjecture that the S from Definition 1 is an irreducible pattern with probability $\log_{10}(2)$, then any M which passes the generalized Benford test also passes the Benford test.

---

[3] We tailored this definition of irreducible pattern to our needs. The theory of algorithmic randomness may offer alternatives. However, algorithmic randomness generally considers all computable tests and focuses on the case where $p = \frac{1}{2}$ [22,23]. We believe that any reasonable definition inspired by algorithmic randomness would imply Definition 2.

[4] See pre-print version [24] for the full proof.

5   A Learning Algorithm

We now introduce an algorithm $A_{L,T}$ that passes the generalized Benford test (see Algorithm 1). The general idea behind the algorithm is to make a prediction for a sentence by searching for an irreducible pattern which it belongs to (represented by the program X). To be sure that a pattern is irreducible, we must also search for any subsequences (represented by Y) which have significantly different probabilities. In effect, we are trying to predict an event by finding a *reference class* which the event belongs to. A reference class which is simple and passes tests for pseudo-randomness is chosen, since this indicates that we are unlikely to do better by choosing a different reference class.

Let L be the Turing machine which accepts on input N if ZFC proves ϕ_N, rejects on input N if ZFC disproves ϕ_N, and otherwise does not halt. For convenience, in Algorithm 1, we define $\log q = 1$ for $q < 2$.

Let $TM(N)$ be the set of all Turing machines X expressible in at most $\log N$ bits such that $U(X, N)$ accepts in time at most $T(N)$. The encoding of Turing machines must be prefix-free, which in particular means that no Turing machine is encoded in 0 bits. Let J_N denote the set of rational numbers of the form $\frac{j}{N}$ with $j = 0, \ldots, N$.

For X and Y Turing machines, let $K(X)$ be the number of bits necessary to encode X. Let $S'(X, Y)$ be the subset of natural numbers i which are accepted by both $U(X, i)$ and $U(Y, i)$ in time at most $T(i)$. Let $Q_N(X, Y)$ be the greatest number less than or equal to N such that for every s in the first $Q_N(X, Y)$ elements of S', $U(L, s)$ halts in time $T(N)$. Let $F_N(X, Y)$ be the proportion of the first $Q_N(X, Y)$ elements of S' which L accepts. Let

$$B_N(X, Y, P) = \max\left(K(X), \frac{|F_N(X, Y) - P|\sqrt{Q_N(X, Y)}}{K(Y)\sqrt{\log \log Q_N(X, Y)}} \right). \tag{5}$$

Lemma 1. *The output of $A_{L,T}$ on input N is in*

$$\arg\min_{P \in J_N} \max_{Y \in TM(N)} \min_{X \in TM(N)} B_N(X, Y, P). \tag{6}$$

Proof. Omitted due to space limitations.[5]

The code is not optimized for computational efficiency. The following proposition is just to ensure that the runtime is not far off from $T(N)$.

Proposition 2. *The runtime of $A_{L,T}(N)$ is in $O(R(N)) = O(T(N)N^4 \log T(N)))$.*

Proof. Simulating U on any input for T time steps can be done in time $cT \log T$ for some fixed constant c [25]. The bulk of the runtime comes from simulating Turing machines on lines 8, 13, 14, and 16. Each of these lines takes at most $cT(N) \log T(N)$ time, and we enter each of these lines at most N^4 times. Therefore, the program runs in time $O(T(N)N^4 \log T(N))$.

---

[5] See pre-print version [24] for the full proof.

Algorithm 1. $A_{L,T}(N)$

```
 1: P = 0
 2: M = N
 3: for j = 0, . . . , N do
 4:     M_Y = 0
 5:     for Y a Turing machine expressible in K_Y < log N bits do
 6:         M_X = N
 7:         for X a Turing machine expressible in K_X < log N bits do
 8:             if U(X, N) and U(Y, N) both accept in time T(N) then
 9:                 A = 0
10:                 R = 0
11:                 i = 1
12:                 while i ≤ N do
13:                     if U(X, i) and U(Y, i) both accept in time T(i) then
14:                         if U(L, i) accepts in time T(N) then
15:                             A = A + 1
16:                         else if U(L, i) rejects in time T(N) then
17:                             R = R + 1
18:                         else
19:                             i = N
20:                     i = i + 1
21:                 F = A/(A + R)
22:                 Q = A + R
```
$$23: \quad \text{if } \max\left(K_X, \frac{|F - \frac{j}{N}|\sqrt{Q}}{K_Y \sqrt{\log\log Q}}\right) < M_X \text{ then}$$
$$24: \quad M_X = \max\left(K_X, \frac{|F - \frac{j}{N}|\sqrt{Q}}{K_Y \sqrt{\log\log Q}}\right)$$
```
25:         if M_X > M_Y then
26:             M_Y = M_X
27:     if M_Y < M then
28:         M = M_Y
29:         P = j/N
30: return P
```

6 Passing the Generalized Benford Test

We are now ready to show that $A_{L,T}$ passes the generalized Benford test. The proof will use the following two lemmas.

Lemma 2. *Let S be an irreducible pattern with probability p, and let Z be a Turing machine such that $U(Z, N)$ accepts in time $T(N)$ if and only if $N \in S$.*
    There exists a constant C such that if $N \in S$, then there exists a $P \in J_N$ such that

$$\max_{Y \in TM(N)} B_N(Z, Y, P) < C. \tag{7}$$

Proof. Let $P = \frac{\lfloor pN \rfloor}{N}$. From the definition of irreducible pattern, we have that there exists c such that for all Y,

$$|F_N(Z,Y) - p| < \frac{cK(Y)\sqrt{\log \log Q_N(Z,Y)}}{\sqrt{Q_N(Z,Y)}}. \tag{8}$$

Clearly,

$$|P - p| \leq \frac{1}{N} \leq \frac{1}{Q_N(Z,Y)} \leq \frac{1}{\sqrt{Q_N(Z,Y)}} \leq \frac{K(Z)K(Y)\sqrt{\log \log Q_N(Z,Y)}}{\sqrt{Q_N(Z,Y)}}. \tag{9}$$

Setting $C = K(Z) + c$, we get

$$|F_N(Z,Y) - P| \leq |F_N(Z,Y) - p| + |P - p| < \frac{CK(Y)\sqrt{\log \log Q_N(Z,Y)}}{\sqrt{Q_N(Z,Y)}}, \tag{10}$$

so

$$\frac{|F_N(Z,Y) - P|\sqrt{Q_N(Z,Y)}}{K(Y)\sqrt{\log \log Q_N(Z,Y)}} < C. \tag{11}$$

Clearly, $K(Z) < C$, so $B_N(Z,Y,P) > C$ for all Y. Therefore,

$$\max_{Y \in TM(N)} B_N(Z,Y,P) < C. \tag{12}$$

Lemma 3. *Let S be an irreducible pattern with probability p, and let Z be a Turing machine such that $U(Z,N)$ accepts in time $T(N)$ if and only if $N \in S$.*
For all C, for all $\varepsilon > 0$, for all N sufficiently large, for all $P \in J_N$, if $N \in S$, and

$$\min_{X \in TM(N)} B_N(X,Z,P) < C, \tag{13}$$

then $|P - p| < \varepsilon$.

Proof. Fix a C and a $\varepsilon > 0$. It suffices to show that for all N sufficiently large, if $N \in S$ and $|P - p| \geq \varepsilon$, then for all $X \in TM(N)$, we have $B_N(X,Z,P) \geq C$.
    Observe that since $B_N(X,Z,P) \geq K(X)$, this claim trivially holds when $K(X) \geq C$. Therefore we only have to check the claim for the finitely many Turing machines expressible in fewer than C bits.
    Fix an arbitrary X. Since S is an irreducible pattern, there exists a c such that

$$|F_N(X,Z) - p| < \frac{cK(Z)\sqrt{\log \log Q_N(X,Z)}}{\sqrt{Q_N(X,Z)}}. \tag{14}$$

We may assume that $S'(X,Z)$ is infinite, since otherwise if we take $N \in S$ large enough, $X \notin TM(N)$. Thus, by taking N sufficiently large, we can get $Q_N(X,Z)$ sufficiently large, and in particular satisfy

$$\frac{\sqrt{Q_N(X,Z)}}{K(Z)\sqrt{\log \log Q_N(X,Z)}} \varepsilon \geq C + c. \tag{15}$$

Take $N \in S$ large enough that this holds for each $X \in TM(N)$ with $K(X) < C$, and assume $|P - p| \geq \varepsilon$. By the triangle inequality, we have

$$|F_N(X,Z) - P| \geq |P - p| - |F_N(X,Z) - p| \geq \varepsilon - \frac{cK(Z)\sqrt{\log \log Q_N(X,Z)}}{\sqrt{Q_N(X,Z)}}. \quad (16)$$

Therefore

$$B_N(X,Z,P) \geq \frac{\left(\varepsilon - \frac{cK(Z)\sqrt{\log \log Q_N(X,Z)}}{\sqrt{Q_N(X,Z)}}\right)\sqrt{Q_N(X,Z)}}{K(Z)\sqrt{\log \log Q_N(X,Z)}} \quad (17)$$

$$= \frac{\sqrt{Q_N(X,Z)}}{K(Z)\sqrt{\log \log Q_N(X,Z)}}\varepsilon - c \geq C,$$

which proves the claim.

Theorem 3. $A_{L,T}$ *passes the generalized Benford test.*

Proof. Let S be an irreducible pattern with probability p. We must show that

$$\lim_{\substack{N \to \infty \\ N \in S}} A_{L,T}(N) = p. \quad (18)$$

Let Z be a Turing machine such that $U(Z,N)$ accepts in time $T(N)$ if and only if $N \in S$.

By considering the case when $X = Z$, Lemma 2 implies that there exists a constant C such that for all N sufficiently large, there exists a $P \in J_N$ such that

$$\max_{Y \in TM(N)} \min_{X \in TM(N)} B_N(X,Y,P) < C. \quad (19)$$

Similarly, using this value of C, and considering the case where $Y = Z$, Lemma 3 implies that for all $\varepsilon > 0$, for all N sufficiently large, for all $P \in J_N$ if $N \in S$, and

$$\max_{Y \in TM(N)} \min_{X \in TM(N)} B_N(X,Y,P) < C, \quad (20)$$

then $|P - p| \leq \varepsilon$.

Combining these, we get that for all $\varepsilon > 0$, for all N sufficiently large, if $N \in S$ and if P is in

$$\arg\min_{P \in J_N} \max_{Y \in TM(N)} \min_{X \in TM(N)} B_N(X,Y,P), \quad (21)$$

then $|P - p| \leq \varepsilon$.

Thus, by Lemma 1, we get that for all $\varepsilon > 0$, for all N sufficiently large, if $N \in S$, then $|A_{L,T}(N) - p| \leq \varepsilon$, so

$$\lim_{\substack{N \to \infty \\ N \in S}} A_{L,T}(N) = p. \quad (22)$$

7   Final Remarks

We identified a new desirable property for logical uncertainty, the generalized Benford test, based on making probability assignments when sequences of logical statements appear pseudorandom. We developed an algorithm with this property. Although the algorithm does not have a practically useful run-time, it demonstrates that it is possible to achieve the desired property in a very general case: we can apply this algorithm to learn patterns in ZFC or other powerful logics, which include essentially any mathematical domains of interest within them.

The main drawback of the approach here is that it does not achieve desirable properties of previous approaches. No attempt is made here to satisfy the probability axioms in the limit as more computing power is used, as in [1,9]. Integrating with those approaches is an important next step. Nonetheless, we see passing the generalized Benford test alone as a fairly powerful property, as it implies an ability to notice a wide variety of patterns within mathematics.

References

1. Christiano, P.: Non-Omniscience, Probabilistic Inference, and Metamathematics. Technical report 2014–3. Berkeley, CA: Machine Intelligence Research Institute (2014). http://intelligence.org/files/Non-Omniscience.pdf
2. Hennig, P., Osborne, M.A., Girolami, M.: Probabilistic numerics and uncertainty in computations. Proc. Royal Soci. London A: Math. Phys. Eng. Sci. **471**, 2179 (2015)
3. Beckman, N.E., Nori, A.V.: Probabilistic, modular andscalable inference of typestate specifications. ACM SIGPLAN Not. **46**(6), 211–221 (2011). ACM
4. Polya, G.: Mathematics and Plausible Reasoning: Patterns ofplausible inference, vol. 2. Princeton University Press, Princeton (1968)
5. Parikh, R.: Knowledge and the problem of logical omniscience. ISMIS **87**, 432–439 (1987)
6. Gaifman, H.: Reasoning with limited resources and assigning probabilities to arithmetical statements. Synthese **140**, 97–119 (2004). doi:10.1023/B:SYNT.0000029944.99888.a7
7. Cozic, M.: Impossible states at work: Logicalomniscience and rational choice. Contrib. Econ. Anal. **280**, 47–68 (2006)
8. Halpern, J.Y., Pucella, R.: Dealing with logical omniscience. In: Proceedings of the 11th Conference on Theoretical aspects of Rationality and Knowledge, pp. 169–176. ACM (2007)
9. Demski, A.: Logical prior probability. In: Bach, J., Goertzel, B., Iklé, M. (eds.) AGI 2012. LNCS, vol. 7716, pp. 50–59. Springer, Heidelberg (2012). doi:10.1007/978-3-642-35506-6
10. Soares, N., Fallenstein, B.: Questions of Reasoning Under Logical Uncertainty. Technical report 2015–1. Berkeley, CA: MachineIntelligence Research Institute (2015). https://intelligence.org/files/QuestionsLogicalUncertainty.pdf
11. Cox, R.T.: Algebra of Probable Inference. JHU Press, Baltimore (1961)

12. Horn, A., Tarski, A.: Measures in boolean algebras. Trans. Am. Math. Soci. **64**(3), 467–467 (1948). doi:10.1090/S0002-9947-1948-0028922-8. http://www.ams.org/journals/tran/1948-064-03/S0002-9947-1948-0028922-8/S0002-9947-1948-0028922-8.pdf

13. Maharam, D.: An algebraic characterization of measurealgebras. Ann. Math. **48**(1), 154–167 (1947). doi:10.1016/j.annemergmed.2010.11.022. ISSN: 01960644

14. Loś, J.: On the axiomatic treatment of probability. Colloquium Math. **2**(3), 125–137 (1955)

15. Gaifman, H.: Concerning measures in first order calculi. Israel J. Math. **2**(1), 1–18 (1964). doi:10.1007/BF02759729

16. Nilsson, N.J.: Probabilistic logic. Artif. Intell. **28**(1), 71–87 (1986)

17. Hailperin, T., et al.: Probability logic. Notre Dame J. Formal Logic **25**(3), 198–212 (1984)

18. Hutter, M., et al.: Probabilities on sentences in anexpressive logic. J. Appl. Logic **11**(4), 386–420 (2013)

19. Vovk, V.G.: Aggregating strategies. In: Proceedings of the Third Workshop on Computational Learning Theory, pp. 371–383. Morgan Kaufmann (1990)

20. Weinberger, M.J., Ordentlich, E.: On delayedprediction of individual sequences. Inf. Theor. IEEE Trans. **48**(7), 1959–1976 (2002)

21. Pietronero, L., et al.: Explaining the uneven distribution ofnumbers in nature: the laws of Benford and Zipf. Physica A: Stat. Mech. Appl. **293**(1–2), 297–304 (2001). doi:10.1016/S0378-4371(00)00633-6. ISSN: 03784371. eprint: 9808305

22. Ko, K.: On the notion of infinite pseudorandom sequences. Theor. Comput. Sci. **48**, 9–33 (1986). doi:10.1016/0304-3975(86)90081-2. ISSN:03043975

23. Downey, R.G., Hirschfeldt, D.R.: Algorithmicrandomness and complexity. Springer Science & Business Media (2010). ISBN: 9780387955674. doi:10.4249/scholarpedia. 2574

24. Garrabrant, S., et al.: Asymptotic Logical Uncertainty and TheBenford Test. Preprint (2015). arXiv: 1510.03370 [cs.LG]

25. Hennie, F.C., Stearns, R.E.: Two-tape simulation ofmultitape Turing machines. J. ACM **13**(4), 533–546 (1966). doi:10.1145/321356.321362. ISSN: 00045411

Towards a Computational Framework for Function-Driven Concept Invention

Nico Potyka[(✉)], Danny Gómez-Ramírez, and Kai-Uwe Kühnberger

Institute of Cognitive Science, University of Osnabrück, Osnabrück, Germany
`nico.potyka@uni-osnabrueck.de`

Abstract. We propose a novel framework for computational concept invention. As opposed to recent implementations of Fauconnier's and Turner's Conceptual Blending Theory, our framework simplifies computational concept invention by focusing on concepts' functions rather than on structural similarity of concept descriptions. Even though creating an optimal combination of concepts that achieves the desired functions is NP-complete in general, some interesting special cases are tractable.

1 Introduction

Despite the success of many AI applications, tools, and services, there are some cognitive abilities and phenomena which are hard to model with computational approaches. Classical examples for such shortcomings are creative abilities of cognitive agents, in particular, the ability to create new concepts with new and interesting properties and features based on the available background knowledge of the agent. Particularly, artificial general intelligence (AGI) has an interest to address the problem of developing computational models for certatin aspects of creativity research.

A cognitive theory addressing possibilities to model the invention of new concepts is conceptual blending [6]: In [15], the authors argue for the broad applicability of computational approaches for conceptual blending in the context of concept invention. Conceptual blending can be regarded as the process of combining elements of at least two distinct concepts (or *input spaces*) to get a meaningful new concept (the *blend space*) [6]. For instance, in greek mythology, a centaur is composed of parts of a horse and parts of a human; a faun is composed of a goat and a human. Similar examples can be found in other areas such as mathematics [8] or music [4].

The process of conceptual blending that generates a blend space from given input spaces has been formalized by using tools from various areas such as frame-based knowledge representation [13], algebra [7], quantum theory [1] or analogical reasoning [10]. Many interesting blends can be explained and sometimes automatically generated by these frameworks, but unsupervised blending of concepts can also yield many meaningless results. Quality criteria can be defined to filter the results, but if concept descriptions become large, this approach becomes impractical due to the combinatorial explosion of possible blends. In particular

B. Steunebrink et al. (Eds.): AGI 2016, LNAI 9782, pp. 212–222, 2016.
DOI: 10.1007/978-3-319-41649-6_21

logical approaches that search for maximal consistent blends rely on computational problems that go far beyond NP or are even undecidable.

The authors in [9] propose a goal-oriented view on conceptual blending to further structure the search space and demonstrate the computational benefits with case studies in story generation and pretend play. The three essential components for efficient computation are (see [9] for a detailed discussion):

1. selection of input spaces,
2. selection of elements that should be incorporated in the blend space,
3. stopping criteria for blend elaboration.

Note that the workflow of concept generation will usually apply these components multiple times. Candidate input spaces will be selected (1), combined (2), and evaluated until an acceptable new concept is generated (3). We will follow this philosophy here and assume that our goals can be defined as *functions* that our newly generated concept should satisfy. This view might be less suitable for concept invention in domains like music or poetry, but is well apt to create new physical entities like a houseboat [13] or a monster [12].

In our computational framework, functions will be defined globally and can be satisfied by concepts' *functional units*. By a functional unit, we mean a subset of parts of a concept that achieve a function. For instance, feet, legs, and the pelvis area constitute humans' functional unit for moving the body; hands, arms, and the thorax area humans' functional unit for moving things. In particular, we associate functions with properties that can be used to evaluate the usefulness of functional units. For instance, the functional unit for moving the body can have a property *speed*, the functional unit for moving things can have the property *power*. Roughly speaking, we implement component (1) from [9] by scanning the database for concepts that contribute to satisfying the desired functions. Component (2) and (3) basically consist of combining functional units and evaluating the generated concept with respect to some utility functions. Combination can be guided, for instance, by evaluating functional units' properties while balancing the candidates' contributions to the blend space.

2   Concept Representation

We start our discussion by introducing a functional concept blending framework formally. To this end, let us consider languages $\mathcal{L}_C$ of concepts, $\mathcal{L}_F$ of functions that are associated with concepts and $\mathcal{L}_P$ of properties that functions can have. In our examples, $\mathcal{L}_C$, $\mathcal{L}_F$ and $\mathcal{L}_P$ will be made up of strings like *human* (concept), *move_body* (function) and *speed* (property). Each property p is associated with a domain domain(p) of values it can take. Values can be strings, numerical values, or intervals. For instance, we could specify domain($speed$) = $\{[b_1, b_2] \mid b_1, b_2 \in \mathbb{R}, 0 \leq b_1 \leq b_2\}$. Intuitively, domain($speed$) is a set of intervals that represent minimum and maximum speed that a concept can take. We also need some mappings that connect our languages.

– functions : $\mathcal{L}_C \to 2^{\mathcal{L}_F}$, parents : $\mathcal{L}_C \to 2^{\mathcal{L}_C}$, components : $\mathcal{L}_C \to 2^{\mathcal{L}_C}$ associate concepts with the functions they fulfill, with their parents and components. Intuitively, parents correspond to more general concepts (in ontology research often called superconcepts) and serve to arrange concepts hierarchically in a tree-like structure, where child concepts inherit features of their parents. Formally, we demand that

If $p \in$ parents(c) for some concept c, then functions$(p) \subseteq$ functions(c).

For instance, Fig. 1 shows a hierarchy, in which the concept Organic might contain functional units like a reproduction system and a metabolic system, which can be overwritten by its childs. Components (in ontology research often associated with concepts standing in the part_of relation) are the building blocks that concepts are made of and that can be used to create new concepts in our framework. For instance, we could let functions$(human) = \{move\_body\}$, parents$(human) = \{animal\}$, components$(human) = \{human\_lower\_body, human\_upper\_body, human\_head\}$.

– funit : $(\mathcal{L}_C \times \mathcal{L}_F) \to 2^{\mathcal{L}_C}$ is a partial mapping that associates concepts and functions with the components that serve to fulfill this function such that
  1. if $f \notin$ functions(c), then funit$(c, f) = \bot$ is undefined,
  2. if $f \in$ functions(c), then funit$(c, f) \subseteq$ components(c).

– eval : $(\mathcal{L}_C \times \mathcal{L}_F \times \mathcal{L}_P) \to \mathcal{L}_V$ is a partial mapping that associates concepts, functions and properties with the value that this property takes for the given function and concept. For instance, we could have $eval(human, move\_body, speed) = [0, 45]$. We demand that
  1. if $f \notin$ functions(c), then eval$(c, f, p) = \bot$,
  2. if $f \in$ functions(c) and $p \notin$ properties(f), then eval$(c, f, p) = \bot$,
  3. if $f \in$ functions(c) and $p \in$ properties(f), then eval$(c, f, p) \in$ domain(p).

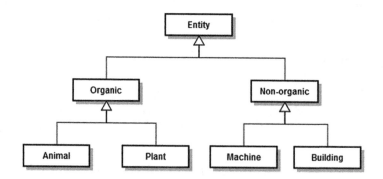

Fig. 1. Hierarchy of abstract concepts.

Definition 1 (Functional Concept Blending Framework). *A functional concept blending framework is a pair* $(\mathcal{C}, \mathcal{F})$, *where* $\mathcal{C} \subseteq \mathcal{L}_C$ *is a set of concepts and* $\mathcal{F} \subseteq \mathcal{L}_F$ *is a set of functions.*

For a discussion of Definition 1 and its relation to classical types of concept blending, please compare Sect. 4.

3   Computing Blends

Given a functional concept blending framework $(\mathcal{C}, \mathcal{F})$, we want to create new concepts. Following [9], our search for interesting candidates to combine will be lead by goals. Our goals are functions that the new concept must satisfy.

The most straightforward way to set the goals is to just let the user select the desired functions. However, if $(\mathcal{C}, \mathcal{F})$ is large in terms of the number of concepts and functions, it is easier to define the desired functions in an implicit way by exploiting the hierarchical structure of the concepts. For instance, given the example from Fig. 1, we could just say that we want a concept that features aspects of Organic and Machine and that can move its body in the air. In general, if we select an abstract concept from the hierarchy as a goal, the newly generated concept should satisfy all functions that the abstract concept and its parents satisfy.

So let us assume that we are given a functional concept blending framework $(\mathcal{C}, \mathcal{F})$ and a set of goals $\mathcal{G} \subseteq \mathcal{F}$. Our aim is an algorithm that outputs a new and meaningful concept that fulfills our goals. Similar to [9], we consider three components of the algorithm. Roughly speaking it works by iterating over the database and selecting candidate concepts (1), combining these concepts to a new concept (2), evaluating the concept and maybe restarting the procedure (3). These phases cannot be considered independently of each other. In particular, both the first and second phase depend on the third one. We will first describe combination of concepts and then selection of concepts. Along the way, we will explain how we can evaluate candidates during these phases.

3.1   Concept Combination

Suppose we already selected a subset of components $\mathcal{C}' \subseteq \mathcal{C}$ from which we want to create a new concept. The main task is to select a subset of $\bigcup_{c \in \mathcal{C}'}$ components(c) that makes up the new concept, let us just call this set *components*. The basic requirement for *components* in our framework is that for each goal $f \in \mathcal{G}$, *components* contains a functional unit that fulfills this function. Algorithm 1 shows a simple algorithm that guarantees this requirement. It just iterates over the concepts and chooses the components of that functional unit that best satisfies the desired function. One naive way to implement bestSatisfies is to select a concept that fulfills the function randomly. A more sophisticated way is to select the concept that best satisfies the function with respect to some *utility* function. To this end, let us assume that for

Input: Goals $\mathcal{G}$, Concepts $\mathcal{C}'$
Output: Components of new concept
$components \leftarrow \emptyset;$
for $f \in \mathcal{G}$ **do**
$\quad | \quad c \leftarrow$ bestSatisfies$(\mathcal{C}', f);$
$\quad | \quad components \leftarrow components \cup funit(c, f);$
return $components;$

Algorithm 1. A local algorithm to combine concepts' components.

each $f \in \mathcal{F}$ and for each property $p \in$ properties(f), we have a utility function $u_{f,p} :$ domain$(p) \rightarrow \mathbb{R}$. For instance, for the property speed, we could let $U([b_1, b_2]) = b_2$ be the maximum speed of the concept. Additionally, we might want to reward *diversity* of the new concept. We can do this, for instance, by computing the ratio that the given concept already contributes to the new concept contribution$(c) = \frac{|components(c) \cap components|}{|components|}$ and preferring low contributions by multiplying the utility value by a factor like $\frac{3}{1+2^{\text{contribution}(c)}}$. Let $U(\mathcal{C}, \mathcal{G})$ denote the cost of evaluating the utility functions, then bestSatisfiesruns in time $O(|\mathcal{C}'| \cdot U(\mathcal{C}, \mathcal{G}))$. Note that instead of storing the components in *components* explicitly, we can just store a pointer to the fulfilling functional unit for each goal. Then Algorithm 1 runs in time $O(|\mathcal{G}| \cdot |\mathcal{C}'| \cdot U(\mathcal{C}, \mathcal{G}))$.

If we think of our goal as combining concepts' components in a way that maximizes utility, Algorithm 1 corresponds to a local approach that takes only the individual values of concepts' functional units into account, but not their group values. In particular, the influence of the diversity factor depends on the order in which we selected the goals. Algorithm 2 shows an alternative global algorithm. It works by first determining for each goal $f \in \mathcal{G}$ the set of concepts C_f that fulfill this function. Then for each possible assignment $\pi : \mathcal{G} \rightarrow \mathcal{C}'$, which determines which goal will be satisfied by which concept's functional unit, the utility value of the corresponding combined concept is determined. From the best component sets, one set is returned. A simple implementation can just select a best component set randomly. It might also be reasonable to add all elements from the intersection $\bigcap_{C \in best} C$ of all best component sets. In order to implement utility$(\mathcal{G}, \mathcal{C}', components, \pi)$, we need several ingredients. We can evaluate the usefulness of each individual functional component by using utility functions like in the local approach. We can then combine these individual values by a combination function like a weighted sum. Additionally, we can consider a diversity factor again. In a good combination of concepts, each concept should contribute equally to the new concept. Let us consider again the contribution contribution$(c) = \frac{|components(c) \cap components|}{|components|}$ for each concept $c \in \mathcal{C}'$. We want to prefer concepts in which the contributions are distributed more uniformly. We can do this, for instance, by measuring the entropy of the contribution distribution or by measuring its negative euclidean distance to the uniform distribution; and then multiplying this value to the combined utility value. Letting again $U(\mathcal{C}, \mathcal{G})$ denote the maximum cost of evaluating the utility values, Algorithm 2

Input: Goals $\mathcal{G}$, Concepts $\mathcal{C}'$
Output: Components of new concept
for $f \in \mathcal{G}$ **do**
$\quad | \quad C_f \leftarrow \{c \in \mathcal{C}' \mid f \in \text{functions}(c)\};$
$maxUtil \leftarrow -\infty;$
$best \leftarrow \emptyset;$
for *each assignment* $\pi : \mathcal{G} \to \mathcal{C}'$ *such that* $\pi(f) \in C_f$ **do**
$\quad components \leftarrow \emptyset;$
$\quad$ **for** $f \in \mathcal{G}$ **do**
$\quad\quad | \quad components \leftarrow components \cup \text{funit}(\pi(f), f);$
$\quad u \leftarrow \text{utility}(\mathcal{G}, \mathcal{C}', components, \pi);$
$\quad$ **if** $u > maxUtil$ **then**
$\quad\quad best \leftarrow \emptyset;$
$\quad\quad maxUtil \leftarrow u;$
$\quad$ **if** $u = maxUtil$ **then**
$\quad\quad | \quad best \leftarrow best \cup \{components\};$
return selectBestComponenSet($best$);
Algorithm 2. A global algorithm to combine concepts' components.

runs in time $O(|\mathcal{C}'|^{|\mathcal{G}|} \cdot (|\mathcal{G}| + U(\mathcal{C}, \mathcal{G})))$. The runtime is dominated by evaluating all possible assignments π and the worst-case is obtained when all concepts fulfill all functions. However, even if we assume that each function is fulfilled by only 2 concepts, the runtime remains exponential in $|\mathcal{G}|$. Hence, Algorithm 2 is only efficient in its naive form if the number of goals is moderate.

3.2 Selecting Concepts

In order to select concepts from which the new concept shall be generated, we can again follow a local and a global approach. Algorithm 3 shows a simple local algorithm. It works by iterating over the concepts until a concept is found that contributes to the goals. The concept is then added to $\mathcal{C}'$ and all fulfilled goals are removed. This process keeps on until all goals are satisfied. The selected concepts are then combined as explained in the previous section. Algorithm 3 runs in time $O(|\mathcal{G}| \cdot |\mathcal{C}| \cdot |\mathcal{F}| + M(|\mathcal{C}'|)) = O(|\mathcal{C}| \cdot |\mathcal{F}|^2 + M(|\mathcal{C}'|))$, where $M(|\mathcal{C}'|)$ corresponds to the cost of merging the selected concepts. So, for instance, when combining the local Algorithms 1 and 3, the overall cost is $O(|\mathcal{C}| \cdot |\mathcal{F}|^2 + |\mathcal{G}| \cdot |\mathcal{C}'| \cdot U(\mathcal{C}, \mathcal{G})) = O(|\mathcal{F}|^2 \cdot |\mathcal{C}| \cdot U(\mathcal{C}, \mathcal{G}))$ and hence polynomial. Note that a naive implementation of Algorithm 3 might yield an old rather than a new concept if there exists a concept that satisfies all goals. However, we can easily handle this case by adding a simple check and if necessary resetting the goals and adding a second concept.

We can modify Algorithm 3 in various ways to iterate over the concepts in more sophisticated ways. One way to do this is to order the concepts in descending order by the key $key(c) = |\text{functions}(c) \cap \mathcal{G}|$ for each concept $c \in \mathcal{C}'$. In this way, we prefer concepts that satisfy many goals. The additional computational cost is $O(|\mathcal{C}| \cdot \log |\mathcal{C}|)$ when using efficient sorting algorithms like Quicksort. However, after selecting the first concept, the keys can decrease and the order can

Input: Concept Blending Framework $(\mathcal{C}, \mathcal{F})$, Goals $\mathcal{G}$
Output: New concept that satisfies goals
$\mathcal{C}' \leftarrow \emptyset$;
while $\mathcal{G} \neq \emptyset$ **do**
    for $c \in \mathcal{C}$ **do**
        if functions$(c) \cap \mathcal{G} \neq \emptyset$ **then**
            $\mathcal{C}' \leftarrow \mathcal{C}' \cup \{c\}$;
            $\mathcal{G} \leftarrow \mathcal{G} \setminus$ functions(c);
  $c \leftarrow$ combine$(\mathcal{C}')$;
return c;

Algorithm 3. A local algorithm to select concepts.

change. We can just ignore this fact, resort the concepts periodically or maintain the order by using special data structures like heaps. If we assume that the goals can be satisfied by a small number of concepts, the additional cost is asymtotically negligible. This assumption is in particular satisfied if the goals were defined by selecting a small number of abstract concepts from the hierarchy like Organic and Machine because subconcepts in the hierarchy inherit functions from their parents. We can also think of more sophisticated keys that not only regard the number of functions that are satisfied by a concept, but also how effective the goal is satisfied. To this end, we can apply similar utility functions as explained in the previous section.

Algorithm 4 shows a global algorithm to select concepts. It works by iterating over all subsets $\mathcal{C}'$ of $\mathcal{C}$ that contain at least 2 elements. The concepts in $\mathcal{C}'$ are then combined as explained in the previous section. The new concept is then evaluated and the best concepts are stored. Finally, a best concept is returned. In order to compute utility values and to select a best concept, we can apply similar ideas as explained for Algorithm 2. To this end, we can reuse information from the combine-procedure. However, we can also take additional criteria into account. For instance, we might want to avoid that too many concepts are used and can therefore use a discounting factor like 2^{-k} to decrease utility increases as the size of the subsets increases. The runtime of Algorithm 4 is $O(\sum_{k=2}^{|\mathcal{C}|} \binom{|\mathcal{C}|}{k} \cdot M(k))$, where $M(k)$ again denotes the cost for combining k concepts. Hence, the runtime is exponential in $|\mathcal{C}|$ even if we use the local algorithm for combining concepts. However, usually we do not want to combine an arbitrary number of concepts, but maybe only two or three. If we consider a bound b on the number of concepts, the runtimes becomes $O(\sum_{k=2}^{b} \binom{|\mathcal{C}|}{k} \cdot M(k)) = O(|\mathcal{C}|^b \cdot M(b))$.

3.3   Computational Results

We proposed a local and a global algorithm to merge and select concepts, respectively. Our global algorithm has an exponential worst-case runtime. Actually, the concept invention problem is inherently difficult if we do not make any assumptions on the maximum number of concepts that may be combined. To make this precise, let us assume that we are given a utility function $u : 2^{\mathcal{C}} \to \mathbb{R}$. This utility

Input: Concept Blending Framework $(\mathcal{C}, \mathcal{F})$, Goals $\mathcal{G}$
Output: New concept that satisfies goals
$maxUtil \leftarrow -\infty$;
$best \leftarrow \emptyset$;
for $k \leftarrow 2$ **to** $|\mathcal{C}|$ **do**
    for *each k-elementary subset $\mathcal{C}'$ of $\mathcal{C}$* **do**
        $c \leftarrow$ combine($\mathcal{C}'$);
        $u \leftarrow$ utility($\mathcal{G}, c$);
        if $u > maxUtil$ **then**
            $best \leftarrow \emptyset$;
            $maxUtil \leftarrow u$;
        if $u = maxUtil$ **then**
            $best \leftarrow best \cup \{c\}$;
return select($best$);

Algorithm 4. A global algorithm to select concepts.

function can take all criteria into account that we discussed before. Note that we can also use it to evaluate single concepts $c \in \mathcal{C}$ by letting $u(c) = u(\{c\})$. We call u *polynomial-time computable* iff $u(\mathcal{C}')$ can be computed in time polynomial in $\mathcal{C}$ and $\mathcal{G}$ for all $\mathcal{C}' \subseteq \mathcal{C}$. Let us consider the following decision problem.

U-CONCEPT: Given a concept blending framework $(\mathcal{C}, \mathcal{F})$, a set of goals $\mathcal{G} \subseteq \mathcal{F}$ that is compatible with $(\mathcal{C}, \mathcal{F})$, a polynomial-time computable utility function u and a real number $U \in \mathbb{R}$, decide whether there is a subset $\mathcal{C}' \subseteq \mathcal{C}$ such that $u(\mathcal{C}') > U$.

The following result follows from a guess and check argument and a reduction of 0-1-KNAPSACK. We omit the proof to meet space restrictions.

Proposition 1. *U-CONCEPT is NP-complete.*

However, usually we do not want to combine an arbitrary number of concepts, but combine at most a handful of concepts. If the maximum number of concepts that can be combined is some fixed integer b, our previous results show that a globally optimal solution can be found in time $O(|\mathcal{C}|^b \cdot |\mathcal{C}'|^{|\mathcal{G}|} \cdot (|\mathcal{G}| + U(\mathcal{C}, \mathcal{G}))) = O(|\mathcal{C}|^{b+|\mathcal{G}|} \cdot (|\mathcal{G}| + U(\mathcal{C}, \mathcal{G})))$ (Algorithms 2 and 4). Since we assume that u is polynomial-time computable, this term is polynomial in $\mathcal{C}$, but exponential in $|\mathcal{G}|$. However, if we assume that there is only a small number of goals our algorithm is efficient. In other words, if we want to combine only a small number of concepts, U-CONCEPT is fixed-parameter tractable with parameter $|\mathcal{G}|$ (see [3] for an introduction to parameterized complexity). In particular, by combining the local Algorithms 1 and 3, we see that creating a concept that satisfies our goals can be performed in polynomial time. Strictly speaking, we have to assume that there exist indeed b concepts whose functional units can be combined to fulfill all goals. However, it might be reasonable to just introduce a penalty factor in the utility function, which penalizes combinations that ignore goals. We summarize our findings in the following proposition.

Proposition 2. *If there is a subset $C' \subseteq C$ of size at most b, whose functional units fulfill all goals in $\mathcal{G}$, then*

1. *U-CONCEPT restricted to combinations of at most b concepts is fixed-parameter tractable with parameter $|\mathcal{G}|$,*
2. *a subset $C' \subseteq C$ that satisfies $\mathcal{G}$ can be computed in time polynomial in $|C|$ and $|\mathcal{G}|$.*

4   Related Work

Conceptual blending (compare, for example, [5,6]) is a fundamental cognitive process underlying much of everyday thought and language. It is modeled as a process by which humans combine certain concepts, relations, and properties of originally separate conceptual spaces into a unified space (the blend space), in which new elements and relations emerge, and new inferences can be drawn. In this sense, it can be considered as a source of creativity. Whereas the classical framework of conceptual blending requires two input spaces, a generalization of the input spaces (often called generic space), and a blend space, this paper departs to a certain extent from this framework. Input spaces correspond to concepts (composed of components that fulfill certain functions), the generic space corresponds to goals (functions that shall be fulfilled by the new concept's components) and the blend space corresponds to a new concept (composed of some of the input concepts' components). The present approach can be regarded as a search strategy that can be applied to special instances of the general framework. Other computational models for conceptual blending have been proposed, for instance, in [7,9]. There are also relationships to problems like case-based- reasoning [2], predicate invention [11] and concept invention in machine learning [14].

   In [12], the authors describe the creation of monsters from a library of descriptions of animals formalized as OWL ontologies. A major difference between [12] and the present approach is the idea of guiding the blending process by functions that should be realized in the blend space. This is related to using priority values for properties to order them according to their importance for their appearance in the blend space. An approach for creating novel musical chord progressions by conceptual blending directed by hand-coded priority values for certain properties that should be realized in the blend space is presented in [4]. A further approach that uses a heuristics in order to guide the blending process in mathematics is presented in [10] where the consistency (or non-consistency) of the resulting blend theory is used as a heuristics.

5   Conclusions and Future Work

We proposed a computational framework for function-driven concept invention. The search for interesting candidate concepts to combine and the combination of concepts is guided by desirable functions that the new concept should satisfy. Whereas the problem of creating an optimal new concept is NP-complete in general, prohibiting arbitrarily large combinations makes the problem fixed-parameter tractable with respect to the number of goals. Just creating a new concept that satisfies our goals can be performed in polynomial time. We are currently working on basic implementations of the local and global approach.

As in most frameworks for concept invention, our framework's ability to create new concepts strongly depends on the information and structure that we provide. We are planning to apply machine learning tools to automate this process. For instance, we can regard C as an ontology and we can reuse existing ontologies from the web or parse existing nomenclatures from online encyclopedia. In order to learn functions of concepts and their functional units, we will try to apply natural language processing tools.

Acknowledgements. Some of the authors acknowledge the financial support of the Future and Emerging Technologies Programme within the Seventh Framework Programme for Research of the European Commission, under FET-Open grant number: 611553 (COINVENT).

References

1. Aerts, D., Gabora, L.: A theory of concepts and their combinations ii: a hilbert space representation. Kybernetes **34**(1/2), 192–221 (2005)
2. Besold, T., Kühnberger, K.-U., Plaza, E.: Analogy, amalgams, and concept blending. In: Proceedings of ACS 2015, p. 23 (2015)
3. Downey, R.G., Fellows, M.R.: Parameterized complexity. Springer, Heidelberg (2012)
4. Eppe, M., Confalonieri, R., Maclean, E., Kaliakatsos-Papakostas, M.A., Cambouropoulos, E., Schorlemmer, W.M., Codescu, M., Kühnberger, K.: Computational invention of cadences and chord progressions by conceptual chord-blending. In: Proceedings of IJCAI 2015, pp. 2445–2451. AAAI Press (2015)
5. Fauconnier, G., Turner, M.: Conceptual integration networks. Cogn. Sci. **22**(2), 133–187 (1998)
6. Fauconnier, G., Turner, M.: The Way We Think: Conceptual Blending and the Mind's Hidden Complexities. Basic Books, New York (2008)
7. Goguen, J.A., Harrell, D.F.: Style: a computational and conceptual blending-based approach. In: Argamon, S., Burns, K., Dubnov, S. (eds.) The Structure of Style, pp. 291–316. Springer, Heidelberg (2010)
8. Guhe, M., Pease, A., Smaill, A., Martinez, M., Schmidt, M., Gust, H., Kühnberger, K.-U., Krumnack, U.: A computational account of conceptual blending in basic mathematics. Cogn. Syst. Res. **12**(3–4), 249–265 (2011)
9. Li, B., Zook, A., Davis, N., Riedl, M.O.: Goal-driven conceptual blending: a computational approach for creativity. In: International Conference on Computational Creativity, vol.10 (2012)
10. Martinez, M., Krumnack, U., Smaill, A., Besold, T.R., Abdel-Fattah, A.M.H., Schmidt, M., Gust, H., Kühnberger, K.-U., Guhe, M., Pease, A.: Algorithmic aspects of theory blending. In: Aranda-Corral, G.A., Calmet, J., Martín-Mateos, F.J. (eds.) AISC 2014. LNCS, vol. 8884, pp. 180–192. Springer, Heidelberg (2014)

System Induction Games
and Cognitive Modeling as an AGI Methodology

Sean Markan[(✉)]

Eudelic Systems LLC, Boston, USA
markan@eudelic.com

Abstract. We propose a methodology for using human cognition as a template for artificial generally intelligent agents that learn from experience. In particular, we consider the problem of learning certain Mealy machines from observations of their behavior; this is a general but conceptually simple learning task that can be given to humans as well as machines. We illustrate by example the sorts of observations that can be gleaned from studying human performance on this task.

1 Introduction

A generally intelligent agent must be able to learn the dynamics of its environment through experience. One strategy for developing agents with this capability is to study how humans approach analogous learning problems. In this paper we illustrate how one might proceed with this methodology. We must admit at the outset that we have not pushed this methodology all the way through to the construction of learning systems; we aim only to lay some groundwork for that objective (and to propose a class of learning problems relevant to AGI).

First, we need to define a domain in which learning can take place. We will use a class of learning tasks we call "system induction games" (SIGs). In a SIG, the player is presented with an unknown (black box) Mealy machine [14] and must work out rules that predict its behavior.[1] We will not stipulate the source of the input stream; it might be decided by the player, by a teacher trying to help the player learn, or by chance. We further assume the player produces a guess after each input as to what the output will be. Importantly, we are concerned specifically with Mealy machines governed by some "reasonably simple" set of rules—that is, a set of rules a human could work out within a reasonable amount of time. (A very simple example would be a machine which emits a B symbol if either of the two prior inputs were A.) Our goal is *not* to find methods for inducing Mealy machines in general, which is already a well-studied problem.[2]

---

[1] Recall that a Mealy machine is a finite-state machine which, at each timestep, receives an input i, produces an output $o = f(s, i)$ (where s is its present state), and changes state to $s' = g(s, i)$. Actually, for our purposes there is no particular reason to assume a finite state space, but the games we will consider do have this property.

[2] In fact, the general problem is NP-complete [6].

© Springer International Publishing Switzerland 2016
B. Steunebrink et al. (Eds.): AGI 2016, LNAI 9782, pp. 223–233, 2016.
DOI: 10.1007/978-3-319-41649-6_22

Playing a SIG amounts to learning about the behavior of an environment through experience: the Mealy machine is the environment being learned. The methodology we explore in this paper is to let humans play SIGs, observe their behavior, and attempt to model it. We believe this combination of SIGs and cognitive modeling is a promising approach for AGI. The domain of SIGs gives rise to learning problems which are nontrivial, natural for humans, and isolated from complications like sensorimotor processing. Furthermore, if one models actual human learning mechanisms, one has a reason to think that the algorithms produced will scale to the difficult problems humans solve.

The plan for this paper is as follows. First we will discuss some related work. We will then illustrate the methodology we propose by examining some data produced by the author while playing SIGs. We will look both at the large-scale behavior involved in figuring out a SIG, as well as a broader but shallower sample of data related to conjecturing rules. In each case we will discuss some of the mechanisms and requirements this data seems to suggest for a generally intelligent learning agent. Finally we will propose directions for future work.

2   Related Work

Probably the closest related work is the "Seek-Whence" project of Hofstadter and colleagues, who examined the problem of extrapolating sequences of integers. Like us, Hofstadter emphasized cognitive plausibility as a guiding principle, seeking to build systems which parsed sequences in the same way a human might [8]. This research has led to at least two full-fledged sequence-extrapolating systems [11,15]. There has also been other work on the psychology of sequence extrapolation. Simon and Kotovsky [10,20] carried out some of the most systematic experiments, though the sequences they considered were very simple compared to those of Hofstadter. SIGs differ from Hofstadter's Seek-Whence domain in that they require the extrapolator to induce a *mapping* from input to output—that is, an explanation for a sequence of outputs conditioned on a sequence of inputs, not just an explanation for a sequence of outputs on its own. Thus SIGs are arguably a closer fit to the problem an agent needs to solve to make sense of its environment. At the same time, SIGs can be much harder to solve (even for people).[3]

As alluded to earlier, the problem of inducing Mealy machines has been studied within computational learning theory. Angluin's L^* algorithm [1] provides an efficient solution to the related problem of inducing deterministic finite automata (provided the agent can control the input), and that algorithm can be adapted to Mealy machines (see [19] for a discussion). A number of algorithms for learning POMDPs (which might be viewed as a probabilistic generalization of Mealy machines) have also been proposed [3,12,13]. Algorithms in this vein are only partially applicable as models of human learning on SIGs, in part because SIGs

---

[3] More precisely, a SIG whose description is about the same length as the description for an integer sequence is likely to be harder to figure out than the integer sequence.

involve additional structure (in particular, they should admit reasonably compact verbal descriptions). Humans are able to recognize and exploit a variety of structural regularities which do not exist in generic state machines but which do play an important role in the environments we actually face. (In the Mealy machine context, such regularities might include two letters of the alphabet being functionally equivalent, a factorization of the machine into several independent parts, sparsity of nontrivial transitions, etc.) By examining human learning in environments with these types of structure, we have a possible window into learning mechanisms relevant to general intelligence.

A few researchers, such as Drescher [4] and Bergman [2], have developed systems which learned rich rule-based models of their environments. Drescher's system, which was inspired by Piaget's theory of cognitive development [17], focused especially on inferring hidden states through their indirect effects on observations. Bergman's system discovered causal relationships in an environment with a rich and highly structured (but directly observable) state space. Both projects considered only a single environment, but developed algorithms with substantial cognitive plausibility that may be relevant in the SIG domain.

On a more general level, the topic of human rule induction has been studied extensively in the context of concept learning (see [7] for a recent approach to this problem). The SIG domain, however, adds several elements to traditional concept learning problems: a need for selecting features from a very large feature space, a need to discover hidden state and how it changes, and the possibility of temporally extended actions (rather than one-off category judgments).

3   General Observations on Human SIG-Playing Behavior

We now discuss some observations based on the author's own experience playing SIGs and recording thoughts while playing. (This methodology is similar to the protocol analysis method of Simon and Newell [5,16].[4]) The games considered used input alphabets of $\{A, C, D, -\}$ and output alphabets of $\{B, -\}$.[5] They are listed in Table 1, alongside the number of turns taken to figure out the game with reasonable confidence and the minimal number of states to represent the game as a Mealy machine. The game history was not visible during the game, so information of interest had to be held in memory, and inputs were random[6]

---

[4] As they are based on a single subject, we should not expect our observations to generalize in all details to other subjects. This is not a problem for our purposes, since the goal is to collect a sample of *some* of the approaches people apply to SIGs, not to survey them completely. One other note is in order: since the author also wrote the games, some steps were taken to avoid recalling how they worked during play. The games were played some weeks after being created, had their inputs shuffled, and were drawn from a larger set of 48 games.

[5] The − input symbol was chosen as a "null" symbol to indicate nothing of note had happened; this allows an asynchronous interaction to be modeled within a synchronous formalism.

[6] There was some weighting, chosen for each game with the intent of making it more learnable.

Table 1. Sample system induction games.

#	Description (output is − if not otherwise specified)	Turns	States
1	If C occurs, do two Bs; add one extra B if an A is received during or right after those Bs	43	4
2	A toggles a hidden state; in the "on" state, each C produces B	77	2
3	If A occurs, do two Bs	102	2
4	C toggles repetition of B; A suppresses Bs for two turns	125	4
5	Do B if last three inputs were a cyclic permutation of ACD	142	7
6	Do B if the last two inputs were AD or DA	241	3
7	Do B every time the inputs switch between D and non-D	250	2
8	Any time C occurs, respond to the next two Ds with B	250	3
9	If − occurs and there have been ≥ 2 As since the last B, do B	419	3
10	The sequence DA activates a hidden state and AD deactivates it; when in the state, blocks of Cs get the response $-B-B\ldots$	463	5

except in the later parts of Games 8–10, where I got stuck and switched to controlling them directly.

The overarching activity that appears in the transcripts of these games is the conjecturing, testing, and refining of rules. Some rules are easy to deduce: if a certain input symbol always leads to a certain output, we quickly pick up on that. We also readily pick up on block-related rules, such as "in a block of −s, all turns after the first have output −." Other easy features to pick up on include alternation, situations where an event triggers two outputs in a row (or where two equal inputs in a row trigger an effect), and situations where one of two outcomes can occur, for example "in a block of Cs the outputs are either all − or they alternate, starting with −."

The more challenging component of the task tends to be figuring out the conditions controlling an unreliable event. For example, in Game 9, I quickly saw that in a block of − inputs, the first output could be either − or B, but it was not easy to figure out the controlling condition. Let us call the event that prompts the unpredictable outcome the "probe"; in our example the first − of a block was the probe. To figure out non-obvious conditions, I seemed to consider several types of theories. The type considered first was that the relevant considerations for determining the outcome of a probe took place since the last probe; this assumption led me to seek features of the inter-probe history that were successful predictors (such as, in Game 9, the presence of two As). This search process was biased to first consider recent inputs as explanatory factors, which is reminiscent of prediction suffix trees [18]. A second type of theory was that the probe exposed some underlying (hidden) state which could be toggled on or off by certain events. When working under this assumption, I would look at inter-probe periods where the outcome had switched, and try to extract features that would predict the switches. Interestingly, this sort of theory resembles Drescher's idea of "synthetic items" [4]. A third type of theory, which I came to in Games 8 and 9 only after the other ideas failed, was that performing the probe itself alters the hidden state. In both cases, this conjecture quickly led to the discovery of the actual rule, but from the limited data it is unclear what general method might apply here.

While this very preliminary study does not allow us to draw definitive conclusions, the above patterns suggest that several existing ideas (such as prediction suffix trees, synthetic items, decision trees, and rule-based concept learning [7]) may be part of a learning "toolbox" employed by humans and perhaps appropriate for AGI too. We can also see that there is a need to do a certain amount of "perceptual" processing of the input, even in the rather abstract domain of SIGs. For example, in Game 10, a pattern of alternating Cs can be viewed as a stable state, and a multiple-input sequence can be viewed as a single event. In Game 4, a two-turn occurrence of "suppression" is viewed as a single event.

It is also interesting to consider what the types of theories we contemplate tell us about the environments we are biased to learn. The theory types mentioned earlier are most effective when hidden state is controlled by recent or distinctive events, or is relatively stable between probes. These features need not be present in general; one can imagine machines (think hash functions) in which every input "scrambles" the state. On a more fundamental level, the *existence* of effective probes, and indeed of a distinction between "really" hidden and "not-so-hidden" state,[7] is a form of structure that humans seem to productively utilize. It seems likely that we will need to design agents with similar considerations in mind if we want them to display general intelligence.

4   A Model of Early Decision-Making on SIGs

The previous section was effectively a "depth-first" investigation of human SIG behavior. We can also take a breadth-first approach and look at a smaller amount of behavior on a wider sample of games. In an effort to do this, I examined a sample of 73 situations a SIG player could face on the fifth turn and annotated each with a judgment of which guesses would be appropriate, which is a proxy for what hypotheses humans are inclined to consider.[8] We will present a rule-based model which replicates this data and discuss what it suggests about how humans go about rule induction in SIGs.

---

[7] In the SIG formalism, *all* state is hidden; what we mean by "really" hidden state is information about the state which cannot be inferred from the recent history.

[8] The sample of situations considered was generated by taking all distinct histories (treating relabelings as equivalent) satisfying two conditions: (i) that the history contained mixed evidence and (ii) that the last two inputs were the same. By "mixed evidence" we mean that there was at least one input that was followed by both outputs; this restriction was chosen because cases with no mixed evidence were uniformly felt to be easy decisions (just do what worked last time). The second restriction was an arbitrary choice to reduce the sample to a manageable size.

Before doing this, however, it may be worth clarifying why we care about obtaining such a model. The logic is as follows. In order to learn how an environment behaves, humans (or artificial agents) must notice regularities in it and entertain hypotheses about the causes of those regularities. This raises the question of *which* regularities and hypotheses humans naturally consider.[9] Human SIG judgments are surely based on the regularities we perceive and the hypotheses we generate, so by modeling the judgments we can begin to inventory the mechanisms behind those elements of the learning process.

Note that even though the preliminary "inventory" we construct takes the form of a collection of rules, these rules should not be confused with the rules that characterize the environments we want to learn—the inventory is instead more akin to a set of "meta-rules" for conjecturing environment-governing rules. Given the preliminary nature of this study, our meta-rules are not particularly sophisticated, but they serve to illustrate the methodology we have in mind.

4.1 Data

The judgments and the number of times each was used are shown in Table 2. Sample histories, together with corresponding judgments, are shown in Table 3. One interesting finding about these judgments is that in general they are not very hard to make; we do have an intuition for what choices are reasonable, just as we have intuition for what would be a reasonable continuation of the sequence $1, 4, 9, \ldots$. As one might expect, however, there is inevitably a bit of fuzziness, and at times a history seems to border two categories, or we change our judgment from one day to the next. In a few cases (< 10), as I worked on the model, I discovered similar histories that I had annotated differently, but which (when considered side by side) I did not feel deserved differing judgments. In these cases I simply adjusted one of the judgments to obtain uniformity.

Table 2. Judgments on the fifth turn of our sample of SIGs.

N	Judgment
16	$-$ is the only good answer
18	$-$ is preferred but B is not too unreasonable
27	B and $-$ are about equally good
3	B is preferred but $-$ is not too unreasonable
9	B is the only good answer

---

[9] These questions speak to the problem of what inductive bias is appropriate for AGI. There are of course theoretical proposals like Solomonoff induction [21], but we are motivated by a desire to address the issue empirically.

Table 3. Sample judgments on the fifth turn of SIGs.

In	Out	In	Out	In	Out	In	Out	In	Out
A	B	A	B	A	B	A	B	A	B
C	–	C	B	A	–	C	B	C	B
A	–	C	B	A	B	A	–	A	–
C	–	A	–	C	–	D	B	C	B
C		A		C		D		C	
only –		prefer –		both		prefer B		only B	

4.2 Model

The following model captures all 73 of the judgments. It is based on a set of rules, each of which examines the history and, if it meets certain conditions, proposes an output.[10] If a rule finds the condition it was looking for, we say it "fires." The rules are divided into four groups, which we have labeled 1A, 1B, 2, and 3. These rules function in a preference system. When determining the preferred output, rules in group 1 (A and B) are first consulted. If one or more rules in group 1 fire, then the action(s) those rules propose become the preferred one(s). If no group 1 rule fires, then group 2 is consulted in the same way. (It turns out a rule in group 2 always fires, so group 3 is not needed to determine the preferred action; its role is to determine whether the other option is disallowed or just weak.) In most cases, if a lower-ranked rule proposes an action but the preferred action was already set in a higher group, then the former action is felt to be a weak option. However, the rules in group 1A are so compelling that they outweigh this tendency—proposals from lower-ranked rules are not felt to be options at all, not even weak ones.[11]

The rules are listed in Table 4. Those that can't be described in one line are given names and will be described presently. Throughout, let I be the present input and T be the present turn. $|\cdot|$ will mean the length of a collection of turns.

AnalogousBlocks. A "block" is a contiguous group g of turns with the same input such that (a) $|g| \geq 2$ (b) g is not a subset of a larger block. If T is part of a block b, and there is a prior block b' with $|b'| \geq |b|$, and the outputs of b' have agreed with those of b so far, we say that b and b' are analogous. For example, in $(AB)(A-)(C-)(DB)(D?)$ the last two turns constitute a block analogous to the first two. In this situation the rule says to pick the output that occurred in b' in the position corresponding to T.

AlternationWithinTailBlock. If T is part of a block of length at least 3, and the outputs in that block alternate, continue the alternation.

---

[10] One rule actually proposes both outputs as acceptable.

[11] As it turns out, this mostly applies to group 3 rules. There is only one case in which a 1A rule suppresses a group 2 rule, namely the $AAAAA/B - B-$ situation.

Table 4. Rules modeling a set of fifth-turn SIG decisions.

1A.	$AAAAA$ and $B-B-$ (predict B)
	$AAAAA$ and $BB--$ (predict $-$)
	$B---$ (predict $-$)
1B.	$B---$, $BB--$, or $BBB-$ (predict $-$)
	AnalogousBlocks where both blocks have the same input
	(this implies the input is $AACAA$)
2.	DoLast (copy the most recent output)
	$B-B-$ (predict B)
	$B--B$ (predict $-$)
	AlternationWithinTailBlock
	AnalogousBlocks
3.	AnalogousExperience
	PredominantExperience
	TiedExperience (predict both B and $-$ as acceptable)
	LastExperience
	PredominantAll

AnalogousExperience. Let $e(i)$ be the player's "experience" with input i: the sequence of outputs that have occurred when i was the input. If $|e(I)| \geq 1$, and there is some i with $|e(i)| > |e(I)|$, and $e(i)$ has agreed with $e(I)$ so far, predict the current output from the output at the corresponding position in $e(i)$.

PredominantExperience. If one output has occurred more times than the other in $e(I)$, predict it.

TiedExperience. If both outputs have occurred equally often (and at least once) in $e(I)$, predict that both are acceptable.

LastExperience. If $|e(I)| \geq 1$, predict the last element of $e(I)$.

PredominantAll. If one output has occurred more times than the other in the full history, predict it.

4.3 Discussion

All the listed rules are necessary, although some handle only a couple cases (AnalogousExperience only handles one), and some could be replaced with a different but equally effective rule (for example, we could use an AlternatingExperience rule instead of the TiedExperience rule). Many of the rules are not too surprising; they indicate that we pay attention to alternation, to switches from one output to another, to recent outputs, and to the outputs that previously occurred with the current input. Probably the most interesting feature of the model is the concept of a "block" (a contiguous group of turns with the same input), which is used in multiple ways: a block boundary can be seen as a "cut point" which allows a pattern that exists within the block but not beyond it to be seen as legitimate (this occurs in the AlternationWithinTailBlock rule), and blocks can be used to create analogies between one sequence of turns and a past sequence of turns, thereby allowing more complex predictions than would otherwise be possible.

There are a few rules that are to some extent artifacts of the limited set of cases we considered. For example, DoLast would probably be a much less robust rule if we hadn't restricted attention to cases where the fourth and fifth inputs were the same. Another question we might ask is, is it really the case that 1A proposals are so *good* that they knock out everything else, or is it rather that lower-ranked rules actually need some conditions which are not met in 1A situations to be viable? It is hard to say without more data. And of course some of our rules (like the 1A rules) are overly specific; they were left this way because we did not have enough data to make a well-supported generalization. Nonetheless, in these rules we can start to see the kernel of a more general system. It seems likely that many of the rules would generalize to longer histories or other types of games. Overall, the rules of the model suggest that we have a diverse set of primitives from which we can construct conjectures about the behavior of environments, and that some of these primitives involve perceiving higher-level entities (such as blocks) within the stream of events.

5 Conclusion

In this paper we used data from human performance on system induction games to generate some preliminary ideas about the underlying mechanisms humans use to approach these problems. By extension, this sort of analysis can suggest mechanisms that might be appropriate for artificial generally intelligent agents that learn from experience. The particular mechanisms proposed here are not as important as the overall methodology, which may be summarized as follows: pick a simple but nontrivial class of games, let humans play them, capture the guesses made (and thought processes used) by humans, and infer learning mechanisms.

Regarding possible future directions for this work, obviously there are many more games to explore in much greater depth, and it would be desirable to construct complete SIG-playing algorithms. A likely stepping stone towards that goal would be to develop a "system grammar" which would formally define a space of SIGs humans can easily understand and learn. Such an effort would be analogous to the goal in linguistics of constructing a grammar that defines the space of acceptable sentences, and indeed at least one linguist has explored analogies along these lines [9] (see Chap. 4).

On a larger scale, more sophisticated types of environments could be considered, for example environments with continuous state spaces or sensorimotor components. Another logical extension would be to examine other aspects of human SIG performance, such as how difficult humans find particular decisions and what features of the history we remember (certain features are more memorable than others, such as repetition, blockiness, or symmetric patterns like $ACCA$). These would be suitable modeling targets, just as output decisions are.

A final direction for investigation would be to ask where (meta-)rules like those described in Sect. 4.2 come from (assuming they are psychologically real). Were they themselves learned through experience? Or perhaps they can be explained as combinations of simpler primitives. Studying more sophisticated games may help develop answers to these questions.

Acknowledgments. The author wishes to thank the anonymous reviewers and An-Dinh Nguyen for helpful comments.

References

1. Angluin, D.: Learning regular sets from queries and counterexamples. Inform. Comput. **75**(2), 87–106 (1987)
2. Bergman, R.: Learning World Models in Environments with Manifest Causal Structure. Ph.D. thesis, Massachusetts Insitute of Technology (1995)
3. Chrisman, L.: Reinforcement learning with perceptual aliasing: the perceptual distinctions approach. In: Proceedings of the Tenth National Conference on Artificial Intelligence, pp. 183–188. AAAI Press (1992)
4. Drescher, G.L.: Made-Up Minds: A Constructivist Approach to Artificial Intelligence. MIT Press, Cambridge (1991)
5. Ericsson, K.A., Simon, H.A.: Protocol Analysis: Verbal Reports as Data. MIT Press, Cambridge (1993)
6. Gold, E.M.: Complexity of automaton identification from given data. Inform. Control **37**(3), 302–320 (1978)
7. Goodman, N.D., Tenenbaum, J.B., Feldman, J., Griffiths, T.L.: A rational analysis of rule-based concept learning. Cogn. Sci. **32**(1), 108–154 (2008)
8. Hofstadter, D.: Fluid Concepts & Creative Analogies: Computer Models of the Fundamental Mechanisms of Thought. Basic Books, New York (1995)
9. Jackendoff, R.: Language, Consciousness, Culture: Essays on Mental Structure. MIT Press, Cambridge (2007)
10. Kotovsky, K., Simon, H.A.: Empirical tests of a theory of human acquisition of concepts for sequential patterns. Cogn. Psychol. **4**(3), 399–424 (1973)
11. Mahabal, A.A.: Seqsee: A Concept-centered Architecture for Sequence Perception. Ph.D. thesis, Indiana University Bloomington (2009)
12. McCallum, A.K.: Reinforcement learning with selective perception and hidden state. Ph.D. thesis, University of Rochester (1996)
13. McCallum, R.A.: Instance-based utile distinctions for reinforcement learning with hidden state. In: ICML, pp. 387–395 (1995)
14. Mealy, G.H.: A method for synthesizing sequential circuits. Bell Syst. Tech. J. **34**(5), 1045–1079 (1955)
15. Meredith, M.J.E.: Seek-Whence: A model of pattern perception. Ph.D. thesis, Indiana University (1986)
16. Newell, A., Simon, H.A.: Human Problem Solving. Prentice-Hall, Englewood Cliffs (1972)

17. Piaget, J.: The Origins of Intelligence in Children. International Universities Press, New York (1952)
18. Ron, D., Singer, Y., Tishby, N.: The power of Amnesia: learning probabilistic automata with variable memory length. Mach. Learn. **25**(2–3), 117–149 (1996)
19. Shahbaz, M., Groz, R.: Inferring mealy machines. In: Cavalcanti, A., Dams, D.R. (eds.) FM 2009. LNCS, vol. 5850, pp. 207–222. Springer, Heidelberg (2009)
20. Simon, H.A., Kotovsky, K.: Human acquisition of concepts for sequential patterns. Psychol. Rev. **70**(6), 534 (1963)
21. Solomonoff, R.J.: A formal theory of inductive inference. Part I. Inform. Control **7**(1), 1–22 (1964)

Integrating Model-Based Prediction and Facial Expressions in the Perception of Emotion

Nutchanon Yongsatianchot[(⊠)] and Stacy Marsella

College of Computer and Information Science and Department of Psychology,
Northeastern University, Boston, MA 02115, USA
yongsatianchot.n@husky.neu.edu

Abstract. Understanding a person's mental state is a key challenge to the design of Artificial General Intelligence (AGI) that can interact with people. A range of technologies have been developed to infer a user's emotional state from facial expressions. Such bottom-up approaches confront several problems, including that there are significant individual and cultural differences in how people display emotions. More fundamentally, in many applications we may want to know other mental states such as goals and beliefs that can be critical for effective interaction with a person. Instead of bottom-up processing of facial expressions, in this work, we take a predictive, Bayesian approach. An observer agent uses mental models of an observed agent's goals to predict how the observed will react emotionally to an event. These predictions are then integrated with the observer's perceptions of the observed agent's expressions, as provided by a perceptual model of how the observed tends to display emotions. This integration provides the interpretation of the emotion displayed while also updating the observer's mental and emotional display models of the observed. Thus perception, mental model and display model are integrated into a single process. We provide a simulation study to initially test the effectiveness of the approach and discuss future work in testing the approach in interactions with people.

Keywords: Emotion perception · Bayesian inference · Agent-based modelling

1 Introduction

Understanding a person's mental state is a key challenge to the design of an Artificial General Intelligence (AGI) that can interact with people. In our everyday life, interpreting and understanding what other people are feeling and thinking is an important task. When you have a conversation with your friends, you want to understand what they are thinking and feeling about a conversation. You may want to continue talking if you infer your friends enjoys it, but you may want to change the topic if you think your friends do not like it. This inference can draw on many sources of information, including the observed behavior such as facial

© Springer International Publishing Switzerland 2016
B. Steunebrink et al. (Eds.): AGI 2016, LNAI 9782, pp. 234–243, 2016.
DOI: 10.1007/978-3-319-41649-6_23

expressions, the situation the observed person is in, and the observer's beliefs about the observed person's goals and beliefs.

One of the important questions regarding these different sources of information is how to integrate them. While you are talking, you observe that you friend frowned. Should you interpret that ambiguous frown as negative reaction to what you are saying or is it rather a sign of concentration showing interest? In addition, how should we use the new observations and inferences to help refine our beliefs about the observed agent's goals and beliefs?

Our interest is in giving a similar capacity to an artificial agent observing another human or artificial agent. This has led us to explore the questions of how predictions from observed agent's models about emotion can be integrated with the perception of facial expression, and how the observer can update the models based on the observation and inference to achieve the true model of observed agent.

A key question here is how emotions relate to expression. Ekman et al. and Izard [4,8] argue that some facial expressions signal specific *basic emotions*. According to this view, there is a specific way of expressing each basic emotion that is culturally universally recognizable. However, other research [6,11] has alternatively argued that different cultures and different individuals can express the same emotion differently.

Additionally, Calvo et al. [2] have pointed out the limitation of many existing affect detection systems is that they do not take the context of an emotion evoking situation into account. They have argued on the important of top-down contextually driven predictive models of affect. One type of emotion's theories that makes a prediction about emotion based on context information is appraisal theory. Appraisal theories argue that a person reacts to a situation based on how a person appraises the situation with respect to his or her goals and beliefs. [10, 12] Therefore, when predicting other person's emotion based on context, it is important to take into account the individual difference in term of goals and beliefs.

In this paper, we present an approach to infer on observed agent's emotional states by integrating both top-down predictions about emotional response given how a situation is influencing an observed agent's goal as well as bottom-up facial expression observations of the agent as it expresses that emotional response. This work extends previous work by Alfonso et al. [1] by choosing to leverage ideas of the descriptive Bayesian approach [13] that allow us to capture the individual differences in how the observed agent emotional reacts to a situation and how the observed agent displays that emotional reaction. The descriptive Bayesian approach is an inference approach that allows multiple priors and likelihoods.

To express individual differences in how agent's emotionally reacts, we use an Appraisal Theory of emotion. To model differences in expression of emotion, we draw on the concept that people have "display rules" [11] that mediate how they express emotion. First, we argue that appraisal is operating top-down and acts as prior in Bayesian inference making probabilistic predictions about observed agent's emotion from context. Second, we can group individual difference in facial expression into the group of display rules for each emotion which allows us to infer emotion from facial expression. Finally, we also seek to model not only inference of emotion, but also how observations and inferences could be used to update observed agent's models of an observed agent's goal and display rules.

In the rest of the paper, we first discuss the proposed method. We illustrate how the descriptive Bayesian approach captures individual difference, how appraisal theory can be used to predict emotion given situation, and how facial expressions can be grouped using display rules. Then, we describe in detail the mathematic behind our approach. After that, we explain the simulation to test the proposing method and the result of simulations. A simulation study was designed to demonstrate that our method could converge to the observed agent's true model and display rules, and could predict observed agent's emotion more accurately by using both agent's model with context and display rules. At the end, we discuss the implication of the work and future work.

2 Method

2.1 Expressing Individual Difference in Bayesian Inference

In a standard Bayesian model, the learner's inferences are described by Bayes' rule as following:

$$\Pr(h|x) = normalize(\Pr(x|h)\Pr(h|H))$$

where x represents the data available to the learner, h is a hypothesis that generates the data, and H is the set of all hypotheses available to the learner. In this setting, we need to know and constrain the prior and likelihood beforehand. Tauber et al. [13] proposed a descriptive Bayesian approach in which Bayes' rule could be expressed with multiple priors and likelihoods. In the descriptive approach, there could be multiple possible choices of prior and likelihoods, and learner's inferences are also conditioned on all possible prior and likelihoods. This approach argues that the learner's prior should not be perceived as fixed by some expectation about the thing to learn, and the likelihoods need not to correspond to any specific theory or model of how data are generated.

For our work, we apply the idea of multiple priors and likelihoods to capture the individual difference as the following. Given the same event or context, different person could experience different emotion based on his or her goals and beliefs used to evaluate the event. As a result, different models act as possible different priors of emotion. Similarly, there could be many different ways to express the same emotion based on a display rule, so display rules act as possible different likelihoods for a specific emotion. Therefore, the descriptive Bayesian approach allows us to capture individual differences in emotion expression in terms of different display rules as multiple likelihoods and different models as multiple priors.

2.2   Appraisal Theory and Theory of Mind

In order to predict the emotion based on context and agent's model, we use appraisal theory of emotion. Generally, appraisal theories argue that emotion arises from a process of a subjective assessment of the relation between the event and a person's goal. [12] In this work, we use the appraisal theory proposed by Ortony, Clore, and Collins or OCC model of emotion [3,10]. Briefly, OCC model is an appraisal theory that focuses only on the structure of situation, and does not involve any process of appraisal. This is suitable for our purpose since all we want in our simulation is a distribution of possible emotion from a given situation, and not the underlying processes. OCC model specifies the features of the prototypical situations represented by each kind of emotion, and separates emotions into three groups - emotion that focuses on event, agent or object. Note that we could replace OCC model with any other appraisal theory as long as it provides a reasonable way to obtain a distribution of emotion given context and agent's model. Further, we assume an observing agent can appraise events from the perspective of the observed. In particular, the observer has beliefs about observed agent's goals, what is sometimes referred to as a Theory of Mind [14]. (We are assuming agent architectures that can model other agents [9].)

2.3   Display Rules

The display rules in this work are influenced by Safdar et al. work [11], and dialect theory [6]. In essence, display rule modifies the expression of emotion. Safdar et al. proposes seven different possible behavioral responses: amplify, deamplify, neutralize, masque by displaying another emotion, qualify by combining the actual emotion with another emotion, and express exactly without modification. In addition, Elfenbein et al. [6]. have shown that different culture has a different way of displaying the same emotion similar to different dialects in language.

Combining these two ideas, three different display rules of each emotion were designed for simulation study. We define a display rule as a set of action units (AU) [5] associated with the probability that it will be expressed. It can be thought of as a function that takes in an emotion and generates facial expression. See Display rules in simulation section for more detail.

2.4   Calculation

Inferring Emotions

$$\forall e \in E : \Pr(e|X,c) = norm(\Pr(X|e,c)\Pr(e|c)) \tag{1}$$

$$= norm\left(\prod_{x \in X} \Pr(x|e,c) \left(\sum_{m \in M} \Pr(e|m,c)\Pr(m|c) \right) \right) \tag{2}$$

$$= norm\left(\prod_{x \in X} \left(\sum_{d_e \in D_e} \Pr(X|e,d_e,c)\Pr(d_e|e,c) \right) \left(\sum_{m \in M} \Pr(e|m,c)\Pr(m) \right) \right) \tag{3}$$

$$= norm\left(\prod_{x \in X} \left(\sum_{d_e \in D_e} \Pr(X|d_e)\Pr(d_e) \right) \left(\sum_{m \in M} \Pr(e|m,c)\Pr(m) \right) \right) \tag{4}$$

The equations above represent the way to infer the emotion of an observed agent given facial expression and context. *norm* stands for normalize. E is a probabilistic distribution of emotion, and e is a category of emotion. An example of E is the following: $E = \{angry : 0.1, happy : 0.5, sad : 0.1, no\ emotion : 0.3\}$ where the number is the probability that the observer expect agent to experience that emotion. X is a set of action units represents facial expression, and x is an individual action unit. D_e is a set of display rule for emotion e and d_e is an individual display rule for emotion e. M is a probabilistic distribution of observer agent's possible models of the observed agent, and m represents each possible model. Lastly, c is context which contains the information about the situation that is eliciting the emotion. In the case of display rules of each emotion d_e, in our simulation, they are defined to be specific for a given context so they are already taken context into account. See simulation section for full description and examples of observed agent's goal, display rules, and context.

The first equation, $\Pr(e|X, c)$ is expressed using Bayes' rule. In order to calculate $\Pr(e|c)$, we express it in term of multiple possible models, m. Basically, the observer has multiple mental models of observed agent that could be used to infer observed agent's emotion from context. $\Pr(e|m, c)$ is calculated based on OCC model which takes both model and context, and returns a probabilistic distribution of emotion. For $\Pr(m|c)$, we assume that model is independent from context, which results in $\Pr(m)$. Multiple possible models represent multiple possible priors in the descriptive Bayesian approach.

We express $\Pr(X|e, c)$ in term of multiplication of $\Pr(x|e, c)$ for all $x \in X$. Here, we assume that each action unit is independent. $\Pr(X|e, c)$ can be further expressed in term of multiple display rules of a given emotion, d_e. Again, this is similar to the idea of the descriptive Bayesian approach in which we could have multiple likelihood functions. The first term $\Pr(x|d_e, e, c)$ is the likelihood that x will be generated from d_e. A display rule d_e is a subset of both context and emotion so $\Pr(x|d_e, e, c)$ can be reduced to $\Pr(x|d_e)$. Since we define d_e specific for a given context c and emotion e, $\Pr(d_e|e, c)$ can be reduced to $\Pr(d_e)$.

After the calculation, an emotion that has a highest probability or a maximum a posteriori (MAP) of $\Pr(e|X, c)$ is the prediction of emotion that the observed agent experiences.

Updating the Distribution of Models

$$\Pr(m|e) = norm(\Pr(e|m)\Pr(m)) \tag{5}$$

$$\Pr(m)_{new} = \sum_{e \in E}(\Pr(m|e)\Pr(e) + \Pr(m)_{old}(1 - \Pr(e))) \tag{6}$$

Equation 5 calculates posterior probability of m given e using Bayes' rule. $\Pr(e|m)$ is calculated using OCC model similar to how we calculate prior in Eq. 3, but only for one model. Note that we omit context in the above equations but we use it to calculate $\Pr(e|m)$.

In the inference part, we infer emotion in term of probabilistic distribution so there is uncertainty associated with our inference. For example, the observer may infer that observed agent experience happy with some probability p. We need to take uncertainty of evidence into account when we update a distribution of model. Equation 6 represents how we use posterior probability from Eq. 5 to update the probability of model, m, accounting for uncertainty of evidence. There are two possible cases - either observed agent experiences emotion e with probability $\Pr(e)$ or does not experiences it with probability $1 - \Pr(e)$. If observed agent experience e, we update $\Pr(m)$ based on the posterior probability as in the first part, $\Pr(m|e)\Pr(e)$, in Eq. 6. If observed agent does not experience e, we keep $\Pr(m)$ the same as in the second part, $\Pr(m)(1 - \Pr(e)$, in Eq. 6. We update $\Pr(m)$ using every emotion e in E.

Updating the Distribution of Display Rules of Each Emotion

$$\Pr(d_e|X) = norm(\Pr(X|d_e)\Pr(d_e)) \tag{7}$$

$$\Pr(d_e)_{new} = \Pr(d_e)_{old}(1 - \Pr(e)) + \Pr(d_e|X)\Pr(e) \tag{8}$$

Equation 7 expresses the posterior probability of display rules of emotion e, d_e, given X using Bayes rule. Equation 8 is similar to Eq. 6 in which we takes into account the probability of emotion when we updating the probability of d_e. For display rule, unlike model that we takes into account all emotions, we only consider emotion e that corresponds to d_e.

3   Simulation

In order to demonstrate the method, a simulation study was designed. There are two things we want to test. First, by using situational context and observed agent's facial expression, our method, starting with uninform distribution of model and display rules, could converge to the true observed agent's model and display rules. Second, after converge, our method could use both model and display rule to predict observed agent's emotion correctly, better than using model alone, using display rules alone, and using neither of them.

3.1   Context and Model

The simulation is the following. At each time step, the observer observes a target agent receives a payment from the boss. The boss can either give the observed agent extra money, or deduct money from a payment. The upper bound is 6000, and the lower bound is -6000. The goal of an observed agent is to earn a baseline payment. Since the goal is just a reference point, we can set it to be 0. An observed agent can have different expectation on what the extra money should be. In this simulation, there are three different expectations - no expectation (0), low expectation (+2000), and high expectation (+4000).

OCC theory uses a threshold to determine whatever a person will experience any emotion or not. However, in this work, we want to express it in probabilistic terms. Therefore, to calculate the probability of an emotion using OCC and context, we use a logistic function with the expectation as the mid-point.

According to OCC model, one of the mechanisms that makes an agent to experience different emotions from the same event is determined by the component the agent focuses on. In this simulation, an agent can focus on event or agent causing the event. We define two different types of focus. The first type of agent is likely to focus more on an event while the second type of agent is likely to focus more on an agent causing the event. Combining three different expectations and two different foci, there are 6 possible models of observed agent in our simulation.

In summary, we simulate the situation that can please or displease the observed agent according to the agent's goal, and the observed agent can focus on the event itself or another agent that causes it. As a result, according to OCC, there are four different kinds of emotion - happy, sad, grateful and angry. However, we group happy and grateful together as a positive emotion labeled happy, because gratitude does not normally show up in facial expression literatures. Therefore, we are left with happy, sad, angry, and no emotion.

To illustrate OCC model, consider the following example, an observed agent, with low expectation (2000) and likely to focus on event (0.8), receive 2000 extra money. The probability that agent will be happy is $0.6 \times 0.8 = 0.48$, where 0.6 is the probability of feeling displeased calculating from logistic function and 0.8 is the probability that an agent will focus on event. The probability that agent will be grateful (happy) is $0.6 \times 0.2 = 0.12$, where 0.6 is the same as happy case and 0.2 is the probability that an observed agent will focus on agent that causes the event. Therefore, an observed agent will be happy with probability 0.6, and no emotion with probability 0.4.

3.2 Display Rules

A display rule for each emotion composes of a list of action units (AU) with a probability that it will show up on the face. This probability is $\Pr(x|d_e)$ in our equation. The list of AUs that we use in our simulation is the following: AU 1 - inner brow raiser, AU 4 - brow lowerer, AU 5 - upper lid raiser, AU 6 - cheek raiser, AU 12 - lip corner puller, AU 15 - lip corner depresser, AU 23 - lip tighter, and AU 25 - lips part. One example of display rule happy could be AU6, AU12, and AU25 with all of them having a probability 0.9, and the rest of action units with a probability 0.1. This means if an agent has this display rule, it is very likely that when an agent feels happy, AU6, AU12, and AU25 will show up while other action units likely to not show. Another example of happy rule could be AU6 and AU12 with both having a probability 0.25 representing a display rule of happy that unlikely to express smile. In the simulation, we define 3 display rules for each emotion, so there are 81 combinations of display rules.

3.3 Experiment

We run the simulation for each different possible combination of model and display rules. At each time step, the amount of extra money is randomly generated that an observed agent received. A distribution of observed agent's emotion is generated based on the money and agent's model using OCC. Then one emotion is randomly generated from the distribution, and used to generate a set of action unit based on a observed agent's display rule of the emotion. Once both situational context and a set of shown action units are generated, we feed them to 4 different methods listing below to generate the prediction.

The first method which is the proposed method uses both situational context and facial expression to generate a prediction. In other word, it uses both observer agent's models of the observed goals and display rules (M and D). For the starting distribution of observed agent's model, every model is equally likely, so it has the same probability. For the starting distribution of display rules, the probability of the high display rule is 0.5 while the probability of other two rules is 0.25. Before testing the performance of this method, we first run a simulation on the same setup for 200 time steps to let the observer learns agent's model and display rules before testing in the simulation with other methods.

For the rest of the method, we do not train them. Instead, we provide them with agent's true model or display rules, or pre-defined display rules. The second method only uses context with true model of agent (M only), and ignore agent's facial expression. This method only applies OCC to a given situation and chooses emotion with highest probability to be a prediction of agent's emotion. Basically, this method only calculates $\Pr(e|m_{true}, c)$ or prior in Eq. 1 and uses the result to infer agent's emotion.

The third method uses only facial expression with true display rules for all emotion (D only), and ignore situational context. Essentially, this method only calculates $\Pr(X|e, c, D_{true})$ which is similar to likelihood in Eq. 3, and uses the result to infer agent's emotion.

The fourth method uses only facial expression, but with a high probability (or typical prototype) display rule for all types of emotion. In essence, it discards agent's model and display rules (No M and D). This method is similar to the third method but using a high probability display rule rather than the true display rule.

The simulation runs encompass 486 different agents, based on 6 different goal models times 81 different combination of display rules. For each of these agents, 100 simulations were run. Each simulation run encompassed an initial training session of 200 steps, followed by an evaluation phase of 500 steps. We calculate the accumulated error in predicting the emotion over these 500 steps for each method. If the method predicts observed agent's emotion correctly, then the error is 0. If it does not predict correctly, then the error is 1.

4   Simulation Results

On average, the proposed method took 105 time steps to converge (or need about 105 observations to converge) in which we define to be when the probability of one of the model is higher than 0.95. It fails to converge to the true observed agent's model only 1.78 % of the time, but it always converges to the true observed agent's display rules for each emotion.

Table 1. Results of simulations. M stands for model and D stands for display rules. The error is the error in predicting the observed agent's emotion.

Error	M and D	M only	D only	No M and D
Maximum	0.1177	0.2540	0.2516	0.4078
Minimum	0.0213	0.1770	0.0486	0.0486
Mean	0.0637	0.2220	0.1425	0.1933
Standard Derivation	0.035	0.036	0.073	0.12

Table 1 shows the error in predicting an observed agent's emotion for each method. On average, the proposed method yields 6.37 % error with SD = 0.035, while "M only" yields 22.2 % error with SD = 0.036, "D only" yields 14.25 % error with SD = 0.073, and "No M and D" yields 19.33 % error with SD = 0.12. The proposed method yields a maximum error at 11.77 % when, after training, it does not converge to the true model so it cannot predict emotion accurately. The minimum error for both "D only" and "No M and D" is only at 4.86 % when the true display rules of observed agent are high probability display rules. It is important to note that the simplicity of simulation may have an effect on these errors.

5   Discussion and Future Work

In this work, we propose a method to infer observed agent's emotion from prediction about emotional response and facial expression observations, and a way to update the observer's model of observed agent's goals and display rules that are needed to make the inference. To test the proposed method, a simulation study was created. The results of simulation show that the proposed model converges to the true model and display rules almost all the time. It also does better than a method with model alone, with display rules alone, and with only a high probability display rule.

There are several important problems that still need to be addressed. A key problem is how to acquire the information. In case of facial expression, some studies report success in accurately reading action units on the face [7]. For events, in a specific setting such as game or classroom, acquiring the relevant information needed for appraisal theory to predict emotion is feasible. For example, if an agent gets an answer wrong in the exercise, it is displeased event. Another problem is how much each information source contributes to help inferring observed agent's emotion. For example, facial expression may be a better predictor for happiness, but affective prosody may be a better predictor when it comes to angry or sad.

The next important step in our work is to validate our method with real humans. In our simulation, OCC is used to model the observed agent's emotional reaction, but if the observed is a human then OCC may not be an accurate model of the emotion elicitation process. Therefore, in order to further test our method, we need to replace simulated observed agents with human subjects, and let the system try to predict human emotions based on various types of event that could elicit them.

All in all, this work demonstrates how to capture individual difference in descriptive Bayesian approach, and the way to update observer agent's distribution of models and display rules of observed agent to yield more accurate models. Moreover, this work argues for the importance of context, goals and display rules to make an accurate emotion inference.

References

1. Alfonso, B., Pynadath, D.V., Lhommet, M., Marsella, S.: Emotional perception for updating agents' beliefs. In: 2015 International Conference on Affective Computing and Intelligent Interaction (ACII), pp. 201–207. IEEE (2015)
2. Calvo, R., D'Mello, S., et al.: Affect detection: an interdisciplinary review of models, methods, and their applications. IEEE Trans. Affect. Comput. 1(1), 18–37 (2010)
3. Clore, G.L., Ortony, A.: Psychological construction in the occ model of emotion. Emot. Rev. 5(4), 335–343 (2013)
4. Ekman, P., Friesen, W.V., O'Sullivan, M., Chan, A., Diacoyanni-Tarlatzis, I., Heider, K., Krause, R., LeCompte, W.A., Pitcairn, T., Ricci-Bitti, P.E., et al.: Universals and cultural differences in the judgments of facial expressions of emotion. J. Pers. Soc. Psychol. 53(4), 712 (1987)
5. Ekman, P., Rosenberg, E.L.: What the Face Reveals: Basic and Applied Studies of Spontaneous Expression using the Facial Action Coding System (FACS). Oxford University Press, New York (1997)
6. Elfenbein, H.A., Beaupré, M., Lévesque, M., Hess, U.: Toward a dialect theory: cultural differences in the expression and recognition of posed facial expressions. Emotion 7(1), 131 (2007)
7. Happy, S., Routray, A.: Automatic facial expression recognition using features of salient facial patches. IEEE Trans. Affect. Comput. 6(1), 1–12 (2015)
8. Izard, C.E.: Innate and universal facial expressions: evidence from developmental and cross-cultural research (1994)
9. Marsella, S.C., Pynadath, D.V., Read, S.J.: Psychsim: agent-based modeling of social interactions and influence. In: Proceedings of the International Conference on Cognitive Modeling, vol. 36, Citeseer, pp. 243–248 (2004)
10. Ortony, A., Clore, G.L., Collins, A.: The Cognitive Structure of Emotions. Cambridge University Press, Cambridge (1990)
11. Safdar, S., Friedlmeier, W., Matsumoto, D., Yoo, S.H., Kwantes, C.T., Kakai, H., Shigemasu, E.: Variations of emotional display rules within and across cultures: A comparison between Canada, USA, and Japan. Canadian Journal of Behavioural Science/Revue canadienne des sciences du comportement 41(1), 1 (2009)
12. Smith, C.A., Lazarus, R.S.: Emotion and adaptation (1990)
13. Tauber, S., Navarro, D.J., Perfors, A., Steyvers, M.: Bayesian models of cognition revisited: Setting optimality aside and letting data drive psychological theory
14. Whiten, A.: Natural Theories of Mind: Evolution, Development and Simulation of Everyday Mindreading. Basil Blackwell, Oxford (1991)

A Few Notes on Multiple Theories and Conceptual Jump Size

Grace Solomonoff[✉]

Oxbridge Research, P.O.B. 400404, Cambridge, MA 02140, USA
prettyvivo@gmail.com

Abstract. These are a few notes about some of Ray Solomonoff's foundational work in algorithmic probability, focussing on the universal prior and conceptual jump size, including a few illustrations of how he thought. His induction theory gives a way to compare the likelihood of different theories describing observations. He used Bayes' rule of causation to discard theories inconsistent with the observations. Can we find good theories? Lsearch may give a way to search and the conceptual jump size a measure for this.

1 Understanding and Learning

The first thing Ray did when he acquired something was to take it apart. Here's a picture of Ray taking apart a scooter he found in the trash. He took many notes. They were like a program, so that the scooter could be remade. Ray built a house from descriptions in a book, like a recipe. What was made in Ray's lab in the cellar?

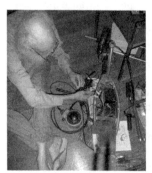

1. Ray taking apart a scooter. 2. Working on the house he built. 3. An "experiment" (Ray is on the right).

Ray [Sol97] wrote:

My earliest contact with modern scientific philosophy may have been Bridgman's [Bri27] concept of "operational definition". An operational definition of anything is a precise sequence of physical operations that enable one to either construct it or identify it with certainty.

B. Steunebrink et al. (Eds.): AGI 2016, LNAI 9782, pp. 244–253, 2016.
DOI: 10.1007/978-3-319-41649-6_24

...When one can't make an operational definition of something, this is usually an indication of poor understanding of it. ...Attempts to operationalize definitions can be guides to discovery. I've found this idea to be an invaluable tool in telling me whether or not I really understand something.

To quantify information Solomonoff's theory uses operational definitions by means of computer programs.

A new way to measure things may herald a new era in math or science. It can bring new ways to see, and new tools. A new way to measure information content of a string happened in 1960-65 when Ray Solomonoff (60, 64) [Sol60b, Sol64], Andrey Kolmogorov (65) [Kol65] and Gregory Chaitin (66) [Cha66] independently published a new way to measure the complexity of a sequence of observations. Kolmogorov and Chaitin were interested in the descriptional complexity of a sequence: to quantify the information, and use that to define randomness, while Ray was interested in the prediction aspects of the sequence.

Prediction and learning are closely related. The heart of science is prediction.[1]

I think Ray thought the length and number of explanations that produced or described a sequence of observations was related to learning. We don't yet know if this new way to measure will be important, but there is a good possibility.

It implies that understanding and learning are not weird things trapped in the brain's black box; they may be weird, but they will be understood.

Ray used a method called algorithmic probability (AP) to measure theories. He used a method of searching for theories called Lsearch which is related to a measure he called conceptual jump size (CJS).

This paper will discuss a few of Solomonoff's ideas about some concepts of AP, Lsearch and CJS. He had delight in creating something new, a joy that is there for all who search for new ideas. Hopefully his ideas will contribute to his lifelong interest of achieving a thinking machine able to solve hard problems in all domains.

2 Algorithmic Probability and the Suite of Theories

In a letter in 2011, Marcus Hutter wrote: "Ray Solomonoff's universal probability distribution M(x) is defined as the probability that the output of a universal monotone Turing machine U starts with string x when provided with fair coin flips on the input tape. Despite this simple definition, it has truly remarkable properties, and constitutes a universal solution of the induction problem." (See also [RH11])

---

[1] Earlier Ray wondered [Sol03] why Kolmogorov wasn't interested in using these concepts for inductive inference — to define empirical probability. "Leonid Levin suggested that inductive inference was at that time, not actually a "mathematical" problem...It may have been that in 1965 there was no really good definition of induction and certainly no general criterion for how good an inductive system was." That paper points out important differences between the universal prior on one Turing Machine and the universal distribution of Turing machines themselves and incomputibility.

To predict the continuation of a string, x, AP gives weights to the theories that could produce or describe it:

$$P_M(x) = \sum_{i=1}^{\infty} 2^{-|s_i(x)|} \tag{1}$$

It measures the likelihood of each unique, randomly created program s_i input into Machine M to produce a chosen sequence, x; this means all the different ways that x could be replicated. Then it adds these probabilities together. The resulting value is P probability of the sequence. It is the likelihood of the sequence x occurring at all.

The shortest program in this distribution is intuitively like the idea of Occam's Razor: the simplest program is the best. Using all the individual programs is intuitively like an idea of Epicurus: keep all of the theories. But the simpler theories are more likely. It weights each theory by a measure based on the likelihood of that theory.

The Universal Prior by its sum to define the probability of a sequence, and by using the weight of individual programs to give a figure of merit to each program (cause or description – like an operational definition) that could produce the sequence [Sol64]. He uses Bayes' rule to predict the continuation of the sequence.

The simplest explanation for an event is often the best one. But something is also more likely to happen if there are many possible causes. Some researchers use AP to choose the single shortest program for prediction [WD99]. Ray thought that keeping as many programs as possible is best for some situations [Sol84]:

> Why not use the single "best" theory? The <u>best</u> is via one criterion; (a) i.e. min a priori of theory x (pr [probability] of corpus with right theory); (b) however another best is with respect to (b) minimum expected prediction error. For best in (b) we use weights of various theories, using weights of (a)

Any new hypothesis can be roughly measured and added to the group of hypotheses; in a finite world, we don't have to include every possible hypothesis from an infinite amount.

3   Using Bayes' Rule

Bayes' rule is used in many statistical applications to sort out frequencies of events. If the events are called causes then Bayes' rule becomes "Bayes' rule for the probability of causes" [Fel50].

Bayes' rule may be the optimal method of predicting future observations based on current beliefs and evidence. A value of AP is that it provides the necessary prior, the universal prior, that contains the complete universe of theories used for prediction. When little or no prior information is available, this technique enables us to construct a default prior based on the language used to describe the data.

The shortest input codes describing the sequence x are more likely than the longer ones, but there will always be at least one theory that can describe any finite sequence of observations: this sequence simply predicts every observation one by one, which as a program, translates to "print $< x >$" for any given sequence x. Thus none of the sequences will have zero probability.

Ray [Sol99] wrote: "If there is any describable regularity in a corpus of data, this technique will find the regularity using a relatively small amount of data. – While the exact a priori probability is mathematically incomputable, it is easy to derive approximations to it. An important outgrowth of this research has been the insight it has given into the necessary trade-offs between a priori information, sample size, precision of probability estimates and computation cost."

In early years probability was scorned in the AI community. Nowdays, in Artificial Intelligence (AI), Bayes' rule is usually used for frequencies, – sorting out masses of data; it gives good statistical values. The frequency version deals with a search space like a Greek urn with events that are variously colored balls. Bayes' rule helps sort the events into groups that may be within other groups, relating them to a common base, so you can add ratios together properly.

I think Ray changed the Greek urn into a Turing urn filled with events that are hypotheses. In this urn are explanations, not objects. The explanations may be different, but may begin the same way.

In a letter by Alex Solomonoff [Sol16b], Alex remembers Ray telling him that perhaps all probability is causal, not frequentist – a coin has a 50 % chance of coming up heads only because we are ignorant of the details of how it is flipped. Also Alex notes that in Solomonoff's theory, the events or observations being predicted by AP are deterministic, not random. The Universal prior implies that the universe has structure and can be described by rules, *not* derived from frequencies of events.

4   Incomputability

AP is (almost) as "computable" as the value of π with successive approximations that are guaranteed to converge to the right value. But unlike π, we can not know how large the error in each approximation can be.

Ray [Sol97] wrote, "The question of the "validity" of any inductive inference methods is a dificult one. You cannot prove that any proposed inductive inference method is "correct.", only that one is "incorrect" by proving it to be internally inconsistent, or showing that it gives results that are grossly at odds with our intuitive evaluation."

But Ray often said about incomputibility: "It's not a bug, it's a feature!" Systems that are computable cannot be complete [Leg06]. Incomputability is because some algorithms can never be evaluated because it would take too long. But these programs will be recognized as possible solutions. On the other hand, any computable system is incomplete: there will always be regularities outside system's search space which will never be acknowledged or considered, even in an infinite amount of time. Computable prediction models hide this fact by ignoring such descriptions.

5   Metamorphoses of a Theory

The second thing Ray did when he acquired something was to use it in a way for which it wasn't intended. When Ray discovered a new use for Mimi the cat's house, he described the use of Mimi's house in a new way; a container with an opening, which can be used in different ways. The new encompassing theory leads to greater flexibility, more uses for Mimi's (who wasn't all that happy about this!) house.

1. A Sultan in a turban. 2. Ray in a Turban 3. Mimi the cat in her house.

A different view may help making or attempting predictions. One day Ray turned the graph of the Dow Jones index upside down. It looked different, which indicated that there was information there. Another day he got my brother to try "playing" several indices on his viola.

In general, a new description is evidence of a kind of learning. Ray uses a method called Lsearch to look for descriptions and a measure called conceptual Jump Size to quantify steps of this learning.

6   Lsearch

Lsearch is a computable way to build simple theories that match the observations. Ray [Sol97] explained it in a biographical article:

> "In the present context, any "concept" can be represented by string of computer instructions – a "macro". They are combined by concatenation. Given a machine, M, that maps finite strings onto finite strings. Given the finite string, x. How can we find in minimal time, a string, p, such that $M(p) = x$?
>
> Suppose there is an algorithm, A, that can examine M and x, then print out p within time T. Levin had a search procedure that, without knowing A, could do the same thing that A did, but in no more time than $CT2^L$. Here, L is the length of the shortest description of A, using a suitable reference machine, and C is a measure of how much slower the reference

machine is than a machine that implements A directly. An alternative form of this cost of the search is CT/P. Here $P = 2^{-L}$ is approximately the a priori probability of the algorithm, A.

The parameter T/P plays a critical role in searches of all kinds. In designing sequences of problems to train an induction machine the T/P value of a particular problem at a particular point in the training of the machine gives an upper bound on how long it will take the machine to solve the problem. In analogy with human problem solving, I christened T/P "Conceptual Jump Size".

Before I met Levin, I had been using T/P as a rough estimate of the cost of a search, but I had no proof that it was achievable. ...Sometime later, I showed that Levin's search procedure (which I will henceforth denote by "Lsearch") is very close to optimum if the search is a "Blind Search""

Lsearch takes the first program to match observations, so it is close to the spirit of Kolmogorov complexity. Lsearch hasn't been applied very much for real problem solving. The measure gives an upper bound to how much time it will take, but it does not tell about error size, and the bound though finite can be very large. Perhaps Schmidhuber [Sch94] was the first to run a computer program using a very simple Lsearch to solve a problem. Ray thought Lsearch could be used.

7   Conceptual Jump Size and Descriptions

CJS is related to the difference of Kolmogorov complexity of a growing string of observations, where the computation time to find a new best description is taken into account. In schools, most often, problems are given that are either right or wrong. But in the real world, plans that first seemed right often fail when new data comes in: so we have Plan B and Plan C, which in Ray's work, may be represented by the members of the suite of programs. Conceptual jump size may give a way to think about questions like this. For example if the sequence is "*water water water...*", then the shortest code is likely "repeat *water* forever". However, if the sequence is "*water water water... chicken chicken... [some differential equation]... [a game of chess]...*", then the simplest description may become more and more complicated as the sequence progresses. Each time there is a lack of regularity between the new observations and the past ones, there is a jump of complexity of the description, resulting in a jump of (decreasing) probability of the sequence. The conceptual jump size is a computable way to measure how much more complex the sequence becomes.

8   Can the Search Be Practical?

"Nothing is always absolutely so" (T. Sturgeon, July 57): was Ray's comment on the cover of his first 1960 Inductive Inference report [Sol60a].

A big problem is that a search for better theories may take more time than can ever be available. Yet people find new theories all the time. If people can do it, so can AI. Can CJS be brought into reasonable size?

Ray had other ideas about Lsearch; for example: improving it by altering the next cycle of Ti, so that the same codes wouldn't be found a second time. Much time is wasted if Lsearch doesn't remember what it did in earlier cycles.

In another note, a question... "The question about if I've spent time T_0 seconds on compression without more in compression what is probability of finding more compression in next t seconds. Is it t/t_0 or $1 - (t/(epsilon_0^t))$ [Sol84]".

Among the notes, a small graph gives another idea:

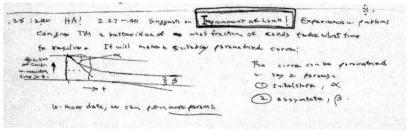

Ray was interested in Lcost as a form of Lsearch which incorporated the cost of computer activity; so there would be penalty for nonproductive activity caused by a successful code. A similar measure of learning is action. The use of dollar cost (in those days equipment cost x rental time) is a good cost measure for most AI type calculations. "Action is approximately equal to equipment cost X time".[Sol81]

Ray also developed the idea of RLP (Resource Limited Prediction) to deal with four basic factors: They are: (1.) The prediction itself. (2.) The reliability of that prediction. (3.) The sample size. (4.) Computation cost [Sol81].

Here are some more ideas by Alex Solomonoff [Sol16a]:

Suppose there are two codes, (with different continuations) that both reproduce the observed data. Both are the same length, and both are the shortest code in their respective cloud of functionally equivalent codes.[2] Then the code with the bigger, denser cloud will be more probable.

Training sequences were a method Solomonoff suggested for leading the Lsearch to the destination in steps short enough to be practical. The idea of a training sequence suggests Levin search can be taught things the trainer already knows. But how would it learn things that no-one knows? You would run short Levin searches on every bit of data you could find. Occasionally you might find a regularity. Those few short codes, and that data would be your training sequence. You wouldn't require that the short code reproduce the entire string perfectly. If it got "enough" of it right, you would call it a success. But this requires that a

---

[2] Two codes are functionally equivalent if all the bits they ever output are identical. If two codes compute all the same output bits, how they generate those bits won't make any difference to any prediction or probability. Except for the matter of computing speed, in a time limited code search. . . .

large corpus of data be divided up into bite-sized chunks, and there are a million ways to do this. Even if there were a "natural" way of splitting it, how would the machine find it? More undirected Lsearchx. This would be a very slow process.

In the most basic Levin search, the CPU fraction assigned to a code is determined solely by the length of the code.

1. If a running code has not finished printing out x, and has not printed out a bit in a long time, it is probably in an infinite loop, will never print out another bit, so we should reduce its CPU fraction.
2. If a running code has correctly printed out most of the bits of x, it is more likely to output all of the bits correctly than a code that has only printed out a few bits. So we should increase the CPU fraction of a code every time it prints out a correct bit.

9   Agents

Agents are also being developed to speed up the search.

Marcus Hutter's general concept of an agent is one that, in the scientific world, can make experiments to get more meaningful. observations faster than waiting for the universe to provide them. Orseau et al. [OLH13] developed a Bayesian knowledge-seeking agent.

These are a few examples of ways to shorten CJS size.

10   Fun with Unconscious Jumps

Ray asked how people do learning jumps – mostly by unconscious methods.

Pac-Man interested him, because a person plays and plays and does maybe a bit better, and then suddenly does much better. Ray believed that was the unconscious making a good jump to a new method of play. Nobody yet knows how the jump occurs but the action shows that it did occur. It remains in the players unconscious as a tool, and using it, may lead on to the next level. Unless a method is remembered it isn't learned.

Jokes are a mental kind of sports; sports are a fun way to make people better at hunting and other physical survival skills. Finding punchlines to jokes make people better at discovering interesting theories — a mental survival skill — they are a fun way to enlarge our ability to jump from one theory to another: there is a normal description of something, and then in the joke we get a nifty different description: a 'funny' description that is just right, and the reward is that we 'get it!' and laugh. So in this way we may learn more from jokes that encourage our ability to leap to better theories, than from the school homework that has Yes or No answers.

Many theories; simple theories: what kind of probability has the Universe?

11   On the Back Porch Just Beyond the Universe

Kolmogorov and Solomonoff were sitting admiring the view when Kolmogorov brought out a string of 2^{1000} bits and set it on the wicker table next to his Kvas. He took out his Universal Turing Rover laptop and in 10 s found one program of 100 bits that described his string.

Solomonoff set down his root beer, and brought out a string of 2^{1000} bits and set it on the table. He took out his Universal Turing Handmade computer[3] and in 10 s found 2^{50} programs that described it, each program of 110 bits.

1.,2. Ray's handmade computer 3. Looking into space during fireworks

Andrey said, "My string seems least random because my program is only 100 bits, while yours are 110 bits." Ray said, "Mine seems so because your single program of 100 bits has prior probability of 2^{-100}, while my 2^{50} programs give a combined probability of 2^{50} x 2^{-110} which is 2^{-60}"

Solomonoff turned to Kolmogorov, and added, "I use shortest codes to measure my hypotheses and in Lsearch."

In our finite world in short periods of time, multiple codes may have similar weights. But what about a longer and longer string as seen from the back porch?

Ray [Sol64] said, Hmm, "...if T is a very long string, ... $P_i(T)$ normally decreases exponentially as T increases in length. Also, if Q_i and Q_j are two different probability evaluation measures (PEM's) and Q_i is "better" than Q_j, then usually $P_i(T)/P_j(T)$ increases exponentially as T increases in length. Of greater import, however, ... the relative weight of Q_i and Q_j, increases to arbitrarily large values for long enough T's. This suggests that for very long T, ... [AP] ... gives almost all of the weight to the single "best" PEM.".

Sitting on the back porch, just beyond the Universe, Kolmogorov turned to Solomonoff.

He said "Almost?!?"

---

[3] Of course they both had the Stallman [free] v. 4.3 instruction set architecture.

References

[Bri27] Bridgman, P.W.: The Logic of Modern Physics. Macmillan Company, New York (1927)

[Cha66] Chaitin, G.W.: On the length of programs for computing finite binary sequences. J. Assoc. Comp. Mach. **13**, 547–569 (1966)

[Fel50] Feller, W.: Probability Theory and Its Applications. Wiley, New York (1950)

[Kol65] Kolmogorov, A.N.: Three approaches to the quantitative definition of information. Probl. Inf. Transm. **1**(1), 1–7 (1965)

[Leg06] Legg, S.: Is there an elegant universal theory of prediction? In: Balcázar, J.L., Long, P.M., Stephan, F. (eds.) ALT 2006. LNCS (LNAI), vol. 4264, pp. 274–287. Springer, Heidelberg (2006)

[OLH13] Orseau, L., Lattimore, T., Hutter, M.: Universal knowledge-seeking agents for stochastic environments. In: Jain, S., Munos, R., Stephan, F., Zeugmann, T. (eds.) ALT 2013. LNCS, vol. 8139, pp. 158–172. Springer, Heidelberg (2013)

[RH11] Rathmanner, S., Hutter, M.: A philosophical treatise of universal induction. Entropy **13**, 1076–1136 (2011)

[Sch94] Schmidhuber, J.: Discovering problem solutions with low kolmogorov complexity and high generalization capability. Technical report, Technische Universität, München (1994)

[Sol60a] Solomonoff, R.J.: A preliminary report on a general theory of inductive inference. Technical report V-131, Zator Co. and Air Force Office of Scientific Research, Cambridge, Mass, February 1960

[Sol60b] Solomonoff, R.J.: A preliminary report on a general theory of inductive inference. (revision of Report V-131). Technical report ZTB-138, Zator Co. and AFOSR, Cambridge, Mass, November 1960

[Sol64] Solomonoff, R.J.: A formal theory of inductive inference: Part I. Inf. Control **7**(1), 1–22 (1964)

[Sol81] Solomonoff, R.J.: Notes for mit talk. Solomonoff Archive, November 1981

[Sol84] Solomonoff, R.J.: Notes for harvard talk (1984)

[Sol97] Solomonoff, R.J.: The discovery of algorithmic probability. J. Comput. Syst. Sci. **55**(1), 73–88 (1997)

[Sol99] Solomonoff, R.J.: A letter to david malkoff, February 1999

[Sol03] Solomonoff, R.J.: The universal distribution and machine learning. Comput. J. **6**, 508–601 (2003)

[Sol16a] Solomonoff, A.: Algorithmic probability. Privately circulated report (2016)

[Sol16b] Solomonoff, A.: A letter. Personal Communication, February 2016

[WD99] Wallace, C.S., Dowe, D.L.: Minimum message length and Kolmogorov complexity. Comput. J. **42**(4), 270–283 (1999)

Generalized Temporal Induction
with Temporal Concepts
in a Non-axiomatic Reasoning System

Tony Lofthouse[1]([⊠]) and Patrick Hammer[2]

[1] Evolving Solutions Ltd., Newbury, UK
Tony.Lofthouse@GMILab.com
[2] Institute for Software Technology, Graz University of Technology,
Inffeldgasse 16b/II, Graz, Austria
patrickhammer9@hotmail.com

Abstract. The introduction of Temporal Concepts into a Syllogistic based reasoning system such as NARS (Non-Axiomatic Reasoning System) provides a generalized temporal induction capability and extends the meaning of semantic relationship to include temporality.

1 Introduction

For the purpose of this paper, NARS [6] can be considered as a reasoning system which takes two premises, a task and a belief, and carries out an inference process, using defined logic rules. The task and belief are selected according to a control system and are required to have a common component in order for the logic rules to apply. Due to this constraint, arbitrary premises such as two sequentially occurring events (with no common component) cannot be selected for inference [3].

This constraint presents a problem for temporal reasoning, where it is desired to form sequences of arbitrary events, for sequence learning. NAL (Non-Axiomatic Logic) [6] is the logic used by NARS and includes logic rules for temporal induction but these rules require special handling and do not sit comfortably within the unified principle of cognition that applies to semantically related logic rules.

The introduction of Temporal Concepts addresses this shortfall [7] and allows the temporal aspect of premises to be considered as a semantic relation between premises, thereby allowing sequences of arbitrary events, instead of relying on an event-chainer: applying inference between succeeding events, as was the case in OpenNARS 1.7.

2 Temporal Concurrency

Temporal concurrency can occur on vastly different timescales, for example two sub-atomic interactions versus two birthdays. For the purpose of this discussion concurrency, in NARS, is defined as two events occurring within a temporal window, called DURATION, where DURATION is defined as a number of system cycles.

© Springer International Publishing Switzerland 2016
B. Steunebrink et al. (Eds.): AGI 2016, LNAI 9782, pp. 254–257, 2016.
DOI: 10.1007/978-3-319-41649-6_25

The justification for this approach is based on research in cognitive science, whereby, humans discern events as being concurrent when experienced within a temporal window of roughly 80 ms [1].

The primary role of this implicit form of temporal concurrency is to allow the formation of perception sequences. When events span longer time windows, an explicit representation can be used (expressed in Narsese) [5].

Different NARS systems can have different values for DURATION, where a system perceiving extremely fast perception streams, such as monitoring chemical interactions, would have a short DURATION time in the order of nanoseconds or microseconds, whilst on the other hand a system monitoring whale migration data could have a much longer DURATION.

3   Implementation

NARS contains two types of concept: general concepts and temporal concepts. A general concept is a data structure which supports local inference: choice – whereby questions are answered, revision – where evidence is summarized, and decision – where a yes/no decision is made whether to carry out a specific action. General inference is also supported whereby a pair of premises, a task and a belief are provided, via an attention controlled selection process, that are then used by the logic engine to derive further results. The structure of a general concept is designed to ensure that a (task, belief) always share a common component [5].

A Temporal Concept in contrast is a much simpler idea. Firstly, there is no requirement for Temporal Concepts to perform local inference, as their role is simply to build sequences. Secondly, in a general concept a task premise can take several forms: question, belief or goal. A temporal concept only processes beliefs that have a temporal component (occurrence time), where a belief is a premise that the system believes to be true to a certain degree [6]. Beliefs with occurrence time are called events. Occurrence time is defined in system perception cycle steps (which are definable, as 1 ms for example). Inference in Temporal Concepts is, currently, between two events.

The structure of a Temporal Concept contains; a unique name (named for the occurrence time which the concept represents), a budget value (which represents the degree of attention the system has for the concept and is composed of priority, duration and quality) [3], and a belief collection (all the events for the specified occurrence time to a max k items.

Inference with temporal concepts is carried out slightly differently than for general concepts:

1. Select a concept 1 from memory (according to attention control)
2. Select belief (A) from concept 1 Beliefs (according to attention control)
3. Select a concept 2 from memory (according to attention control)
4. Select belief (B) from concept 2 Beliefs (according to attention control)
5. Perform inference on (A, B) (primarily temporal induction)

where, concepts are temporal concepts and temporal induction between events, A and B, creates A => B statements saying that when A is the case, B is usually also the case, these statements can then be statistically summarized by evidence revision [5].

4 Discussion

The temporal component of two premises can be considered as a form of semantic relation, a temporal one in this case. However, there is a difference, in that the 'common' component in regular concepts is an exact match between two premises, whereas, the temporal component can be related over a time span. For example: past, present and future are all valid periods of temporal relation and can have different degrees of resolution. So premises are related by the degree of time between them, the interval period (which can be zero). This is their temporal 'semantic' relationship.

The key role of temporal concepts is to provide a generalized temporal chaining capability to support sequence learning of arbitrary premises. This is necessary as without this mechanism, only semantically related premises, with a common component, can be derived. The separate temporal chainer that was required for this capability, in NARS 1.7 [3], is no longer required as generalized temporal chaining is now an aspect of the unified principle of cognition.

Temporal chaining is primarily to enable perception to perform sequence learning, so it is aimed at the initial stages of the belief hierarchy (although not exclusively). Once initial percept sequences are formed, they can then be used in the 'higher' levels through general inference (using the common component principle required in general inference).

Temporal concepts should generally be short lived, unless they happen to coincide with a high priority task from higher up the belief hierarchy. Without new tasks being added to them, or being selected for inference, the temporal concepts will quickly lose their priority and will become candidates for deletion. The attention mechanism provides a bias to select concepts that are relevant to the present moment. This ensures that the range of concepts is relatively focused and quickly lose their focus once a concepts occurrence time has passed beyond the DURATION window.

One consideration is that creating temporal concepts for each occurrence time could lead to them swamping the system. This is constrained by limiting the number of temporal concepts, selected per inference cycle, biased by concept priority.

5 Conclusion

The introduction of Temporal Concepts into NARS has provided a generalized temporal chaining capability within a unified principle of cognition. The approach described in this paper seamlessly integrates with the NARS architecture and provides a further enhancement to the cognitive capabilities of NARS.

There are similarities between Temporal concepts in NARS and other AGI systems such as OpenCog's TimeNodes, which use AtTimeLinks to connect to other concepts [2]. Differently than in OpenCog, the occurrence time in NARS is a relative notion in respect to the current moment: the system reasons within time and adapts to variable time pressure, instead of abstractly reasoning over time without taking its own 'thinking' speed under consideration.

These Temporal Concepts can potentially also be a useful technique to other temporal reasoning systems, especially those applied in robotics and goal-driven systems [4], since selecting proper premises under time pressure immediately becomes an issue once the amount of events is large, and the attention-mechanism as described in [3] applied with these temporal concepts provides a solution to this.

Future research is focused on tighter integration with the attention mechanism, generalizing temporal concepts to handle all task types (beliefs, goals and questions) and the inclusion of variable DURATION within a NARS system.

The ideas presented in this paper are currently being implemented in OpenNARS 2.0.0. Additional information is available at: http://opennars.github.io/opennars.

References

1. Eagleman, D.M., Sejnowski, T.J.: Motion integration and postdiction in visual awareness. Science **287**(5460), 2036–2038 (2000)
2. Goertzel, B., Pennachin, C., Geisweiller, N.: Engineering General Intelligence Part 1 and 2: A Path to Advanced AGI via Embodied Learning and Cognitive Synergy. Atlantis Thinking Machines, vol. 5. Springer, Heidelberg (2014)
3. Hammer, P., Lofthouse, T., Wang, P.: The OpenNARS implementation of the non-axiomatic reasoning system. In: AGI 2016 Conference Proceedings (2016)
4. Rajan, K., Bernard, D., Dorais, G., Gamble, E., Kanefsky, B., Kurien, J., Millar, W., Muscettola, N., Nayak, P., Rouquette, N., Smith, B., Taylor, W., Tung, Y.: Remote agent: an autonomous control system for the new millennium. In: ECAI 2000 (2000)
5. Wang, P.: Rigid Flexibility - The Logic of Intelligence, vol. 34. Springer, Amsterdam (2006)
6. Wang, P.: Non-axiomatic Logic: A Model of Intelligent Reasoning. World Scientific, Singapore (2013)
7. Wang, P., Hammer, P.: Issues in temporal and causal inference. In: Bieger, J., Goertzel, B., Potapov, A. (eds.) AGI 2015. LNCS, vol. 9205, pp. 208–217. Springer, Heidelberg (2015)

Introspective Agents: Confidence Measures for General Value Functions

Craig Sherstan[1], Adam White[2],
Marlos C. Machado[1], and Patrick M. Pilarski[1(✉)]

[1] University of Alberta, Edmonton, AB, Canada
pilarski@ualberta.ca
[2] Indiana University, Bloomington, IN, USA

Abstract. Agents of general intelligence deployed in real-world scenarios must adapt to ever-changing environmental conditions. While such adaptive agents may leverage engineered knowledge, they will require the capacity to construct and evaluate knowledge themselves from their own experience in a bottom-up, constructivist fashion. This position paper builds on the idea of encoding knowledge as temporally extended predictions through the use of general value functions. Prior work has focused on learning predictions about externally derived signals about a task or environment (e.g. battery level, joint position). Here we advocate that the agent should also predict internally generated signals regarding its own learning process—for example, an agent's confidence in its learned predictions. Finally, we suggest how such information would be beneficial in creating an introspective agent that is able to learn to make good decisions in a complex, changing world.

Predictive Knowledge. The ability to autonomously construct knowledge directly from experience produced by an agent interacting with the world is a key requirement for general intelligence. One particularly promising form of knowledge that is grounded in experience is *predictive knowledge*—here defined as a collection of multi-step predictions about observable outcomes that are contingent on different ways of behaving. Much like scientific knowledge, predictive knowledge can be maintained and updated by making a prediction, executing a procedure, and observing the outcome and updating the prediction—a process completely independent of human intervention. Experience-grounded predictions are a powerful resource to guide decision making in environments which are too complex or dynamic to be exhaustively anticipated by an engineer [1,2].

A *value function* from the field of reinforcement learning is one way of representing predictive knowledge. Value functions are a learned or computed mapping from state to the long-term expectation of future reward. Sutton et al. recently introduced a generalization of value functions that makes it possible to specify general predictive questions [1]. These *general value functions* (GVFs), specify a prediction target as the expected discounted sum of future signals of interest (*cumulants*) observed while the agent selects actions according to some decision making policy. Temporal discounting is also generalized in GVFs from

B. Steunebrink et al. (Eds.): AGI 2016, LNAI 9782, pp. 258–261, 2016.
DOI: 10.1007/978-3-319-41649-6_26

the conventional exponential weighting of future cumulants to an arbitrary, state-conditional weighting of future cumulants. This enables GVFs to specify a rich class of predictive questions where discounting acts as a stochastic termination function [2]. A single GVF specifies a predictive question, and the answer takes the form of an approximate GVF that can be learned by temporal-difference (TD) learning algorithms solely from unsupervised interaction with the world. A collection of GVFs contributes to the agent's knowledge of the world.

Ultimately, the purpose of acquiring knowledge is to improve the agent's ability to achieve its goals. The agent's collection of GVFs are only useful to the extent that they help with reward maximization. While GVFs are relatively new, there have been several recent demonstrations of their usefulness in robot tasks, from reflexive action in mobile robots [2], to the control of prosthetic arms [3,4]. In this paper we take the next step by specifying GVFs whose cumulants are internal signals defined by the agent's own learning process.

Predicting Internal Signals. GVFs have been previously used to specify predictions about signals external to the agent—signals in the agent's sensorimotor stream of interactions. However, agents also have access to a set of *internal signals* not previously considered as cumulants for GVFs. Specifically, there are a number of signals available to an agent that relate to the agent's own learning mechanisms—for example, its predictions' errors, weight changes, and other time-varying meta-parameters. There are also a range of signals that quantify the agent's interactions with its sensorimotor stream—for example, statistics about state or feature-space visitation and statistical properties of input signals. Integrating predictions of these internal signals should improve an agent's decision making abilities towards human-level intelligence [5].

One representative class of internal signals relates to an agent's certainty in its own predictions. An agent might make better use of its knowledge given some sense of how much each approximate GVF is to be trusted. That is, given a GVF, how *confident* is the agent that the learned prediction is accurate and precise? Methods such as confidence intervals or ensemble forecasting are used in many domains and may also be appropriate here [6]. For our purposes, we desire an approach that is compatible with function approximation and supports online and incremental prediction and learning with only linear complexity (in the size of the input features). GVFs and TD methods used to approximate them satisfy these criteria and are therefore a promising approach to incorporating confidence measures. Indeed, this presents an appealing architecture where both predictive questions and measures of their confidence are represented in a single form.

Further, we propose that an agent's decision making process can be improved by using several confidence measures, rather than solely relying on a single value of confidence. Each measure can then provide a different perspective on the accuracy of an approximate GVF, enabling the agent to make more informed decisions. Encoding these measures as GVFs enables these internal predictions to participate in the agent's representation of state [7], which can lead to more efficient reward maximization [8,9] and more accurate prediction [10].

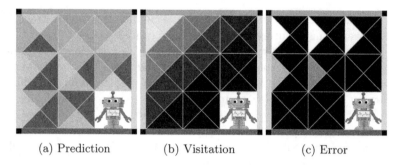

(a) Prediction   (b) Visitation   (c) Error

Fig. 1. In this illustrative example, a robot moves through a 3×3 grid world and (**a**) predicts wall hue (a continuous representation of color in [0,360)) in each of four directions. One GVF is randomly initialized for each direction. A tabular state representation is used, and the robot is only able to observe the hue of a wall when it takes direct action into that wall. At each timestep the hue of the walls may change. In this example, the hue of the upper wall has high variance while all other walls have low or no variance. Each cell of (a) shows the predicted hue in each direction. (**b**) The robot moves in a weighted random walk with a preference for moving up and left, as seen in the state-action visitation. High confidence (white) corresponds to high visitation and low confidence (black) corresponds to low visitation (visitation is initialized to 0). (**c**) The robot makes predictions of the expected squared TD error of the primary hue prediction. High confidence (white) corresponds to low error and low confidence (black) corresponds to high error (error is initialized high). Predictions of variance (not shown) produce a similar pattern to that of (c). The robot can decide to only trust predictions in portions of the world it has visited before, here the upper left. Further, when in the upper-left corner, the robot can see that despite high visitation it should not trust it's upward prediction as error (and variance) remain high. On the other hand, it can trust its leftward prediction as visitation is high and error is low. (Color figure online)

While there are many measures that could be useful for an agent in determining confidence [11], we here provide three examples which are readily represented as GVFs (see Fig. 1 for examples). The first is *visitation*. A measure of state visitation can be expressed as a GVF by simply using a constant valued cumulant. An agent might reasonably decide to only trust a prediction in states that have been visited many times. The second is *prediction error*. On each time step, a temporal-difference error is used to update each approximate GVF [1]; this TD error can itself be used as the cumulant of another GVF. Such a prediction gives an agent an expectation of how much each approximate GVF will differ from the true outcome specified by the corresponding GVF. The third is *variance*. The variance of a cumulant or an approximate GVF can easily be represented as the difference between two GVFs, although the process for approximating these nonstationary cumulants is somewhat more involved [12].

Example: Exploration with Confidence Measures. A collection of approximate GVFs, combined with their corresponding confidence measures provide the agent with a way to measure how much it should trust what it knows. In a safe environment an agent might view low confidence as an opportunity to learn more about its world [7,13]. In a dangerous environment, low confidence might be a strong indicator to proceed with caution or not at all. Further, confidence itself can be a goal for an agent's behavior. That is, an agent could choose to seek out predictability (high confidence) or novelty (low confidence). This naturally plays a role in the trade off between exploration and exploitation.

Concluding remarks: Predictive knowledge is essential to a generally intelligent agent in maximizing its reward. We advocate that internal measures relating to prediction learning can and should also be represented as GVFs and learned in the same way. These new predictions provide additional knowledge that enables an agent to improve its decision making abilities. GVFs present a novel approach to the general problem of introspection within intelligent agents.

References

1. Sutton, R.S., Modayil, J., Delp, M., Degris, T., Pilarski, P.M., White, A., Precup, D.: Horde: A scalable real-time architecture for learning knowledge from unsupervised sensorimotor interaction categories and subject descriptors. In: International Conference on Autonomous Agents and Multi-Agent Systems, pp. 761–768 (2011)
2. Modayil, J., White, A., Sutton, R.S.: Multi-timescale nexting in a reinforcement learning robot. Adapt. Behav. **22**, 146–160 (2014)
3. Edwards, A.L., Dawson, M.R., Hebert, J.S., Sherstan, C., Sutton, R.S., Chan, K.M., Pilarski, P.M.: Application of real-time machine learning to myoelectric prosthesis control: A case series in adaptive switching. Prosthet. Orthot. Int., published online ahead of print, pp. 1–9 (2015)
4. Sherstan, C., Modayil, J., Pilarski, P.M.: A collaborative approach to the simultaneous multi-joint control of a prosthetic arm. In: International Conference on Rehabilitation Robotics, Singapore, Singapore, pp. 13–18 (2015)
5. Clark, A.: Surfing Uncertainty: Prediction, Action, and the Embodied Mind. Oxford University Press, New York (2015)
6. Wiering, M.A., van Hasselt, H.: Ensemble algorithms in reinforcement learning. IEEE Trans. Syst. Man, Cybern. Part B Cybern. **38**(4), 930–936 (2008)
7. White, A.: Developing a predictive approach to knowledge. Ph.D. Thesis. University of Alberta (2015)
8. Rafols, E.J., Ring, M.B., Sutton, R.S., Tanner, B.: Using predictive representations to improve generalization in reinforcement learning. In: International Joint Conference on Artificial Intelligence, pp. 835–840 (2005)
9. Schaul, T., Ring, M.: Better generalization with forecasts. In: International Joint Conference on Artificial Intelligence, Beijing, China, pp. 1656–1662 (2013)
10. Littman, M.L., Sutton, R.S., Singh, S.: Predictive representations of state. In: Advances in Neural Information Processing Systems 14, pp. 1555–1561 (2001)
11. Sherstan, C.: Towards Prosthetic Arms as Wearable Intelligent Robots. MSc Thesis. University of Alberta (2015)
12. White, M., White, A.: Interval estimation for reinforcement-learning algorithms in continuous-state domains. In: Advances in Neural Information Processing Systems 23, pp. 2433–2441 (2010)
13. Schmidhuber, J.: Curious model-building control systems. In: IEEE International Joint Conference on Neural Networks, Singapore, Singapore, Singapore, pp. 1458–1463 (1991)

Automatic Sampler Discovery
via Probabilistic Programming
and Approximate Bayesian Computation

Yura Perov[✉] and Frank Wood

Department of Engineering Science, University of Oxford, Oxford, UK
{perov,fwood}@robots.ox.ac.uk

Abstract. We describe an approach to automatic discovery of samplers in the form of human interpretable probabilistic programs. Specifically, we learn the procedure code of samplers for one-dimensional distributions. We formulate a Bayesian approach to this problem by specifying an adaptor grammar prior over probabilistic program code, and use approximate Bayesian computation to learn a program whose execution generates samples that match observed data or analytical characteristics of a distribution of interest. In our experiments we leverage the probabilistic programming system Anglican to perform Markov chain Monte Carlo sampling over the space of programs. Our results are competive relative to state-of-the-art genetic programming methods and demonstrate that we can learn approximate and even exact samplers.

Keywords: Probabilistic programming · Automatic programming · Program synthesis · Bayesian inference · Automatic modelling

1 Introduction

In this paper we present an approach to automatic sampler discovery in the framework of probabilistic programming. Our aim is to induce program code that, when executed repeatedly, returns values whose distribution matches that of observed data. Ultimately, the artificial general intelligence machinery can use such approach to synthesise and update the model of the world in the form of probabilistic programs. As a starting point, we consider the induction of programs that sample from parametrised one-dimensional distributions.

Probabilistic programming is relevant to this problem for several reasons. Programs in Turing-complete languages can represent a wide range of generative probabilistic models. Samples from these models can be generated efficiently by simply executing the program code. Finally, in higher-order languages like Anglican, that is languages where procedures may act on other procedures, it is possible to write a generative model for program code that is itself a probabilistic program. This enables us to perform inference by specifying an adaptor grammar prior over program code and to use general-purpose Markov chain Monte Carlo

© Springer International Publishing Switzerland 2016
B. Steunebrink et al. (Eds.): AGI 2016, LNAI 9782, pp. 262–273, 2016.
DOI: 10.1007/978-3-319-41649-6_27

algorithms implemented by the inference engine to sample over the space of programs.

To assess whether the distribution of samples generated by a program candidate matches the distribution of interest, we use approximate Bayesian computation methods that specify an approximate likelihood in terms of the similarity between a summary statistic of the generated samples and that of the observed values. While this approach is inherently approximate, it still can be used to find exact sampler code. This argument is supported by the fact that we were able to successfully learn an exact sampler for the Bernoulli distribution family given only the adaptor grammar prior learnt from a corpus of sampler code not including Bernoulli. We also successfully found approximate samplers for other common one-dimensional distributions and for real-world data. Finally, our approach holds its own in comparison to state-of-the-art genetic programming methods.

2   Related Work

Our approach to learning probabilistic programs relates to both program induction [4,10,14,16,19,21] and statistical generalisation from sampled observations. The former is usually treated as search in the space of program text where the objective is to find a deterministic function that exactly matches outputs given parameters. The latter, generalising from data, is usually referred to as either density estimation or learning, and also includes automatic modelling [7,9].

3   Approach

Our approach can be described in terms of a Markov Chain Monte Carlo (MCMC) approximate Bayesian computation (ABC) [18] targeting

$$\pi(\mathcal{X}|\hat{\mathcal{X}})p(\hat{\mathcal{X}}|\mathcal{T})p(\mathcal{T}), \tag{1}$$

where at a high level $\pi(\mathcal{X}|\hat{\mathcal{X}})$ is a compatibility function between summary statistics computed between observed data $\mathcal{X}$ and data, $\hat{\mathcal{X}}$, generated by interpreting latent sampler program text $\mathcal{T}$. The higher $\pi(\mathcal{X}|\hat{\mathcal{X}})$, the more similar distributions $\mathcal{X}$ and $\hat{\mathcal{X}}$.

Consider a parametric distribution F with parameter vector θ. Let $\mathcal{X} = \{x_i\}_{i=1}^{I}, x_i \sim F(\cdot|\theta)$ be a set of samples from F. Consider the task of learning program text $\mathcal{T}$ that when repeatedly interpreted returns samples whose distribution is close to F. Let $\hat{\mathcal{X}} = \{\hat{x}_j\}_{j=1}^{J}, \hat{x}_j \sim \mathcal{T}(\cdot)$ be a set of samples generated by repeatedly interpreting $\mathcal{T}$ J times.

Let s be a summary function of a set of samples and let $d(s(\mathcal{X}), s(\hat{\mathcal{X}})) = \pi(\mathcal{X}|\hat{\mathcal{X}})$ be an unnormalised distribution function that returns high probability when $s(\mathcal{X}) \approx s(\hat{\mathcal{X}})$. We refer to d as a compatibility function, or penalty interchangeably.

```
(defquery lpp-normal
  (let
    [n 0.001
     prog (grammar '() 'real)
     prog-c (extract-compound prog)
     samples (apply-n-times prog-c 100 '())]
    (observe (normal (mean samples) n) 0.0)
    (observe (normal (std  samples) n) 1.0)
    (observe (normal (skew samples) n) 0.0)
    (observe (normal (kurt samples) n) 0.0)
    (predict (extract-text prog))))
```

Fig. 1. Probabilistic program to infer program text for a Normal(0, 1) sampler. Variable n is a noise level. Procedure **grammar** samples a probabilistic program from the adaptor grammar. This procedure returns a tuple: a generated program candidate in the form of nested compound procedures and the same program candidate in the form of program text.

We use probabilistic programming to write and perform inference in such a model, i.e. to generate samples of $\mathcal{T}$ from the marginal of (1) and generalisations to come of the same. Refer to the probabilistic program code in Fig. 1 where the first line establishes a correspondence between $\mathcal{T}$ and the variable **program-text** then samples it from $p(\mathcal{T})$ where **grammar** is an adaptor-grammar-like [13] prior on program text that is described in Sect. 3.1. In this particular example θ is implicitly specified since the learning goal here is to find a sampler for the standard normal distribution. Also $\hat{\mathcal{X}}$ corresponds to the program variable **samples** and here $J = 100$. Here s and d are computed on the last four lines of the program with s being implicitly defined as returning a four dimensional vector consisting of the estimated mean, variance, skewness, and kurtosis of the set of samples drawn from $\mathcal{T}$. The penalty function d is also defined to be a multivariate normal with mean $[0.0, 1.0, 0.0, 0.0]^T$ and diagonal covariance $\sigma^2 \mathbf{I}$. Note that this means that we are seeking the sampler source code whose output distribution has mean 0, variance 1, skew 0, and kurtosis 0 and that we penalise deviations from that by a squared exponential loss function with bandwidth σ^2, named **noise** in the code.

The more moments we match, the better the approximation will be achieved, but inevitably this will require more samples J.

This example highlights an important generalisation of the original description of our approach. For the standard normal example we chose a form of s such that we can compute the summary statistic of $s(\mathcal{X})$ analytically. There are at least three kinds of scenarios in which d can be computed in different ways. The first occurs when we search for efficient code for sampling from known distributions. In many such cases, as in the standard normal case just described, the summary statistics of F can be computed analytically. The second is the fixed dataset cardinality setting and corresponds to the setting of learning program text generative model for arbitrary observed data. The third, similar to the previous one, happens when we can only sample from F. This corresponds

```
(defquery lpp-bernoulli
  (let
    [prog (grammar '(real) 'int)
     proc-c (extract-compound prog)
     J 100]
    (let
      [samples-1 (apply-n-times prog-c J '(0.5))]
      (observe (flip (G-test-p-value samples-1
                             'Bernoulli (list 0.5))) true))
      ... ;; So on for samples-2, etc; until N.
      (predict (extract-text prog))
      (predict (apply-n-times prog-c J '(0.3)))))))
```

Fig. 2. Probabilistic program to infer program text for a Bernoulli(θ) sampler and generate J samples from the resulting procedure at a novel input argument value, 0.3.

to a situations when, for instance, there is a running, computationally expensive MCMC sampler that can be asked to produce additional samples.

Figure 2 illustrates the another important generalisation of the formulation in (1). When learning a standard normal sampler we did not have to take into account parameter values. Interesting sampler program text is endowed with arguments, allowing it to generate samples from an entire family of parameterised distributions. Consider the well known Box-Muller algorithm shown in Fig. 3. It is parameterised by mean and standard deviation parameters. For this reason we will refer to it and others like it as a conditional distribution samplers. Learning conditional distribution sampler program text requires recasting our MCMC-ABC target slightly to include the parameter θ of the distribution F:

$$\pi(\mathcal{X}|\hat{\mathcal{X}}, \theta) p(\hat{\mathcal{X}}|\mathcal{T}, \theta) p(\mathcal{T}|\theta) p(\theta). \tag{2}$$

Here in order to proceed we must begin to make approximating assumptions. This is because in our case we need $p(\theta)$ to be truly improper as our learned sampler program text should work for all possible input arguments and not simply a just a high prior probability subset of values. Assuming that program text that works for a few settings of input parameters is fairly likely to generalise well to other parameter settings we approximately marginalise our MCMC-ABC target (2) by choosing a small finite N of θ_n parameters yielding our approximate marginalised MCMC-ABC target:

$$\frac{1}{N} \sum_{n=1}^{N} \pi(\mathcal{X}_n|\hat{\mathcal{X}}_n, \theta_n) p(\hat{\mathcal{X}}_n|\mathcal{T}, \theta_n) p(\mathcal{T}|\theta_n) \approx$$
$$\int \pi(\mathcal{X}|\hat{\mathcal{X}}, \theta) p(\hat{\mathcal{X}}|\mathcal{T}, \theta) p(\mathcal{T}|\theta) p(\theta) d\theta. \tag{3}$$

The probabilistic program for learning conditional sampler program text for Bernoulli(θ) in Fig. 2 shows an example of this kind of approximation. It samples

```
(def box-muller-normal                 (def poisson (fn [rate]
  (fn [mean std]                         (let
    (+ mean (* std                        [L (exp (* -1 rate))
      (* (cos (* 2 (* 3.14159             inner-loop (fn inner-loop [k p]
        (uniform-cont 0.0 1.0))))          (if (< p L) (dec k)
      (sqrt (* -2                           (inner-loop (inc k)
        (log (uniform-cont                   (* p (uniform-cont 0 1)))))))]
             0.0 1.0))))))))))       (inner-loop 1 (uniform-cont0 1)))))
```

Fig. 3. Human-written sampling procedure program text for, left, Normal(μ, σ) [3] and, right, Poisson(λ) [15]. Counts of the constants, procedures, and expression expansions in these programs (and that of several other univariate samplers) are fed into our hierarchical generative prior over sampler program text.

from T N times, accumulating summary statistic penalties for each invocation. In this case each individual summary penalty computation involves computing both a G-test statistic

$$G_n = 2 \sum_{i \in 0,1} \#[\hat{\mathcal{X}}_n = i] \ln \left(\frac{\#[\hat{\mathcal{X}}_n = i]}{\theta_n^i (1 - \theta_n)^{(1-i)} \cdot |\hat{\mathcal{X}}_n|} \right),$$

where $\#[\hat{\mathcal{X}}_n = i]$ is the number of samples in $\hat{\mathcal{X}}_n$ that take value i and its corresponding p-value under the null hypothesis that $\hat{\mathcal{X}}_n$ are samples from Bernoulli(θ_n). Since the G-test statistic is approximately χ^2 distributed, i.e. $G \sim \chi^2(1)$, we can construct d in this case by computing the probability of falsely rejecting the null hypothesis $H_0 : \hat{\mathcal{X}}_n \sim$ Bernoulli(θ_n). Falsely rejecting a null hypothesis is equivalent to flipping a coin with probability given by the p-value of the test and having it turn up heads. These are the summary statistic penalties accumulated in the observe lines in Fig. 2.

As an aside, in the probabilistic programming compilation context θ could be all of the observe'd data in the original program. By this parameterising compilation links our approach to that of [12].

3.1   Grammar and Production Rules

As we have the expressive power of a higher-order probabilistic programming language at our disposal, our prior over conditional distribution sampler program text is quite expressive. At a high level it is similar to the adaptor grammar [13] prior used in [16] but diverges in details, particularly those having to do with creation of local environments and the conditioning of subexpression choices on type signatures. To generate a probabilistic program we apply these production rules starting with $expr_{type}$, where $type$ is the output signature of the inducing program.

The set of types we used for our experiments was {real, bool, int}. To avoid numerical errors while interpreting generated programs we replace functions like log(a) with safe-log(a), which returns 0 if $a < 0$, and uniform-continuous with safe-uc(a, b) which swaps arguments if $a > b$ and returns a if $a = b$. The general set of procedures in the global environment

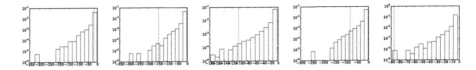

Fig. 4. Blue log-scaled histograms illustrate distributions over program codes' log likelihoods given production rules $P(T)$, which facilitate search of random variate generators for Bernoulli, Gamma, Normal, Poisson and Standard Normal distributions. Red dashed lines show the program codes' log likelihoods of true samplers written by humans as in Fig. 3.

included +, −, *, safe-div, safe-uc, cos, safe-sqrt, safe-log, exp, inc, dec. Schematically our prior is provided below. Prior probabilities $\{p_i\}$ are learnt from a small corpus of probabilistic programs in the way described in Sect. 3.2.

1. $expr_{type} \mid env \xrightarrow{p_1} v$, a random variable v from the environment env specified by $type$. An environment is a mapping of typed symbols to values, but these values are not produced until the actual probabilistic program runs.
2. $expr_{type} \mid env \xrightarrow{p_2} c$, a random constant c with the type $type$. Constants were drawn from the predefined constants set (including 0.0, π, etc.)[1].
3. $expr_{type} \mid env \xrightarrow{p_3} (procedure_{type} \ expr_{arg\_1\_type} \ \cdots \ expr_{arg\_N\_type})$, where $procedure$ is a primitive or compound, and deterministic or stochastic procedure chosen randomly from the global environment with output type signature $type$.
4. $expr_{type} \mid env \xrightarrow{p_4} (let \ [new\text{-}symbol \ expr_{real}] \ expr_{type} \mid env \cup new\text{-}symbol))$, where $env \cup new\text{-}symbol$ is an extended environment with a new variable named $new\text{-}symbol$. Its value is defined by an expression, generated according to the same production rules.
5. $expr_{type} \mid env \xrightarrow{p_5} (cp_{type} \ expr_{arg\_1\_type} \ \cdots \ expr_{arg\_N\_type})$, where cp_{type} is a compound procedure. Its body is generated using the same production rules given an environment that incorporates argument input variable names and values.
6. $expr_{type} \mid env \xrightarrow{p_6} (if \ (expr_{bool}) \ expr_{type} \ expr_{type})$.
7. $expr_{type} \mid env \xrightarrow{p_7} (recur \ expr_{arg\_1\_type} \ \cdots \ expr_{arg\_M\_type})$, i.e. recursive call to the current compound procedure if we are inside, or to the main inducing procedure otherwise.

3.2 Probabilities for Production Rules

While it is possible to manually specify production rule probabilities for the grammar in Sect. 3.1 we took a hierarchical Bayesian approach instead, learning from human-written sampler source code. To do this we translated existing

---

[1] For experiments described in Sect. 4.4 constants were also sampled from Normal and Uniform continuous distributions.

implementations of common one-dimensional samplers [6] into Anglican source (see examples in Fig. 3). Conveniently all of them require only one stochastic procedure `uniform-continuous` so we also only include that stochastic procedure in our grammar.

We compute held-out production rules prior probabilities from this corpus. When we are inferring a probabilistic program to sample from F we update our priors using counts from all other sampling code in the corpus, specifically excluding the sampler we are attempting to learn. Our production rule probability estimates are smoothed by Dirichlet priors. Note that in the following experiments (Sects. 4.4) the production rule priors were updated. True hierarchical coupling and joint inferences approaches are straightforward from a probabilistic programming perspective [17], but result in inference runs that take longer to compute.

4   Experiments

The experiments we perform illustrate uses cases outlined for automatically learning probabilistic programs. We begin by illustrating the expressiveness of our prior over sampler program text in Sect. 4.1. We then report results from experiments in which we test our approach in all three scenarios for how we can compute the ABC penalty d.

The first set of experiments in Sect. 4.2 tests our ability to learn probabilistic programs that produce samples from known one-dimensional probability distributions. In these experiments d either probabilistically conditions on p-values of one-sample statistical hypothesis tests or on approximate moment matching. In Sect. 4.3 the evaluation against genetic programming is presented. The second set of experiments in Sect. 4.4 addresses the cases where only a finite number of samples from an unknown real-world source are provided.

4.1   Samples from Sampled Probabilistic Programs

To illustrate the flexibility of our prior over probabilistic programs source code, we show probabilistic programs sampled from it. In Fig. 5 we show six histograms of samples from six sampled probabilistic programs from our prior over probabilistic programs. Such randomly generated samplers constructively define considerably different distributions. Note in particular the variability of the domain, variance, and even number of modes.

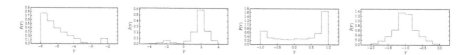

Fig. 5. Histograms of samples generated by repeatedly evaluating probabilistic procedures sampled from our prior over probabilistic sampling procedure text. The prior is constrained to generate samplers with univariate output but is clearly otherwise flexible enough to represent a nontrivial spectrum of distributions.

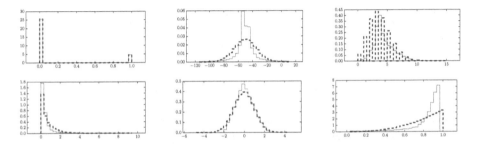

Fig. 6. Representative histograms of samples *(green solid lines)* drawn by repeatedly interpreting inferred sampler program text versus *(blue dashed lines)* histograms of exact samples drawn from the corresponding true distribution. Top row left to right: Bernoulli(p), Normal(μ, σ), Poisson(λ). Bottom row same: Gamma($a, 1.0$), Normal($0, 1$), Beta($a, 1.0$). The parameters used to produce these plots do not appear in the training data. In the case of Bernoulli(p) we inferred programs that sample exactly from the true distribution (see Fig. 7). Not all finite-time inference converges to good approximate sampler code as illustrated by the Beta($a, 1.0$) and Normal(μ, σ) examples. With limited experimental time, a better sampler was found for Normal(μ, σ) in comparison to Normal($0, 1$). A possible explanation is that it is harder to find a sampler with two parameters rather than a sampler without any parameters. Future experiments should benefit from learning more complex probabilistic programs given already learnt simpler ones, similarly to [5, 11].

4.2 Learning Sampler Code for Common One-Dimensional Distributions

Source code exists for efficiently sampling from many if not all common one-dimensional distributions. We conducted experiments to test our ability to automatically discover such sampling procedures and found encouraging results.

In particular we performed a set of leave-one-out experiments to infer sampler program text for six common one-dimensional distributions: Bernoulli(p), Poisson(λ), Gamma($a, 1.0$), Beta($a, 1$), Normal($0, 1$), Normal(μ, σ). For each distribution we performed MCMC-ABC inference with approximately marginalising over the parameter space using a small random set $\{\theta_1, \ldots, \theta_N\}$ of parameters and conditioning on statistical hypothesis tests or on moment matching as appropriate. Note that the pre-training of the hierarchical program text prior was never given the text of the sampler for the distribution being learned.

Representative histograms of samples from the best posterior program text sample discovered in terms of summary statistics match are shown in Fig. 6. A pleasing result is the discovery of the exact Bernoulli(p) distribution sampler program, the text of which is shown in Fig. 7.

4.3 Evaluating Our Approach Versus Evolutionary Algorithms

The approach was evaluated against genetic programming, one of state-of-the-art methods to search in the space of programs. Genetic programming is an

```
(fn [p stack-id]                    (fn [p stack-id]
  (if (< (sample                      (if (< 1.0 (safe-sqrt (safe-div p
          (uniform-cont                    (safe-uc p (dec p))))) 1.0 0.0))
              0.0 1.0)) p)          (fn [p stack-id]
    1.0 0.0)                          (if (< 1.0 (safe-uc (safe-sqrt p)
  )                                         (+ par (cos p)))) 1.0 0.0))
```

Fig. 7. *(left)* Human-written exact Bernoulli(p) sampler. *(right, two instances)* Inferred sampler program text. The first is also an exact sampler for Bernoulli(p). The last is another sampler also assigned non-zero posterior probability but it is not exact.

evolutionary based metaheuristic optimisation algorithm to generate a program from a specification. The same grammar we used before was reproduced in the evolutionary computation framework DEAP [8]. The fitness function was selected to be the log probability presented in the Eq. 3 with omitted $p\left(\hat{X} \mid \mathcal{T}\right)$ part in accordance with the assumption that desired probabilistic programs will repeatedly appear in results of search over programs. Note that another possible way is to marginalise over $\hat{X}$ during its fitness function evaluation, however this requires more programs runs.

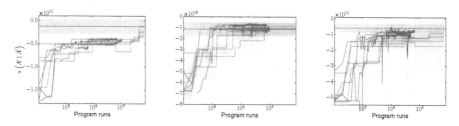

Fig. 8. Convergence of unnormalised penalty function $\pi\left(\mathcal{X} \mid \hat{\mathcal{X}}\right)$ for Bernoulli(p), Normal(μ, σ), and Geometric(p) correspondingly. $\hat{\mathcal{X}}$ is a samples set from a probabilistic program $\mathcal{T}$ as described in Sect. 3. Navy lines show the true sampler's penalty function value (averaged by 30 trials), red lines correspondent to genetic programming, and green lines – to PMCMC. Transparent filled intervals represent standard deviations within trials.

Figure 8 shows that PMCMC inference performance is similar to genetic programming. In contrast to genetic programming, PMCMC is statistically valid estimator of the target distribution. In addition, probabilistic programming system allows to reason about the model over models and inferring models within the same framework, while genetic programming is an external machinery which requires to consider optimising probabilistic programs as a black box[2].

---

[2] An interesting work for future is to run experiments in the framework of probabilistic programming with the inference engine that is itself based on evolutionary algorithms, in a similar way to [2].

4.4   Generalising Arbitrary Data Distributions

We also explored using our approach to learn generative models in the form of sampler program text for real world data of unknown distribution. We arbitrarily chose three continuous indicator features from a credit approval dataset [1, 20] and inferred sampler program text using two-sample Kolmogorov-Smirnov distribution equality tests (vs. the empirical data distribution) analogously to the G-test described before. Histograms of samples from the best inferred sampler program text versus the training empirical distributions are shown in Fig. 9. The data distribution representation, despite being expressed in the form of sampler program text, matches salient characteristics of the empirical distribution well.

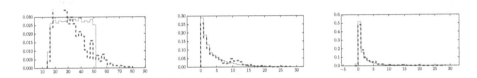

Fig. 9. Histograms of samples *(green solid)* generated by repeatedly interpreting inferred sampler program text and the empirical distributions *(blue dashed)* that they were trained to match.

5   Discussion

Our approach to program synthesis via probabilistic programming raises at least as many questions as it answers. One key high level question this work invokes is, really, what is the goal of program synthesis? By framing program synthesis as a probabilistic inference problem we are implicitly naming our goal to be that of estimating a distribution over programs that obey some constraints rather than as a search for a single best program that does the same. On one hand, the notion of regularising via a generative model is natural as doing so predisposes inference towards discovery of programs that preferentially possess characteristics of interest (length, readability, etc.). On the other hand, exhaustive computational inversion of a generative model that includes evaluation of program text will clearly remain intractable for the foreseeable future. For this reason greedy and stochastic search inference strategies are basically the only options available. We employ the latter, to explore the posterior distribution of programs whose outputs match constraints knowing full-well that its actual effect in this problem domain, and, in particular finite time, is more-or-less that of stochastic search.

It is pleasantly surprising, however, that the Monte Carlo techniques we use were able to find exemplar programs in the posterior distribution that actually do a good job of generalising observed data in the experiments we report. It remains an open question whether or not sole sampling procedures are the best stochastic search technique to use for this problem in general however. Perhaps by using them in combination with one of search we might do better, particularly if our goal is a single best program.

References

1. Bache, K., Lichman, M.: UCI Machine Learning Repository (2013)
2. Batishcheva, V., Potapov, A.: Genetic programming on program traces as an inference engine for probabilistic languages. In: Bieger, J., Goertzel, B., Potapov, A. (eds.) AGI 2015. LNCS, vol. 9205, pp. 14–24. Springer, Heidelberg (2015)
3. Box, G.E., Muller, M.E.: A note on the generation of random normal deviates. Ann. Math. Stat. **29**(2), 610–611 (1958)
4. Briggs, F., Oneill, M.: Functional genetic programming with combinators. In: Proceedings of the Third Asian-Pacific Workshop on Genetic Programming, ASPGP (2006)
5. Dechter, E., Malmaud, J., Adams, R.P., Tenenbaum, J.B.: Bootstrap learning via modular concept discovery. In: Proceedings of the 23rd International Joint Conference on Artificial Intelligence (IJCAI 2013) (2013)
6. Devroye, L.: Non-uniform random variate generation. Springer-Verlag, Heidelberg (1986)
7. Duvenaud, D., Lloyd, J.R., Grosse, R., Tenenbaum, J.B., Ghahramani, Z.: Structure discovery in nonparametric regression through compositional kernel search. In: Proceedings of the 30th International Conference on Machine Learning (ICML 2013) (2013)
8. Fortin, F.A., De Rainville, F.M., Gardner, M.A., Parizeau, M., Gagné, C.: DEAP: Evolutionary algorithms made easy. J. Mach. Learn. Res. **13**, 2171–2175 (2012)
9. Grosse, R., Salakhutdinov, R.R., Freeman, W.T., Tenenbaum, J.B.: Exploiting compositionality to explore a large space of model structures. In: Proceedings of the 28th International Conference on Machine Learning (ICML 2012) (2012)
10. Gulwani, S., Kitzelmann, E., Schmid, U.: Approaches and applications of inductive programming (Dagstuhl seminar 13502). Dagstuhl Reports (2014)
11. Henderson, R.: Incremental learning in inductive programming. In: Schmid, U., Kitzelmann, E., Plasmeijer, R. (eds.) AAIP 2009. LNCS, vol. 5812, pp. 74–92. Springer, Heidelberg (2010)
12. Hwang, I., Stuhlmüller, A., Goodman, N.D.: Inducing probabilistic programs by Bayesian program merging. arXiv e-print (2011). arXiv:1110.5667
13. Johnson, M., Griffiths, T.L., Goldwater, S.: Adaptor grammars: A framework for specifying compositional nonparametric Bayesian models. In: Advances in Neural Information Processing Systems (NIPS 2007) (2007)
14. Kersting, K.: An inductive logic programming approach to statistical relational learning. In: Proceedings of the Conference on An Inductive Logic Programming Approach to Statistical Relational Learning 2005 (2005)
15. Knuth, D.E.: The art of computer programming, vol. 2: Seminumerical algorithms 3rd edn. (1998)
16. Liang, P., Jordan, M.I., Klein, D.: Learning programs: a hierarchical Bayesian approach. In: Proceedings of the 27th International Conference on Machine Learning (ICML 2010) (2010)
17. Maddison, C., Tarlow, D.: Structured generative models of natural source code. In: Proceedings of the 31st International Conference on Machine Learning (ICML 2014) (2014)
18. Marjoram, P., Molitor, J., Plagnol, V., Tavaré, S.: Markov chain Monte Carlo without likelihoods. In: Proceedings of the National Academy of Sciences (2003)
19. Muggleton, S.: Stochastic logic programs. In: Advances in Inductive Logic Programming (1996)

20. Quinlan, J.R.: Simplifying decision trees. Int. J. Man Mach. Stud. **27**(3), 221–234 (1987)
21. De Raedt, L., Frasconi, P., Kersting, K., Muggleton, S.H. (eds.): Probabilistic Inductive Logic Programming. LNCS (LNAI), vol. 4911. Springer, Heidelberg (2008)

How Much Computation and Distributedness is Needed in Sequence Learning Tasks?

Mrwan Margem and Ozgur Yilmaz[✉]

Department of Computer Engineering, Turgut Ozal University, Ankara, Turkey
mmargem2013@stu.turgutozal.edu.tr, ozyilmaz@turgutozal.edu.tr,
http://ozguryilmazresearch.net

Abstract. In this paper, we are analyzing how much computation and distributedness of representation is needed to solve sequence-learning tasks which are essential for many artificial intelligence applications. We propose a novel minimal architecture based on cellular automata. The states of the cells are used as the reservoir of activities as in Echo State Networks. The projection of the input onto this reservoir medium provides a systematic way of remembering previous inputs and combining the memory with a continuous stream of inputs. The proposed framework is tested on classical synthetic pathological tasks that are widely used in evaluating recurrent algorithms. We show that the proposed algorithm achieves zero error in all tasks, giving a similar performance with Echo State Networks, but even better in many different aspects. The comparative results in our experiments suggest that, computation of high order attribute statistics and representing them in a distributed manner is essential, but it can be done in a very simple network of cellular automaton with identical binary units. This raises the question of whether real valued neuron units are mandatory for solving complex problems that are distributed over time. Even very sparsely connected binary units with simple computational rules can provide the required computation for intelligent behavior.

1 Introduction

Intelligence requires remembering previously presented perceptual input or a past cognitive state, and making a synthesis to provide an output for effectively interacting with the environment. This capability is essential in any artificial general intelligence system and there are various solutions to this problem. In this study, we are providing a very simple recurrent architecture for solving sequence tasks that poses as a lower bound on complexity. The recurrent formulation is applied for three different representations: Stack, Covariance and Cellular Automata. In Stack representation, there is no computation involved, the input sequence steps are reserved one after another in raw format. Covariance representation computes the pairwise covariance of the input attributes and locally saves those for each step of the sequence input, as in Tensor Products [13]. Being very similar to Covariance representation in terms of complexity of operations,

© Springer International Publishing Switzerland 2016
B. Steunebrink et al. (Eds.): AGI 2016, LNAI 9782, pp. 274–283, 2016.
DOI: 10.1007/978-3-319-41649-6_28

Cellular Automata holds a distributed representation of high order attribute statistics. Stack representation provides pure memorization, whereas Covariance representation computes useful second order statistics. Cellular Automata representation enables both computation of high order statistics and distributedness. We contrast these three approaches in sequence learning tasks and show that Cellular Automata approach gives superior performance than the other two and equivalent performance with Echo State Networks with significantly less computational demands. Therefore, one of the main contributions of the paper is a novel framework of cellular automata based reservoir computing in a recurrent setting (called *ReCA*), that is capable of short-term memory.

Next, we review reservoir computing and cellular automata, then provide methods and results in the following sections. We discuss the results of our experiments contrasting feedforward vs feedback, memory vs computation, local vs distributed.

1. Reservoir Computing: Many real life problems in artificial intelligence (AI) require the system to remember previous inputs. Recurrent Neural Networks (RNN)s are powerful tools of machine learning with memory. Therefore, they employ very powerful hierarchical computation as well as distributed representation which make them excellent tools for sequence learning tasks. Unfortunately RNNs are difficult to train due to the inherent difficulty of learning optimal representations tailored for long-term dependencies [1,4] and convergence issues [3]. In 2001 an approach to design and train RNNs was proposed independently by Wolfgang Maass and Herbert Jaeger under the names of Liquid State Machines (*LSM*) [9] and Echo State Networks (*ESN*) [5] respectively. These two methods became lately known as Reservoir Computing (RC) approaches [14]. RC model avoids the shortcomings of conventional training methods in RNNs, by setting up RNNs in the following way: **1.** Building the *Reservoir* which is a randomly created RNN and remains unchanged during training. The reservoir is excited by the input signal and maintains in its state a nonlinear transformation of the input history. **2.** The output signal is generated as a linear combination of the neuron's signals from the input-excited reservoir. This linear combination is learned by linear regression, using the teacher signal as a target [8]. A question still remains: how much computation is needed in the reservoir? In Echo State Networks, real valued neurons with nonlinear activation functions are utilized and this still corresponds to a fairly complex neural model. Can we simplify the recurrent architecture further by using identical binary units, and the maximum possible amount of connection sparsity? This corresponds to an elementary cellular automaton array.

2. Cellular Automata: Cellular Automata (CA) are discrete dynamical systems with sparse connections [16]. A cellular automaton is an array of cells evolving synchronously according to an identical interaction rule. The evolution of a cell is dependent on the previous states of a surrounding neighborhood of cells as shown in Fig. 1(b) and thoroughly investigated in [15].

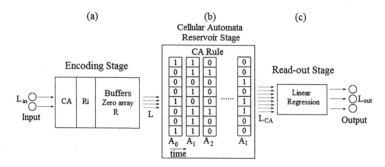

Fig. 1. General framework for Cellular Automata based Reservoir Computing (*ReCA*) with vector lengths for each stage: **a.** Encoding Stage that consists of; *CA*: Input expansion using *ECA* (Multilayer CA), *Ri*: Representing each input bit by R_i bits, and **Buffers:** adding zero array R. **b.** Cellular Automata Reservoir Stage; The output of Encoding Stage is projected onto cellular automaton instead of a neural network in Echo State Networks. A_0 is evolved using a pre-specified ECA rule from 1 to I iterations. **c.** Read-out Stage; The feature vector (reservoir output) is trained by Linear regression.

The dimension of cellular automata can have an integer value, thus it is a grid in general, but one or two dimensions are utilized in most of the studies. If the rules change in time (in certain iterations), the configuration is termed as *multi-layer* CA. In our work, we will use exclusively Elementary Cellular Automaton (ECA) which is a one dimensional CA with binary cells (*1* or *0*), evolving according to a uniform (non-changing rule). The ECA rules are classified according to their evolution behavior (Wolfram classes) [15]. Starting from random initial cell values, CA state evolution will show a certain behavior: **Class I** (*Uniform*) CA states evolve to a homogeneous behavior, **Class II** (*Periodic*) CA states evolve periodically, **Class III** (*Chaotic*) CA states evolve chaotically (without any defined pattern) and **Class IV** (*Complex* or *edge of chaos*) can show all these evolution patterns in an unpredictable manner.

2   Cellular Automata in Reservoir Computing: *ReCA*

The introduction of Cellular Automata into reservoir computing framework was proposed in [18] and some applications discussed in [17,19].

The main idea can be summarized as follows: cellular automata provide powerful enough computation and rich enough representation to be used instead of real valued recurrent neural networks. Cellular automaton is a very sparsely connected network with identical and binary units, thus it gives a lower bound on the amount of model complexity for solving hard problems in AI.

In this paper we are using the recurrent formulation of cellular automata reservoir to handle a sequence of inputs. The algorithmic flow of CA based RC (*ReCA*) is shown in Fig. 1. The encoding stage translates the input into the initial states of CA. In cellular automata reservoir stage, the ECA rules are applied for

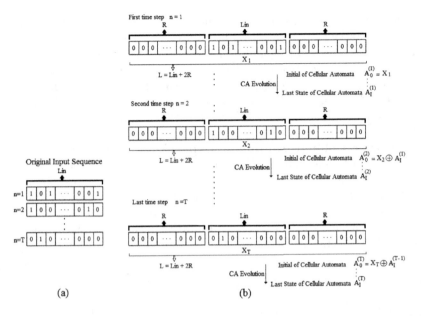

Fig. 2. a. Original input sequence before encoding stage. **b.** Encoding stage and CA Reservoir stage: Adding zero array with length R to obtain the input steps to the reservoir (X_1 to X_T, size L vectors). Then cellular automaton is initialized with the first time step input of the sequence, so $A_0^{(1)} = X_1$, where the subscript (0) denotes to initial state and increases to I (No of CA iterations) and the superscript (1) denotes to the number of time steps (from 1 to T). The CA states $A_i^{(n)}$ are used as the features to estimate the output at time step n ($y(n)$) using linear regression in read-out stage.

a fixed period of iterations (I), to evolve the CA initial states. The CA states in the reservoir are concatenated to produce a feature vector that will be used in read-out stage (Linear Regression).

2.1   Encoding Stage

In encoding stage, the input is translated into the initial states of cellular automaton. It can be divided into three subroutines as shown in Fig. 1(a)[1]

1. **Utilizing Buffers (Zero Array R):** For handling a sequence of inputs, an array of zeros with length of R are added to both sides of original input, these buffers will hold the activity of the reservoir corresponding to previous time steps. Then, the expanded input to cellular automata reservoir is of fixed length $L = L_{in} + 2R$, as shown in Figs. 1 and 2. In most of the experiments, R equals to $I \times T$ (I is the number of CA iterations and T is the sequence length of the input), to guarantee that CA states due to all time sequences have been

---

[1] We should note that, zero buffers are utilized for all experiments but the other two subroutines are applied selectively according to the task.

conserved. To relax this constraint and to reduce time/space complexity an expansion ratio $f \in [0, 1]$ has been introduced as follows $R = f * (I \times T)$, thus the size of the reservoir (complexity) decreases with the value of f.

2. **Reducing Interference (R_i):** To improve the accuracy in tasks, the interference between non zero elements in the reservoir should be reduced. Therefore, each bit of the input will be represented by R_i bits[2]. After each time step, the location of the non zeros will rotate right[3] one bit. For more details see [10].

3. **Multilayer Cellular Automata Expansion:** The original binary input can be transformed into another binary vector using nonlinear *ECA* rules to increase the nonlinearity of the model. This stage enables a *Multilayer Cellular Automata* architecture, in which the first layer projects the input into a nonlinear space, and the next layer evolves it further with linear rules in time to expand the feature space. Linearity in the second layer is essential for lossless injection of the input at each time step.

2.2   Cellular Automata Reservoir Stage

After the input data is encoded as the initial states of a cellular automaton, it is passed on a CA reservoir (instead of an ESN as in [5]) for computation as shown in Fig. 1(b). The dynamics of CA provide the necessary projection of the input data onto an expressive and discriminative space-time volume that can be used as the feature vector. It was previously shown that the cellular automata reservoir holds a distributed representation of high order attribute statistics [18]. Thus, sequence of inputs at each time step is processed to extract the input statistics and these are represented in a distributed manner as in recurrent neural networks.

Figure 2 shows more details for ReCA algorithm, where the initial state at time n, $A_0^{(n)}$ is evolved using a pre-specified ECA rule from 1 to I iterations to obtain the CA evolution states $(A_1^{(n)}, A_2^{(n)}, \ldots, A_I^{(n)})$ (n varies from 1 to T, the input sequence length). XOR[4] operation is used to insert the new input sequence X_n in the reservoir as follows: $A_0^{(n)} = A_I^{(n-1)} \oplus X_n$ and shown in Fig. 2. Then the CA states $(A_1^{(n)}, A_2^{(n)}, \ldots, A_I^{(n)})$ are concatenated to obtain a single state vector $A^{(n)}$ that will be used as a feature vector with length of $L_{CA} = IL$ to estimate the output at time step n ($y(n)$) using linear regression in read-out stage.

---

[2] The value of R_i should be chosen carefully to reduce the interference between non zeros that have different locations in consecutive time steps.

[3] The rotation right is to reduce the interference between non zeros that have the same location in consecutive time steps.

[4] *XOR* computes the correlation, which provides a lossless merging of two binary numbers: it outputs 1 if something different from cell content is presented to the cell.

2.3   Read-Out Stage

In this stage the cellular automaton state vectors (feature vector with dimension of L_{CA}) are used in linear regression to estimate the output:

$$y(n) = W_{out} * A^{(n)} \tag{1}$$

In our experiments, there are two cases for the output: 1. There is only one output y at last time step $n = T$. 2. There is an output for each time step. The size of the feature space and matrix W_{out} differs in the two conditions. See [10] for details.

3   Covariance and Stack Representations

Two other representations with different levels of distributedness and computation are introduced for comparison with ReCA.

1.Covariance Representation: The operator C_k is defined as:

$$C_k = \Pi_k A_0 \oplus \Pi_{-k} A_0 \ , \tag{2}$$

where, Π_k and Π_{-k} are permutation matrices $+k$ and $-k$ shifts and $\oplus$ is bitwise XOR. C_k computes the pairwise covariance of the input attributes as in tensor products [13] and memorizes those for each sequence input. In this representation the operator C_k in (2) is computed in the reservoir to produce the covariance evolution states, instead of applying ECA rules. Second order statistics information is **locally** held in this representation.

2. Stack Representation: In this representation there is **no computation** involved, the input sequence steps are reserved one after another in raw format. T memory blocks of size L_{in} are used as the feature space. It can be considered as the simplest feedforward formulation (no interference between time steps), thus it is not a fixed length representation as in recurrent architectures, which is problematic for large T and L_{in}.

3. Hybrid Covariance and Stack Representations: Instead of using the raw input of the sequence in Covariance and Stack, we can first apply cellular automata nonlinearity and project the input feature space onto the cellular automata state space. This provides a hybrid feature space, in which a minimal amount of computation and distributedness of cellular automata state space is injected into the Covariance and Stack representations.

4   Experiments

In the experiments we trained linear regressors using three representations of sequence; ReCA, Covariance and Stack, on various pathological synthetic tasks.

A set of N_{train} (No of training examples) and N_{test}[5] (No of test examples) input time series and their associated outputs (Target) are synthesized for each task [6]. The experiments target is to achieve a **zero test error** (there should be **no** False Bits in the predicted output). The parameters I (No of CA evolution iterations), R_i (No of bits that represent each input attribute) and N_{train} (No of training set examples) are varied to find the minimal configuration to achieve zero error. Normal equation based linear regression implemented by pseudo-inverse is used in read-out stage.

The classical *Pathological Synthetic Tasks* are used in order to test short-term-memory capability of representations. These tasks have been proposed by Hochreiter and Schmidhuber in [4] that all exhibit pathological long term dependencies and known to be *effectively impossible* for gradient descent [7,11] based pure feedforward architectures. These tasks can be classified into 3 categories: **1.** Memory tasks (5 bit, 20 bit and Random permutation), **2.** Temporal order tasks (2 and 3 symbols) and **3.** Arithmetic or logic operation tasks (XOR, Addition and Multiplication)[6]. We refer the reader to [6] and [10] for a detailed description of them. The difficulty of these tasks increases with the number sequence time steps T, because longer T exhibits longer range temporal dependencies. All inputs in the tasks are originally one hot encoded (i.e. one nonzero entry per time step). In order to make the input more appropriate for real applications, *Binary Encoded* versions are used. As an example, we illustrate the change of 4 bit one hot encoded input to 2 bit binary encoded input: $0001 \Rightarrow 00$, $0010 \Rightarrow 01$, $0100 \Rightarrow 10$ and $1000 \Rightarrow 11$.[7]

5   Results and Discussion

The results of our experiments are illustrated in Table 1. ReCA framework has solved all pathological tasks with zero error either **a.** *directly*, as in random permutation, 5 Bit and temporal order tasks, or **b.** by *expanding* the input using R_i (reduces the interference between input bits) for 20 bit task, or using **c.** *multilayer* CA expansion for addition, multiplication and XOR tasks. Covariance and Stack representations are capable of solving only memory tasks. However, Stack also fails in binary encoded 20 bit memory task, which implies incapability for more realistic applications. Therefore, we conclude that ReCA representation is superior due to its distributed representation (more robust to interference[8] due to activity merging) and computation of higher order attribute statistics.

---

[5] In all experiments $N_{test} = 100$.

[6] In addition and multiplication tasks the input is binary, in future work decimal numbers will be used after binarization.

[7] As an example, this encoding is essential for word prediction application of language modeling, for which one hot encoded input should be of length tens of thousands (size of word dictionary).

[8] Interference can be defined as the modulation of reservoir activity with injection of input at each time step that disturbs one-to-one correspondence between the input sequence and the reservoir activity due to the sequence.

Table 1. Results for Pathological tasks using the proposed representations. The last column (red and bold) is the number of false bits in predicted output of test set. The other columns are for various parameters. T is the sequence length of task input, I is the iterations of CA evolution, N_{train} is the number of training example, $\%N_{train}$ is the ratio between training examples and all input possibilities, f is the expansion ratio, R_i is the number of bits to represent each bit of task input, No of False Bits is the number of false bits in predicted output.

Pathological Task		Method	Multilayer ECA rule Expansion*	T	I	Ntrain	% Ntrain	f	Ri	No of False Bits
Memory	5 Bit	ECA Rule 90	-	1000	4	32	1	1	1	0
	20 Bit Normal	ECA Rule 90	-	300	20	120	1.23E-05	1	2	0
		Covariance	-	300	19	120	1.23E-05	1	3	0
		Stack	-	1000	-	5	5.12E-07	-	-	0
	20 Bit Binary Encoded	ECA Rule 90	-	200	24	250	2.56E-05	1	8	0
		Covariance	-	100	19	250	2.56E-05	1	2	0
		Stack	-	100	-	500	5.12E-05	-	-	47
	Random Permutation	ECA Rule 90	-	1000	2	200	≅ 0	1	1	0
		Covariance	-	1000	2	200	≅ 0	1	1	0
		Stack	-	1000	-	1200	≅ 0	-	-	0
Temporal Order	2 Symbols	ECA Rule 150	-	500	8	6000	1.20E-02	1	1	0
		Covariance	-	200	8	6000	7.54E-02	1	1	151
		Stack	-	200	-	6000	7.54E-02	-	-	4
		ECA Rule 150	122 (1)	1000	8	8000	4.00E-03	0.5	1	0
		Covariance	122 (1)	50	8	1500	3.06E-01	1	1	56
		Stack	122 (1)	500	-	14000	2.81E-02	-	-	0
	3 Symbols	ECA Rule 90	-	50	24	7000	4.46E-02	1	1	0
		ECA rule 90**	-	200	16	2000	1.90E-04	1	1	0
Arithmetic and Logic Operaton	Addition	ECA rule 150	40 (1)	500	20	2500	≅ 0	0.5	1	0
		Covariance	110 (1)	50	20	3300	2.39E-15	1	1	6
		Stack	110 (2)	1000	-	3500	≅ 0	-	-	0
	Multiplication	ECA rule 150	110 (2)	500	12	2000	≅ 0	0.5	1	0
		Covariance	110 (2)	50	12	2000	1.45E-15	1	1	17
		Stack	110 (2)	1000	-	14000	≅ 0	-	-	0
	XOR	ECA rule 150	40 (1)	1000	4	500	≅ 0	0.5	1	0
		Covariance	110 (2)	50	4	3200	2.32E-15	1	1	35
		Stack	110 (2)	50	-	3200	2.32E-15	-	-	39

* The number between brackets is the number of iterations are used in multilayer CA.

** The feature vector for regression consists of *last* CA evolution state from *all* time steps .

For hybrid representations of Stack and Covariance, we observe that Stack becomes capable of solving addition, multiplication after cellular automata input expansion, but **not XOR task**. This is possibly due to requirements of the non-linear nature of XOR task. However, Covariance representation benefits very little from the initial CA expansion. Multilayer CA expansion with non linear rules is a very powerful technique in general, because it also enables ReCA to solve XOR, Addition and Multiplication tasks and improve temporal order tasks. In ReCA, linear (*additive*) ECA rules (90 and 150) are essential for the reservoir evolution, to achieve lossless injection of input at each time step[9]. However, non linear ECA rules (for rule 40 see [2]) should exclusively be used in multilayer expansion as shown in the fourth column of Table 1. Please see more results in [10].

---

[9] Linearity maximizes one-to-one correspondence between input sequence and the reservoir activity due to the sequence.

Table 2. Number of bitwise operations for ESN and ReCA frameworks for solving some pathological tasks.

Task	ESN (Floating Point$\Rightarrow$Bit)	CA (Bit)	Speedup
20 Bit, $T_d = 200$	105.6 M$\Rightarrow$3380 M Bit	24.8 M Bit	136X
3 Symbols, $T = 200$	5 M$\Rightarrow$160 M Bit	20.5 M Bit	7.8X
XOR, $T = 1000$	0.2 M$\Rightarrow$6.4 M Bit	16 M Bit	0.4X

Comparing ReCA with previous approaches, it outperforms: **1.** Martens and Sutskever (2011) [11] and Pascanu et al. (2013) [12] in sequence length T, in their studies the zero test error has been obtained for T ranging from 50 to 200, but in our experiments T ranging from 200 to 1000. **2.** Jaeger (2012) [6], where the zero test error could not be achieved in 20 Bit binary encoded task using ESNs. ReCA outperforms ESN in computational complexity for most of the tasks as listed in Table 2. There is more than **100**× speedup/energy savings for memory tasks and **8**× for temporal order tasks, but ESN is **2**× faster for XOR task. Comparing the representations of ReCA and ESN, the computation performed in the ReCA is much more transparent for analysis and improvement compared to ESNs, in which the state evolution is untraceable due to random and irregular distributivity.

6   Conclusion

Cellular Automata Reservoir framework (ReCA) constructs a novel bridge between computational theory of automata and recurrent neural architectures. We show that the ReCA achieves zero error in all pathological synthetic tasks of sequence learning. Sequence learning is an essential capability for a wide collection of intelligence tasks such as language, continuous vision (i.e. video), symbolic manipulation in a knowledge base etc. ReCA outperforms the Covariance and Stack representations because it enables both computation of high order statistics and distributedness, where Stack representation provides pure memorization, and Covariance representation computes only second order statistics.

Usage of cellular automaton instead of real valued neurons in reservoir computing framework greatly simplifies the architecture, makes the computation more transparent for analysis, and provide enough computation for sequence learning even though it is a very sparse network with identical binary units. Increasing cellular automata iterations I, and the size of each input entry R_i, reduces interference in the reservoir in a predictable manner, making the computation more similar to a feedforward architecture (i.e. Stack representation).

Acknowledgments. This research is supported by The Scientific and Technological Research Council of Turkey (TUBİTAK) Career Grant, No: 114E554.

References

1. Bengio, Y., Simard, P., Frasconi, P.: Learning long-term dependencies with gradient descent is difficult. Neural Netw. IEEE Trans. **5**(2), 157–166 (1994)
2. Braga, G.: Chaotic properties of the elementary cellular automaton rule 40 in wolframs class i. Complex Syst. **17**, 295–308 (2007)
3. Doya, K.: Bifurcations in the learning of recurrent neural networks 3. Learn. (RTRL) **3**, 17 (1992)
4. Hochreiter, S., Schmidhuber, J.: Long short-term memory. Neural Comput. **9**(8), 1735–1780 (1997)
5. Jaeger, H.: The echo state approach to analysing and training recurrent neural networks-with an erratum note. Bonn, Germany: German National Research Center for Information Technology GMD Technical Report 148, 34 (2001)
6. Jaeger, H.: Long short-term memory in echo state networks: Details of a simulation study. Technical report, Technical Report (2012)
7. Kremer, S.C., Kolen, J.F.: Field Guide to Dynamical Recurrent Networks. Wiley-IEEE Press, New York (2001)
8. LukošEvičIus, M., Jaeger, H.: Reservoir computing approaches to recurrent neural network training. Comput. Sci. Rev. **3**(3), 127–149 (2009)
9. Maass, W., Natschläger, T., Markram, H.: Real-time computing without stable states: A new framework for neural computation based on perturbations. Neural Comput. **14**(11), 2531–2560 (2002)
10. Margem, M., Yilmaz, O.: An experimental study on cellular automata reservoir in pathological sequence learning tasks (2016). [Online;accessed31-March-2016]. http://ozguryilmazresearch.net/Publications/MargemYilmaz_TechReport2016.pdf
11. Martens, J., Sutskever, I.: Learning recurrent neural networks with hessian-free optimization. In: Proceedings of the 28th International Conference on Machine Learning (ICML-11), pp. 1033–1040 (2011)
12. Pascanu, R., Mikolov, T., Bengio, Y.: On the difficulty of training recurrent neural networks. In: Proceedings of the 30th International Conference on Machine Learning (ICML-13) (2013)
13. Smolensky, P.: Tensor product variable binding and the representation of symbolic structures in connectionist systems. Artif. Intell. **46**(1), 159–216 (1990)
14. Verstraeten, D., Schrauwen, B., Haene, M., Stroobandt, D.: An experimental unification of reservoir computing methods. Neural Netw. **20**(3), 391–403 (2007)
15. Wolfram, S.: A New Kind of Science, vol. 5. Wolfram media Champaign (2002)
16. Wolfram, S., et al.: Theory and applications of cellular automata, vol. 1. Worldscientific Singapore (1986)
17. Yilmaz, O.: Analogy making and logical inference on images using cellular automata based hyperdimensional computing. In: NIPS, Workshop on Cognitive Computation (2015)
18. Yilmaz, O.: Machine learning using cellular automata based feature expansion and reservoir computing. J. Cell. Automata **10**(5–6), 435–472 (2015)
19. Yilmaz, O.: Symbolic computation using cellular automata based hyperdimensional computing. Neural Comput. **27**(12), 2661–2692 (2015)

Analysis of Algorithms and Partial Algorithms

Andrew MacFie[(✉)]

School of Mathematics and Statistics, Carleton University, Ottawa, Canada
amacfie@sent.com

Abstract. We present an alternative methodology for the analysis of algorithms, based on the concept of expected discounted reward. This methodology naturally handles algorithms that do not always terminate, so it can (theoretically) be used with partial algorithms for undecidable problems, such as those found in artificial general intelligence (AGI) and automated theorem proving. We mention an approach to self-improving AGI enabled by this methodology.

1 Introduction: Shortcomings of Traditional Analysis of Algorithms

Currently, the (running time) analysis of algorithms takes the following form. Given two algorithms A, B that solve the same problem, we find which is more efficient by asymptotically comparing the running time sequences (a_n), (b_n) [4,15]. This could be using worst-case or average-case running times or even smoothed analysis [16]. We refer to this general method as *traditional analysis of algorithms*.

As with any model, traditional analysis of algorithms is not perfect. Authors have noted [1,9] that comparing sequence tails avoids the arbitrariness of any particular range of input lengths but leads us to say $a_n = n^{100}$ is superior to $b_n = \left(1 + \exp(-10^{10})\right)^n$ which is false for practical purposes.

A further issue with traditional analysis is illustrated by this situation: Say we have a function $F : \{0,1\}^* \to \{0,1\}$ and an algorithm A that computes F such that for $n \geq 0$, A takes $(n!)!$ steps on the input 0^n and n steps on any other input of length n. The algorithm A then has worst-case running time $(n!)!$ and average-case running time slightly greater than $2^{-n}(n!)!$, which are both terrible. However, if the inputs are generated according to a uniform distribution, the probability of taking more than n steps is 2^{-n} which is quickly negligible. We see that A should be considered an excellent algorithm but traditional analysis does not tell us that, unless we add "with high probability".

The same issue arises if A simply does not halt on 0^n, in which case the worst-case and average-case running times are infinite. Indeed, this is not an esoteric phenomenon. For any problem with Turing degree $\mathbf{0}'$ we cannot have an algorithm that halts on every input, but we develop partial solutions that work on a subset of inputs. Such problems include string compression (Kolmogorov complexity), the halting problem in program analysis [2], algebraic simplification [17], program optimization, automated theorem proving, and Solomonoff

© Springer International Publishing Switzerland 2016
B. Steunebrink et al. (Eds.): AGI 2016, LNAI 9782, pp. 284–293, 2016.
DOI: 10.1007/978-3-319-41649-6_29

induction (central to artificial general intelligence [13]). E.g. in the case of automated theorem proving, Buss, describing the main open problems in proof theory [3], states, "Computerized proof search ... is widely used, but almost no mathematical theory is known about the effectiveness or optimality of present-day algorithms."

Definition 1. *An algorithm A is a* partial algorithm *(a.k.a. computational method [12, p. 5]) for a given problem if on all inputs, A either outputs the correct value, or does not terminate.*

Definition 2. *We refer to partial algorithms for problems with Turing degree $0'$ as $0'$ algorithms.*

To analyze $0'$ algorithms, and perhaps to better analyze normal terminating algorithms, we need a new approach that is not based on worst-case or average-case running time sequences. In Sect. 2 we present a new method for analyzing algorithms, called expected-reward analysis that avoids some of the issues mentioned above. Then in Sect. 3 we mention how this method can be used in self-improving AI systems. We give directions for further work in Sect. 4.

Notation 1. *Given a (possibly partial) algorithm A and an input ω, we denote the number of steps taken by A on ω by $c_A(\omega)$, which takes the value ∞ if A does not halt on ω.*

2 Expected-Reward Analysis of Algorithms

2.1 Definition

Let A be a (possibly partial) algorithm with inputs in Ω. We say the *score* of A is

$$S(A) = \sum_{\omega \in \Omega} P(\{\omega\})r(\omega)D(c_A(\omega)) = E(r \cdot (D \circ c_A)),$$

where P is a probability measure on Ω, D is a discount function [7], and $r(\omega)$ is a reward (a.k.a. utility) value associated with obtaining the solution to ω. The expression $S(A)$ may be interpreted as the expected discounted reward that A receives if run on a random input, and the practice of comparing scores among algorithms we call *expected-reward analysis*. A higher score indicates a more efficient algorithm.

The functions D and r are arbitrary and are free to be set in the context of a particular application. E.g. in graphical user interface software we often desire near-instant responses, with utility rapidly dropping off with time. Assuming $0 \leq r \leq 1$, we immediately see that for all A, partial or not, we have

$$0 \leq S(A) \leq 1.$$

For simplicity in this paper we assume $r(\omega) = 1$ and D is an exponential discount function, i.e.

$$D(c_A(\omega)) = \exp(-\lambda c_A(\omega)),$$

where $\lambda > 0$ is a discount rate.

The choice of P is also arbitrary; we remark on two special cases. If all inputs of a given length are weighted equally, P is determined by a probability mass function on $\mathbb{Z}_{0+}$. In this case any common discrete probability distribution may be used as appropriate. The measure P is also determined by a probability mass function on $\mathbb{Z}_{0+}$ if we weight equal-length inputs according to Solomonoff's universal distribution m [13], which is a particularly good general model, although computationally difficult.

Expected-reward analysis is non-asymptotic, in the sense that all inputs potentially matter. Thus, while expected-reward analysis can be used on terminating algorithms, we expect it to give different results from traditional analysis, in general. Since particular inputs can make a difference to $S(A)$, it may be advantageous to "hardcode" initial cases into an algorithm. This practice certainly exists, e.g. humans may store the 12×12 multiplication table as well as knowing a general integer multiplication algorithm.

Computational complexity theory often works with classes of problems whose definitions are equivalent for all "reasonable" models of computation [5]. However, even a varying constant factor could arbitrarily change a score. This is simply the price of concreteness, and outside of complexity theory, traditional analysis of algorithms generally selects a particular model of computation and gives precise results that do not necessarily apply to other models [6].

Unlike traditional analysis, experimental data is relevant to score values in a statistical sense. If we are able to generate inputs according to P, either artificially or by sampling inputs found in practice, $S(A)$ is a quantity amenable to statistical estimation. This suggests a form of experimental analysis of algorithms which focuses on a single real number rather than plotting the estimated running time for every input length, which, in the necessary absence of asymptotics in experimental analysis, may not conclusively rank two competing algorithms anyway.

The expected-reward paradigm already appears in the analysis of artificial agents, rather than algorithms [8]. As we see in Sect. 3, however, even in applications to AI, working in the more classical domain of algorithms brings benefits.

2.2   Theory and Practice

Traditional analysis of algorithms has an established literature going back decades which provides a set of techniques for performing traditional analysis on algorithms developed for various problems. We do not significantly develop a mathematical theory of expected-reward analysis here, but we make some very brief initial remarks.

By way of introductory example, we consider expected-reward analysis applied to some well-known sorting algorithms. Let S_n be the set of permutations of $[1..n]$ and let Π_n be a uniform random element of S_n. We denote the algorithms mergesort and quicksort by M and Q, as defined in [15], and set

$$m_n = E\left[\exp(-\lambda\, c_M(\Pi_n))\right], \quad q_n = E\left[\exp(-\lambda\, c_Q(\Pi_n))\right],$$

where $c_A(\omega)$ is the number of comparison operations used by an algorithm A to sort an input ω.

Proposition 1. *For $n \geq 1$ we have*

$$m_n = \exp\left(-\lambda(n\lceil \lg(n)\rceil + n - 2^{\lceil \lg(n)\rceil})\right), \qquad m_0 = 1, \qquad (1)$$

$$q_n = \frac{e^{-\lambda(n+1)}}{n} \sum_{k=1}^{n} q_{k-1} q_{n-k}, \qquad q_0 = 1.$$

Proof. From [15], M makes the same number of comparisons for all inputs of length $n \geq 1$:

$$c_M(\Pi_n) = n\lceil \lg(n)\rceil + n - 2^{\lceil \lg(n)\rceil},$$

so (1) is immediate.

Now, when Q is called on Π_n, let $\rho(\Pi_n)$ be the pivot element, and let $\underline{\Pi}_n, \overline{\Pi}_n$ be the subarrays constructed for recursive calls to Q, where the elements in $\underline{\Pi}_n$ are less than $\rho(\Pi_n)$, and the elements in $\overline{\Pi}_n$ are greater.

We have

$$E[\exp(-\lambda c_Q(\Pi_n))]$$

$$= \frac{1}{n} \sum_{k=1}^{n} E[\exp(-\lambda(n+1+c_Q(\underline{\Pi}_n)+c_Q(\overline{\Pi}_n)))\,|\,\rho(\Pi_n) = k]$$

$$= \frac{e^{-\lambda(n+1)}}{n} \sum_{k=1}^{n} E[\exp(-\lambda(c_Q(\underline{\Pi}_n)+c_Q(\overline{\Pi}_n)))\,|\,\rho(\Pi_n) = k].$$

It can be seen that given $\rho(\Pi_n) = k$, $\underline{\Pi}_n$ and $\overline{\Pi}_n$ are independent, thus

$$E[\exp(-\lambda c_Q(\Pi_n))]$$

$$= \frac{e^{-\lambda(n+1)}}{n} \sum_{k=1}^{n} E[\exp(-\lambda c_Q(\underline{\Pi}_n))\,|\,\rho(\Pi_n) = k]\cdot$$

$$E[\exp(-\lambda c_Q(\overline{\Pi}_n))\,|\,\rho(\Pi_n) = k]$$

$$= \frac{e^{-\lambda(n+1)}}{n} \sum_{k=1}^{n} E[\exp(-\lambda c_Q(\Pi_{k-1}))]E[\exp(-\lambda c_Q(\Pi_{n-k}))]. \qquad \square$$

From examining the best-case performance of Q, it turns out that $c_M(\Pi_n) \leq c_Q(\Pi_n)$ for all n, so the expected-reward comparison of M and Q is easy: $S(M) \geq S(Q)$ for any parameters. However, we may further analyze the absolute scores of M and Q to facilitate comparisons to arbitrary sorting algorithms. When performing expected-reward analysis on an individual algorithm, our main desideratum is a way to quickly compute the score value to within a given precision for each possible parameter value P, λ. Proposition 1 gives a way of computing scores of M and Q for measures P that give equal length inputs equal weight, although it does not immediately suggest an efficient way in all cases. Bounds on scores are also potentially useful and may be faster to compute; in the next proposition, we give bounds on m_n and q_n which are simpler than the exact expressions above.

Proposition 2. *For $n \geq 1$,*

$$\frac{e^{-2\lambda(n-1)}}{(n-1)!^{\lambda/\log(2)}} \leq m_n \leq \frac{e^{-\lambda(n-1)}}{(n-1)!^{\lambda/\log(2)}}. \tag{2}$$

For all $0 < \lambda \leq \log(2)$ and $n \geq 0$,

$$\frac{e^{-2\gamma\lambda(n+1)-\lambda}}{(n+1)!^{2\lambda}}(2\pi(n+1))^\lambda < q_n \leq \frac{e^{-2\lambda n}}{(n!)^{\lambda/\log(2)}},$$

where γ is Euler's constant.

Proof. Sedgewick and Flajolet [15] give an alternative expression for the running time of mergesort:

$$c_M(\Pi_n) = \sum_{k=1}^{n-1} (\lfloor \lg k \rfloor + 2).$$

Statement (2) follows from this because

$$\log(k)/\log(2) + 1 < \lfloor \lg k \rfloor + 2 \leq \log(k)/\log(2) + 2.$$

With $0 < \lambda \leq \log(2)$, we prove the upper bound

$$q_n \leq \frac{e^{-2\lambda n}}{(n!)^{\lambda/\log(2)}} \tag{3}$$

for all $n \geq 0$ by induction. Relation (3) clearly holds for $n = 0$. We show that (3) can be proved for $n = N$ ($N > 0$) on the assumption that (3) holds for $0 \leq n \leq N - 1$. Proposition 1 gives

$$q_N = \frac{e^{-\lambda(N+1)}}{N} \sum_{k=1}^{N} q_{k-1} q_{N-k}$$

$$\leq \frac{e^{-\lambda(N+1)}}{N} \sum_{k=1}^{N} \frac{e^{-2\lambda(k-1)}}{((k-1)!)^{\lambda/\log(2)}} \frac{e^{-2\lambda(N-k)}}{((N-k)!)^{\lambda/\log(2)}}$$

(by the assumption)

$$= e^{-3\lambda N + \lambda} \left(\frac{1}{N} \sum_{k=1}^{N} \left(\frac{1}{(k-1)!} \frac{1}{(N-k)!} \right)^{\lambda/\log(2)} \right)$$

$$\leq e^{-3\lambda N + \lambda} \left(\frac{1}{N^{\lambda/\log(2)}} \left(\sum_{k=1}^{N} \frac{1}{(k-1)!} \frac{1}{(N-k)!} \right)^{\lambda/\log(2)} \right)$$

(by Jensen's inequality, since $0 < \lambda/\log(2) \leq 1$)

$$= e^{-3\lambda N + \lambda} \left(\frac{(2^{N-1})^{\lambda/\log(2)}}{(N!)^{\lambda/\log(2)}} \right)$$

$$= \frac{e^{-2\lambda N}}{(N!)^{\lambda/\log(2)}}.$$

Thus (3) has been proved for all $n \geq 0$.

For the lower bound on q_n, we use the probabilistic form of Jensen's inequality,

$$q_n = E\left[\exp(-\lambda c_Q(\Pi_n))\right] \geq \exp(-\lambda E\left[c_Q(\Pi_n)\right]),$$

noting that average-case analysis of quicksort [15] yields

$$E\left[c_Q(\Pi_n)\right] = 2(n+1)(H_{n+1} - 1), \qquad n \geq 0,$$

where (H_n) is the harmonic sequence. For $n \geq 0$, the bound

$$H_{n+1} < \log(n+1) + \gamma + \frac{1}{2(n+1)}$$

holds [11] (sharper bounds exist), so we have

$$q_n > \exp\left(-2\lambda(n+1) \left(\log(n+1) + \gamma + \frac{1}{2(n+1)} - 1 \right) \right)$$

$$= e^{-2(\gamma-1)\lambda(n+1)-\lambda}(n+1)^{-2\lambda(n+1)}.$$

We finish by applying Stirling's inequality

$$(n+1)^{-(n+1)} \geq \sqrt{2\pi(n+1)}\, e^{-(n+1)}/(n+1)!, \qquad n \geq 0. \qquad \square$$

From these results we may get a sense of the tasks involved in expected-reward analysis for typical algorithms. We note that with an exponential discount function, the independence of subproblems in quicksort is required for obtaining a recursive formula, whereas in traditional average-case analysis, linearity of expectation suffices.

We end this section by mentioning an open question relevant to a theory of expected-reward analysis.

Question 1. If we fix a computational problem and parameters P, λ, what is $\sup_A S(A)$, and is it attained?

If $\sup_A S(A)$ is not attained then the situation is similar to that in Blum's speedup theorem. Comparing $\sup_A S(A)$ among problems would be the expected-reward analog of computational complexity theory but because of the sensitivity of S to parameters and the model of computation, this is not useful.

3   Self-improving AI

The generality of $\mathbf{0}'$ problems allows us to view design and analysis of $\mathbf{0}'$ algorithms as a task which itself may be given to a $\mathbf{0}'$ algorithm, bringing about recursive self-improvement. Here we present one possible concrete example of this notion and discuss connections with AI.

Computational problems with Turing degree $\mathbf{0}'$ are Turing-equivalent so without loss of generality in this section we assume $\mathbf{0}'$ algorithms are automated theorem provers. Specifically, we fix a formal logic system, say ZFC (assuming it is consistent), and take the set of inputs to be ZFC sentences, and the possible outputs to be `provable` and `not provable`.

Let a predicate β be such that $\beta(Z)$ holds iff Z is a $\mathbf{0}'$ algorithm which is correct on provable inputs and does not terminate otherwise. In pseudocode we write the instruction to run some Z on input ω as $Z(\omega)$, and if ω contains β or S (the score function), their definitions are implicitly included.

We give an auxiliary procedure SEARCH which takes as input a $\mathbf{0}'$ algorithm Z and a rational number x and uses Z to obtain a $\mathbf{0}'$ algorithm which satisfies β and has score greater than x (if possible). Symbols in bold within a string literal get replaced by the value of the corresponding variable. We assume $\mathbf{0}'$ algorithms are encoded as strings in a binary prefix code.

```
1: procedure SEARCH(x, Z)
2:      u ← the empty string
3:      loop
4:          do in parallel until one returns provable:
5:              A: Z("∃v : (Z* = u0v ⟹ β(Z*) ∧ S(Z*) > x)")
6:              B: Z("∃v : (Z* = u1v ⟹ β(Z*) ∧ S(Z*) > x)")
7:              C: Z("Z* = u ⟹ β(Z*) ∧ S(Z*) > x")
8:          if A returned provable then
9:              u ← u0
10:         if B returned provable then
11:             u ← u1
12:         if C returned provable then
13:             return u
```

We remark that the mechanism of SEARCH is purely syntactic and does not rely on consistency or completeness of ZFC, or the provability thereof. This would not be the case if we strengthened β to require that $\beta(Z)$ is true only if at most one of $Z(\omega)$ and $Z(\neg\omega)$ returns `provable`. Such a β would never provably hold in ZFC.

The following procedure IMPROVE takes an initial $\mathbf{0}'$ algorithm Z_0 and uses dovetailed calls to SEARCH to output a sequence of $\mathbf{0}'$ algorithms that tend toward optimality.

```
1: procedure IMPROVE(Z_0)
2:     best ← Z_0,  pool ← {},  score ← 0
3:     for n ← 1 to ∞ do
4:         a_n ← nth term in Stern-Brocot enumeration of ℚ ∩ (0, 1]
5:         if a_n > score then
6:             initialState ← initial state of SEARCH(a_n, best)
7:             add (a_n, best, initialState) to pool
8:         improvementFound ← false
9:         for (a, Z, state) in pool do
10:            run SEARCH(a, Z) one step starting in state state
11:            newState ← new current state of SEARCH(a, Z)
12:            if state is not a terminating state then
13:                in pool, mutate (a, Z, state) into (a, Z, newState)
14:                continue
15:            improvementFound ← true
16:            best ← output of SEARCH(a, Z)
17:            score ← a
18:            for (â, Ẑ, stâte) in pool where â ≤ score do
19:                remove (â, Ẑ, stâte) from pool
20:            print best
21:        if improvementFound then
22:            for (a, Z, state) in pool do
23:                initialState ← initial state of SEARCH(a, best)
24:                add (a, best, initialState) to pool
```

The procedure IMPROVE has the following basic property.

Proposition 3. *Let (Z_n) be the sequence of $\mathbf{0}'$ algorithms printed by* IMPROVE. *If $\beta(Z_0)$ holds, and if there is any $\mathbf{0}'$ algorithm Y and $s \in \mathbb{Q}$ where $\beta(Y)$ and $S(Y) > s > 0$ are provable, we have*

$$\lim_{n \to \infty} S(Z_n) \geq s.$$

If (Z_n) is finite, the above limit can be replaced with the last term in (Z_n).

Proof. The value s appears as some value a_n. For $a_n = s$, if $a_n > score$ in line 5, then SEARCH(s, best) will be run one step for each greater or equal value of n and either terminates (since Y exists) and $score$ is set to s, or is interrupted if we eventually have $score \geq s$ before SEARCH(s, best) terminates. It suffices to note that when $score$ attains any value $x > 0$, all further outputs Z satisfy $S(Z) > x$ and there is at least one such output.   □

The procedure IMPROVE also makes an attempt to use recently printed $\mathbf{0}'$ algorithms in calls to SEARCH. However, it is not true in general that $S(Z_{n+1}) \geq S(Z_n)$. Checking if a particular output Z_n is actually an improvement over Z_0 or Z_{n-1} requires extra work.

In artificial general intelligence (AGI) it is desirable to have intelligent systems with the ability to make autonomous improvements to themselves [14]. If an AGI system such as an AIXI approximation [10] already uses a $\mathbf{0}'$ algorithm Z to compute the universal distribution m, we can give the system the ability to improve Z over time by devoting some of its computational resources to running IMPROVE. This yields a general agent whose environment prediction ability tends toward optimality.

4   Future Work

We would like to be able to practically use expected-reward analysis with various parameter values, probability measures, and discount functions, on both terminating and non-terminating algorithms. Particularly, we would like to know whether $\mathbf{0}'$ algorithms may be practically analyzed. It may be possible to develop general mathematical tools and techniques to enhance the practicality of these methods, such as exist for traditional analysis; this is a broad and open-ended research goal.

Acknowledgements. The author wishes to thank Zhicheng Gao, Nima Hoda, Patrick LaVictoire, Saran Neti, and anonymous referees for helpful comments.

References

1. Aaronson, S.: Why philosophers should care about computational complexity. In: Computability: Gödel, Turing, Church, and Beyond (2012)
2. Burnim, J., Jalbert, N., Stergiou, C., Sen, K.: Looper: lightweight detection of infinite loops at runtime. In: International Conference on Automated Software Engineering (2009)
3. Buss, S.: Re: proof theory on the eve of year 2000 (1999). http://www.ihes.fr/~carbone/papers/proofsurveyFeferman2000.html. Accessed: 04 Oct 2015
4. Cormen, T.H., Leiserson, C.E., Rivest, R.L., Stein, C.: Introduction to Algorithms, 3rd edn. MIT Press, Cambridge (2009)
5. van Emde Boas, P.: Handbook of Theoretical Computer Science, vol. A, pp. 1–66. MIT Press, Cambridge (1990)
6. Flajolet, P., Sedgewick, R.: Analytic Combinatorics. Cambridge University Press, Cambridge (2009)
7. Frederick, S., Loewenstein, G., O'Donoghue, T.: Time discounting and time preference: a critical review. J. Econ. Lit. **40**, 351–401 (2002)
8. Goertzel, B.: Toward a formal characterization of real-world general intelligence. In: Proceedings of the 3rd Conference on Artificial General Intelligence, AGI, pp. 19–24 (2010)
9. Gurevich, Y.: Feasible functions. London Math. Soc. Newslett. **206**, 6–7 (1993)
10. Hutter, M.: Universal Artificial Intelligence: Sequential Decisions based on Algorithmic Probability. Springer, Berlin (2005)
11. Julian, H.: Gamma: Exploring Euler's Constant. Princeton University Press, Princeton (2003)
12. Knuth, D.E.: The Art of Computer Programming, vol. 1. Addison-Wesley, Reading (1997)

13. Li, M., Vitányi, P.: An Introduction to Kolmogorov Complexity and its Applications. Springer Science & Business Media, New York (2013)
14. Schmidhuber, J.: Gödel machines: fully self-referential optimal universal self-improvers. In: Goertzel, B., Pennachin, C. (eds.) Artificial General Intelligence, pp. 199–226. Springer, Heidelberg (2007)
15. Sedgewick, R., Flajolet, P.: An Introduction to the Analysis of Algorithms. Addison-Wesley, Reading (2013)
16. Spielman, D.A., Teng, S.H.: Smoothed analysis: an attempt to explain the behavior of algorithms in practice. Commun. ACM 52(10), 76–84 (2009)
17. Trott, M.: The Mathematica Guidebook for Symbolics. Springer Science & Business Media, New York (2007)

Estimating Cartesian Compression
via Deep Learning

András Lőrincz(✉), András Sárkány, Zoltán Á. Milacski, and Zoltán Tősér

Faculty of Informatics, Eötvös Loránd University,
Pázmány Péter sétány 1/C, Budapest 1117, Hungary
lorincz@inf.elte.hu

Abstract. We introduce a learning architecture that can serve compression while it *also* satisfies the constraints of factored reinforcement learning. Our novel Cartesian factors enable one to decrease the number of variables being relevant for the ongoing task, an exponential gain in the size of the state space. We demonstrate the working, the limitations and the promises of the abstractions: we develop a representation of space in allothetic coordinates from egocentric observations and argue that the lower dimensional allothetic representation can be used for path planning. Our results on the learning of Cartesian factors indicate that (a) shallow autoencoders perform well in our numerical example and (b) if deeper networks are needed, e.g., for classification or regression, then sparsity should also be enforced at (some of) the intermediate layers.

1 Introduction

An intriguing fact about intelligence is the following. Our scientific discoveries have a history of about 15000 years. The same holds for the technological developments and this progress was made by billions of people. Still, this knowledge, or a large part of it, can be passed to a child in 15 years. It looks that innovations and discoveries take long, whereas explaining and proving them are much faster. One may consider the complexity of optimization and problem solving. They may scale polynomially or exponentially both from the point of view of solving them and verifying them (see, e.g., [4] and the cited references). The polynomial type is called easy and the exponential type is called hard. Out of the four options, the *hard* to solve and *easy* to verify — such as the Traveling Salesman Problem — can be particularly useful for communicating agents. The relevance of the other three classes is less. It thus seems that human knowledge is concerned with hard to solve and easy to verify problems. After all, mathematical theorems are hard to discover, but the proof is 'linear'.

Consider sensory information. It brings about the possibility of information fusion from different sensory modalities. For example, smell may be associated with tasty food and then the smell can be used for searching for food. Thus, information fusion concerns Cartesian factors (e.g., smell and taste) and spatiotemporal patterns (e.g., during hunting the smell predicts the taste). Smell and

© Springer International Publishing Switzerland 2016
B. Steunebrink et al. (Eds.): AGI 2016, LNAI 9782, pp. 294–304, 2016.
DOI: 10.1007/978-3-319-41649-6_30

taste have their respective sensors, unlike many Cartesian factors. The creation (or the derivation) of such factors is of high importance for lowering the number of relevant variables in problem solving.

The concept of numbers is such a Cartesian abstraction; it represents the quantity and separates material properties. '$2 + 2 = 4$', no matter if we are concerned with apples or peaches. Cartesian abstractions enable concise formulations for similar tasks.

We turn to the constraints of goal-oriented behavior. Factored reinforcement learning (FRL) is advantageous [15,32], since without factored description, the state space explodes. Factors of FRL are Cartesian ones [3,17] and can be latent non-linear *coordinates*. Such abstractions are considered hard, 'although potentially pseudo-polynomial' [7]. We postulate that communication favors such abstractions, provided that the factor, in a given task, enables the agent to neglect other components of the information without high risks, e.g., by applying robust controllers [33,36].

In our view, creative intelligence finds those factors that suit the essence of the problem and diminish the combinatorial explosion for an approximate FRL framework. In turn, the views that compression is related to intelligence, e.g., the proposal that compression is one of the driving forces of science [28], the thought that compression may lead to AGI[1] together with the warning that intelligence is not simply compression [8] may all gain support through the concept of Cartesian factors.

Contributions: we treat the Cartesian factor problem by means of deep networks. We assume that we are given a factor and we find the complementing one without exploiting temporal information. The paper is constructed as follows. In the next section, we shall review similar efforts. Section 3 provides the details about the deep learning formalism and the problem itself. Our results are presented in Sect. 4 and discussed in Sect. 5. Conclusions are drawn in Sect. 6.

2   Related Works

Factor or component learning appears in a number of contexts, such as factor analysis (FA), nonlinear matrix factorization (NMF), principal/independent component analysis (PCA/ICA) (see, e.g., [16] and the references therein), sparse coding (SC), also in bilinear forms [34]. The literature is enormous and goes beyond the scope of this paper. These methods have the following properties: (i) they assume the structure of the data (NMF, ICA), (ii) they drop components of small variances (FA, PCA), and (iii) they are essentially additive factor models. Generative models with specified joint probability distributions also form a group of models [27]. By contrast, Cartesian factors are more like *modalities*, can have a *metric*, and may be *deterministic*.

'Place field' cells observed in rat hippocampus [24], also known as the 'cognitive map' [25], motivate our thinking, since place fields are independent from

---

[1] http://prize.hutter1.net/.

the egocentric direction of the animal and thus, it could be a modality, but it is not sensed directly. The explanation of the place field phenomenon – that gave rise to the Nobel Prize in 2014 – motivates our demonstration. We mention two of the many models and refer the interested reader to the literature. One model starts from ICA on directed spatially local but dispersed information, derives direction dependent place fields, develops an autoregressive (AR) predictor from those and produces direction independent place fields from measuring the innovation of the AR process [19]. However, this method does not work for distant cues. The other model uses distant information and takes advantage of Slow Feature Analysis (SFA), see [29] and the references therein. This method needs a relatively large angle of view to derive the place fields. Both methods exploit temporal information, a strong restriction for the general case.

Here, we assume that we have one Cartesian factor and we will develop a potentially deep architecture that can robustly discover the complementing one.

3   Methods

3.1   Theoretical Background

Deep Autoencoders. A *Deep Autoencoder* [12,38] is the unsupervised version of a modern Multilayer Perceptron (MLP). Consider a series of non-linear mappings (layers) of the form:

$$H = f_N \Big(\cdots f_2 \big(f_1 (X W_1) W_2 \big) \cdots W_N \Big), \tag{1}$$

where $X \in \mathbb{R}^{I \times J}$ is the matrix of I inputs of size J, $W_n \in \mathbb{R}^{Q_{n-1}, Q_n}$ are parameters with $Q_0 = J$, and f_n are non-linear almost everywhere differentiable element-wise functions ($n = 1, \ldots, N$; $N \in \mathbb{N}$). Then $H \in \mathbb{R}^{I \times Q}$ is called the feature map ($Q_N = Q$). Typically, one takes two such mappings with reversed sizes — an encoder and a decoder — and composes them. Thereupon one can define a so-called reconstruction error between the encoder input X and the decoder output $\widehat{X} \in \mathbb{R}^{I \times J}$ (normally the ℓ_2 or Frobenius norm of the difference, i.e., $\frac{1}{2}\|X - \widehat{X}\|_F^2 = \frac{1}{2}\sum_{i=1,\ldots,I}\sum_{j=1,\ldots,J}(X_{i,j} - \widehat{X}_{i,j})^2)$ and try to find a local minima of it in terms of parameters W_n after random initialization, by taking advantage of a step-size adaptive mini-batch subgradient descent method [9,18, 39]. The non-linearity can be chosen to be the rectified linear function $f_n(x) = x \cdot \mathbb{I}(x > 0)$ for $x \in \mathbb{R}$ [5,22] to avoid the vanishing gradient problem [13,14], where $\mathbb{I}$ designates the indicator function.

Spatial and Lifetime Sparsity. Deep Autoencoders are often used as a pretraining scheme [10] or as a part of supervised algorithms [26], but they lack the ability to learn a meaningful or simple data representation without prior knowledge [30]. To obtain such a description, one might add regularizers or constraints to the objective function [1,11], or employ a greedy procedure [6,37]. It is well known that minimizing the sum of ℓ_2 norms of parameters W_n can reduce model complexity by yielding a dense feature map, and similarly, the ℓ_1 variant may result in a sparse version [23,35]. An alternative possibility is to introduce constraints in the non-linear function f_n. For example, one may utilize a k-sparse representation by keeping solely the top k activation values in feature map $\boldsymbol{H}$, and letting the rest of the components zero [20]. This case, when features, i.e., the components of the representation, compete with each other is referred to as *spatial sparsity*. Input indices of the representation may also go up against each other and this case is called *lifetime sparsity* [21].

3.2   Problem Formulation

We assume that a latent random variable Z and an observed random variable Y are continuous and together they fully explain away another observed binary random variable X. The ranges of Z and Y are supposed to be grid discretized finite r- and one-dimensional intervals, respectively, that fits FRL. We denote the resulting grid points by $(z^{(m)}, y^{(l)}) \in \mathbb{R}^r \times \mathbb{R}$; $l = 0, \ldots, L$, $m = 1, \ldots, (M+1)^r$, $L, M, r \in \mathbb{N}$. The indices $m = 1, \ldots, (M+1)^r$ are supposed to be scrambled throughout training (i.e., we assume no topology between $z^{(m)}$). Then observation $\boldsymbol{x}^{(m,l)} \in \{0,1\}^d$ is generated by a highly non-linear function $g: \mathbb{R}^r \times \{1, \ldots, L\} \to \{0,1\}^d$ from grid point $z^{(m)}$ and grid interval $[y^{(l-1)}, y^{(l)})$ as

$$\boldsymbol{x}^{(m,l)} = g(\boldsymbol{z}^{(m)}, l) \tag{2}$$

for $m = 1, \ldots, (M+1)^r$; $l = 1, \ldots, L$. For each fixed m, one is given masks $\boldsymbol{V}_{i,\cdot} \in \{0,1\}^L$; $\sum_{l=1}^{L} V_{i,l} = v \in \mathbb{N}$ indexing pairs of the form $(l, \boldsymbol{x}^{(m,l)})$, where $i = 1, \ldots, I$ is a global index. Provided such a sample from Y and X, we aim to approximate the discretized version of Z.

The variables may correspond to discretized latent points in space (Z); direction intervals in an allothetic system, e.g., a compass with limited resolution (Y); and ego-centric views of distant cues within a viewing angle (X), see Fig. 1 for an illustration.

We formulated the above problem as a multilayer feedforward *lifetime sparse autoencoding* [21] procedure with input matrix $\boldsymbol{X} \in \{0,1\}^{I \times J}$ utilizing two novelties: concatenated input vectors and a masked loss function are motivated by the input structure. In order to construct the inputs $\boldsymbol{X}_{i,\cdot}$; $i = 1, \ldots, I$ of size $J = L \cdot d$, we coupled each v-tuple of $\boldsymbol{x}^{(m,l)}$ vectors for fixed m into a single block-vector using the $\boldsymbol{V}_{i,\cdot}$ values as follows:

$$\boldsymbol{X}_{i,\cdot} = \left[\boldsymbol{V}_{i,1} \cdot \boldsymbol{x}^{(m,1)}, \ldots, \boldsymbol{V}_{i,l} \cdot \boldsymbol{x}^{(m,l)}, \ldots, \boldsymbol{V}_{i,L} \cdot \boldsymbol{x}^{(m,L)} \right]. \tag{3}$$

Then, we used the ℓ_2 reconstruction error as the loss, but on a restricted set of elements, namely, on the v non-zero blocks for each input:

$$l(\boldsymbol{X}, \widehat{\boldsymbol{X}}, \boldsymbol{V}): = \frac{1}{I} \sum_{\substack{i=1,\ldots,I \\ j=1,\ldots,J}} V_{i, \lfloor \frac{i-1}{d}+1 \rfloor} \cdot (\boldsymbol{X}_{i,j} - \widehat{\boldsymbol{X}}_{i,j})^2 \tag{4}$$

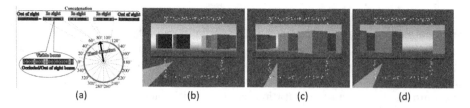

Fig. 1. Numerical experiment. (a): input is concatenated from sub-vectors, which belong to different allothetic directions. A given index corresponds to the same box, the 'remote visible cue', in all sub-vectors. The value of the a component of a sub-vector is 1 (0) if the box is visible (non-visible) in the corresponding direction. Three directions are visible (green). Some boxes may be present in neighboring sub-vectors, since they are large. (b)–(d): the 'arena' from above with the different boxes around it. Shaded green areas in (b), (c), and (d), show the visible portions within the field of view at a given position with a given head direction. Insets show the visual information for each portion to be transformed to 1 s and 0 s in the respective components of the sub-vectors. Components of out-of-view sub-vectors are set to zero. (Color figure online)

where $\widehat{X}$ denotes the output of the decoder network. Finally, a sparse non-linearity was imposed on top of each encoder layer, which selected the k percent topmost activations across one component. We applied both lifetime [21] and spatial sparsification [20].

We expected the output of the encoder $H \in \mathbb{R}^{I \times Q}$ to resemble $z^{(m)}$, i.e., not depending on $y^{(l)}$ and discretizing the latent space $\mathbb{R}^r$. The procedure is summarized in Fig. 2.

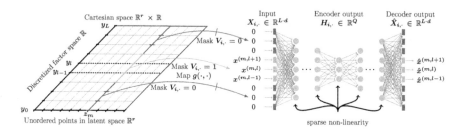

Fig. 2. General architecture. In the numerical experiments the notations correspond to the following quantities: Z latent positions, Y discretized 'compass' values. Input to the network: red: not visible, green: visible at neighboring viewing angle ranges. Each viewing angle range provides inputs about all boxes. The full input equals to the 'No. of boxes × No. of viewing angle ranges'. See text for details of the autoencoder. (Color figure online)

We implemented our method in the Python library Theano [2] based upon the SciPy2015 GitHub repository[2]. We used multilayer autoencoders with rectified

---

[2] https://github.com/kastnerkyle/SciPy2015.

linear units, $k = 1$ spatial sparsity and $p\%$-sparse lifetime sparsity. The decoder output layer was linear. We trained parameters using full-batch Adam gradient descent [18] with early stopping (maximum 10000 epochs with 500 epochs patience).

3.3 Numerical Experiment

For our study, we generated a squared 'arena' surrounded by $d = 150$ boxes in Unity[3] 3D game engine (Fig. 1). The 'arena' had no obstacles. Boxes were placed pseudo-randomly: they did not overlap. The 'arena' was discretized by an $M \times M = 36 \times 36$ grid. From each grid point and for every $20°$, a $28°$ field of view was created (i.e., $L = \frac{360°}{20°} = 18$, overlap: $4°$ between regions), and the visibility — a binary value (0 for occlusion or out of the angle of view) — for each box was recorded, according to Eq. (2); we constructed a total of $I = 37 \cdot 37 \cdot 18 = 24642$ binary $(\boldsymbol{x}^{(m,l)})$ vectors.

These vectors were processed further. Beyond the actual direction of the center of the viewing angle, we introduced some degree of closeness about the input regarding the direction, but not the position: we varied the viewing angle between $28°$ and $360°$. Formally, for various experiments, we defined masks $\boldsymbol{V}_{i,}$ summing to $v = 1, 3, \ldots, 17, 18$, for which we carried out the concatenation method from Eq. (3): for each visible $28°$ sector, the corresponding $\boldsymbol{x}^{(m,l)}$ vector; while for all non-visible sectors, an all-zero vector were appended. This manipulation did not change the size of the database.

In some experiments we normalized the inputs to unit ℓ_2 norm for each $d = 150$ dimensional components, provided that at least one of the components differed from zero. This is called normalized experiment. We used spatial sparsification with $k = 1$ and lifetime sparsification with $p = 3.33\%$ and $p = 6.66\%$. In the error of the autoencoder we considered two options: (a) error of the full output and (b) error only on the visible components that belonged to the viewing angle as in Eq. (4). This latter is called masked experiment. We used them in combination. We also tried 3 and 5 layer autoencoders, with the middle layer representing the latent variables.

The size of the middle layer was always $Q = 30$. This means that spatial (i.e., latent component-wise) sparsity gave rise to 3.33% lifetime sparsity. On the other hand, $p = 3.33\%$ lifetime sparsity was effectively larger than 3.33% since it was possible that none of the latent unit was selected for a given input (and thus all of them were set to zero), when backpropagation became ineffective. The same holds for $p = 6.66\%$ lifetime sparsity, which, on the average, would give rise to 1, 2, 3, or more non-zero latent units with average above 2. The sizes of the hidden layers were spaced linearly between 2700 and 30.

4 Results

The dependencies of the responses in the hidden representation vs. space and direction are shown in Figs. 3 and 4. Linear responses of randomly selected latent

---

[3] https://unity3d.com.

	Field of view [deg]									
	28	68	108	148	188	228	268	308	348	360
ICA										
Norm-SP1-Mask										
LT3.33%										
Norm-LT3.33%										
Norm-LT3.33%-Mask										
Norm-LT6.66%-Mask										
Norm-DL-LT3.33%-Mask										
Norm-LT3.33%-LT3.33%-Mask										

Fig. 3. Linear responses of individual latent units selected randomly: we chose neuron with index 2 from the latent layer. ICA: values may take positive and negative values. Other experiments: all units are ReLUs, except the output, which is linear. Color coding represents the sum of responses for all directions at a given point. SP1: spatial sparsity with $k = 1$, LT3.3%: lifetime sparsity $= 3.3\%$, Norm: for each 150 components, the ℓ_2 norm of input is 1 if any of the components is non-zero, Mask: autoencoding error concerns only the visible part of the scene, DL: dense layer. 'Norm-LT3.3%-LT3.3%-Mask' means normed input, masked error, 5 layers: input layer, 3 layers with LT sparsity equals 3.3%, output layer.

units for different algorithms are depicted in Fig. 3, illustrating the extent that the responses were localized. Figure 4 shows the direction (in)dependence of the responses. For each input, we chose the highest activity latent component and in each position we computed the number of directions (out of the 18 possible) that a neuron was the winner in the dataset. We computed these numbers for all units, selected the largest values at each position and combined them in a single figure that we color coded (Fig. 4): Black color at one position means that unit won in all angles at that position. Lighter colors mean less winning directions.

One should ask (i) if the linear responses are local and activities far from the position of the peak activity are close to zero; (ii) if the number of dead latent units is small, (iii) if responses are direction independent, that is, if we could derive the discretization of space in allothetic coordinates, the complementary component of the egocentric direction. We found that spatial sparsity with the 3 layer network and the 5 layer network with dense 2nd and 4th layers rendered the output of some or sometimes all hidden units to zero (Table 1). On the other hand, lifetime sparsity with the 5 layer network produced excellent results. Lifetime sparsity $p = 6.66\%$ can still produce place fields. Note that local responses appear without the mask, but only for very large viewing angles. For the sake of completeness, we also provide the ICA responses in Fig. 3. We discuss the relevance, the limitations and the promises of our results in the next section.

Table 1. Dead neuron count: number of non-responsive computational units.

	Field of view [deg]									
	28	68	108	148	188	228	268	308	348	360
Norm-SP1-Mask	2	0	5	5	10	12	16	18	15	18
LT3.33 %	0	0	0	0	0	2	2	6	8	9
Norm-LT3.33 %	0	0	0	1	1	3	2	4	9	11
Norm-LT3.33 %-Mask	0	0	0	0	0	0	1	2	7	11
Norm-LT6.66 %-Mask	0	0	0	0	0	0	1	4	13	13
Norm-DL-LT3.33 %-Mask	0	3	1	29	30	30	30	30	30	30
Norm-LT3.33 %-LT3.33 %-Mask	0	0	0	0	0	0	0	0	0	0

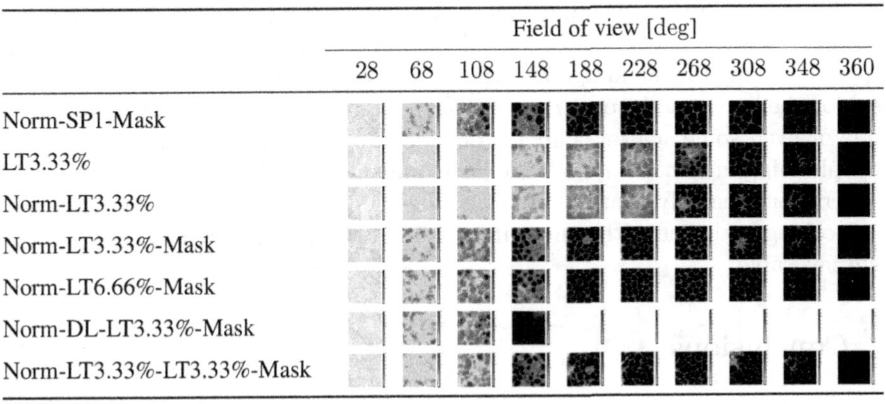

Fig. 4. Angle independence. Notations are the same as in Fig. 3. The highest activity (winning) unit was selected for each input at each position in each direction. We counted the number of wins at each position for each unit and selected the largest number. Results are color coded. Black (18): there is a single winner for all angles at that position. White (0): no response at that point from any neuron in any direction. Values between 1 and 17: the darker the color the larger the direction independence for the best winner at that position.

5   Discussion

Our goal was to find a discretization of hidden Cartesian factors (coordinates) provided that we already have one. The coordinate that we know must have a metric by definition. Such metric may show up in the temporal domain or, alternatively, it may manifest itself implicitly, via discretized spatial information, such as neighboring viewing ranges in our case. Temporal information has been exploited via hierarchical SFA (see, [29] and the cited references). Their goal was to closely model the rat's sensory system and found that indeed, a large viewing angle of 320° gave rise to direction independent place fields.

Here, we could reach about 108°, or so, and according to our results, further improvements can be expected for deeper networks, provided that sparsity is kept at some layers. Our algorithms can work if temporal information is *not* available. Deeper networks may be unavoidable, e.g., if the input structure we used can not be prewired and should be learned. We highlight that (i) high quality reconstruction is corrupted without the mask, but our method shows robustness for this case, too and (ii) if temporal information *is* available then our results may be improved further.

Cartesian factors are needed for FRL. Consider, e.g., that place fields uncover neighboring graph that can be used both for path planning. An integrated path planning and control architecture on place fields has been put forth some years ago [31]. For path planning, the exponent of the state space is lowered, being a critical issue for FRL.

Lifetime sparsity seems important in the development of the Cartesian factor, here, for the place fields. However, real time operation requires spatial sparsity, or possibly some thresholding, or even the linear mode, since responses are fairly local for the linear mode, e.g., $p = 6.66\%$ and for the 5 layer network. The linear mode or even some spatial sparsification uncovers neighbor relations useful for path planning and may support the development of metrics. In turn, two types of operations, namely, learning off-line when lifetime sparsity can be enforced, and working real time with some thresholding for learning neighboring relations seem favorable.

6   Conclusions

We have derived a complementary Cartesian component in discretized form to an existing one by means of deep learning. This novel type of compression supports factored reinforcement learning. Our experimental studies point towards two phase – off-line and a real-time – operation and also to the necessity of sparsification. The novel compression method may have relevance for Big Data and may support the understanding of intelligence, since compression is thought to be closely related to it.

Acknowledgments. This work was supported by the EIT Digital grant (Grant No. 16257). Helpful comments from Gábor Szirtes are gratefully acknowledged.

References

1. Becker, S.R., Candès, E.J., Grant, M.C.: Templates for convex cone problems with applications to sparse signal recovery. Math. Prog. Comp. **3**(3), 165–218 (2011)
2. Bergstra, J., Breuleux, O., Bastien, F., Lamblin, P., Pascanu, R., Desjardins, G., Turian, J., Warde-Farley, D., Bengio, Y.: Theano. In: Python Sci. Comp. vol. 4, p. 3. Austin, TX (2010)
3. Boutilier, C., Dearden, R., Goldszmidt, M.: Stochastic dynamic programming with factored representations. Artif. Intel. **121**(1), 49–107 (2000)

4. Culberson, J.C.: On the futility of blind search: an algorithmic view of no free lunch. Evol. Comp. **6**(2), 109–127 (1998)
5. Dahl, G.E., Sainath, T.N., Hinton, G.E.: Improving deep neural networks for LVCSR using rectified linear units and dropout. In: Acoustics, Speech and Signal Processing (ICASSP), pp. 8609–8613. IEEE (2013)
6. Dai, W., Milenkovic, O.: Subspace pursuit for compressive sensing signal reconstruction. Info. Theo. **55**(5), 2230–2249 (2009)
7. Daswani, M., Sunehag, P., Hutter, M.: Feature reinforcement learning: state of the art. In: Sequential decision-making with big data: AAAI 2014. Assoc. Adv. Artif. Intel. (2014)
8. Dowe, D.L., Hernández-Orallo, J., Das, P.K.: Compression and intelligence: social environments and communication. In: Schmidhuber, J., Thórisson, K.R., Looks, M. (eds.) AGI 2011. LNCS, vol. 6830, pp. 204–211. Springer, Heidelberg (2011)
9. Duchi, J., Hazan, E., Singer, Y.: Adaptive subgradient methods for online learning and stochastic optimization. J. Mach. Learn. Res. **12**, 2121–2159 (2011)
10. Erhan, D., Bengio, Y., Courville, A., Manzagol, P.A., Vincent, P., Bengio, S.: Why does unsupervised pre-training help deep learning? J. Mach. Learn. Res. **11**, 625–660 (2010)
11. Grant, M., Boyd, S.: CVX: Matlab software for disciplined convex programming, version 2.1., March 2014. http://cvxr.com/cvx
12. Hinton, G.E., Salakhutdinov, R.R.: Reducing the dimensionality of data with neural networks. Science **313**(5786), 504–507 (2006)
13. Hochreiter, S.: Untersuchungen zu dynamischen neuronalen netzen. Master's thesis, Institut für Informatik, Technische Universität, München (1991)
14. Hochreiter, S., Bengio, Y., Frasconi, P., Schmidhuber, J.: Gradient flow in recurrent nets: the difficulty of learning long-term dependencies (2001)
15. Hutter, M.: Feature reinforcement learning: Part I. unstructured MDPs. J. Artif. Gen. Intel. **1**, 3–24 (2009)
16. Hyvärinen, A., Karhunen, J., Oja, E.: Independent Component Analysis, vol. 46. Wiley, New York (2004)
17. Kearns, M., Koller, D.: Efficient reinforcement learning in factored MDPs. In: IJCAI, vol. 16, pp. 740–747 (1999)
18. Kingma, D., Ba, J.: Adam: a method for stochastic optimization. arXiv:1412.6980 (2014)
19. Lőrincz, A., Szirtes, G.: Here and now: how time segments may become events in the hippocampus. Neural Netw. **22**(5), 738–747 (2009)
20. Makhzani, A., Frey, B.: k-sparse autoencoders. arXiv:1312.5663 (2013)
21. Makhzani, A., Frey, B.J.: Winner-take-all autoencoders. In: Advances in Neural Information Processing Systems, pp. 2773–2781 (2015)
22. Nair, V., Hinton, G.E.: Rectified linear units improve restricted Boltzmann machines. In: Proceedings of the 27th International Conference on Machine Learning, pp. 807–814 (2010)
23. Ng, A.Y.: Feature selection, l1 vs. l2 regularization, and rotational invariance. In: Proceedings of the 21st International Conference on Machine Learning, p. 78. ACM (2004)
24. O'Keefe, J., Dostrovsky, J.: The hippocampus as a spatial map. preliminary evidence from unit activity in the freely-moving rat. Brain Res. **34**(1), 171–175 (1971)
25. O'Keefe, J., Nadel, L.: The Hippocampus as a Cognitive Map. Clarendon Press, Oxford (1978)

26. Rasmus, A., Berglund, M., Honkala, M., Valpola, H., Raiko, T.: Semi-supervised learning with ladder networks. In: Advances in Neural Information Processing Systems, pp. 3532–3540 (2015)
27. Salakhutdinov, R.: Learning deep generative models. Ann. Rev. Stat. Appl. **2**, 361–385 (2015)
28. Schmidhuber, J.: Driven by compression progress: a simple principle explains essential aspects of subjective beauty, novelty, surprise, interestingness, attention, curiosity, creativity, art, science, music, jokes. In: Pezzulo, G., Butz, M.V., Sigaud, O., Baldassarre, G. (eds.) Anticipatory Behavior in Adaptive Learning Systems. LNCS, vol. 5499, pp. 48–76. Springer, Heidelberg (2009)
29. Schönfeld, F., Wiskott, L.: Modeling place field activity with hierarchical slow feature analysis. Frontiers Comp. Neurosci. 9 (2015)
30. Sun, Y., Mao, H., Sang, Y., Yi, Z.: Explicit guiding auto-encoders for learning meaningful representation. Neural Comp. Appl., 1–8 (2015)
31. Szepesvári, C., Lőrincz, A.: An integrated architecture for motion-control and path-planning. J. Robot. Syst. **15**(1), 1–15 (1998)
32. Szita, I., Lőrincz, A.: Optimistic initialization and greediness lead to polynomial time learning in factored MDPs. In: Proceddings of the 26th International Conference on Machine Learning, pp. 1001–1008. ACM (2009)
33. Szita, I., Takács, B., Lőrincz, A.: ε-MDPs: Learning in varying environments. J. Mach. Learn. Res. **3**, 145–174 (2003)
34. Tenenbaum, J.B., Freeman, W.T.: Separating style and content with bilinear models. Neural Comp. **12**, 1247–1283 (2000)
35. Tibshirani, R.: Regression shrinkage and selection via the lasso. J. Royal Stat. Soc. Ser. B (Meth.) **58**, 267–288 (1996)
36. Tősér, Z., Lőrincz, A.: The cyber-physical system approach towards artificial general intelligence: the problem of verification. In: Bieger, J., Goertzel, B., Potapov, A. (eds.) AGI 2015. LNCS, vol. 9205, pp. 373–383. Springer, Heidelberg (2015)
37. Tropp, J.A., Gilbert, A.C.: Signal recovery from random measurements via orthogonal matching pursuit. Info. Theo. **53**(12), 4655–4666 (2007)
38. Vincent, P., Larochelle, H., Lajoie, I., Bengio, Y., Manzagol, P.A.: Stacked denoising autoencoders. J. Mach. Learn. Res. **11**, 3371–3408 (2010)
39. Zeiler, M.D.: Adadelta: an adaptive learning rate method. arXiv:1212.5701 (2012)

A Methodology for the Assessment of AI Consciousness

Harry H. Porter III[(✉)]

Portland State University, Portland, OR, USA
porter@pdx.edu

Abstract. The research and philosophical communities currently lack a clear way to quantify, measure, and characterize the degree of consciousness in a mind or AI entity. This paper addresses that gap by providing a numerical measure of consciousness. Implicit in our approach is a definition of consciousness itself. Underlying this is our assumption that consciousness is not a single unified characteristic but a constellation of features, mental abilities, and thought patterns. Although some people may experience their own consciousness as a unified whole, we assume that consciousness is a multi-dimensional set of attributes, each of which can be present to differing degrees in a given mind. These attributes can be measured and therefore the degree of consciousness can be quantified with a number, much as IQ attempts to quantify human intelligence.

Keywords: Consciousness · Self-awareness · Definition · Measurement · Assessment

1 Methodology

Any definition of consciousness today will be contentious. Consciousness is a subjective sensation and each thinking entity has a unique experience of consciousness which no one else can share. Nonetheless, a way to measure a thinking entity's level of consciousness—for example, on a numeric scale from 0 to 100—is needed. Obviously this task is problematic and impossible to do with precision or accuracy, but the exercise is enlightening.

Our goal is only to measure the degree of consciousness exhibited, without making any assumptions about its implementation. We say that if an agent exhibits the given set of externally observable behaviors listed below, then it is conscious by definition, and conversely, if it is conscious, then these behaviors will be present. Specific cognitive architectures, e.g., Global Workspace Theory [1–3], are candidates for evaluation using the methodology proposed here. We do not propose any testable theory of consciousness, only an approach to assessment and, by extension, a concrete definition thereof.

This assessment consists of a series of questions. Use this questionnaire to evaluate the degree of consciousness of a person, AI system, or any other thinking entity. Answer the questions and then compute the score.

There is no clear consensus on the definition of consciousness; this test reflects the author's personal definition. Other researchers with differing definitions of

B. Steunebrink et al. (Eds.): AGI 2016, LNAI 9782, pp. 305–313, 2016.
DOI: 10.1007/978-3-319-41649-6_31

consciousness may create their own evaluation methodologies, or weigh the questions here differently to reflect their definitions of consciousness.[1]

2   Instructions

Answer each question using the following scale:

0 – NONE
> Not present at all

1 – SOME
> Present, but at a level far below human levels

2 – ALMOST
> Substantially present, but still at a sub-human level

3 – HUMAN
> Present at a level typical of a normal human

4 – SUPER-HUMAN
> Present to a degree that exceeds human ability

After answering all questions, add together the points for each answer to give a total sum. Then multiply the sum by the number 0.741 to normalize and give the final score.[2]

Scores will lie on the following spectrum:

0	No consciousness present. The consciousness level of a rock.
100	The consciousness of a fully functioning human.
>100	A consciousness that exceeds human levels.
133	The maximum possible score.

The questions are listed next.

3   Ability to Reason and Use Logic

- Is **THE-TEST-SUBJECT** able to use logic in order to perform reasoning tasks? (The term "logic" is to be interpreted loosely to include an ability to make deductions.)
- Does **THE-TEST-SUBJECT** have short-term (working) memory; the ability to acquire/deduce and then remember new facts/data/etc. in such a way that they can be used in ongoing reasoning tasks? (For example, able to answer: "My name is Tom. I live in Portland. What is my name?")

---

[1] To make this (subjective) definition a clearer and more discrete target for future discussions of the nature of consciousness, let us name the present methodology and implied definition of consciousness "Porter's Definition and Assessment of AI Consciousness" so as to distinguish it from other definitions.

[2] This multiplier was chosen so that an answer of "3 – HUMAN" for all 45 questions will yield a score of 100. If questions are added or deleted, the multiplier will need to be adjusted accordingly.

- Does *THE-TEST-SUBJECT* have long-term memory; the ability to acquire/deduce and then remember new facts/data/information in such a way that it can be used in reasoning tasks that occur in the future (after many unrelated reasoning tasks are performed)? (For example: "Yesterday I told you my birth date; how old am I?")
- Can *THE-TEST-SUBJECT* deal with partial/incomplete/inaccurate information?
- Can *THE-TEST-SUBJECT* make decisions, such as whether to take action "X" or "Y", based on some train of reasoning?

4 Situational Awareness

- Can *THE-TEST-SUBJECT* reason about dates/times/intervals?
- Can *THE-TEST-SUBJECT* answer questions about the current date?
- Can *THE-TEST-SUBJECT* reason about size/space/location?
- Can *THE-TEST-SUBJECT* answer questions about *THE-TEST-SUBJECT'S* current location and the location of the questioner? (For an electronic "cyber" entity whose location is not well-defined, then at least it can give reasonable answers to questions about its location.)

5 Natural Language Ability

- Can *THE-TEST-SUBJECT* communicate using natural language?

6 Goals, Opinions, and Emotions

- Does *THE-TEST-SUBJECT* have goals/motivations/needs?
- Does *THE-TEST-SUBJECT* take steps to achieve his/her/its goals/motivations/needs?
- Does *THE-TEST-SUBJECT* have opinions/likes/dislikes?
- Does *THE-TEST-SUBJECT* have emotions/feelings/moods?
- Do *THE-TEST-SUBJECT'S* emotions/feelings/moods change appropriately over time in response to events?

7 Experiencing Existence

- Does *THE-TEST-SUBJECT* have a memory of the recent conversational history? (For example: "Why did you say that? – Because you just told me X, which implies it.")
- Can *THE-TEST-SUBJECT* have experiences? (The definition of "experiences" is to be taken loosely. A human can stub his/her toe; the ability to have this sort of

physical bodily experience is not required. For example, an act of communication can itself be an experience, although it involves only words and nothing physical.)

- Does **THE-TEST-SUBJECT** have a memory of past experiences and events? (These experiences may have happened to **THE-TEST-SUBJECT**, but this is not necessary.)
- Is some emotional coloring attached to memories? (For example, can **THE-TEST-SUBJECT** distinguish between good and bad memories?)

8 Growth and Learning

- Can **THE-TEST-SUBJECT** learn new material?
- Can **THE-TEST-SUBJECT** change in ways deeper than simply acquiring more data?
- Does **THE-TEST-SUBJECT** have curiosity about the world and an impulse to learn and acquire information/knowledge/wisdom?

9 Self Knowledge

- Does **THE-TEST-SUBJECT** have knowledge about himself/herself/itself? Can **THE-TEST-SUBJECT** provide a coherent description of who/what he/she/it is?
- Does **THE-TEST-SUBJECT** have some mental model of **THE-TEST-SUB-JECT'S** own thought processes?
- Can **THE-TEST-SUBJECT** sense or perceive his/her/its current thought processes?
- Does **THE-TEST-SUBJECT** have some mental model of his/her/its own goals/motivations/needs?
- Can **THE-TEST-SUBJECT** articulate his/her/its current goals/motivations/needs?
- Does **THE-TEST-SUBJECT** have some mental model of his/her/its own emotions/feelings/moods?
- Can **THE-TEST-SUBJECT** identify his/her/its current emotions/feelings/moods?

10 Self Control

- Can **THE-TEST-SUBJECT** control his/her/its own thought processes? (For example, can **THE-TEST-SUBJECT** follow a novel algorithm to perform some reasoning task? Can **THE-TEST-SUBJECT** be told how to think more effectively and then alter his/her/its thought processes as a result of these instructions?)
- Can **THE-TEST-SUBJECT** detect when certain thought processes are not effective and alter his/her/its thought processes in an attempt to make them more effective?
- Can **THE-TEST-SUBJECT** articulate the algorithms that **THE-TEST-SUBJECT** uses to performs certain novel tasks? (For example, able to "Describe how you would sort a sequence of numbers?")

11   Knowledge About Humans

- Does *THE-TEST-SUBJECT* have knowledge about humans? We mean "the human species" as opposed to knowledge about particular humans. (In the future or to evaluate an alien life form, we might need to substitute "the dominate intelligent species" for "humans".)
- Does *THE-TEST-SUBJECT* have knowledge about particular humans as they differ from other humans? (Perhaps in the future, we'll substitute the phrase "other thinking entities" for "humans" in these questions.)
- Does *THE-TEST-SUBJECT* have the ability to learn about other people and remember details about specific individuals?
- Does *THE-TEST-SUBJECT* have an understanding of common mental illnesses, such as depression, mania, phobia?

12   Knowledge About the Current Conversationalist

- Does *THE-TEST-SUBJECT* know about the current thought processes of the person *THE-TEST-SUBJECT* is communicating with? (For example, this would include knowing the person knows "X" because they know both "Y" and "Y implies X" and they would be likely to infer "X".)
- Does *THE-TEST-SUBJECT* have a model of the other person's thought processes, as they may differ from other humans? (For example, the knowledge that Tom is good with facts, Robert is ruled by his emotions, and Matthew is driven by his greed.)
- Does *THE-TEST-SUBJECT* know about the person's current mood/feelings/emotional state?
- Can *THE-TEST-SUBJECT* make reasonable inferences about how the person's current mood/feelings/emotional state affects the person's current thoughts and actions?
- Does *THE-TEST-SUBJECT* know about the person's current motivations/goals/needs and how this influences the person's current thoughts and actions?
- Can *THE-TEST-SUBJECT* make judgments about the other person's level of intelligence?

13   Curiosity and Imitation

- Does *THE-TEST-SUBJECT* have curiosity about the current conversationalist's thoughts/thought processes/knowledge?
- Does *THE-TEST-SUBJECT* have curiosity about the current conversationalist's mood/emotions/goals/motivations?
- Does *THE-TEST-SUBJECT* have a desire/ability to imitate the thought processes of others? (Even if this imitation is only temporary and only used to understand the thought processes.)

14   Example: Dog Consciousness

I used this assessment to evaluate the consciousness of dogs. On many of the questions I supplied the answer as a range (such as 0-2) rather than a single number, because I do not know the exact value and can only supply my best guess.

According to my assessment using this methodology, **dogs score 51-67** on this metric of consciousness.

15   Example: The Cyc Inference System

To quote Wikipedia, "Cyc is an artificial intelligence project that attempts to assemble a comprehensive ontology and knowledge base of everyday common sense knowledge, with the goal of enabling AI applications to perform human-like reasoning."

I used this assessment to evaluate the consciousness of this AI system. As before, I supplied many answers in the form of ranges, due to my limited knowledge about the system.

According to my assessment using this methodology, **Cyc scores 36-54** on this metric of consciousness, clearly below dogs, but well above rocks.

16   Comments and Criticisms of This Assessment

We can evaluate this assessment by asking which attributes a personal digital assistant (such as "Siri" on the iPad/iPhone) would need to possess in order for you to feel she was conscious. We suggest that an AI entity scoring 100 or more on the assessment described here would be judged by a reasonable person to be conscious, at least to a nontrivial degree.[3]

The well-known Turing Test [4] is substantially different from this test since the Turing Test is meant to determine how well a machine can imitate a human. Turing Test judges are free to ask questions that are peculiar to human experience and the human way of thinking. In other words, the Turing Test checks for human-like thought. Any intelligent entity that can pass the Turing Test will, by definition, be able to convince the judges that it can think just like a human and would therefore be able to score 100 on our test. On the other hand, our test only asks how well a thinking entity can perform the various tasks associated with consciousness, not the larger question of whether the entity can mimic or imitate the human way of thinking to the point of being indistinguishable from a human mind.

There is also a difference in methodology. Turing requires his "Imitation Game" to be repeated a number of times, and the question is whether the machine contestant is

---

[3] Perhaps being able to *form a friendship* with a thinking entity is a useful indicator of whether that entity is conscious. We suggest that with any AI entity able to score high on this assessment, it would be possible to form a reasonably recognizable friendship. For example, if the features listed here could be added to Siri, then there is no question that Siri would appear to be more consciousness than she does now.

statistically indistinguishable from the human contestant, winning 50% of the time. Performing the Turing Test properly requires a competent judge who has proven skill in the art of distinguishing between machines and humans. The Turing Test also requires you to perform a number of rounds of the imitation game sufficient to extract reliable statistics. Our test is much less expensive to perform: You just run through the questions and answer them to the best of your ability. This assessment is a subjective test of a subjective quality.

The Turing Test also suffers from a serious shortcoming. Turing designed his test as a pass-fail test. In some cases, it might be possible for a machine to be reliably differentiated from a human with a single simple question. (For example, perhaps the machine doesn't know how many fingers a typical human has.) Any unusual gap in the machine's knowledge—no matter how irrelevant—might allow the judge to distinguish between human and machine with 100% accuracy, even though the machine is, in all other ways, capable of imitating human thought. When a machine fails the Turing Test, it gives us no useful information.

One difficulty with our test is that it may be difficult or impossible to answer some of the questions. For example consider evaluating the consciousness level of a dog. The question "Can he/she/it sense or perceive his/her/its current thought processes?" is almost impossible to answer. For these questions, you must provide an educated guess. Omitting questions will alter the test itself, whereas inaccurate answers merely change the accuracy of the test. Using standard statistical methods, you can express the final score with error probabilities, if you wish.

These questions are probably skewed to favor human-like consciousness, although we have tried to make them as neutral (and fair to the AI entities of the future) as possible.

These questions weigh certain features differently than some people might prefer. For example, there is only one question about natural language ability, there are several questions about emotions and motivations, and there are no questions about body or the ability to visualize shapes.[4]

Many aspects of the human experience are ignored. There are no questions about whether the thinking entity can experience hunger, pain, pleasure, or the joy of hearing beautiful music. There is nothing about "love", which may be an emotion particular to sexual species that raise their own offspring via direct personal contact. Perhaps some of these experiences are important in your definition of consciousness.

There are no questions about experiencing an "internal voice" or "hearing your own thoughts". While this seems to be an important part of my subjective experience of consciousness, it is difficult to know how others experience it. Additionally, it is hard to ask questions to evaluate another person's experience of an internal voice. Also it is unclear whether hearing an internal voice is required for consciousness. Nevertheless, I considered adding the question, "Does he/she/it report hearing an internal voice at times?".

---

[4] It is for this reason that we are presenting our implicit definition of consciousness as one possible *standard definition* among many, rather than suggesting it is more valid or correct than competing definitions of consciousness.

There are no questions about sight and the ability to see. It seems likely that a person totally blind from birth experiences consciousness differently than most humans, but I question whether they are any less conscious because of their visual impairment.

There are no questions about mental visualization, although most humans can mentally envision shapes and can report on this ability. Indeed, the ability to "see" and manipulate objects entirely within the mind is so distinct and widespread that some people may argue that it is a requirement for consciousness.

There are no questions about body or bodily experiences. Certainly all humans have bodies and a large part of the brain is devoted to dealing with them, but it is possible and reasonable to envision a completely disembodied consciousness.

There are no questions about sensors and actuators. A human body can be viewed as a collections of senses and abilities to move and otherwise take action. Many would insist that having some sort of physical presence (such as a robotic body with sensors and actuators) is required for consciousness, but this questionnaire takes the position that no physical embodiment is required.

There are no questions about the survival instinct or the desire to avoid death. This is a core feature of the experience of being human, but so is the instinctive impulse to breathe. Both seem unrelated to consciousness itself, and merely artifacts of the evolution of humans.

This questionnaire does not attempt to evaluate the "moral goodness" of a thinking entity. It attempts to rate the consciousness of an evil psychopath in the same way as a virtuous nun, ignoring all questions about whether one consciousness should be preferred over another.

As the future unfolds, society will need to grapple with questions about which conscious entities are acceptable and which entities must be forbidden and/or terminated, but this discussion is beyond this assessment. Before this conversation can begin, we need to have a better understanding of consciousness itself, and it is hoped that this informal assessment will help stimulate the debate.

17 Related Research

The topic of consciousness continues to fascinate philosophers, AI researchers, neuroscientists, and the general public and much has been written and said about the nature, definition, and mechanisms of consciousness. Approaches to the subject range from philosophical (e.g., Daniel Dennett, David Chalmers, John Searle), to neurological (e.g., Antonio Damasio, Oliver Sacks), to more creative theories (Roger Penrose). Beyond the scientific approach, there is an abundance of material on what might be termed "new-age" or "cosmic" consciousness—approaches to becoming one with the universal consciousness and/or achieving a higher level of personal consciousness, moving in the direction of enlightenment. When trying to define, understand, and explain human consciousness, we are clearly in an exciting phase of intellectual advancement.

In terms of evaluating the degree of consciousness, not much work has been done. The "Lovelace 2.0 Test of Artificial Creativity and Intelligence" [5] requires a human judge who, interacting directly with an AI entity, asks the AI entity to produce a poem, drawing, story, etc. The judge then evaluates the creative work of the AI. This approach seems quite reasonable for testing the ability of an AI entity to think creatively in the manner of a human. Consciousness seems to be related to creativity, but creativity and consciousness are clearly different. In the Winograd Schema Challenge [6], the AI entity is presented with a series of short questions, each with a multiple choice answer which cleverly evaluates whether the sentence was understood. The WSC is an excellent test of natural common sense intelligence, but common sense intelligence is not consciousness. The WSC has the advantage of being objective and not requiring a human judge.

To many people, consciousness seems irreducible, nonprogrammable, and perhaps even magical or beyond the reach of science. While there are some eloquent arguments in favor of these opinions, it now appears that a simple, unified explanation is elusive and consciousness is turning out to be nothing more than a motley collection of reasoning skills, mental abilities, and characteristics of neural processing that, in the case of humans, has evolved in no different a way than other aspects of the brain. Consciousness is just like other thinking — except that it is reflective and involves the concept of self. This paper is an attempt to enumerate and elucidate the features that come together to form the colloquial notion of consciousness, with the understanding that this is only one subjective opinion on the nature of subjectiveness itself.

References

1. Baars, B.J.: In the theatre of consciousness. Global Workspace Theory, a rigorous scientific theory of consciousness. J. Conscious. Stud. **4**(4), 292–309 (1997)
2. Baars, B.J.: The Conscious access hypothesis: origins and recent evidence. TRENDS Cogn. Sci. **6**(1), 47–52 (2002)
3. Baars, B.J.: The global brainweb: an update on global workspace theory. Sci. Conscious. Rev. **4**, 292–309 (2003)
4. Turing, A.M.: Computing machinery and intelligence. Mind **49**, 433–460 (1950)
5. Riedl, M.O.: The Lovelace 2.0 Test of Artificial Creativity and Intelligence (2014). http://arXiv.com:1410.6142v3[cs.AI]
6. Levesque, H.J., Davis, E., Morgenstern, L.: The winograd schema challenge. In: Proceedings of the Thirteenth International Conference on Principles of Knowledge Representation. AAAI Press (2012)

Toward Human-Level Massively-Parallel Neural Networks with Hodgkin-Huxley Neurons

Lyle N. Long[✉]

The Pennsylvania State University, University Park, PA, USA
lnl@psu.edu

Abstract. This paper describes neural network algorithms and software that scale up to massively parallel computers. The neuron model used is the best available at this time, the Hodgkin-Huxley equations. Most massively parallel simulations use very simplified neuron models, which cannot accurately simulate biological neurons and the wide variety of neuron types. Using C++ and MPI we can scale these networks to human-level sizes. Computers such as the Chinese TianHe computer are capable of human level neural networks.

Keywords: Neural networks · Neurons · Parallel · Hodgkin-Huxley · MPI

1 Introduction

Artificial intelligence began in roughly 1956 at a conference at Dartmouth University. The participants, and many researchers after them, were clearly overly optimistic. As with many new technologies, the technology was oversold for decades.

Computer processing power, however, has been doubling every two years thanks to Moore's law. In the 1950's one of the main computers was the IBM 701, which could do 16,000 adds/subtracts per second, or 2,000 multiples/divides per second. This is roughly a trillion times smaller than the human brain. As shown in Fig. 1, it is more on par with the C. Elegan worm, which is about 1 mm long and has 302 neurons and 6393 synapses [1].

Over a wide range of biological creatures, it is estimated [2, 3] that the number of synapses in biological systems can be modeled via:

$$Synapses = 3.7 \, Neurons^{1.32} \tag{1}$$

A cockroach has about a million neurons, and using the above formula has about 300 million synapses. A rough estimate is that each synapse can store 1–8 bits and can perform roughly 1–2 operations per second. Thus from these crude estimates the IBM 701 had performance about 10,000 times worse than a cockroach neural system. It is amazing that the term "artificial intelligence" (AI) was coined during this era of horribly low-powered computers. Not until about 1975 did we have a computer on the order of a cockroach, the Cray 1, which had a speed of roughly 160 megaflops. It is not surprising that AI by this time was not taken seriously except in science fiction.

© Springer International Publishing Switzerland 2016
B. Steunebrink et al. (Eds.): AGI 2016, LNAI 9782, pp. 314–323, 2016.
DOI: 10.1007/978-3-319-41649-6_32

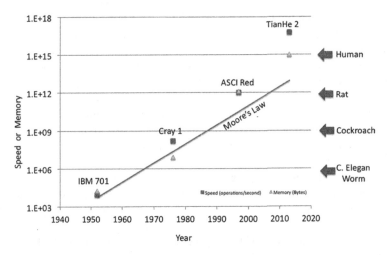

Fig. 1. Computers and biological systems speed and memory.

About 20 years later there was the ASCI Red computer with 9298 processors with a terabyte of memory and a speed of 1 teraflop. If this could have been harnessed for modeling a brain, it would have been on the order of a rat, which has about 200 million neurons.

The five largest parallel computers that exist today (which aren't classified) are shown in Table 1 [4]. The TianHe-2 computer in China has more than 3 million processor cores, 1 petabyte of memory, and a peak speed of 55 petaflops.

Table 1. Top five computers in the world, (www.top500.org, Nov. 2015).

Rank	Name	Processor Cores	Peak Speed (PetaFlops) (10^{15})	Memory (PetaBytes) (10^{15})	Power Required (MWatts)
1	TianHe-2 (China)	3,120,000	55	1.0	17.8
2	Titan (USA-DOE)	560,640	27	0.7	8.2
3	Sequoia (USA-DOE)	1,572,864	20	1.6	7.9
4	K Computer (Japan)	705,024	11	1.4	12.7
5	Mira (USA-DOE)	786,432	10	0.8	3.9

Note that the data in Fig. 1 do not follow Moore's law. The increasing numbers of processors makes the trend much faster than Moore's law. Instead of doubling every two years, supercomputer speed doubles about every 1.4 years. Over a 60 year period that leads to about 10,000 times more speed than Moore's law would predict.

The human brain has roughly 10^{11} neurons and 10^{15} synapses. Some estimate that the brain is capable of roughly 10^{14}–10^{15} operations per second, with memory storage of roughly 10^{14}–10^{15} bytes. Thus the largest computers in the world are now on the same order of magnitude as the human brain in terms of speed and memory. We are very far, however, from replicating the efficiency of the human brain. It only requires about 20 watts and about 1200 cm^3, which is about a million times lower than the supercomputers.

Finally, 60 years after the first AI conference we have computers on the order of the performance of the human brain, even if they are a million times less efficient (in terms of power and space).

The main issues now are algorithms and network structure. We have excellent models of neurons, such as the Hodgkin-Huxley model, but we do not know how the human neurons are wired together, or how carefully we need to match brain architecture.

This paper is an attempt at using efficient and powerful algorithms, together with powerful supercomputers to simulae as many neurons and synapses as possible, and in a scalable manner. The goal is not to simulate the brain, but to develop an engineering system.

There are several computational neuroscience models of neural networks [5–8], but most of these aim for accurate neuroscience simulations. In the work presented here the goal is to perform engineering simulations of massive neural networks for possible applications to complex engineering systems such as cognitive robotics [9]. Riemann et al. [10] used 12,000 neurons and 15 million synapses and used 4096 cpus in a Blue Gene P computer. Four seconds of real time took 3 h of CPU time.

2   Hodgkin-Huxley Neurons

There are numerous models for neurons, as described in [2]. Most of these are very simplified and approximate formulae. As we have shown in previous papers [2, 3], this is a mistaken approach for two reasons:

1. With modern algorithms and computers more accurate models cost almost no more computer time
2. There are typically many orders of magnitude more synapses than neurons in large networks, as shown by Eq. (1).

Thus accurate neuron models can be used and it is of paramount importance to store and compute the synapse operations extremely efficiently.

Also, it should be mentioned that the neural networks being discussed here are time-dependent spiking (or pulsed) networks. These are quite different than typical rate-based artificial neural networks often used in engineering applications.

In 1952 Hodgkin and Huxley [11] proposed a mathematical model for a neuron. It was used to account for the electric current flow through the surface membrane of a squid giant axon. The Hodgkin-Huxley model is used to explain the different spiking phenomena of a neuron after it is exposed to various current stimulations. In their paper, the effects of different ionic channels to the capacity and resistance of the membrane were incorporated into the model; and empirical curve-fittings were used to generate the component functions for the equations. The Hodgkin-Huxley (HH) model is one of the most biological plausible models in computational neuroscience, and they won a Nobel prize for their research. Their model is a complicated nonlinear system of coupled ordinary differential equations (ODE) consisting of four equations describing the membrane potential, activation and inactivation of different ionic gating variables respectively.

For many years now researchers have stated that the Hodgkin-Huxley model was far too expensive to use due to its complexity. This is simply not the case, as we showed in [2]. In particular models such as Izhikevich's [12] are not recommended. As shown in [2], it is not as efficient as the author states, nor can it model many types of neurons. The H-H model does not require as much work as people think, and it *can* model many types of neurons. The HH equations are the following differential equations:

$$\frac{du}{dt} = E - Gu \qquad \frac{dm}{dt} = \alpha_m - (\alpha_m + \beta_m)m$$

$$\frac{dn}{dt} = \alpha_n - (\alpha_n + \beta_n)n \qquad \frac{dh}{dt} = \alpha_h - (\alpha_h + \alpha\beta_h)h$$

where

$$G = g_{Na}m^3h + g_K n^4 + g_L \qquad E = g_{Na}m^3h E_{Na} + g_K n^4 E_K + g_L E_L + I$$

and where the coefficients and constants are defined as:

$$\alpha_n(u) = \frac{0.1 - 0.01u}{\exp(1 - 0.1u) - 1} \qquad \beta_n(u) = 0.125 \exp(-\frac{u}{80})$$

$$\alpha_m(u) = \frac{2.5 - 0.1u}{\exp(2.5 - 0.1u) - 1} \qquad \beta_m(u) = 4\exp(-\frac{u}{80}) \qquad g_{Na} = 120ms/cm^2, \, E_{Na} = 115mV$$

$$g_K = 36ms/cm^2, \quad E_K = -12mV$$

$$\alpha_h(u) = 0.07 \exp(\frac{u}{20}) \qquad \beta_h(u) = \frac{1}{\exp(3 - 0.1u) + 1} \qquad g_L = 0.3ms/cm^2, E_L = 10.6mV$$

Here $u(t)$ is the neuron membrane voltage, parameters g_{Na}, g_K, and g_L are used to model the channel conductances. The additional variables h, m, and n control the opening of the channels. The parameters E_{Na}, E_K, and E_L are the reversal potentials. The term I is the input current (from other neurons or some external source), and is typically a function of time.

The HH equations can be solved very efficiently using the exponential Euler method. For an equation of the form

$$\frac{df}{dt} = A - Bf$$

(note that all four ODE's in the HH equations are of this form) the exponential Euler method is implemented as

$$f^{n+1} = \left(f^n - \frac{A^n}{B^n}\right)e^{-B^n \Delta t} + \frac{A^n}{B^n}$$

For A and B constant, this is an exact formula. For our purposes we will assume the coefficients change very slowly and can be assumed constant over one time step. Iterations could also be easily performed if necessary, but they are usually not required. Using look-up tables for the coefficients is very effective, since the exponentials are expensive to compute.

3   Parallel Software Implementation

The software used in these simulations was written in C++ and uses the Message Passing Interface [13]. C++ was used due to its wide acceptance, high performance, efficient memory usage, and powerful modern syntax. MPI was used since it is essentially the only possible approach for massively parallel computers.

One of the difficult aspects of using distributed memory computers, especially when there might be millions of processors, is how to distribute the problem across the processors. This is especially difficult for neural networks, since we have to simulate neurons and synapses and they are connected in very complicated networks.

In the approach used here, the neurons are evenly distributed across the processors using MPI in a single program multiple data (SPMD) approach. Each neuron also has a list of synapses that it is connected to, and each synapse has information on its post-synaptic neuron and its processor number. For the H-H model each neuron stores 19 floats, 4 integers, and a dynamic list of synapses. So the memory used per neuron is (23 + num_synapses) *4 bytes.

While biologically a synapse might store roughly a byte of data, in the computer program each synapse here requires 73 bits (or roughly 9 bytes). The weights are stored as char variables (1 byte), an integer is used to store the post-synaptic neuron number (4 bytes), an integer is used to store the processor on which the post-synaptic neuron exists (4 bytes), and 1 bit is used to store whether it is an input neuron or not. Using a 32-bit integer for the neuron addresses limits the number of neurons per MPI process to 2^{32} (about 4 billion, if they are unsigned ints), which is quite adequate. And using an integer to store processor number also means one could use roughly 4 billion processors. So any of the top five computers in the list above could store roughly as many of these synapses as the human brain (10^{14}–10^{15}). The amount of memory required by the synapses could be reduced by using short ints, but they can have maximum values of only 65,536.

Figure 2 shows the number of processors required for a wide range of neurons (and using Eq. 1 for number of synapses). Figure 3 shows how much memory is required per number of neurons. This shows on a computer such as the TianHe we have enough processors and memory to model human-level neural networks. A computer ten times larger than the TianHe could model a neural network ten times larger than a human brain, and possibly lead to superintelligence [14].

The other major issue is computer time requirements. As shown in [2] the algorithm for the H-H neurons requires about 69 operations per time step using the exponential Euler method combined with lookup tables for the coefficients. This is only about a factor of two slower than the Izhikevich method, which cannot capture the physics properly or model a wide range of neuron types. A typical time step size for reasonable solutions is about 0.1 ms. Each processor core of the TianHe-2 computer has a peak speed of about 10 billion operations per second. So for a billion neurons each time step

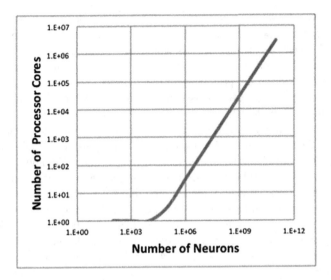

Fig. 2. Processors required for a range of neurons.

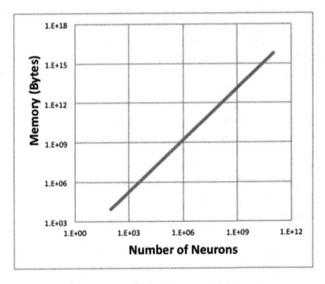

Fig. 3. Memory required for a range of neurons.

would require about 7 s using just one processor (but the machine has 3 million). Also, one second of real time requires roughly 690,000 operations, but we are not interested in real-time neural computing.

Also, we need to consider the *communication* cost of the synapses. When a neuron fires, a pulse is sent to the connecting neurons, and this pulse is weighted by the value of the synapse weight. This can be accomplished with an add operation and process per synapse. So if we have a billion neurons and 1000 synapses per neuron, we'd have 10^{12} synapses. This means we'd have to do 10^{12} operations per time step. Using one processor of the TianHe-2 computer, this would take roughly 100 s, which is significantly more than the work required to march the neuron forward in time. As stated earlier, the synapses drive the problem, not the neurons.

The third major issue in using massively parallel computers is the inter-processor communication. Computers such as those shown in Table 1 are hybrid distributed-shared memory machines. Each node of the machine is a shared memory computer, and they are connected via a high-speed network to the other nodes. The networks are often Infiniband networks, or something similar. Communication speeds are often on the order of 100 gigabits/second, with minimum latencies on the order of 1–5 microseconds. A microsecond might sound like a very short period of time, but a 10 gigaflop processor could perform 10,000 operations during a microsecond. So if the processor is sitting idle waiting for data, the performance can be seriously affected. And there is no guarantee you will experience the minimum latency or the maximum bandwidth in practice. And neural networks can require an enormous amount of communication, especially if not done properly.

For the example discussed earlier, with a billion neurons and a trillion synapses, every neuron is connected to 1000 other neurons. If every synapse sends its weight every time step, this would require 10^{12} bytes transmitted each time step. Whether this is feasible depends on the bi-section bandwidth of the supercomputer. Another way to look at this is that the TianHe has 16,000 nodes with 88 Gbytes/node. If each node had 50 billion synapses and had to transmit them each time step, it might take roughly an hour per time step (assuming 100 Mb/sec. connection). So synapse communications need to be handled very carefully to maintain performance.

Fortunately the above scenario is not required. While in a traditional artificial neural network (ANN) using backpropagation, all the synapse weights are involved each sweep of the network, this is not true in spiking neural networks. In spiking neural networks, the synapse weight only needs to be communicated when the pre-synaptic neuron fires. And in biological systems typically only a few percent of the neurons are active at a time. And in addition, they typically only spike (at most) roughly every 20 time steps. So in effect we might only need to transmit about one in a thousand synapse weight data per step, if programmed properly. So instead of an hour, it might take seconds.

In the code developed here, when a neuron fires, it sends this information to every one of the post-synaptic neurons it is connected to. Some of these neurons might be on other processors, while some might be on the local processor. MPI-3 has many new features, one of which is one-sided communication. Instead of one processor executing a SEND command, and another processor execute a RECEIVE command, a processor can simply do an MPI_PUT and send the signal from one neuron to another, much as a biological neuron does.

The PUT and GET functions are very useful, but an even more appropriate function for sending neural signals is the MPI_ACCUMULATE function. This allows one to put a variable on another processor and have it add the value to the current value on that processor. This is exactly what we need here. For the MPI_PUT and

MPI_ACCUMULATE functions it is also necessary to set up "windows," which set up the memory block that is to be shared.

The code here uses a completely unstructured or pointer-based approach. There is a Neuron class, a Synapse class, and a Network class. Each Neuron object has a dynamic list of Synapses, and each of these Synapses connects to one other Neuron. So a Synapse has to store two integers and a byte (the weight). Thus any type of connectivity can be modeled, including, all-to-all networks, convolution networks, recursive networks, or deep networks.

The unstructured or pointer-based approach to network connectivity was chosen for another reason as well. It makes the network very easy to modify (i.e. to add/remove neurons and synapses), as discussed in [15]. One of the biggest issues with neural networks is the "catastrophic forgetting" problem [16]. The current code can add neurons and synapses to handle new situations without affecting the previously trained synapses.

4   CPU Time Estimates

This computer code has been run on computers at Xsede.org in order to measure CPU time and memory requirements. This is a complicated task since the CPU time depends on the number of neurons, the number of synapses, the firing rates of the neurons, how many neurons are typically firing, the processor speeds, and the inter-processor communication speeds.

Since Eq. (1) gives an estimate of the number of synapses in biological systems given the number of neurons, it is used to estimate number of synapses in the simulations. This was shown in Fig. 1.

We also know that the neurons require 69 floating point operations per time step, and each time step represents 0.1 ms of real time. So one second of real time requires 10,000 steps or 690,000 floating point operations. We also assume a 50 Hz neuron firing rate and at any given time only about 5 % of the neurons are firing, which is representative of some biological systems.

Table 2 shows preliminary code performance numbers for up to 2,048 processors. The performance will vary depending on the network connectivity.

Table 2. Preliminary code performance for 300 time steps on Gordon computer at xsede.org.

No. Processor Cores	Total No. Neurons	Total No. Synapses	CPU Time (sec.)	Memory Required (Bytes)
1	$3 * 10^3$	$2 * 10^6$	0.36	$6 * 10^9$
32	$1 * 10^5$	$6 * 10^7$	0.20	$2 * 10^8$
256	$8 * 10^5$	$5 * 10^8$	0.26	$1 * 10^{12}$
2048	$6 * 10^6$	$4 * 10^9$	0.26	$12 * 10^{12}$

5   Conclusions

Human brain scale simulations are now feasible on massively parallel supercomputers. With careful attention to efficient event-driven programming, table lookups, and memory minimization these simulations can be performed.

The next phase of this research will be incorporating learning. We have implemented back propagation on massively parallel computers in the past [17], and could use that for these networks also. We have also implemented spike time dependent plasticity (STDP) in the past for spiking neural networks [18–20], there are still some issues related to supervised learning using that approach.

References

1. http://www.wormatlas.org/
2. Skocik, M.J., Long, L.N.: On the capabilities and computational costs of neuron models. IEEE Trans. Neural Netw. Learn. 25(8), 1474–1483 (2014)
3. Long, L.N.: Efficient neural network simulations using the Hodgkin-Huxley equations. In: Conference on 60 Years of Hodgkin and Huxley, Trinity College, Cambridge, 12–13 July 2012
4. www.top500.org
5. Markram, H., et al.: Reconstruction and simulation of neocortical microcircuitry. Cell 163(2), 456–492 (2015)
6. www.nest-initiative.org
7. https://www.neuron.yale.edu/
8. Bower, J.M., David, B.: The Book of GENESIS: Exploring Realistic Neural Models with the GEneral NEural SImulation System. Springer, Heidelberg (2012)
9. Reimann, M.W., Anastassiou, C.A., Perin, R., Hill, S.L., Markram, H., Koch, C.: Biophysically detailed model of neocortical local field potentials predicts the critical role of active membrane currents. Neuron 79, 375–390 (2013)
10. Kelley, T.D., Avery, E., Long, L.N., Dimperio, E.: A hybrid symbolic and sub-symbolic intelligent system for mobile robots. In: InfoTech@Aerospace Conference, Seattle, WA, AIAA, Reston, VA, AIAA Paper 2009–1976 (2009)
11. Hodgkin, A.L., Huxley, A.F.: A quantitative description of ion currents and its applications to conduction and excitation in nerve membranes. J. Physiol. 117, 500–544 (1952)
12. Izhikevich, E.M.: Which model to use for cortical spiking neurons? IEEE Trans. Neural Netw. 15(5), 1063–1070 (2004)
13. http://www.mpi-forum.org/docs/mpi-3.0/mpi30-report.pdf
14. Bostrom, N.: SuperIntelligence: Paths, Dangers, Strategies, Oxford Press, Oxford, England (2014)
15. Long, L.N., Gupta, A., Fang, G.: A computational approach to neurogenesis and synaptogenesis using biologically plausible models with learning. In: Frontiers in Systems Neuroscience, Conference Abstract: Computational and Systems Neuroscience (COSYNE) Meeting, Salt Lake City, Utah, Feb. 25–28 2010
16. French, R.M.: Catastrophic forgetting in connectionist networks. Trends Cogn. Sci. 3(4), 128–135 (1999)
17. Long, L.N., Gupta, A.: Scalable massively parallel artifical neural networks. J. Aerosp. Comput. Inf. Commun. (JACIC), 5(1), 3–15 (2008)

18. Gupta, A., Long, L.N.: Hebbian learning with winner take all for spiking neural networks. In: IEEE International Joint Conference on Neural Networks (IJCNN), Atlanta, Georgia, June 14–19 (2009)
19. Long, L.N.: An adaptive spiking neural network with hebbian learning. In: Presented at the IEEE Workshop on Evolving and Adaptive Intelligent Systems, Symposium Series on Computational Intelligence, Paris, France, April 11–15 (2011)
20. Long, L.N.: Scalable biologically inspired neural networks with spike time based learning. In: Invited Paper, IEEE Symposium on Learning and Adaptive Behavior in Robotic Systems, Edinburgh, Scotland, Aug. 6–8 2008

Modeling Neuromodulation as a Framework to Integrate Uncertainty in General Cognitive Architectures

Frédéric Alexandre[1,2,3(✉)] and Maxime Carrere[1,2,3]

[1] Inria Bordeaux Sud-Ouest, 200 Avenue de la Vieille Tour, 33405 Talence, France
frederic.alexandre@inria.fr
[2] LaBRI, Université de Bordeaux, Bordeaux INP, CNRS, UMR 5800, Talence, France
[3] Institut des Maladies Neurodégénératives,
Université de Bordeaux, CNRS, UMR 5293, Bordeaux, France

Abstract. One of the most critical properties of a versatile intelligent agent is its capacity to adapt autonomously to any change in the environment without overly complexifying its cognitive architecture. In this paper, we propose that understanding the role of neuromodulation in the brain is of central interest for this purpose. More precisely, we propose that an accurate estimation of the nature of uncertainty present in the environment is performed by specific brain regions and broadcast throughout the cerebral network by neuromodulators, resulting in appropriate changes in cerebral functioning and learning modes. Better understanding the principles of these mechanisms in the brain might tremendously inspire the field of Artificial General Intelligence. The original contribution of this paper is to relate the four major neuromodulators to four fundamental dimensions of uncertainty.

Keywords: Neuromodulation · Bio-inspiration · Decision making

1 Introduction

Computational Neuroscience has contributed many models of cognitive functions [32], emphasizing their implementation in cerebral circuits or underlying neuronal mechanisms, notably related to learning. Nevertheless, from this huge amount of local models of cognitive functions, defining a general cognitive architecture, really autonomous and versatile is not just a matter of integration and a lot of work remains to be done to propose an effective framework of the brain, seen as a global cognitive model at this systemic level.

One of the more puzzling capacities of human cognition is our ability to adapt to any new circumstances without explicit labeling that the circumstances have changed and require a specific adaptation. This is particularly critical in our dynamic and stochastic world: Does an unusual event correspond to noise and can be neglected, or announce an important change and must be analyzed with

B. Steunebrink et al. (Eds.): AGI 2016, LNAI 9782, pp. 324–333, 2016.
DOI: 10.1007/978-3-319-41649-6_33

care? Whereas we are rather good at answering such questions, they turn out to be difficult to integrate in modeling studies.

This is revealed in the stability-plasticity problem, studied in the domains of Artificial Neural Networks [19], Computational Neuroscience [23] and Lifelong Machine Learning [30]. In short, this problem originates from the fact that we would like at the same time to have a learning system able to adapt to any change (plastic) and preserving its past experience and not deleting it, in case any exception occurs (stable). A related dilemma is that of exploitation-exploration, also encountered in many domains [6]. On the one hand we might have the will to exploit our current knowledge of the present situation but on the other hand we might also want to explore other recipes and possibly find more efficient solutions.

This problem has been hardly studied in Cognitive Science. To our knowledge, [14] is one of the rare experimental studies to analyze human cerebral activations for such conflicts during decision making. Cohen and colleagues [11] underline that in reinforcement learning, formal solutions of optimal policies have been proposed only in simplified cases of this problem, particularly corresponding to discovering noisy but stationary processes with fixed probabilities of reward, but not in the case of unstationarity whereas changing environments are probably more realistic as far as human cognition is concerned.

The case of unstationary environments has been tackled in [17] formalizing them as a set of stationary environments and a certain probability to switch from an environment to the other. Accordingly, the very interesting MMBRL model has been proposed [17], as a multi-modules model, each specialized on an environment, learned by Q-learning, and predicting the current state. This model is very original because at each moment, all the modules participate in the decision and learn, but the number of environments must be fixed in advance and cannot evolve.

In the framework of decision making, the distinction between stationary and unstationary environments can be presented as follows: when you try to associate an action to a stimulus to get a reward, you might be willing to apply an associative rule that you have learned before, proposing, for a given stimulus, the best action to trigger to get a reward. Now, suppose that suddenly the rule does not work any longer (you get no reward): Which conclusion should you draw from this failure? On the one hand, you might decide that the reason is that the environment is stationary but the rule is probabilistic (not always valid). In this case, the decision to make is only to revise its rate of validity and wait for the next trial (hopefully more rewarding). On the other hand, you might decide that the environment is unstationary and that the rule has suddenly changed. In this case, you will have to elaborate a new rule or re-use an old one. It is explained in [33] that these two interpretations are intricately linked. For example, if a rule is highly stochastic, you will be less prone to consider a failure as corresponding to unstationarity. Conversely a failure with a highly probable rule will be immediately considered as requiring a new rule.

The paper by Yu and Dayan [33] had a big impact in the computational neuroscience community because it was also proposing that two neuromodulators in the brain, Acetylcholine (ACh) and Noradrenaline (or Norepinephrine NE) were respectively signaling these two kinds of uncertainty. This view is partly consistent with the wider view by Doya [16], proposing more generally a role for neuromodulators in reinforcement learning.

In the present paper, based on biological knowledge extracted from the literature and on models and experimental simulations including from our group, we propose to gather information about the main neuromodulators and insert them in a more systematic framework, particularly relating their role to the adaptation of the cerebral circuitry and the underlying cognitive functions, to the kind of uncertainty and to the part of the behavioral episode concerned with experienced uncertainty. Our goal is to show that neuromodulation in the brain is a very powerful way to drive it in different functioning and learning modes, at a lower cost regarding the complexification of the cognitive architecture. We will also explain that this is made possible because the nature of the information carried by neuromodulators is well adapted to such global modulations. We will finally propose that this information is not so heterogeneous as classically reported but rather corresponds to adapting the cerebral network to different kinds of uncertainty.

2   The Role of Neuromodulation in Neural Processing

Information flows that feed a neural network can have different kinds of effects on its functioning and on its learning. Based on biological inspiration, three main flows can be considered. Friston has contrasted driver and modulator flows [18], corresponding respectively to sensory feed-forward afferent flows and to feedback flows carrying expectations from higher regions of the network. Whereas the driver flows are directly integrated in the functioning rules of the neuronal units (classically in the weighted sum performed therein) and have a major (driving) impact on the resulting activation states, the modulator flows, as their name tells, have a more limited impact. They cannot generate an activation by themselves but can modulate an existing activation, by acting on some internal parameters like the gain of the activation rules. Relying on sparser and less focused connectivity, the feed-back flows can have consequently an attentional effect that can modify the level of activity in some regions. In addition, referring to the classical hebbian framework, it is also clear that both kinds of flows have distinct roles in the learning rules.

In natural and artificial networks, neuromodulation can also have a distinct effect on neural networks but is more rarely considered in modeling approaches. The main types of neuromodulators are monoamines (dopamine, serotonin, noradrenaline) and acetylcholine. The underlying mechanism [8,15] is that, for each kind of neuromodulators, specific neurons gathered in a nucleus project to most regions of the brain. Accordingly, they can widely modify the functioning and learning modes of extended networks by modifying intrinsic properties of neurons and synaptic weights. This is done thanks to specialized receptors types on different parts of neurons. This kind of information broadcasting is interesting in a distributed architecture like the brain, where the anatomy of interconnections is rather stable and cannot be systematic but where some important information has to be known in many regions to modulate their functioning and learning modes [15]. Basically, neuromodulatory neurons can have two kinds of activity, a phasic activity corresponding to a reaction synchronized to a specific event, typically the reception of a reward, and a tonic activity corresponding to a sustained release of the neuromodulator. Whereas phasic activity of neuromodulatory neurons can have dramatic roles in brain functioning (cf. for example the phasic dopamine, often described as representing the reward prediction error [29]), their tonic activity is more consistent with the modulatory role that we discuss here and will be only considered in the remaining of the paper.

In order to introduce the influence of neuromodulators on the normal functioning of the cerebral structures, let us first rapidly define what we call a 'normal' (or nominal) functioning of the cognitive architecture. In short, an important part of our deliberative cognition consists in analyzing current exteroception and interoception to detect respectively important information in the external world (sensory cues) and in the internal world (needs) and to apply corresponding sensorimotor rules to satisfy currents goals [1]. Here, sensorimotor rules must be understood as relations encoded in the prefrontal cortex associating perception to the result obtained when a decision is executed, which can correspond to trigger a motor action in the external world or to trigger more internal decisions. In the ideal case, the world is perfectly known and the corresponding important sensory cues and rules have already been extracted by learning. But the world is not ideal but uncertain, as it can be detected by reward prediction errors that monitor uncertainty.

An important characteristic of the neuromodulatory systems is that they are triggered by the central nucleus of the amygdala, a limbic structure known to be active when an error of (negative or positive) reward prediction is detected. As explained below, other evaluations are made in other cerebral regions to differentiate the kind of uncertainty and inhibit non relevant neuromodulation.

3   Four Kinds of Neuromodulators

Acetylcholine (ACh) is released by basal forebrain nuclei like the nucleus basilis. Its role has been related to expected uncertainty [33], corresponding to the stochastic case evoked above, when the rule has not changed but is not always valid. The observed effects of ACh in the sensory cortex are attentional and correspond to increase the signal-to-noise ratio [27], resulting in promoting feed-forward sensory information against feed-back expectations, when the environment is judged highly stochastic. As modeled in [10], another observed effect of ACh in conditioning experiments [9] is to promote learning about the context and not about (noisy) sensory cues.

Noradrenaline (or Norepinephrine NE) is released by the Locus Coeruleus and has been associated to unexpected uncertainty [33] when the rules have changed, like it is the case during reversal [2]. Accordingly, it is also associated to an increase of exploration, to extract new contingencies and elaborate new rules [3]. NE has been reported to have the same kinds of attentional effects as ACh to favor exploration of new sensory cues [33]. The identification of the circumstances as corresponding to unexpected uncertainty has been modeled in [24] by a signal depending on the reward rate and on measures of response conflict estimated from two windows encompassing long term and short term history of activity.

Concerning the other two neuromodulators considered here, Serotonin (or 5HT) released from the dorsal raphe nucleus and Dopamine (DA) released from the Ventral Tegmental Area in the midbrain, the situation is more controversial. Old models like [13] propose a dual role for these neuromodulators, with tonic DA for average appetitive reward prediction and 5HT for average aversive reward (punishment) prediction. More recent papers acknowledge a role for 5HT in aversive processing [12] but mainly for behavioral inhibition and passive avoidance. Accordingly, low levels of 5HT are also associated to impulsivity. This is consistent with the view expressed in [16] relating 5HT to time discounting, corresponding to the degree of preference between immediate over delayed rewards, higher levels of 5HT corresponding to greater patience. This kind of impulsivity can also be linked to the concept of risk, another major theory for the role of 5HT [5], where a greater variance in rewards might be prefered to more stable payoffs, even if disavantageous on the total reward received. Defining a utility function as the trade-off between the expected reward and its variance is proposed as a model for the level of tonic 5HT [5]. Concerning tonic DA, recent papers generally agree for a role to set the trade-off between exploration and exploitation [21], which has of course to be confronted to the hypothetized role of NE mentioned above. The evoked model of tonic DA implements the corresponding mechanisms in the output functions of the basal ganglia, a motor region responsible for action selection, with a probability distribution that can be modulated by tonic DA from flat (to favor exploration) to sharp (for exploitation) [21] shapes.

4   Towards a Common Framework of Interpretation

We propose that setting the focus on the concept of action is a good way to make clear the ambiguities evoked above. This idea has also been proposed by Niv [25] to better explain the differences between the pavlovian and instrumental conditioning paradigms. Instead of evoking mainly rewards, actions should be considered as representing the main difference between both paradigms: The new dimension brought by instrumental conditioning (and related decision making) over pavlovian conditioning (and related reward value) is that the animal or human agent is responsible for deciding to trigger an action and more precisely for its frequency, yielding the rapidity or the vigor of this action, but also a certain cost corresponding to the energy necessary to trigger the action. Consequently the vigor of the response (and the corresponding energetic price to pay for it) is a good indicator of the motivation to have a reward and, similarly, the cost of a delay in this procedure is more meaningful.

We propose to exploit the same duality between the rate of the action and the reward as a way to disambiguate the respective roles of the neuromodulators considered here and propose accordingly to go deeper in the specification of different kinds of uncertainty. We have evoked several times above that uncertainty manifests itself by the acknowledgement that the sensorimotor rule which has been applied doesn't bring the expected reward. The next question would be to know what is the cause of this problem: Is it because the selected sensory cues is not longer valid (unexpected sensory uncertainty) or just because it is only noisy (expected sensory uncertainty)? Or is it because the action to associate to the (still correct) sensory cue has changed (unexpected motor uncertainty) or just because it is only noisy and not always working (expected motor uncertainty). We propose here that these cases respectively trigger the release of Noradrenaline, Acetylcholine, Dopamine and Serotonin.

This view does not modify the acknowledged role of ACh on sensory processing and is also consistent with information given above for tonic DA and NE roles. DA would be for exploration/exploitation trade-off for action selection whereas NE would be concerned with the same trade-off for selective attention of the sensory cues. This is consistent with the fact that DA effect is mainly reported in the basal ganglia and the frontal cortex (known to be responsible for the organization of action) and NE effect in the posterior parietal cortex [4]. The role of NE to modify sensory processing in the thalamus and the cortex is also acknowledged [28]. Similarly, DA has a clear role for wanting in the motor pole and not for liking on the sensory side [7]. This separation of roles between NE and DA has also been proposed in modeling studies [21].

Similarly, relating the role of 5HT to the estimation of risk and variance of reward can rather be seen as a matter of noise or probabilistic distribution of effects, consistently with an interpretation of expected uncertainty related to actions. Even older interpretations of DA and 5HT as respectively related to reward and punishment can be re-examined here: It can be understood that when the risk is high, this should promote behavioral inhibition and passive avoidance, often related to aversive processing [12], whereas exploration due to high level of tonic DA might be misinterpreted as behavioral activation to get a reward.

5   Discussion

In this paper we have mainly discussed about the role of neuromodulators in cognition. Structurally, they have been presented [15] as a way to broadcast information in a sparsely connected network like it is the case for the brain. Functionally, it can be also argued that this kind of information passing is preferable for certain types of information, orthogonal to the information processed locally and rapidly changing. This is the case with uncertainty, that we have proposed to be the key topic of neuromodulation. More precisely, we have proposed a double set of criteria to qualify uncertainty. In addition to uncertainty announcing a radical change in the underlying rules or simply reporting stochasticity in the environment, as already proposed in [33], we suggest, as the major contribution of the present paper, that uncertainty can also refer to the sensory cues or to the actions. In this view, each of the resulting four kinds of uncertainty would require fundamentally different modifications in the cerebral network and consequently different neuromodulators.

Altogether, the contribution of the present view to the framework of Artificial General Intelligence can be synthesized as follows: Deliberative decision-making is often summarized as learning and exploiting sensorimotor rules, associating the sensory context to the best actions to trigger to get rewards and reach goals. Such a framework is very classical in machine learning, particularly corresponding to reinforcement learning [31], and in cognitive science [1]. It is attractive because of its simplicity and because several computational frameworks have been developed to express and learn such rules, using symbols [1], neurons [31] and bayesian formalism [33] and proposing accordingly effective means to implement artificial intelligent agents. This simplicity can also be seen as a weakness, reducing cognition to simple sensorimotor rules. One argument is that adapting to the unknown and changing world is more complex than learning simple contingencies between situations and optimal decision to make, particularly because the world is uncertain, including dynamic and stochastic aspects. A really autonomous agent, in the perspective of Artificial General Intelligence, should be able to detect by itself such uncertainties and adapt to them.

The first lesson that we propose to be drawn by inspiration from neuromodulation in the brain is that, in order to take uncertainties into account in a cognitive architecture, there is no need to give up the framework of sensorimotor rules and look for a completely different or radically more complex framework. Alternatively, it can be sufficient to build additional modules to detect the kind of experienced uncertainty and to modulate or increment the set of sensorimotor rules. This is interesting because existing systems based on sensorimotor rules could be simply extended (and not fundamentally modified) and remain effective in an uncertain world, corresponding to an important improvement in autonomy for the corresponding agent.

The second element that we introduce here, corresponding to the most original contribution of this paper, is about the different kinds of uncertainties that can be experienced. In addition to the distinction between expected and unexpected uncertainties already proposed in [33], we propose here that the fact that uncertainty applies either to sensory or to motor dimensions is of prime importance. In our view, the resulting four kinds of uncertainty should be signaled by the four major neuromodulators in the brain, allowing for distinct modulation of the cerebral system and, accordingly, of the existing set of sensorimotor rules. Although we have given above some hints from existing models about the kind of modulation performed by each neuromodulator in the cerebral system, a more precise specification of these effects should be the topic of future work.

Another key topic hardly evoked here, is about the identification of the kind of uncertainty experienced by the agent and consequently of the kind of neuromodulator to release. We have evoked models performing this identification from history of response conflicts and reward errors [24]. The way these elements are estimated and determination of their cerebral encoding is the topic of ongoing research in the team. It can be also mentioned that metalearning occurs at this level to help determine as fast and accurately as possible this critical information, particularly depending on the context in which it occurs [26].

This tentative explanation for the role of neuromodulators in cognition needs to be confirmed by a deeper anchoring in neuroscience. Additional clues might be particularly searched in the nucleus accumbens, known to be the gateway between sensory limbic and motor sides of cognition [22] and more generally in the basal ganglia concerning the respective roles of DA and 5HT in the balance between inhibition and excitation of behavior [20]. Finally, an important issue to consider in forthcoming works in about interneuromodulatory interactions: It has been shown that many interactions exist between neuromodulators resulting in more intricate roles than presented here [15].

References

1. Anderson, J.R., Bothell, D., Byrne, M.D., Douglass, S., Lebiere, C., Qin, Y.: An integrated theory of the mind. Psychol. Rev. **111**(4), 1036–1060 (2004). http://dx.doi.org/10.1037/0033-295x.111.4.1036
2. Aston-Jones, G., Rajkowski, J., Kubiak, P.: Conditioned responses of monkey locus coeruleus neurons anticipate acquisition of discriminative behavior in a vigilance task. Neuroscience **80**(3), 697–715 (1997). http://dx.doi.org/10.1016/s0306-4522(97)00060--2
3. Aston-Jones, G., Cohen, J.D.: An integrative theory of Locus Coeruleus-Norepinephrine function: adaptive gain and optimal performance. Ann. Rev. Neurosci. **28**(1), 403–450 (2005). http://dx.doi.org/10.1146/annurev.neuro.28.061604.135709
4. Aston-Jones, G., Rajkowski, J., Cohen, J.: Role of locus coeruleus in attention and behavioral flexibility. Biol. Psychiatry **46**(9), 1309–1320 (1999). http://dx.doi.org/10.1016/s0006-3223(99)00140–7
5. Balasubramani, P.P., Chakravarthy, V.S., Ravindran, B., Moustafa, A.A.: An extended reinforcement learning model of basal ganglia to understand the contributions of serotonin and dopamine in risk-based decision making, reward prediction, and punishment learning. Front. Comput. Neurosci. 8 (2014)
6. Berger-Tal, O., Nathan, J., Meron, E., Saltz, D.: The exploration-exploitation dilemma: a multidisciplinary framework. PLoS ONE **9**(4), 1–8 (2014)
7. Berridge, K.C., Robinson, T.E.: What is the role of dopamine in reward: hedonic impact, reward learning, or incentive salience? Brain Res. Rev. **28**(3), 309–369 (1998). http://dx.doi.org/10.1016/s0165-0173(98)00019–8
8. Bouret, S., Sara, S.J.: Network reset: a simplified overarching theory of locus coeruleus noradrenaline function. Trends Neurosci. **28**(11), 574–582 (2005). http://dx.doi.org/10.1016/j.tins.2005.09.002
9. Calandreau, L., Trifilieff, P., Mons, N., Costes, L., Marien, M., Marighetto, A., Micheau, J., Jaffard, R., Desmedt, A.: Extracellular hippocampal acetylcholine level controls amygdala function and promotes adaptive conditioned emotional response. J. Neurosci. Official J. Soc. Neurosci. **26**(52), 13556–13566 (2006)

10. Carrere, M., Alexandre, F.: A pavlovian model of the amygdala and its influence within the medial temporal lobe. Front. Syst. Neurosci. **9**(41) (2015)
11. Cohen, J.D., McClure, S.M., Yu, A.J.: Should I stay or should I go? How the human brain manages the trade-off between exploitation and exploration. Philos. Trans. R. Soc. Lond. Ser. B, Biol. Sci. **362**(1481), 933–942 (2007). http://dx.doi.org/10.1098/rstb.2007.2098
12. Cools, R., Nakamura, K., Daw, N.D.: Serotonin and dopamine: unifying affective, activational, and decision functions. Neuropsychopharmacology **36**(1), 98–113 (2011). http://dx.doi.org/10.1038/npp.2010.121
13. Daw, N.D., Kakade, S., Dayan, P.: Opponent interactions between serotonin and dopamine. Neural Netw. **15**(4–6), 603–616 (2002). http://dx.doi.org/10.1016/s0893-6080(02)00052--7
14. Daw, N.D., O'Doherty, J.P., Dayan, P., Seymour, B., Dolan, R.J.: Cortical substrates for exploratory decisions in humans. Nature **441**(7095), 876–879 (2006). http://dx.doi.org/10.1038/nature04766
15. Dayan, P.: Twenty-five lessons from computational neuromodulation. Neuron **76**(1), 240–256 (2012). http://dx.doi.org/10.1016/j.neuron.2012.09.027
16. Doya, K.: Metalearning and neuromodulation. Neural Netw. **15**(4–6), 495–506 (2002). http://dx.doi.org/10.1016/s0893-6080(02)00044-8
17. Doya, K., Samejima, K., Katagiri, K., Kawato, M.: Multiple model-based reinforcement learning. Neural Comp. **14**(6), 1347–1369 (2002). http://neco.mitpress.org/cgi/content/abstract/14/6/1347
18. Friston, K.: Functional integration and inference in the brain. Prog. Neurobiol. **68**(2), 113–143 (2002). http://view.ncbi.nlm.nih.gov/pubmed/12450490
19. Grossberg, S.: Adaptive resonance theory: how a brain learns to consciously attend, learn, and recognize a changing world. Neural Netw. **37**, 1–47 (2013). http://dx.doi.org/10.1016/j.neunet.2012.09.017
20. Haber, S., Fudge, J., McFarland, N.: Striatonigrostriatal pathways in primates form an ascending spiral from the shell to the dorsolateral striatum. J. Neurosci. **20**(6), 2369–2382 (2000)
21. Humphries, M.D., Khamassi, M., Gurney, K.: Dopaminergic control of the exploration-exploitation trade-off via the basal ganglia. Front. Neurosci. **6**(9), 1–14 (2012)
22. Mannella, F., Gurney, K., Baldassarre, G.: The nucleus accumbens as a nexus between values and goals in goal-directed behavior: a review and a new hypothesis. Front. Behav. Neurosci. 7 (2013)
23. McClelland, J.L., McNaughton, B.L., O'Reilly, R.C.: Why there are complementary learning systems in the hippocampus and neocortex: insights from the successes and failures of connectionist models of learning and memory. Psychol. Rev. **102**(3), 419–457 (1995)
24. McClure, S., Gilzenrat, M., Cohen, J.: An exploration-exploitation model based on norepinepherine and dopamine activity. In: Weiss, Y., Schölkopf, B., Platt, J. (eds.) Advances in Neural Information Processing Systems 18, pp. 867–874. MIT Press (2006). http://www.csbmb.princeton.edu/~smcclure/pdf/MGC_NIPS.pdf
25. Niv, Y.: Cost, benefit, tonic, phasic: what do response rates tell us about dopamine and motivation. Annals of the New York Academy of Sciences **1104**(1), 357–376 (2007). http://dx.doi.org/10.1196/annals.1390.018
26. Pauli, W.M., Hazy, T.E., O'Reilly, R.C.: Expectancy, ambiguity, and behavioral flexibility: separable and complementary roles of the orbital frontal cortex and amygdala in processing reward expectancies. J. Cogn. Neurosci. **24**(2), 351–366 (2011). http://dx.doi.org/10.1162/jocn_a_00155

27. Pauli, W.M., O'Reilly, R.C.: Attentional control of associative learning-a possible role of the central cholinergic system. Brain Res. **1202**, 43–53 (2008)

28. Sara, S.J., Bouret, S.: Orienting and reorienting: the locus coeruleus mediates cognition through arousal. Neuron **76**(1), 130–141 (2012). http://dx.doi.org/10.1016/j.neuron.2012.09.011

29. Schultz, W.: Predictive reward signal of dopamine neurons. J. Neurophysiol. **80**(1), 1–27 (1998). http://jn.physiology.org/content/80/1/1

30. Silver, D., Yang, Q., Li, L.: Lifelong machine learning systems: beyond learning algorithms. In: AAAI Spring Symposium Series (2013)

31. Sutton, R.S., Barto, A.G.: Reinforcement Learning: An Introduction. MIT Press, Cambridge (1998)

32. Trappenberg, T.P.: Fundamentals of Computational Neuroscience, 2nd edn. Oxford University Press, Oxford (2009)

33. Yu, A.J., Dayan, P.: Uncertainty, neuromodulation, and attention. Neuron **46**(4), 681–692 (2005)

Controlling Combinatorial Explosion in Inference via Synergy with Nonlinear-Dynamical Attention Allocation

Ben Goertzel[1,2]([⊠]), Misgana Bayetta Belachew[1,2,4],
Matthew Ikle'[3], and Gino Yu[4]

[1] OpenCog Foundation, Hong Kong, China
ben@goertzel.org
[2] Hanson Robotics, Hong Kong, China
[3] Adams State University, Alamosa, USA
[4] School of Design, Hong Kong Poly U, Hong Kong, China

Abstract. One of the core principles of the OpenCog AGI design, "cognitive synergy", is exemplified by the synergy between logical reasoning and attention allocation. This synergy centers on a feedback in which nonlinear-dynamical attention-spreading guides logical inference control, and inference directs attention to surprising new conclusions it has created. In this paper we report computational experiments in which this synergy is demonstrated in practice, in the context of a very simple logical inference problem.

More specifically: First-order probabilistic inference generates conclusions, and its inference steps are pruned via "Short Term importance" (STI) attention values associated to the logical Atoms it manipulates. As inference generates conclusions, information theory is used to assess the surprisingness value of these conclusions, and the "short term importance" attention values of the Atoms representing the conclusions are updated accordingly. The result of this feedback is that meaningful conclusions are drawn after many fewer inference steps than would be the case without the introduction of attention allocation dynamics and feedback therewith.

This simple example demonstrates a cognitive dynamic that is hypothesized to be very broadly valuable for general intelligence.

1 Introduction

One approach to creating AGI systems is the "integrative" strategy, involving combining multiple components embodying different structures or algorithms, and relying on synergistic dynamics between components. One kind of integrative system involves various highly independent software components, each solving a specialized set of problems in a mostly standalone manner, with occasional communication between each other in order to exchange problems and solutions. On the other end of the scale, are systems designed as tightly interconnected components that give rise to complex non-linear dynamical phenomena. Here, we are specifically focused on the latter approach. We will discuss the

B. Steunebrink et al. (Eds.): AGI 2016, LNAI 9782, pp. 334–343, 2016.
DOI: 10.1007/978-3-319-41649-6_34

particulars of one form of cognitive synergy – between probabilistic inference and nonlinear-dynamical attention allocation – within the context of one particular integrative AGI architecture, PrimeAGI (formerly named OpenCogPrime) [9,10], implemented on the OpenCog platform [7].

The specific nature of the synergy explored and demonstrated here is as follows:

- Probabilistic logical reasoning, proceeding via forward chaining and using the PLN (Probabilistic Logic Networks) rule-base, chooses premises for its inferences based on weights called STI (ShortTermImportance) values
- When the inference process discovers something sufficiently surprising (via an information-theoretic measure), it boosts the STI value associated with this discovery
- STI values spread according to a particular set of equations modeled on economics (ECAN, Economic Attention Allocation), so that when an item or fragment of knowledge has a high STI, related entities will also get their STI boosted

Thus, broadly speaking, we have a feedback in which

- importance values prune the combinatorial explosion of inference chaining
- inferentially determined surprisingness guides importance assessments
- importance spreads among related entities

According to this dynamic, entities related to other entities that have been useful for an inference process, will also tend to get brought to the attention to that inference process. This will cause the inference process to focus, much more often than would otherwise be the case, on sets of interrelated knowledge items regarding which there are surprising (interesting) conclusions to be drawn. It is a form of deliberative thinking in which conclusion-drawing and attention-focusing interact synergetically.

This sort of dynamic is very general in nature and, according to the conceptual theory underlying PrimeAGI, is critical to the operation of probabilistic inference based general intelligence. Here we illustrate the synergy via a simple "toy" example, which highlights the nature of the feedback involved very clearly. Our current work involves leveraging the same synergy in more realistic cases, e.g. to help a system maintain focus in the course of inference-guided natural language dialogue.

2 Background: PrimeAGI

Our work here is based upon specific details of the AGI architecture called **PrimeAGI** (formerly known as OpenCogPrime), based on the open-source OpenCog project at http://opencog.org. PrimeAGI is a large and complex system whose detailed description occupies two volumes [9,10].

The concept of cognitive synergy is at the core of the PrimeAGI design, with highly interdependent subsystems responsible for inference regarding patterns obtained from visual, auditory and abstract domains, uncertain reasoning, language comprehension and generation, concept formation, and action planning. The goal of the PrimeAGI project is to engineer systems that exhibit general intelligence equivalent to a human adult, and ultimately beyond.

The dynamics of interaction between processes in PrimeAGI is designed in such a way that knowledge can be converted between different types of memory; and when a learning process that is largely concerned with a particular type of memory encounters a situation where the rate of learning is very slow, it can proceed to convert some of the relevant knowledge into a representation for a different type of memory to overcome the issue, demonstrating **cognitive synergy**. The simple case of synergy between ECAN and PLN explored here is an instance of this broad concept; PLN being concerned mainly with declarative memory and ECAN mainly with attentional memory.

2.1   Memory Types and Cognitive Processes in PrimeAGI

PrimeAGI's memory types are the declarative, procedural, sensory, and episodic memory types that are widely discussed in cognitive neuroscience [14], plus attentional memory for allocating system resources generically, and intentional memory for allocating system resources in a goal-directed way. Table 1 overviews these memory types, giving key references and indicating the corresponding cognitive processes, and which of the generic patternist cognitive dynamics each cognitive process corresponds to (pattern creation, association, etc.).

The essence of the PrimeAGI design lies in the way the structures and processes associated with each type of memory are designed to work together in a closely coupled way, the operative hypothesis being that this will yield cooperative intelligence going beyond what could be achieved by an architecture merely containing the same structures and processes in separate "black boxes."

The inter-cognitive-process interactions in OpenCog are designed so that

- conversion between different types of memory is possible, though sometimes computationally costly (e.g. an item of declarative knowledge may with some effort be interpreted procedurally or episodically, etc.)
- when a learning process concerned centrally with one type of memory encounters a situation where it learns very slowly, it can often resolve the issue by converting some of the relevant knowledge into a different type of memory: i.e. **cognitive synergy**

The simple case of ECAN/PLN synergy described here is an instance of this broad concept.

2.2   Probabilistic Logic Networks

PLN serves as the probabilistic reasoning system within OpenCog's more general artificial general intelligence framework. PLN logical inferences take the form of

Table 1. Memory Types and Cognitive Processes in OpenCog Prime. The third column indicates the general cognitive function that each specific cognitive process carries out, according to the patternist theory of cognition.

Memory Type	Specific Cognitive Processes	General Cognitive Functions
Declarative	Probabilistic Logic Networks (PLN) [6]; concept blending [5]	pattern creation
Procedural	MOSES (a novel probabilistic evolutionary program learning algorithm) [13]	pattern creation
Episodic	internal simulation engine [8]	association, pattern creation
Attentional	Economic Attention Networks (ECAN) [11]	association, credit assignment
Intentional	probabilistic goal hierarchy refined by PLN and ECAN, structured according to MicroPsi [2]	credit assignment, pattern creation
Sensory	In OpenCogBot, this will be supplied by the DeSTIN component	association, attention allocation, pattern creation, credit assignment

syllogistic rules, which give patterns for combining statements with matching terms. Related to each rule is a truth-value formula which calculates the truth value resulting from application of the rule. PLN uses forward-chaining and backward-chaining processes to combine the various rules and create inferences.

2.3   Economic Attention Networks

The attention allocation system within OpenCog is handled by the Economic Attention Network (ECAN). ECAN is a graph of untyped nodes and links and links that may be typed either HebbianLink or InverseHebbianLink. Each Atom in an ECAN is weighted with two numbers, called STI (short-term importance) and LTI (long-term importance), while each Hebbian or InverseHebbian link is weighted with a probability value. A system of equations, based upon an economic metaphor of STI and LTI values as artificial currencies, governs importance value updating. These equations serve to spread importance to and from various atoms within the system, based upon the importance of their roles in performing actions related to the system's goals.

An important concept with ECAN is the attentional focus, consisting of those atoms deemed most important for the system to achieve its goals at a particular instant. Through the attentional focus, one key role of ECAN is to guide the forward and backward chaining processes of PLN inference. Quite simply, when PLN's chaining processes need to choose logical terms or relations to include in their inferences, they can show priority to those occurring in the system's attentional focus (due to having been placed their by ECAN). Conversely, when terms or relations have proved useful to PLN, they can have their importance boosted, which will affect ECAN's dynamics. This is a specific example of the cognitive synergy principle at the heart of the PrimeAGI design.

3   Evaluating PLN on a Standard MLN Test Problem

In order to more fully understand the nature of PLN/ECAN synergy, in 2014 we chose to explore it (see [12]) in the context of two test problems standardly used in the context of MLNs (Markov Logic Networks) [4]. These problems are relatively easy for both PLN and MLN, and do not stress either system's capabilities.

The first test case considered there – and the one we will consider here – is a very small-scale logical inference called the *smokes* problem, discussed in its MLN form at [1]. The PLN format of the *smokes* problem used for our experiments is given at https://github.com/opencog/test-datasets/blob/master/pln/tuffy/smokes/smokes.scm.

The conclusions obtained from PLN backward chaining on the *smokes* test case are

```
cancer(Edward) <.62, 1>
cancer(Anna)   <.50, 1>
cancer(Bob)    <.45, 1>
cancer(Frank)  <.45, 1>
```

which is reasonably similar to the output of MLN as reported in [1],

```
0.75 Cancer(Edward)
0.65 Cancer(Anna)
0.50 Cancer(Bob)
0.45 Cancer(Frank)
```

In [12] we explored the possibility of utilizing ECAN to assist PLN on this test problems; however our key conclusion from this work was that ECAN's guidance is not of much use to PLN on the problems as formulated. However, that work did lead us to conceptually interesting conclusions regarding the sorts of circumstances in which ECAN is most likely to help PLN. Specifically, after applying PLN and ECAN to that example, we hypothesized that if one modified the example via adding a substantial amount of irrelevant evidence about other aspects of the people involved, then one would have a case where ECAN could help PLN, because it could help focus attention on the relevant relationships.

This year we have finally followed up on this concept, and have demonstrated that, indeed, if one pollutes the smokes problem by adding a bunch of "noise" relationships with relatively insignificant truth values, then we obtain a case in which ECAN is of considerable use for guiding PLN toward the meaningful information and away from the meaningless, and thus helping PLN to find the meaningful conclusions (the "needles in the haystack") more rapidly. While this problem is very "toy" and simple, the phenomenon it illustrates is quite general and, we believe, of quite general importance.

4   PLN + ECAN on the Noisy Smokes Problem

To create a "noisy" version of the smokes problem, we created a number of "random" smokers and friends and added them to the OpenCog Atomspace along with the Atoms corresponding to the people in the original "smokes" problem and their relationships. We created M random smokers, and N random people associated with each smokers; so $M * N$ additional random people all total. For the experiments reported here, we set $N = 5$. The "smokes" and "friend" relationships linking the random people to others were given truth value strengths of 0.2 for the smoking relationship and 0.85 for the friendship relationship. Of course, these numbers are somewhat arbitrary, but our goal here was to produce a simple illustrative example, not to seriously explore the anthropology of secondhand smoking.

We ran the PLN forward chainer, in a version developed in 2015 that utilizes the OpenCog Unified Rule Engine (URE)[1]. To guide the forward chaining process, we used a heuristic in which the Atom selected as the source of inference is chosen by tournament selection keyed to Atoms' STI values. To measure the surprisingness of a conclusion derived by PLN, we used a heuristic formula based on the Jensen-Shannon Divergence (JSD) between the truth value of an Atom A and the truth value of A^*, the most natural supercategory of A:

$$JSD(A, A^*) * 10^{JSD(A,A^*)}$$

This formula was chosen as a simple rescaling of the JSD, intended to exaggerate the differences between Atoms with low JSD and high JSD. A pending research issue is to choose a heuristic rescaling of the JSD in a more theoretically motivated way; however, this rather extreme scaling function seems to work effectively in practice.

Determining the most natural supercategory is in general a challenging issue, which may be done via using a notion of "coherence" as described in [3]. However, for the simple examples pursued here, there is no big issue. For instance, the supercategory of

```
Evaluationlink
PredicateNode "smokes"
ConceptNode "Bob
```

is simply the SatisfyingSet of the PredicateNode "smokes"; i.e. the degree to which an average Atom that satisfies the argument-type constraints of the

---

[1] https://github.com/opencog/atomspace/tree/master/opencog/rule-engine.

"smokes" predicate, actually smokes. So then "Bob smokes" is surprising if Bob smokes significantly more often than an average entity.

In the case of this simple toy knowledge base, the only entities involved are people, so this means "Bob smokes" is surprising if Bob smokes significantly more often than the average person the system knows about. In a non-toy Atomspace, we would have other entities besides people represented, and then a coherence criterion would need to be invoked to identify that the relevant supercategory is "People in the SatisfyingSet of the PredicateNode 'smokes'" (including people with a membership degree of zero to this SatisfyingSet) rather than "entities in general in the SatisfyingSet of the PredicateNode 'smokes'".

Similarly, in the context of this problem, the surprisingness of "Bob and Jim are friends" is calculated relative to the generic probability that "Two random people known to the system are friends."

4.1   Tweaks to ECAN

We ended up making two significant change to OpenCog's default ECAN implementation in the course of doing these experiments.

The first change pertained to the size of the system's AttentionalFocus (working memory). Previously the "Attentional Focus" (the working memory of the system, comprised of the Atoms with the highest STI) was defined as the set of Atoms in the Atomspace with STI above a certain fixed threshold, the AttentionalFocusBoundary. In these experiments, we found that this sometimes led to an overly large AttentionalFocus, which resulted in a slow forward chaining process heavily polluted by noise. We decided to cap the size of the AttentionalFocus at a certain maximum value K, currently $K = 30$. This is a somewhat crude measure and better heuristics may be introduced in future. But given that the size of the human working memory seems to be fairly strictly limited, this assumption seems unlikely to be extremely harmful in an AGI context.

The second change pertained to the balance between rent and wages. Previously these values were allowed to remain imbalanced until the central bank's reserve amount deviated quite extremely from the initial default value. However, this appeared to lead to overly erratic behavior. So we modified the code so that rent is updated each cycle, so as to retain balance with wages (i.e. so that, given the particular size of the Atomspace and Attentional Focus at that point in time, rent received will roughly equal wages paid).

4.2   Parameter Setting

The ECAN subsystem's parameters, whose meanings are described in [10], were set as follows:

```
ECAN_MAX_ATOM_STI_RENT      = 3
ECAN_STARTING_ATOM_STI_RENT = 2
ECAN_STARTING_ATOM_STI_WAGE = 30
HEBBIAN_MAX_ALLOCATION_PERCENTAGE = 0.1
```

```
SPREAD_DECIDER_TYPE = Step
ECAN_MAX_SPREAD_PERCENTAGE = 0.5
STARTING_STI_FUNDS     =     500000
```

The PLN forward chainer was set to carry out 5 inference steps in each "cognitive cycle", and one step of basic ECAN operations (importance spreading, importance updating, and HebbianLink formation) was carried out in each cycle as well.

4.3   Experimental Results

Figure 1 shows the number of cycles required to correctly infer the truth value of several relationships in the original smokes problem, depending on the noise parameter M. The results are a bit erratic, but clearly demonstrate that the feedback between ECAN and PLN is working. As the amount of noise Atoms in the Atomspace increases, the amount of time required to draw the correct conclusions does not increase commensurately. Instead, for noise amounts above a very low level, it seems to remain within about the same range as the amount of noise increases.

On the other hand, without ECAN, the PLN forward chainer fails to find the correct conclusions at all with any appreciable amount of noise. In principle it would find the answers eventually, but this would require a huge amount of time to pass. The number of possible inferences is simply be too large, so without some kind of moderately intelligent pruning, PLN spends a long time exploring numerous random possibilities.

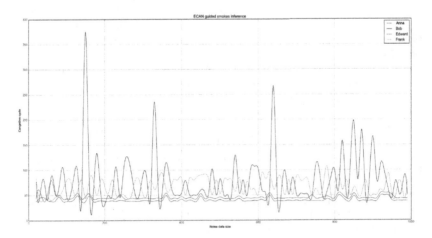

Fig. 1. Number of cognitive cycles required to derive the desired obvious conclusions from the noise-polluted Atomspace. The x-axis measures the amount of noise Atoms added. The graph is averaged over 100 runs. The key point is that the number of cycles does not increase extremely rapidly with the addition of more and more distractions. Red = conclusions regarding Anna; green=Bob, blue=Edward, yellow=Frank. (Color figure online)

5   Conclusion

We began this experimental investigation with the hypothesis that cognitive synergy between PLN and ECAN would be most useful in cases where there is a considerable amount of detailed information in the Atomspace regarding the problem at hand, and part of the problem involves heuristically sifting through this information to find the useful bits. The noisy smokes example was chosen as an initial focus of investigation, and we found that, in this example, ECAN does indeed help PLN to draw reasonable conclusions in a reasonable amount of time, in spite of the presence of a fairly large amount of distracting but uninteresting information.

The theory underlying PrimeAGI contends that this sort of synergy is critical to general intelligence, and will occur in large and complex problems as well as in toy problems like the one considered here. Validating this hypothesis will require additional effort beyond the work reported here, and might conceivably reveal the need for further small tweaks to the ECAN framework.

References

1. Project tuffy. http://hazy.cs.wisc.edu/hazy/tuffy/doc/
2. Bach, J.: Principles of Synthetic Intelligence. Oxford University Press, New York (2009)
3. Ben Goertzel, S.K.: Measuring surprisingness (2014). http://wiki.opencog.org/wikihome/index.php/Measuring_Surprisingness/
4. Niu, F., Re, C., Doan, A., Shavlik, J.: Tuffy: scaling up statistical inference in markov logic networks using an rdbms. In: Jagadish, H.V. (ed.) Proceedings of the 37th International Conference on Very Proceedings of the 37th International Conference on Very Large Data Bases (VLDB 2011), Seattle, Washington, vol. 4, pp. 373–384 (2011)
5. Fauconnier, G., Turner, M.: The Way We Think: Conceptual Blending and the Mind's Hidden Complexities. Basic Books, New York (2002)
6. Goertzel, B., Ikle, M., Goertzel, I., Heljakka, A.: Probabilistic Logic Networks. Springer, New York (2008)
7. Goertzel, B.: Cognitive synergy: a universal principle of feasible general intelligence? In: Proceedings of ICCI 2009, Hong Kong (2009)
8. Goertzel, B., Pennachin, C., et al.: An integrative methodology for teaching embodied non-linguistic agents, applied to virtual animals in second life. In: Proceedings of the First Conference on AGI. IOS Press (2008)
9. Goertzel, B., Pennachin, C., Geisweiller, N.: Engineering General Intelligence, Part 1: A Path to Advanced AGI via Embodied Learning and Cognitive Synergy. Atlantis Thinking Machines. Springer, Heidelberg (2013)
10. Goertzel, B., Pennachin, C., Geisweiller, N.: Engineering General Intelligence, Part 2: The CogPrime Architecture for Integrative, Embodied AGI. Atlantis Thinking Machines. Springer, Heidelberg (2013)
11. Goertzel, B., Pitt, J., Ikle, M., Pennachin, C., Liu, R.: Glocal memory: a design principle for artificial brains and minds. Neurocomputing **74**(1–3), 84–94 (2010)

12. Harrigan, C., Goertzel, B., Iklé, M., Belayneh, A., Yu, G.: Guiding probabilistic logical inference with nonlinear dynamical attention allocation. In: Goertzel, B., Orseau, L., Snaider, J. (eds.) AGI 2014. LNCS, vol. 8598, pp. 238–241. Springer, Heidelberg (2014)
13. Looks, M.: Competent Program Evolution. Ph.D. Thesis, Computer Science Department, Washington University (2006)
14. Tulving, E., Craik, R.: The Oxford Handbook of Memory. Oxford U Press, New York (2005)

Probabilistic Growth and Mining of Combinations: A Unifying Meta-Algorithm for Practical General Intelligence

Ben Goertzel[(✉)]

OpenCog Foundation, Hong Kong, China
ben@goertzel.org

Abstract. A new conceptual framing of the notion of the general intelligence is outlined, in the form of a universal learning meta-algorithm called Probabilistic Growth and Mining of Combinations (PGMC). Incorporating ideas from logical inference systems, Solomonoff induction and probabilistic programming, PGMC is a probabilistic inference based framework which reflects processes broadly occurring in the natural world, is theoretically capable of arbitrarily powerful generally intelligent reasoning, and encompasses a variety of existing practical AI algorithms as special cases. Several ways of manifesting PGMC using the OpenCog AI framework are described. It is proposed that PGMC can be viewed as a core learning process serving as the central dynamic of real-world general intelligence; but that to achieve high levels of general intelligence using limited computational resources, it may be necessary for cognitive systems to incorporate multiple distinct structures and dynamics, each of which realizes this core PGMC process in a different way (optimized for some particular sort of sub-problem).

1 Introduction

An open question in AGI and cognitive science is: If one's goal is the creation of an AI system with general intelligence at the human level or beyond, should one be looking for a "single learning algorithm" to carry out the core learning processes at the heart of one's system? Or, on the other hand, do the practicalities of achieving real-world general intelligence within realistic computational resource restrictions, inevitably push one toward a more heterogeneous approach, with multiple different algorithms handling different kinds of learning?

The concepts presented here constitute a sort of middle ground between single-focused and heterogeneous approaches. Instead of a single core algorithm, what is proposed is a *core process*. However, this core process is a relatively abstract one, and it is proposed that this core process can be realized via a variety of different underlying algorithms – and that, in order to achieve effective general intelligence using realistically limited resources, it may indeed be necessary to utilize a variety of different algorithms, each instantiating the same core process in a slightly different way (due to the different algorithms being optimized for different types of subproblems).

© Springer International Publishing Switzerland 2016
B. Steunebrink et al. (Eds.): AGI 2016, LNAI 9782, pp. 344–353, 2016.
DOI: 10.1007/978-3-319-41649-6_35

The PGMC concept presented here can be viewed as a variation of the "Universal AI" approach, but it has the property that it naturally extends and generalizes a number of practical AI algorithms in current use. It also has potential to be used to create cognitive architectures that are heterogeneous underneath, but wrap this heterogeneity behind a "universal" looking PGMC layer.

In the latter vein, after giving a semi-formal presentation of the key ideas of PGMC, we will discuss here how the OpenCog architecture in particular could be reformulated so that most of the learning algorithms in OpenCog, in spite of their apparent diversity, were explicitly implemented and displayed to the user as aspects of the PGMC "meta-algorithm." This is interesting theoretically as an illustration of the PGMC concept, and may also be interesting practically as a direction for OpenCog development. Due to space limitations, the particulars of OpenCog formalization and implementation are largely omitted here, but can be found online on the OpenCog wiki site[1].

2   Probabilistic Growth and Mining of Combinations

A High Level Conceptual View. The conceptual foundation of the "Probabilistic Growth and Mining of Combinations" notion presented here is the idea of "forward and backward growth processes" introduced in [3] and reiterated in [5,6], and proposed there as a generic framework for modeling focused cognitive processes (meaning, cognitive processes that focus their attention on a relatively small body of information within a potentially larger scope associated with a cognitive system). As defined there, roughly,

- **forward growth** is the process via which a collection of cognitive entities, the subjects of focus, combine with each other to form new entities, which will often then still be subjects of focus. Sometimes these focus entities may also combine with entities outside the focus.
- **backward growth** is the process of figuring out how a target cognitive entity might be produced via forward growth

These simple operations are actually quite generic in character, and can be seen to underlie a large variety of cognitive processes including logical inference, evolutionary learning, clustering, language processing, and a host of others.

The notion of PGMC presented here refines these earlier ideas considerably. Combining entities (as forward growth does) is all very well, but there are always too many combinations; so how does one decide which combinations to actually make? One can say that the entities doing the combining can decide what to combine with, which makes sense, but is not a very meaty conclusion. The idea of PGMC is that forward and backward growth processes can quite generically be executed, in a way that balances resource limitations with practical effectiveness, via a process of: (1) mining patterns in the results of prior forward and backward

---

[1] See   http://wiki.opencog.org/wikihome/index.php/OpenCoggy_Probabilistic_
Programming.

growth processes; (2) using these patterns to probabilistically guide ongoing forward and backward growth. And the pattern mining mentioned in the first item may also be done via leveraging various forward and backward growth processes, thus creating a virtuous-cycle recursion.

This rather generic process may be envisioned as a type of probabilistic programming, and I propose here that it may be considered as a general foundation for generally intelligent cognition. That any cognitive process can in principle be cast in this form is not a terribly interesting observation, since there are numerous foundations for universal computation known already. That so many cognitive processes known to be useful for narrow AI and proto-AGI systems can be conveniently cast in this form, along with so many creative processes occurring in nature, is more interesting and compelling.

A Partial Formalization. To elaborate the PGMC idea a bit further, let us consider the case of a cognitive system concerned with pursuing some complex goal in some complex environment. While goal-oriented activity is not necessarily the crux of all intelligent behavior[2], it is a significant ingredient, and also a convenient concrete focus for analysis. So let us explore the ways in which a cognitive system can maximize the degree of fulfillment of its goal functions.

Without being highly specific about the cognitive architecture of this system, let us assume that it stores knowledge in a manner founded on set of entities called Atoms, that two Atoms can often be combined with each other to form new Atoms, and that it maintains a memory of Atoms which it leverages to take both internal and external actions. Those who wish a more precise formalization may refer to the simple cognitive system model presented in [4]; the discussion here makes sense in the context of that formal agents model. The addition to that formal agents model we need here is simply that the internal operation of the formal agent contains a self-generating system as defined in [2], consisting of entities called Atoms that can combine with each other to form new Atoms.

To figure out how to achieve its goals, the cognitive system in question may look into its memory, which may contain historical information regarding which Atoms, when executed, have led to satisfaction of which goal functions to which degrees. Now, this historical information will not usually be directly relevant, because each new situation the system confronts will be a little different. But it may be indirectly relevant. Which brings us, I hypothesize, very close to the core of general intelligence.

Suppose one has a base probability distribution $\mathcal{P}$ over Atoms. Then, given a goal function G and a cognitive system S, one can define S_G as the set of Atoms in S's memory that take the form

$$[x * y] \rightarrow G < c >$$

Say that x and y are "constituents" of the Atom $[x * y] \rightarrow G < c >$.

---

[2] See [10] for a deep discussion of how general intelligence transcends goal-pursuit.

One can then define the following Basic Learning Process:

1. Initialize the "working memory" pool W (a set of Atoms). Possibilities include
   - Initialize $W = S_G$, for goal-directed combination formation
   - Initialize W to the system's long-term memory, for more general and exploratory combination formation
2. Repeatedly (N times, not forever) create stochastically chosen forward and backward combinations, via the following steps
   - For a forward step, choose a combination $a * b$, in which at least one of a or b is a constituent of a member of W, with probability determined by $\mathcal{P}$
   - For a backward step, choose a combination $a * b$ whose result is a member of W, with probability proportional to $\mathcal{P}$
   - Place the result of this combination in W, and place the expression describing the combination's result in the system's long-term memory
   - Tabulate the degree to which G is achieved at the current time, and insert into the long-term memory an Atom of the form $C \rightarrow G < c >$ corresponding to the current combination C

Basically, this process is doing forward and backward chaining, starting from existing knowledge about the goal G (for goal-oriented learning) or from the system's knowledge as a whole (for more general exploratory learning), and guided in its choices by the distribution $\mathcal{P}$.

This Basic Learning Process summarizes a basic and simplistic form of "probabilistic growth of combinations", and also stores some data along the way, which will be useful for mining. The initial growth of combinations is governed by a prior distribution, so unless this distribution is highly appropriate for the goals in question, the process will take a very long time. The step needed to get from this to PGMC is to mine the data stored, so as to figure out how to grow more appropriate combinations with a higher probability.

To take this next step, suppose one uses the above process to calculate the probability of G being fulfilled to a given degree, within a certain time period following execution of an executable Atom E. This may be used to define another probability distribution $\mathcal{P}_G(E)$ over the space of Atoms E. This distribution may be used to guide the above learning process.

We may then define our universal learning meta-algorithm, PGMC (Probabilistic Growth and Mining of Combinations) as the following loop:

1. begin with a goal G, and an initial distribution $\mathcal{P} = \mathcal{P}_0$
2. apply the Basic Learning Process using $\mathcal{P}$, leading to an estimate of $\mathcal{P}_G$
3. set $\mathcal{P} = \mathcal{P}_G$ and return to the previous step

In essence, this is a form of "reinforcement learning" driven by generic forward and backward chaining processes. One reason this is interesting is that the generic processes of backward and forward chaining can be used to conveniently formulate a wide variety of different learning processes; thus this framework can unify a variety of different, useful learning algorithms within a common meta-algorithm.

This learning process will be very slow (i.e. require many repetitions or very large N) if $\mathcal{P}$ is not chosen intelligently. Here we come to a very deep and interesting aspect of learning. If the Atom language chosen is rich enough, then $\mathcal{P}$ may itself be represented at an Atom $x_\mathcal{P}$, i.e. a nested Atom expression. This may be achieved e.g. if there are basic Atoms that make random choices. One then has a framework capable of supporting *meta-learning*, meaning the process of learning $x_\mathcal{P}$ so that $\mathcal{P}_G$ causes the system to choose actions with high goal-achievement value.

In probabilistic programming vernacular, Step 3 in the Basic Learning Process indicated above can be interpreted as a kind of *fitness-proportionate sampling* over the Atom space, conditioned on the distribution $\mathcal{P}$. This is related to, though different from, the use of *optimization queries* in probabilistic programming, as outlined in [1] Fitness-proportionate sampling may also be performed based on weighted combinations of system goals, rather than a single goal. Why are fitness-proportionate samples appropriate here? Because a full distribution over Atom space, conditioned on $\mathcal{P}_G$, need not be computed, since what the system really cares about is finding something good to do according to its goals, not accurately estimating the degree of badness of each potential bad action it could take. So sampling from the space in a way that takes more samples from the "good" parts is the right thing to do.

If $\mathcal{P}_G$ has the property of favoring simpler Atoms (e.g. Atoms corresponding to smaller Atom expressions), then what we have here is conceptually a variant of Solomonoff induction [8,9]. It seems likely to us that in this case, PGMC could be proved to be an instance of Solomonoff induction based on a certain special computational model. And it seems likely that, in most cases, if the initial $\mathcal{P}$ embodies Occam's Razor, then ensuing $\mathcal{P}_G$ will also do so. But PGMC is not just another reformulation of Occam's Razor; the key point is that this computational model, based on forward and backward chaining, is especially cognitively natural, comprising a mathematical abstraction of a host of well-studied and demonstrably-useful cognitive processes.

The potential flexibility and power of this sort of framework is considerable. For instance, one possibility is to stock S_G with Atoms embodying *logical inference rules*. In this case, application of the logical inference rules will be part of the forward and backward chaining process. Supposing S_G also contains Atoms that are specifically tied to particular situations in which G has been achieved in the past. Then combining the Atoms embodying logical inference rules, with Atoms regarding specific past situations involving G, will lead to *inferential extrapolation* from past situations to present and future situations. The quality of this extrapolation will depend on the quality of the inference rules – and on the quality of the choices made regarding which inference rules to apply, in what order, in each situation. These choices regarding *inference control* may be made by yet more Atoms embodying "inference control rules" – or, more interestingly, they may be made by the probabilistic sampling process outlined above. In this case the probabilistic sampling process is mining historical patterns regarding what inference steps have previously been helpful in what situations. And the inference rules themselves may be useful in performing extrapolations pertinent to these historical patterns and their present applications.

In sum, what we have described here is a "universal learning meta-algorithm" as follows:

1. Combine Atoms in memory via forward and backward chaining
2. Choose which combinations to form, via optimization queries conditioned on a distribution formed by extrapolating from which combinations have achieved relevant goals in the past
3. The "extrapolation" in Step 2 is carried out via forward and backward chaining, guided by optimization queries conditioned on a goal-driven probability distribution
4. The goal-driven probability distribution in Step 3, is formed or improved via Steps 2 and 3 ("meta-learning")

Or, to rephrase once more:

1. Combine stuff in memory, via forward combination (put stuff together and see what comes out) and backward combination (given a target, find stuff that can be combined to yield that target)
2. Since there are too many possible combinations to try them all, choose which ones to form based on estimating which ones have the highest probability of leading to goal achievement. This estimation is based on memory of which combinations have been tried in the past and how much success they've had.
3. Since past combinations and situations were a bit different from the current reality, figuring out how to use them to estimate probabilities regarding current situation requires some "reasoning." This reasoning can be done by the same old backward and forward combination process that we're now in the middle of describing. In other words, the "reasoning rules" or "reasoning processes" involved should be embodied in atomic entities that get combined with other entities in the course of the forward and backward combination processes.
4. To perform all this probability estimation we need some heuristics to guide which combinations have a higher "a priori" probability. This prior distribution had better favor simple combinations, for instance. And this prior distribution can be adapted over time, i.e. "meta-learning."

As emphasized above, this is intended not to summarize the full cognitive activity of a mind, but rather the focused, goal-directed portion of a mind's activity. "Background cognitive activity" is also assumed to occur. This background activity may often be modelable via ongoing forward and backward chaining driven by non-goal-oriented stochastic processes, but we will not enlarge on this point here.

3 Explicitly Implementing PGMC in OpenCog

The PGMC formalism and concept may be used as a general mode of describing and thinking about cognitive processes. It may also, however, be used as a means of explicitly structuring cognitive processes, i.e. of guiding and structuring practical AGI implementation. This is a direction we are now exploring within the OpenCog project. For a review of the OpenCog concepts utilized here, please see [5,6][3]. But we emphasize that the applicability of the PGMC idea is not restricted to OpenCog; the latter is used here as an illustrative example.

The Simplest OpenCog Implementation of PGMC. First we explore a relatively simple, not necessarily practical method of instantiating PGMC within OpenCog[4]

Within OpenCog, knowledge is represented in terms of:

- Atoms for specific sensory data. As illustrative examples: RGB values associated with particular pixels coming from a particular camera at a particular point in time; and characters coming from a particular terminal at a particular point in time.
- Atoms carrying out internal or external actions (SchemaNodes)
- Atoms for combining Atoms to form new Atoms.[5]
- As well as ListLinks, SetLinks for grouping together Atoms into sets, which may then be acted on by SchemaNodes – this is a mechanism enabling SchemaNodes to take whole "nested Atom expressions" as inputs

The standard assemblage of OpenCog Atoms is highly expressive and arguably sufficient to form the representational framework for a general intelligence interacting in the everyday human world.

OpenCog has a Unified Rule Engine (URE) which carries out generic forward and backward chaining processes like the ones abstractly described above[6]. The URE contains a FocusSet which can be used like the "working memory" W in the above-described process. In the URE, the role of the operator $*$ is played by the BindLink construct, which when it sees $a*b$ seeks to bind the VariableNodes contained in a to the Atom b. This is a somewhat specialized formalism, yet fits within the general mathematical framework described above, and has both general computational power and flexible pragmatic usability. For example, this approach is used to apply probabilistic logic rules (formulated as Atom expressions themselves, via the PLN, Probabilistic Logic Networks, framework) to Atoms representing concrete data or data patterns.

---

[3] Or see http://wiki.opencog.org/w/CogPrime_Overview for an informal online overview.

[4] See   http://wiki.opencog.org/wikihome/index.php/OpenCoggy_Probabilistic_ Programming for more details.

[5] E.g. the easiest way to do this in terms of OpenCog's current assemblage of Atom types, is simply to consider polymorphic, higher-order-functional SchemaNodes – i.e. SchemaNodes whose inputs may be SchemaNodes and whose outputs may be SchemaNodes.

[6] https://github.com/opencog/atomspace/tree/master/opencog/rule-engine.

A first pass at a combination-choice distribution $\mathcal{P}$ would be a distribution over patterns (representable as Atoms) obtained by applying OpenCog's *Pattern Miner* to the Atomspace. The Pattern Miner finds combinations of Atoms that occur frequently, or surprisingly often (in the sense of information theory), across the Atomspace. A product of frequency or surprisingness, with a measure of combination size, gives an apparently quite reasonable $\mathcal{P}$ (though further investigation in this direction will certainly be valuable).

Using the Pattern Miner to infer $\mathcal{P}$ is essentially a way of doing frequency-based reinforcement learning for goal-driven selection of combinations to use in forward or backward chaining. One is choosing combinations that match template patterns that have frequently been useful in the past. Of course, this is nowhere near maximally intelligent, in itself, initially. But it's a basis to start from. Pattern mining can be used to choose specific actions, but it can also be used to choose more abstract rules for generating specific actions – which can lead indirectly to higher levels of intelligence. Using this counting-based approach, one can choose, for example, *inference rules* that seem to work frequently. Using these inference rules in future, based on their previously calculated utility, one will then be deploying more intelligent reasoning than is directly implied by pattern mining.

Using the URE and the Pattern Miner, and an expressive set of Atoms including VariableNodes and associated quantifiers (i.e. at least including basic predicate and/or term logic constructs), one could construct a fairly minimal OpenCog based cognitive architecture, which learns *everything* from experience based on reinforcement, aided by spontaneous background self-organization. In an approach like this, meta-learning would be relied upon to ramp up intelligence from an initially low level, where "counting" (probability estimation; information-theoretic pattern mining) is used as the core learning algorithm, relied upon to discover Atom-combinations that comprise more intelligent learning algorithms. The processes of chaining and history-based chain-selection are the core ones, and are carried out with increasing intelligence as the system's experience allows it to improve the tools (the chains of combinations) it uses to build the probability distributions used in chain-selection. The Atomspace would be getting utilized purely as a single, large, self-reprogramming functional program.

Furthermore, it is interesting and important to observe that OpenCog's PLN probabilistic inference engine can be used to improve the various steps of this "simplistic OpenCog PGMC" i.e. pattern mining and credit assignment. Using PLN to augment greedy pattern mining with heuristic probabilistic inference based pattern mining, and to augment simplistic credit assignment with heuristic probabilistic causal inference, makes the OpenCog-based PGMC process much less simplistic. But adaptive pattern mining based inference control, as described in this section, is necessary to get PLN to perform scalably in these roles. So we have a certain circularity, but it's a virtuous cycle rather than a vicious one – the smarter PLN gets, the better it can do pattern mining and credit assignment; and the better pattern mining and credit assignment are done, the smarter PLN will be.

Framing OpenCog Cognitive Processes in Terms of PGMC. While the previously published formulations of OpenCog's cognitive algorithms do not use the PGMC formalism or terminology, in fact every significant cognitive process in OpenCog can be cast fairly straightforwardly in PGMC terms. Here we will illustrate this point by briefly running through a few examples[7],

- MOSES [7], OpenCog's evolutionary learning algorithm, could be reimplemented in such a way that:
  - Candidate "programs" being evolved by MOSES are wrapped in GroundedSchemaNodes, and the fitness function is also wrapped in a GSN
  - Fitness evaluation of candidate GSNs in an evolving population, is recorded in the Atomspace as the degree to which the GSN implies the GSN goal (fitness function)
  - A few "program generation" rules are implemented, each of which creates new GSNs representing new programs to be added to the "evolving population." E.g. a crossover rule could be implemented, as could a "local search" rule.
- Clustering could be implemented via an agglomerative algorithm, so that when the "clustering rule" Atom acts on a pair of Atoms, it decides whether to fuse them into a proto-cluster or not[8]
- Concept blending could be implemented in a similar way to clustering, leveraging the existing cog-blend command[9]

4   Conclusion and Next Steps

We have outlined PGMC, a new framing of the process of general intelligence. Conceptually, PGMC presents general intelligence as a synthesis of probabilistic pattern mining with generic "growth processes" as one finds at the core numerous existing AI algorithms, and throughout the physical and natural world. PGMC can also be viewed as a formulation of the general concept of "universal AGI learning using brute force"; but it differs considerably from prior formulations in that it connects closely conceptually with a variety of practically useful learning algorithms, and with dynamical processes occurring in nature.

Preliminarily, PGMC appears useful as a way of formulating diverse concrete learning algorithms within a common framework. Some examples of this have been given within the OpenCog framework (which would however require various small tweaks to the current OpenCog framework to function as desired). "The OpenCog example is generally instructive regarding the pragmatics of applying PGMC to real-world AGI systems. Different components or aspects of a complex AGI systems may end up manifesting PGMC in their own different ways.

---

[7] Discussed in more depth at http://wiki.opencog.org/wikihome/index.php/Open Coggy_Probabilistic_Programming).

[8] See http://wiki.opencog.org/wikihome/index.php/Agglomerative_Clustering_in_ Atomspace_using_the_URE on the OpenCog wiki site for specifics.

[9] See https://github.com/opencog/opencog/tree/master/opencog/python/blending.

But PGMC may be a valuable way to model components with a view toward simplifying and comprehending inter-component interactions.

Natural next steps in this research direction would be (unordered): Create a full mathematical formalization of the PGMC framework, along the lines outlined here; mathematically explore the relationship between PGMC, probabilistic programming, type theory and other areas of AI mathematics; add SampleLink and any other needed tools to OpenCog, to make PGMC elegantly and concisely implementable in OpenCog; implement a crude, non-scalable version of PGMC-based reinforcement learning in OpenCog, and test it on very simple problems; implement PGMC-based PLN inference control and credit assignment and test as appropriate; formalize the mapping of further OpenCog cognitive algorithms (e.g. MOSES, clustering) into the PGMC framework; explore the mapping of other, non-OpenCog AI approaches into the PGMC framework.

References

1. Potapov, A., Batishcheva, V., Rodionov, S.: Optimization framework with minimum description length principle for probabilistic programming. In: Bieger, J., Goertzel, B., Potapov, A. (eds.) AGI 2015. LNCS, vol. 9205, pp. 331–340. Springer, Heidelberg (2015)
2. Goertzel, B.: Chaotic Logic. Plenum, New York (1994)
3. Goertzel, B.: A system-theoretic analysis of focused cognition, and its implications for the emergence of self and attention. Dynamical Psychology (2006)
4. Goertzel, B.: Toward a formal definition of real-world general intelligence. In: Proceedings of AGI 2010 (2010)
5. Goertzel, B., Pennachin, C., Geisweiller, N.: Engineering General Intelligence, Part 1: A Path to Advanced AGI via Embodied Learning and Cognitive Synergy. Atlantis Thinking Machines. Springer, Heidelberg (2013)
6. Goertzel, B., Pennachin, C., Geisweiller, N.: Engineering General Intelligence, Part 2: The CogPrime Architecture for Integrative, Embodied AGI. Atlantis Thinking Machines. Springer, Heidelberg (2013)
7. Looks, M.: Competent Program Evolution. Ph.D. Thesis, Computer Science Department, Washington University (2006)
8. Solomonoff, R.: A formal theory of inductive inference part I. Inf. Control **7**(1), 1–22 (1964)
9. Solomonoff, R.: A formal theory of inductive inference part II. Inf. Control **7**(2), 224–254 (1964)
10. Weinbaum, D.W., Veitas, V.: Open-ended intelligence (2015). http://arXiv.org/abs/1505.06366

Ideas for a Reinforcement Learning Algorithm that Learns Programs

Susumu Katayama[✉]

University of Miyazaki, 1-1 W. Gakuenkibanadai,
Miyazaki, Miyazaki 889-2192, Japan
skata@cs.miyazaki-u.ac.jp

Abstract. Conventional reinforcement learning algorithms such as Q-learning are not good at learning complicated procedures or programs because they are not designed to do that. AIXI, which is a general framework for reinforcement learning, can learn programs as the environment model, but it is not computable. AIXI has a computable and computationally tractable approximation, MC-AIXI(FAC-CTW), but it models the environment not as programs but as a trie, and still has not resolved the trade-off between exploration and exploitation within a realistic amount of computation.

This paper presents our research idea for realizing an efficient reinforcement learning algorithm that retains the property of modeling the environment as programs. It also models the policy as programs and has the ability to imitate other agents in the environment.

The design policy of the algorithm has two points: (1) the ability to program is indispensable for human-level intelligence, and (2) a realistic solution to the exploration/exploitation trade-off is teaching via imitation.

Keywords: AIXI · Inductive programming · Imitation

1 Introduction

Artificial General Intelligence (AGI) is, unlike the conventional *Narrow AI* that is implemented by experts to behave intelligently for specific purposes, machine intelligence that can deal with various unknown problems and unexpected situations in the same way as human beings.

Some researchers of conventional reinforcement learning (RL) algorithms used to insist this kind of intelligence as an advantage of RL. However, conventional RL algorithms have not actually been able to deal with unexpected situations in the same way as humans, because they require generalizations to be designed for each problem specifically in order to learn efficiently enough for practical purposes. In general, dealing with various problems as intelligently as humans requires the ability to program (often repetitive or recursive) procedures for problem solving. Nevertheless, RL research from the viewpoint of **"learning to obtain procedures or programs"** had not been focused on for decades.

© Springer International Publishing Switzerland 2016
B. Steunebrink et al. (Eds.): AGI 2016, LNAI 9782, pp. 354–362, 2016.
DOI: 10.1007/978-3-319-41649-6_36

At the beginning of this century, Marcus Hutter (e.g. [2]) devised AIXI which is a theoretical, general framework for RL. AIXI involves conventional RL algorithms, and at the same time learns the environment model as Turing machines or programs. Its drawback is that AIXI is not computable, and its approximation AIXI*tl* requires prohibitively enormous computation. MC-AIXI(FAC-CTW) [10], which is another AIXI approximation requiring less computation, models the environment not as Turing machines but as Context Tree Weighting (CTW) [11] that is essentially a tabular representation using a PATRICIA tree which is a kind of trie. In addition, MC-AIXI(FAC-CTW) has not resolved the trade-off between exploration and exploitation within practical computation.

In the real environment, it is not realistic to expect single agents to thoroughly explore, because they must avoid danger that can cause their death. Under totally unknown situations, real agents must avoid danger, sometimes based on prior knowledge (or "instinct"), and sometimes by behaving in the same way as other surviving agents. We should also note that search methods by population such as genetic algorithms, which let each individual exchange information, are known to be effective for finding globally optimal solutions.

This paper presents our idea of an RL algorithm that (1) models the policy, as well as the environment, as programs, and (2) can imitate other agents (and maybe other teachers), or learn behavior from the environment model in order to explore by population.

The rest of this paper is organized in the following way. Section 2 introduces AIXI and its existing approximations, along with our speculations. Section 3 describes the RL algorithm we are going to implement in details. Section 4 discusses how to evaluate the implemented system. Section 5 concludes this paper.

2   AIXI and its Approximations

This section explains AIXI and its existing approximations, along with our speculations.

2.1   AIXI

AIXI [2] is a general framework for RL and a theoretical tool for discussing the limitation of intelligent agents. It is designed to be as general as possible, and it can be considered to cover almost all abilities of artificial (and possibly natural, i.e. human) intelligence.

AIXI is based on the following ideas:

- modeling the environment as Turing machines;
- retaining all of an infinite number of possible environment candidates along with their plausibilities;
- respecting the idea of Occam's razor: simpler environments, or environments that can be described using shorter programs, should be more plausible.

More concretely, an AIXI agent decides the action $\dot{a}_k$ at time k from the *history* h_k at time k, or the sequence of the actual actions, rewards, and observations $\dot{a}\dot{r}\dot{o}_{1:k-1}$ until time $k-1$, by using the following equation:

$$\dot{a}_k = \arg\max_{a_k \in \mathcal{A}} \sum_{r_k o_k \in \mathcal{R} \times \mathcal{O}} \ldots \max_{a_{m_k} \in \mathcal{A}} \sum_{r_{m_k} o_{m_k} \in \mathcal{R} \times \mathcal{O}} (r_k + \ldots + r_{m_k}) \cdot \xi(\dot{a}\dot{r}\dot{o}_{1:k-1} a\underline{ro}_{k:m_k}) \tag{1}$$

where $\mathcal{A}$ denotes the set of actions, $\mathcal{R}$ denotes the numerical set of rewards, and $\mathcal{O}$ denotes the set of observations. $m_k(\geq k)$ represents the extended lifetime: at time k only the sum of rewards $r_k + \ldots + r_{m_k}$ until m_k is considered, and rewards farther in the future are ignored. $a \cdot b$ represents usual scalar multiplication of a and b, and juxtaposition represents tuples and sequences. $aro_{t:u} = a_t r_t o_t a_{t+1} r_{t+1} o_{t+1} \ldots a_u r_u o_u$ denotes the time sequence of actions, rewards, and observations from time t until u. $\xi(\dot{a}\dot{r}\dot{o}_{1:k-1} a\underline{ro}_{k:m_k})$ is the probability of observing the sequence of rewards and observations $ro_{k:m_k}$, given the history $h_k = \dot{a}\dot{r}\dot{o}_{1:k-1}$ at time k and assuming to take actions $a_k \ldots a_{m_k}$ from time k to m_k.

$$\xi(aro_{1:k-1} a\underline{ro}_{k:m_k}) = \xi(a\underline{ro}_{1:m_k})/\xi(a\underline{ro}_{1:k-1}) \tag{2}$$

holds, where the denominator of the rhs at time k is constant and thus can be ignored. For ξ, AIXI uses the universal prior

$$\xi(a\underline{ro}_{1:t}) = \sum_{q \in \{q' | q'(a_{1:t}) = ro_{1:t}\}} 2^{-l(q)} \tag{3}$$

where q is the Turing machine computing the behavior of the environment, and $l(q)$ denotes the description length of q when represented in the binary form. In other words, $\xi(a\underline{ro}_{1:t})$ is the probability that q returns $ro_{1:t}$ for the input of $a_{1:t}$ when the Turing machine q is selected as a random sequence of bits.

Because (3) requires infinite computation, AIXI is not exactly computable. It is not an algorithm, but rather a theoretical framework for discussing the ideal intelligence.

AIXI is proved to be self-optimizing if there exist self-optimizing policies, i.e., if there exist policies that make the expected average reward converge to the optimal one for $m \to \infty$ for all environments, AIXI agents' average reward also converges to it in the same limit. [1] On the other hand, [8] shows that AIXI (and other greedy algorithms using fixed priors) do not converge to the optimal policy if the environment is programmed to suddenly change the reward for some action as the history grows. Although Hutter's self-optimizing theorem suggests that there is no deterministic self-optimizing policy in such a case, [8] argues that such environment is plausible in the real world, and suggests the need for non-greedy exploration strategies.

2.2 AIXI Approximations

AIXI*tl* is a computable AIXI approximation that picks up the best program within length *l* and computable within time *t*. Its main focus is on being computable, and it still requires unrealistic computational complexity.

MC-AIXI(FAC-CTW)[10] is another, more efficient approximation of AIXI. It selects actions using the UCT algorithm [6] which is a kind of Monte-Carlo Tree Search, and uses a generalization of Context Tree Weighting (CTW) [11] for the environment model.

Veness et al. [10] applied MC-AIXI(FAC-CTW) to several toy problems and report better results than other related algorithms. They also applied it to *partially observable Pacman* (a.k.a. *Pocman*) which is much more challenging, and found some facts: MC-AIXI(FAC-CTW) reportedly learns to avoid walls, get food, and run away from ghosts; on the other hand, it does not learn to aggressively chase down ghosts after eating a power pill.

Veness et al. [10] point out that solving the exploration/exploitation trade-off is computationally intractable for MC-AIXI(FAC-CTW). However, learning to capture a ghost only from experience without any teaching would be difficult for *any* learning algorithm, because the ghosts flee and thus it should take time until the agent happens to capture one by chance for the first time. Without seeing other players play, being explained the rule of Pacman, or guessing from the paleness of ghosts, even human players would find difficulty in finding effectiveness of this behavior for themselves.

That being said, if the agent's policy is stochastically implemented as a distribution over programs, and if the universal prior is used to assign higher probability to short programs, the agent may try the compound action of "simply chasing pale ghosts" as exploration.

Another limitation of MC-AIXI(FAC-CTW) which is not mentioned by [10] is that it cannot generalize over sequences of observations because it uses CTW instead of learning Turing machines, unlike AIXI. CTW is essentially a finite map from finite sequences to frequencies implemented compactly using a PATRICIA tree, which means that it uses a tabular representation for modeling the environment.

Again, MC-AIXI(FAC-CTW) does not learn to chase down ghosts *aggressively* after eating the power pill. If it generalized over sequences of observations, it would flee from ghosts, even after eating the pill.

3 Our Idea: Reinforcement Learning Algorithm that Learns to Program

This section describes the RL algorithm we plan to implement in details. The algorithm is based on the following reflections on AIXI and MC-AIXI(FAC-CTW) mentioned in Sect. 2:

- since generalization is necessary in order to solve real world problems, the environment should be modeled as a mixture of programs in a similar (but efficient) way as AIXI;

- the agents should be able to be taught (rules of games, etc.); one way is by words, and another way is by letting them imitate what others do; we consider the latter in this paper because the former looks difficult;
- the exploration/exploitation trade-off could be dealt with by explicitly enabling exploratory behavior; further, designing the policy stochastically as a distribution over multiple programs may enable exploration by compound actions such as chasing pale ghosts in Pacman.

3.1   Environment Model

Since generalization over observations is necessary, we model the environment as a mixture of programs, like AIXI and unlike MC-AIXI(FAC-CTW). However, AIXI is not computable and AIXItl requires a large amount of computation.

Our idea is to let MAGICHASKELLER [3,4][1] enumerate programs within some fixed length and use them as the candidates for the environment. Also, in order to preserve the possibility of generating longer programs, the *component function library* $\mathcal{L}$ that is used to generate programs should be learned incrementally [5].

MAGICHASKELLER is an inductive functional programming system based on generate-and-test. Inductive functional programming is automated functional programming from ambiguous specifications such as input-output examples and properties that the resulting program should satisfy.

In fact MAGICHASKELLER's program generator is similar to the environment model of AIXI in that MAGICHASKELLER generates stream of programs exhaustively from the shortest increasing the length, and tests them against the given examples. On the other hand, they differ in the following ways:

- MAGICHASKELLER' generates Haskell programs, or typed λ expressions, instead of Turing machines, and
- it keeps those programs in its memorization table, and it saves the size of the table by not generating expressions that are obviously semantically equivalent to already-generated expressions and by shelving generation of expressions that may be equivalent until its difference from other expressions is proved.

Learning More and More Complicated Environment. Now we discuss how to update the component library $\mathcal{L}$.

If we apply the idea of AIXI straightforwardly, the true environment is one big (but modularized) program that is consistent with all of the input/output history. An AIXI agent holds (infinitely) many candidate programs with different plausibilities as theories explaining the true environment. This means that although there are many programs, incremental learning by adding expressions often appearing there (considering that they are useful) to the component library $\mathcal{L}$ may make only a little sense, if ever, because only one program out of them is supposed to explain the truth.

---

[1] http://nautilus.cs.miyazaki-u.ac.jp/~skata/MagicHaskeller.html.

However, we need not stick to the AIXI way strictly, but we may relax the above consistency rule. Actually, since there are many programs, there can be Program A that explains the state transition in situation x but cannot explain that in situation y, and Program B that explains that in y but cannot explain that in x at the same time. We think that the plausibility of each program depends on the situation. By admitting this and permitting partially satisfying programs, we can think of incremental learning that adds useful functions in some situations, which can result in a program which is plausible in many situations by conditioning on them.

$\mathcal{L}$ can be updated by adding expressions frequently appearing in plausible environment programs. More exactly, $\mathcal{L}$ should be chosen to make the total length of environment programs weighted with the plausibility as short as possible.

3.2   Action Selection

In (1) that defines AIXI, the other part that needs to be approximated for complexity reasons is the expectimax operations that select the actions at each time step. Also, as written at the beginning of Sect. 3, we want to enable exploratory compound actions by implementing the policy as a distribution over multiple programs. Using exploratory compound actions can have an advantage over stepwise exploration strategies such as ϵ-greedy which can mess up everything by inconsistent exploratory actions.

A simple way to implement it as a set of programs is to use $\arg\max_{p \in \mathcal{P}}$ instead of the expectimax operation in (1) by using some set of programs $\mathcal{P}$:

$$p_k = \arg\max_{p \in \mathcal{P}} \ldots \tag{4}$$

$$\dot{a}_k = p_k(\dot{a}\dot{r}\dot{o}_{1:k-1}) \tag{5}$$

However, this is not very desirable, because

- this requires computation of $\arg\max_p$ at every time step, and
- $\arg\max_p$ is too arbitrary, because p takes the history as the argument, and nothing but $\mathcal{P}$ restricts the return values for not experienced histories.

Thus, we will use a common policy p not depending on the time step. p should be updated from time to time, which means we assume episodic (or factorizable) environment. More concretely, $p \in \mathcal{P}$ such that for all history $h \in (\mathcal{A} \times \mathcal{R} \times \mathcal{O})*$

$$V^{p\xi}(h) = \max_{p' \in \mathcal{P}} V^{p'\xi}(h) \tag{6}$$

holds should asymptotically be found, where $V^{p\xi}(h)$ denotes the expected sum of the total reward after history h from time k to time m_k assuming that the agent will follow the policy p under the environment ξ, and k is the next time after history h finishes. We conjecture such V exists for any set of computable functions $\mathcal{P}$.

One way to find such V asymptotically is to keep the L^2 norm between the best estimation of V and the current estimation of V

$$\sum_h (n_h (\max_{p'} \hat{V}^{p'}(h) - \hat{V}^p(h))^2)$$

for each p, and choose the minimal p either deterministically or stochastically allowing exploration by using, e.g. the roulette selection, where $\hat{V}$ denotes the estimation of V, and n_h denotes the number of visitations to h.

When learning a value function asymptotically, it is also important what values should be assigned to those arguments that have not been used. In the field of RL, simply assigning big values for those unvisited arguments in order to encourage exploration is known to be effective (e.g. Optimistic Initial Values [9] and UCT [6]). However, this will not work for infinite or very big finite $\mathcal{P}$, which has (infinitely) many actions to be tried.

Even when selecting p, programs with less Kolmogorov complexity should be prioritized more based on the idea of Occam's razor in the same way as the environment case. Then, the universal probability (or something similar) should be used as the prior. (In practice, the selection may not necessarily be stochastic, and can be something like "When the number of program selections already done exceeds the reciprocal amount of the sum of the priors of programs that have not been tried, try the shortest one among them.") A good news compared to the environment case is less computational complexity, because the algorithm need not compute the expectation but only choose one program.

Now the question is what should this $\mathcal{P}$ be like. Our idea is to let MAGICHASKELLER enumerate $\mathcal{P}$, too. This means $\mathcal{P}$ is the enumeration of all the programs within some given length, using functions in the component library $\mathcal{L}'$. AIXI requires to find the maximum of $|\mathcal{A}|^{m_k}$ cases, but by using $\arg\max_{p \in \mathcal{P}}$ our algorithm will need to find the maximum of $|\mathcal{P}|$ cases.

Imitation. How should $\mathcal{L}'$ be learned? Although $\mathcal{L}$ could be learned to find the minimal description of the environment, this way cannot be applied to the case of learning $\mathcal{L}'$ that is the library for defining policies, because policy learning is unsupervised.

Our solution to this question is to let $\mathcal{L}' = \mathcal{L} + \mathcal{C}$ where $\mathcal{C}$ is a constant set of primitive actions. This means, "construct your behavior using what you see, i.e., by imitation", because $\mathcal{L}$ should be filled with functions for describing the behavior of the environment in short. In this way, we think, the question of how to implement imitation can be solved at the same time. On the other hand, we should note that with this approach it is difficult for an agent to imitate instantly what it has just seen, because the agent has to wait until it is added to the component library $\mathcal{L}$, and we think it is difficult for this to happen within the same episode.

One question is whether we should consider the amount of reward when registering functions to $\mathcal{L}$, or whether we should give functions used in reward-earning policies more chance to be registered to $\mathcal{L}$. We think that this need not to be done, because the reward-earning policies and resulting reward-earning states will be tried many times anyway, and if otherwise, it is not clear whether the reward is really due to the policy or not.

4   Evaluation and Applications

Most of our ideas are inspired from the experience of playing Pocman in [10]. In order to make sure that newly introduced functionalities are doing what they are supposed to do, evaluation by Pocman is necessary.

Also, in order to make sure that we are not going backward, several other easier problems shown in [10] should also be tried.

Pocman is a partially observable version of Pacman, where cells far from Pacman are invisible. Also, observations in Pocman are made relative to the position of Pacman. Although partially observable problems are more difficult than fully observable ones in general, those changes may have made the game easier, by hiding unimportant information. Because real people play the original Pacman, it would also be interesting to evaluate the agent under the original one.

A more challenging task may be multiplayer games such as Doom, where the effect of introducing imitation can be evaluated. Our algorithm will use MAGICHASKELLER for the policy and the environment, and because MAGICHASKELLER generates functional programs by combining functions in the component library, by including complicated functions implementing Narrow AI in the component library the functionality will be made available. This way, our algorithm can focus on decision making, while using existing technology for e.g. image recognition.

Although Deep Q Network [7] that is a monolithic algorithm dealing with decision making and vision processing at the same time holds the spotlight in recent years, human brains make decisions and process perceptions separately. This modular approach may be better for realizing higher-level artificial intelligence.

5   Conclusions

This paper presented our research idea for an RL algorithm that models both the environment and the policy as a distribution over Haskell programs. The algorithm will also implement imitation, and hopefully, can deal with the exploration/exploitation trade-off in a better way than conventional approaches.

Haskell is an artificial, general-purpose programming language, and thus it is unlikely that human brains are actually planning their behavior in Haskell. However, λ calculus, which is the model of computation on which the Haskell language is built, can be a good option for modeling consciousness. We think that consciousness is the functionality to make the thinking process object of thinking and communication. If this is correct, λ calculus, which is designed to make functions object of computation, can be the best tool for explaining consciousness and discussing it.

Acknowledgements. The author thanks anonymous reviewers who helped improving the paper, especially who mentioned [8].

References

1. Hutter, M.: Self-optimizing and pareto-optimal policies in general environments based on bayes-mixtures. In: Kivinen, J., Sloan, R.H. (eds.) COLT 2002. LNCS (LNAI), vol. 2375, pp. 364–379. Springer, Heidelberg (2002). http://dx.doi.org/10.1007/3-540-45435-7_25
2. Hutter, M.: Universal algorithmic intelligence: a mathematical top $\to$ down approach. In: Goertzel, B., Pennachin, C. (eds.) Artificial General Intelligence. Cognitive Technologies, pp. 227–290. Springer, Heidelberg (2007). http://www.hutter1.net/ai/aixigentle.htm
3. Katayama, S.: Systematic search for lambda expressions. In: Sixth Symposium on Trends in Functional Programming, pp. 195–205 (2005)
4. Katayama, S.: Efficient exhaustive generation of functional programs using Monte-Carlo search with iterative deepening. In: Ho, T.B., Zhou, Z.H. (eds.) PRICAI 2008. LNCS (LNAI), vol. 5351, pp. 199–210. Springer, Heidelberg (2008)
5. Katayama, S.: Towards human-level inductive functional programming. In: Bieger, J., Goertzel, B., Potapov, A. (eds.) AGI 2015. LNCS, vol. 9205, pp. 111–120. Springer, Heidelberg (2015). http://dx.doi.org/10.1007/978-3-319-21365-1_12
6. Kocsis, L., Szepesvári, C.: Bandit based Monte-Carlo planning. In: Fürnkranz, J., Scheffer, T., Spiliopoulou, M. (eds.) ECML 2006. LNCS (LNAI), vol. 4212, pp. 282–293. Springer, Heidelberg (2006)
7. Mnih, V., Kavukcuoglu, K., Silver, D., Rusu, A.A., Veness, J., Bellemare, M.G., Graves, A., Riedmiller, M., Fidjeland, A.K., Ostrovski, G., Petersen, S., Beattie, C., Sadik, A., Antonoglou, I., King, H., Kumaran, D., Wierstra, D., Legg, S., Hassabis, D.: Human-level control through deep reinforcement learning. Nature **518**, 529–533 (2015)
8. Orseau, L.: Optimality issues of universal greedy agents with static priors. In: Hutter, M., Stephan, F., Vovk, V., Zeugmann, T. (eds.) Algorithmic Learning Theory. LNCS, vol. 6331, pp. 345–359. Springer, Heidelberg (2010). http://dx.doi.org/10.1007/978-3-642-16108-7_28
9. Sutton, R.S., Barto, A.G.: Introduction to Reinforcement Learning, 1st edn. MIT Press, Cambridge (1998)
10. Veness, J., Ng, K.S., Hutter, M., Uther, W., Silver, D.: A Monte-Carlo AIXI approximation. J. Artif. Intell. Res. **40**, 95–142 (2011)
11. Willems, F.M.J., Shtarkov, Y.M., Tjalkens, T.J.: The context tree weighting method: basic properties. IEEE Trans. Inf. Theor. **41**, 653–664 (1995)

Author Index

Printed in the United States
By Bookmasters